W9-BSZ-727

the
Income Tax
is
Obsolete

the Income Tax is Obsolete

JOSEPH S. DUARTE

BRIAR CLIFF COLLEGE
LIBRARY

SIOUX CITY, IOWA

ARLINGTON HOUSE·PUBLISHERS
NEW ROCHELLE, N. Y.

Copyright© 1974 by Joseph S. Duarte

All rights reserved. No portion of this book may be reproduced
without written permission from the publisher except by a reviewer
who may quote brief passages in connection with a review.

Library of Congress Catalog Card Number HJ2381.D8

ISBN 0-87000-286-4

Manufactured in the United States of America

Library of Congress Cataloging in Publication Data

Duarte, Joseph S.
    The income tax is obsolete.

Includes bibliographical references.
1. Taxation — United States.
2. Taxation of articles of consumption — United States.
3. Income tax — United States. I. Title.
HJ2381.D8   336.2'00973   74-18366
ISBN 0-87000-286-4

HJ
2381
.D8

To

P. M. Grieve

74696

Contents

Introduction

This work deals with the political basis of taxation and is concerned primarily with Federal taxes and American tax policy — past, present, and future. The economic factor in taxation is not disregarded, but is treated as secondary to the political uses for which tax revenues are used and to the political methods employed for collection and compliance. Economist Henry C. Simons[1], one of the greatest authorities on American taxation, stated that the tax system is only a small part of the larger political framework of society and that taxes cannot be understood apart therefrom. I have written this report from that point of view, not from the standpoint of the tax specialist; therefore, no technical knowledge, legal or economic, is necessary to read it and understand it.

Although taxation is a subject that affects the vital interest and deep concern of every adult member of society, surprisingly little is written on the subject, except in accounting and legal manuals and in a few books that treat the subject either in the lurid manner of a journalistic exposé or in the technical jargon of the professional economist.

It may be, as students have often complained, that taxation is a very dull part of what has been called the dismal science of economics, but I think this criticism reveals a lack of understanding of its true nature. Taxation is not just an economic problem; it is also a political, family, legal, corporate, and individual problem. When studied in all its ramifications, taxation is far from dull. On the contrary, it is a complex and vital subject, sometimes politically explosive, often personally painful, and always a constant, inescapable, and cruel reminder that civilization has its costs.

Throughout history taxes have been the catalyst that has triggered many violent uprisings and revolutionary transfers of power and wealth. Taxes are political dynamite. The imposition of ship taxes by Charles I in defiance of Parliament brought on the English civil war and cost Charles his head. The stamp tax and other British duties arbitrarily levied by Parliament ignited the American Revolution. The efforts by the bankrupt French treasury of Louis XVI to levy more taxes triggered the French Revolution. The Tariff Act of 1828 caused the first abortive attempt at secession by South Carolina and laid the Southern strategy for the Civil War — Calhoun's doctrine of nullification.

Historians have played up the heroic political and military battles and personalities in all these revolutionary movements. Beneath the surface the underlying unrest, however, was probably caused by the spur of cruel and oppressive taxes that goaded the people into rebellion. Oppressive taxes are a form of despotism; throughout history the struggle for personal liberty has been linked with efforts to nullify or limit the coercive tax power of the government. Burke in his "Speech on Conciliation with America" argued that:

"Abstract liberty, like other mere abstractions, is not to be found. Liberty inheres in some sensible object; and every nation has formed to itself some favorite point, which by way of eminence becomes the criterion of their happiness. It happened, you know, Sir, that the great contests for freedom in this country were from the earliest time chiefly on the question of taxing. Most of the contests in the ancient commonwealths turned primarily on the right of election of magistrates, or on the balance among the several orders of the state. But in England it was otherwise. On this point of taxes the ablest pens and the most eloquent tongues have been exercised, the greatest spirits have acted and suffered.... They took infinite pains to inculcate, as a fundamental principle, that in all monarchies the people must in effect themselves, mediately or immediately, possess the power of granting their own money, or no shadow of liberty could subsist. The colonies draw from you, as with their life-blood, these ideas and principles. Their love of liberty, as with you, fixed and attached on this specific point of taxing. Liberty might be safe or might be endangered in twenty other particulars without their being much pleased or alarmed. Here they felt its pulse; and as they found that beat, they thought themselves sick or sound."[2]

Liberty is not considered a factor in economics. It cannot be quantified and given a numerical value. Since the times of Walras and Keynes, the fashion has been to reduce economics to a mathematical science, with problems stated in algebraic symbols and equations of aggregates. Political liberty is not a factor in Keynesian equations, and most social costs are classified as "externalities" outside the sphere of economics. In Marxist economics, political liberty is considered a bourgeois fiction, and only material or economic factors are counted as "real." It is not strange, therefore, that taxation today is seldom discussed as a political problem. Economists such as Milton Friedman and Henry Hazlitt, who raise the question of individual freedom in connection with taxation, are considered outdated. The "progressive" principle in taxation, according to the Keynesian school, is ability to pay and reduction of income inequality. Most politicians have been converted to this view, and even such moderate Republicans as Richard Nixon declare that "We are all Keynesians now." The overriding considerations in tax legislation are economic, not political.

However, the problem of taxation cannot be divorced from politics. Tax laws are the result of a political, not an economic, process; a basic political problem, as old as Plato, is the question of individual freedom versus government authority, or as Bertrand Russell put it, "Freedom Versus Organization." One may not believe with Burke that taxation is the focal point around which this political struggle between freedom and authority always revolves. However, if political considerations are disregarded, a tax law may be enacted for the best economic reasons and then degenerate into an instrument of political despotism, enforced by electronic surveillance, inquisitorial methods of auditing and investigation, paid informers, and court proceedings in which the individual citizen is confronted by the naked power of the state. This has been the fate of the income tax law.

Taxation has grown to a point where it now takes about 40 per cent of the average American's income. Taxation not only provides the financial lifeblood of the government, but also serves as a means for directing and controlling the economy. Large-scale transfers of wealth and power that formerly could be effected only by conquest or revolution are now achieved by tax legislation. The tax powers of the government have grown to a point where they severely restrict individual rights and freedoms, not only because of the sheer size and weight of the bureaucratic tax structure, but because of the inquisitorial and coercive methods used for the collection of income taxes.

When first introduced by Pitt in England in 1799, the income tax was resented by the people as an intolerable invasion of personal rights. In both England and the United States it could be imposed initially only as an emergency wartime measure and was repealed after the war in both countries. The income tax was ruled unconstitutional by the United States Supreme Court in 1895. It required a constitutional amendment, the 16th, to overrule the Supreme Court and make the income tax legal in 1913. Today, the income tax has both acquired legality and moral respectability and become the main support of the government. It has also become a textbook dogma. Nothing is so firmly established in the orthodoxy of economic science as the doctrine that the income tax is the fairest and the most "progressive" of all taxes; nothing is so vehemently defended by most liberal politicians as the theory that the income tax is the levy best suited to correct the gross inequities of the capitalist system.

If the politicians and economists are correct, then why do we see a growing hostility toward the income tax from workers, who formerly supported it, but now find themselves locked into a withholding system that puts them at a cruel disadvantage? Why has the public sector bureaucracy grown to a point where the average American works four months of the year to support it? Why has the market become so weakened that it can no longer function without political guidelines and controls? Why does the Federal government find it necessary to print devaluated dollars and resort to deficit financing because of insufficient tax revenues? Why is it that the income tax, although it brings in more than $100 billion in revenue, is still unable to finance the social programs considered necessary or desirable? While not all of these vexatious problems can be blamed on the income tax, it is hardly logical to disregard the possibility that it may be a major causative factor.

It is my considered opinion that the income tax law *is* a major cause of many of our economic problems. Income taxation has failed to realize the egalitatian ideals of its original advocates; it has developed Orwellian tendencies that contravene basic constitutional rights; and it appears to be unable to cope with the revenue demands imposed upon it by the welfare state. The income tax law may have been justified under 19th century economic conditions, but it has become obsolete; no structural reforms, such as closing the loopholes, will make it compatible with the political goals of a modern democratic society. The reasons for this incompatibility are discussed in the first chapter.

This critical view of the income tax may raise some eyebrows but, since

13

nobody loves taxes, the normal reaction is a shrug of the shoulders. What is there to replace it that will raise the same volume of revenue, that is equally fair, and will be equally useful as a means of reducing inequality of income?

This study is an attempt to answer those questions. The answer given here may not satisfy everyone, and I certainly do not think it is a final answer or panacea. What I have sought to do is to indicate some new approaches to the study of taxation and its relationship to politics, a kinship that is obvious, but has not been given the attention it deserves. This relationship is explored in the fifth chapter, which is a brief review of American tariff history.

Justice Oliver Wendell Holmes once observed that taxes are the price we pay for civilized society. In other words, the costs we pay for social life — social costs — are paid for in taxes. However, taxes also have a direct and indirect effect on market prices, so that many social or noneconomic costs are paid for through the price system. In the third chapter I have analyzed some of the social costs that are included in market prices and others that are excluded. The failure of market prices to embrace all social and energy costs has been a major factor in bringing about our present energy and environmental crisis. The higher the gross national product climbs and the more affluent the nation becomes, the more the environment is impoverished and the poorer the nation becomes in natural resources. This perversion of values is the result of a price and tax system that fails to incorporate all social costs.

In the fourth chapter the role played by the Federal government in setting priorities through taxation is studied in connection with the tax legislative process and the executive tax policymaking process. The setting of priorities by the government through income tax policy causes unplanned but massive distortions in market prices in the private sector and sometimes leads to unexpected crises.

In the sixth chapter a new tax is introduced which is derived from consumption rather than income and is based on the value criteria of total energy and social costs in a closed ecological system.

The final chapter is devoted to a discussion of how the problem of poverty, dependency, and unemployment would be treated under the new tax law, as compared to the treatment it has had under the income tax system. The problem poses a serious dilemma to the government. How can it plan for full employment and full production without severely restricting individual liberty and private property rights? How can the government provide badly needed social services without making taxation an intolerable burden? There are no easy answers to these questions but, under a tax law based on consumption rather than on income, the questions would be looked at under a different light and the answers would be different and, hopefully, could lead to a better understanding of the problem.

This work is frankly polemic. The sacred cows of the American economy — the free market, the income tax, consumer sovereignty, the labor theory of value, government programs of social welfare, profits as the sole criteria of market success — all are criticized for failing to adapt to values compatible with a closed ecological system. Our economic values are still based on the Ricardo-Marx labor theory of value and on the Benthamite theory of market

14

utility values, which are no longer applicable.

This book is not an exposé or an attempt to debunk conventional wisdom. The remedies suggested are neither revolutionary nor highly original; most of the ideas for tax reform expressed in the following pages may be found in the theories of Alexander Hamilton and Simon Nelson Patten.

The new tax proposed is, in reality, an old form of taxation revised to meet new economic conditions and is already in use, on a limited scale, in the United States and in Europe. The new tax law would restore to the legislative branch greater control over national economic and tax policy, now largely dominated by the executive branch. A major feature of the new tax described in the sixth chapter is the introduction of social and energy costs in market prices by legislative process.

The views expressed in the following pages are those of the author as a private citizen and not as the representative of any association, school, organization, corporation, or party. Some of the ideas expressed may sound unorthodox, but they have been carefully checked and rechecked and buttressed in most cases by competent authorities or historical precedent. Their seeming unorthodoxy may stem from the fact that the author has consistently tried to look at the problem of taxes, not from a specialist or technical viewpoint, but from the standpoint of the ordinary citizen as a taxpayer, as a businessman, as a wage earner, as a family man, and as a voter. This rather broad view of a complex problem may displease tax scholars, but if this book gives the average taxpayer a better understanding of his predicament, then it will have served its purpose. When the American citizen understands his tax problem, he will be in a better position to do something about it. Eventually it is the citizen, as a voter, who is going to have to lick the tax problem — nobody else is going to do it for him.

Chapter

I

TAXES ON INCOME

1. The First Income Taxes

Taxes in the agrarian society were imposed by the stronger on the weak. It was a form of tribute paid by nations, classes, or persons who held an inferior, servile, or subject status. Since money was not commonly used, in most cases payment was in kind. Taxes were levied on the person in proportion to his annual produce from the land, a sort of agricultural income tax. The Bible speaks of the tithe, or a tenth of the produce, as the annual tax. The normal Roman land tax paid by proprietors and by lessees of public land was one-tenth (*decuma*). The Egyptian Pharaohs levied a personal tax on peasants of about 18 per cent of their produce. The tax was paid by the head of the family or household. In both Egypt and Mesopotamia the rulers were god-kings. Temples were used for storage and distribution of grains collected as tax payments. In cases where money was used in the economy, the price of grain was set by the ruler or his representative. The Bible tells the story of Joseph in Egypt and his seven-year plan. The peasants were taxed heavily for seven years to build up a surplus of grain to be stored for years of shortages. This is one of the earliest examples of economic planning through taxation. The practice of taxing income at the source or withholding was known and practiced in ancient times. On collective farms — royal, manorial, seigneurial, patrician estates, or *latifundia* — the field workers were slaves, and the major portion of the produce was withheld by the landlord. Only a small portion was left to the slave for his subsistence.

Taxes were also payable in services. In Europe during feudal times the serf worked a specified number of days for his lord before or after he worked on his own plot. No money was involved, but the economic effect was equivalent to contributing labor time in the form of money deducted from wages.

The Roman colonial tax system was simple and arbitrary. If a country yielded without resistance, the Romans allowed the landowners to retain title to their properties, provided they paid taxes (*tributum*) to the Roman emperor, who now became their supreme landlord. If the country resisted, the Romans might punish the landlords, not only by confiscating their lands, but by taking them to Rome as slaves or killing them. The land titles would then be given to Roman colonists or native collaborators, who paid tribute to Rome. The military operations of the agrarian empires were not revolutionary movements in the modern sense, but wars of conquest for the purpose of acquiring land or for acquiring slaves or gaining tribute.

A census was taken by the Romans to fix personal liability for the tribute. It was because of one such census that Joseph and Mary traveled to Bethlehem to register in the tax rolls. The Bible refers to *publicans*, who were the Roman tax collectors. They paid the taxes to Rome for an amount negotiated *in advance*. What they collected, over or under this amount, they took as a profit or loss. Collection methods were extremely harsh, and *publicans* were hated with a passion reserved for tax collectors. Their victims suffered greatly at their hands, but *publicans* themselves were sometimes beaten and killed by enraged taxpayers.

In the latter days of the Roman Empire the state transferred the duties of tax collection to the civic and military leaders of the district and made them responsible for collecting taxes and remitting them to Rome. This was an honor not eagerly sought.

Taxation in an imperial agrarian state was normally a system of extortion imposed on the militarily weak by the strong. Rostovzeff, an authority on the subject, says of the Roman tax system: "The state was living not on its normal income but on a system of more or less organized robbery."

Extortion was already well established under the republic, as documented by Cicero in his speeches on Sicily under Verres.

Before the advent of the market economy, commodity taxes were not as common as personal taxes. Entry and exit fees were collected by kings at the ports of entry; towns collected taxes (excises) on articles brought from other towns; nobles levied taxes (tolls) on goods transported by roads or rivers that crossed their lands. The Arab rulers of El Tarifa, near Gibraltar, imposed a toll on ships passing into or out of the Mediterranean, a practice from which the word for import tax (tariff) is derived.

When markets, national and international, were established, the opportunity presented itself to tax the commodities that were taken to, or sold in, the mart. The form of tax varied, but today they would be called duties and excises levied by national and city governments on goods entering and leaving the nation's borders or the city's gates.

Commodity taxes or nondirect taxes were the levies most commonly used by national governments until the 20th century. In the United States, nondirect taxes — the tariff — financed the Federal government from 1789 to 1913. However, the tariff left untouched a new source of wealth that developed at the start of the 19th century as a result of the industrial revolution. This new wealth had been accumulated tax-free by factory owners and financiers, whom Marx branded as the capitalist class. In the post-Civil War era in the United States this new class rose to a position of enormous economic power. This concentration of economic power led to certain abuses and injustices that brought on the Populist revolt of the 1870s and the Progressive or reform movement in both major parties that lasted until World War I.

The poverty of the national government of the United States appeared to some congressmen as an abdication of power in the face of an entrenched oligarchy rather than as a sign of democracy in the liberal Jeffersonian tradition. Some of these politicians were demagogues who attacked the "malefactors of great wealth" and the "robber barons" and sought outright confiscation of the "capitalist" interests. Others, more moderate, sought to reform the tax system to enable it to capture some of the great wealth that was being accumulated tax free and to force it to carry some of the burden that was crushing the poor. The income tax seemed to be the only fiscal tool available that offered the government the possibility of improving the condition of the poor and of reducing the gross inequality of income. The income tax was first tried out in England and there evolved into its modern form.

The principles on which the income tax is based — ability to pay and progressive rates — have an ancient and respected tradition. It has been a recognized principle, not always observed, that it is unfair to tax the poor at the same rate as the rich. The Indian sage Manu recognized this principle more than 3000 years ago when he said: "To make the burden of taxes equal... is not affected by a mere numerical proportion. The man who is taxed to the amount of one tenth... of an income of 100 rupees per annum, is taxed far more severely than the man who is taxed an equal proportion of an income of 1000 rupees, and to a prodigious bigness more severely than the man who is taxed an equal proportion of 10,000 rupees per annum."[3]

A popular English historian of taxation wrote: "In the Middle Ages in England the principle was recognized that it would be unfair to tax the rich man and the peasant at the same rate. In the poll tax of 1377 the Duke of Lancaster was rated at 520 times that of the peasant. In 1435 and 1450 a graduated income tax was levied at the rate of 2½ per cent on small incomes, and 10 per cent on large."[4] However, since it was extremely difficult to determine personal income before the advent of banks and checking accounts, this form of taxation was of limited usefulness. It was much easier for governments to tax land and other forms of property that could not be concealed.

The modern income tax was born in 1799 in England as a temporary wartime measure. In a famous speech in Parliament on December 3, 1798, William Pitt proposed an income tax of 10 per cent. The act was passed January 9, 1799. Pitt's strategy was to contain the French Revolution by subsidizing an antirevolution coalition in Europe. This grand design called for huge sums of money. Pitt needed an estimated £20 million from all taxes, of which £10 million was to come from the proposed income tax. "It was clear to Pitt that the old system of taxation, the old land tax and the taxes on consumption, were inadequate for a war of this magnitude. New and untaxed sources of income were in existence. They were the untapped profits created by the Industrial Revolution, the profits of trades and businesses, the income from employment and the dividends from the Funds [government bonds]." Pitt, facing a financial crisis, recognized that the tax laws were unfair and that the new forms of capital accumulation that had come into existence should be taxed to pay their share of the war burden. Pitt caustically observed that there was 'much income, much wealth, great means' untouched by the old tax laws. He wanted the tax burden to be more evenly distributed, an end to 'shameful evasion', and an 'approach as near as circumstances will permit to a fair and equal contribution'."[5]

Pitt's income tax law had serious defects. It was based on a simple voluntary declaration of income or self-assessment, but the law had no provisions for auditing, inspection, or enforcement. Under Pitt's law the taxpayer had merely to submit a return in a form that revealed his total income — "...I am willing to pay the sum of _____ ... and I do declare that the said sum of _____ is not less than one tenth of my income. ..." The word of a British gentleman was not to be doubted, but Pitt discovered, to his great chagrin and dismay, that evasion was common and avoidance of full liability almost universal, despite the call for patriotic sacrifices in the face of national emergency. The chief source of income was rentals from land, and Pitt complained that, of 750,000 families subject to income tax, only 250,000 paid taxes. Pitt's income tax law was repealed in 1802 after the signing of the Peace of Amiens. The repeal was greeted with a universal sigh of relief. The income tax had been one of the most unpopular and onerous of all wartime obligations.

However, when the war with Napoleon was renewed, the income tax was reintroduced by Addington, who had replaced Pitt as chancellor. Addington's Property and Income Tax Act of 1803 is regarded by economists as the prototype of the modern income tax. He introduced the great innovation of taxing income at the source; the idea of exempting minimum income; allowances for dependents; and progressive rates. Among other far-reaching proposals was one for earned income relief, which was not enacted, however, until 1907. Addington did away with the lump sum declaration of income and replaced it with five schedules of income according to source. No general return of income was required. The obligation to make such a return, involving as it did, a disclosure of the taxpayer's circumstances in life, had been regarded as the chief objection to the tax.

Addington's income tax act was more successful than Pitt's in raising revenue. The tenant now paid the tax on the rent by deducting it from his payment to the landlord. The landlord was taxed whether or not he declared the rent income. When the Bank of England deducted the tax at the source from dividends and interest payments, the tax revenues from this one source jumped from under £12 million to £22 million! Under Addington's law opportunities for evasion were severely reduced. It was also felt that this automatic deduction of income tax at the source answered one of the most serious criticisms of Pitt's law — that it was too great an intrusion into the private affairs of the citizen. Total income declarations were no longer required. This feature of the tax, unfortunately, was to reappear later and to give the income tax the reputation, as Adam Smith was the first to observe, of being an "inquisitorial" tax incompatible with the personal liberty of private citizens of a free country. Addington's tax was repealed in 1816 at the end of the Napoleonic wars. Despite its mild form, the income tax was thoroughly detested by the English public, and its repeal was greeted with great relief and popular rejoicing.

The income tax was reintroduced in England by Sir Robert Peel in 1842. It was sorely needed, he said, to pay the huge national debt resulting from deficits under his predecessor, Melbourne. As to the charge that the income tax was inquisitorial, Peel replied:

> "You must either resort to direct or indirect taxation. It is but a comparison of evils. I have never denied that a good deal of inconvenience arising from the enquiries that must be instituted into the properties of men is unavoidable from the imposition of an income tax. You may modify or mitigate the inconveniences, but you are bound to give the honest as much security as you can, that they do not have to pay more on account of the misconduct of the dishonest. A certain degree of inquisitorial scrutiny is, therefore, inseparable from an Income Tax." [6]

This reply did not quiet opposition. Macaulay reminded the House of Adam Smith's position that the income tax was an intolerable invasion of personal liberty; by 1842, Smith had become the revered prophet of free trade and laissez-faire capitalism. The Opposition did not object to the tax levy of 3 per cent, which was minimal; it was the invasion of privacy that was objectionable. Peel met this objection partially by giving taxpayers the right to submit returns to special commissioners, who were faceless bureaucrats, rather than to local commissioners, who might be rivals in business or personal enemies of the taxpayers. The right of appeal to the special commissioners was also granted the taxpayer.

Like Pitt, Peel based his argument in favor of the income tax on social justice. The rich were escaping their share of the tax burden. Taxes on property could be avoided by the rich, but they could not avoid the income tax. Said Peel, "Here is a great proprietor of £50,000 or £60,000 a year. Tax his house 20 per cent and you cannot prevent his closing it, and you will add thus an additional temptation to repair to a foreign capital, where he finds himself free from assessed taxes. By the measure I propose, I reach him by means of an Income Tax. I touch his landed property through the intervention of his tenantry; and if he have no tenants I affect him through the funds." By this Peel meant that the income tax would be deducted automatically at the source in the payment of rents or interest on government securities (the funds).[7]

Peel is better known in history as the champion of free trade than as the author of the 1842 Income Tax Act. It is generally held that the passage of both the "free trade" tariff and the income tax at the same time was an act of political adroitness in which Peel balanced the interests of the rising manufacturing class, who feared being priced out of export markets.

It is interesting to note that the first American income tax law was also passed in conjunction with a reduction in tariff duties and was entitled an "Act to Reduce Tariff Duties and to Provide Revenue for the Government." The introduction of the income tax meant a shifting of the base of taxation from indirect to direct taxes, from consumption to income as a base. This trend, which started in 1799 in England, was finally acknowledged as irreversible in that country in 1874 by John Morley:

> "In 1874 the prosperity of the country and the movement of the revenue gave an opportunity for repeal of the Income Tax. That opportunity never recurred. The election of 1874 was the fall, the curtain . . . It marked the decision of the electorate that the Income Tax — introduced in time of peace by Peel and continued by Mr. Gladstone, for the purpose of simplifying the tariff and expanding trade — should be retained for general objects of government and should be a permanent element of our finance. It marked at the same time the prospect of a new era of indefinitely enlarged expenditure, with the Income Tax as the main engine for raising ways and means."[8]

After all, the potential revenue that can be extracted from import duties is not great, even in a country such as England, compared to the total wealth of the nation measured by income. By shifting the tax base to income, the government is immediately in a position to extract much greater revenues. At the same time the tariff is freed from its revenue function, and tariff duties may be reduced drastically or adjusted to fit any foreign policy the government favors — free trade or protectionist. This power over national income was not given to the United States government until 1913 and was not really implemented until 1934.

In the United States the first personal income tax law was enacted as a wartime measure during the Civil War and repealed thereafter. Because of the inquisitorial nature of its collection, to which the American taxpayer had not yet become accustomed, it had been very unpopular.

The second income tax law was introduced in 1894 after the bloody labor-capital clashes of the preceding year. A radical Populist farm-labor movement threatened to undermine the two-party system. The country was in the grip of a financial panic. The farmers, caught between rising costs and falling farm prices, were desperate. In 1893 Coxey's army of the unemployed marched on Washington. President Cleveland sent Federal troops to Chicago to quell the Pullman strike. Violence exploded, and Eugene Debs, the Socialist labor leader, was arrested. The time was ripe for the revolutionary income tax, which was hailed as a "soak the rich" measure and was one of the key demands of the Populist party and the Progressives of both major parties. The bill became law on August 28, 1894. It imposed a 2 per cent tax on income. Although such a tax had been imposed during the Civil War as a wartime measure, the Supreme Court declared the Act unconstitutional in 1895 on the ground that it was a direct tax. It was a Pyrrhic victory. The time had come for the income tax, and legal or constitutional barriers could not stop its coming. The public had changed its mind and was now prepared to accept the income tax. It was not a question of liberty, but one of survival. The people were desperate. Only the income tax, it seemed to them, offered any hope of lifting the heavy load of debt that was crushing them.

Cordell Hull drafted the provisions of the Income Tax Act of 1913 — the same Cordell Hull who as Secretary of State under Franklin Roosevelt negotiated tariff reductions under the Reciprocal Trade Agreement Act. Hull called the income tax "the fairest, the most equitable system of taxation that has yet been devised."[9]

As in England, the advocates of the income tax stressed social justice. There was in America no need for additional tax revenues parallel to the need in England. The tariff in the United States was based on high protective rates, and the revenues derived from it produced after the Civil War a "Fiscal Dividend" or annual surpluses that caused the Federal government some embarrassment; at that time, it had no social welfare programs on which these surplus funds could be spent. The impulse toward the income tax was not financial need, but social reform. The disparity of income between the rich and the poor was flagrantly unfair, and the income tax was designed to correct this inequity. In 1870 Senator John Sherman of Ohio commented on the injustice of income distribution in the United States:

"Here we have in New York Mr. Astor with an income of millions derived from real estate, accumulated year after year by the mere family pride of accumulation, and we have alongside of him a poor man receiving $1,000 a year. What is the discrimination of the law in that case? It is altogether against the poor man. Everything that he consumes we tax, and yet we are afraid to tax the income of Mr. Astor. Is there any justice in it? Why, sir, the income tax is the only one that tends to equalize these burdens between the rich and the poor."

The argument that the income tax was both a reform measure to fight poverty and a means of shifting the tax base away from consumption was clearly stated by one of its champions, Senator William E. Borah, in a speech to Congress:

"I place my advocacy of the income tax proposition upon a higher plane than that of raising a little revenue for the Government for the next few years. . . . I believe that the Constitution as constructed is the same as granting an exemption to the vast accumulated wealth of the country and saying it shall be relieved from the great burden of taxation. I do not believe that the great framers of the Constitution, the men who were forming a government for the people, of the people, by the people, intended that all the taxes of this government should be placed upon the backs of those who toil, upon consumption . . ."[10]

Cordell Hull repeated the classic argument in favor of the income tax as a reform measure when he said that the protective tariff was an "infamous system of class legislation" that imposed the heavy burden of Federal taxation on the poor while "virtually exempting the Carnegies, the Vanderbilts, the Morgans and the Rockefellers with their aggregated billions of hoarded wealth."

In England Lloyd George fought for progressive income tax rates in 1909 and stated in the House of Commons in an impassioned speech that "it is for raising money to wage implacable warfare against poverty and squalidness."

Thus the champions of the income tax assumed the mantle of social crusaders in the war on poverty and used the income tax as their chosen instrument for winning the struggle.[11] But first it was necessary to overcome the extreme repugnance of the people for all types of direct taxes and especially for the income tax, which they considered inquisitorial, subject to political influence, and a violation of their personal rights. The French and American revolutions, which had been fought against what would be regarded today as relatively mild direct taxes, were still fresh in the minds of the people. Direct taxes were still associated in the public mind with feudal privilege and servitude. They were expressly prohibited by Article 1, Section 2 of the Constitution, except by apportionment among the states. The Roman belief that a direct tax was a badge of slavery was still popular in the 18th and early 19th centuries. The unpopularity of the income tax was such that only under wartime conditions or during a national emergency could the English and American poeple be forced to accept it. After the Napoleonic wars in England and the Civil War in the United States, income tax laws were repealed by popular demand. In the second half of the 19th century a new national emergency brought on, not by war but by the Industrial Revolution, made the income tax more acceptable to the people and made former arguments against income taxation less compelling and somewhat irrelevant.

2. An Inquisitorial Tax

In both England and the United States rapid industrialization had brought with it the twin evils of mass unemployment and agrarian decline. It was to alleviate the suffering and deprivation of the worker and farmer, caught in the periodic crises of depression and hard times, that the income tax was proposed. It was not originally intended that the income tax be an instrument of economic planning or be used for funding elaborate social welfare programs. The income tax law of 1913 was not designed to shift the major tax load to income taxes; at least, this possibility was not generally anticipated. It was also not expected that the income tax would be paid by the working class. The income tax was expected to be paid from the excess or surplus income of very wealthy people and to be applied to specific areas of economic distress. It was expected that the major source of revenue for the Federal government would continue to be consumption taxes — tariff and excise taxes — and this was evidenced by the fact that the first American income tax act was passed as a minor supplement to the major revenue bill, which was the tariff bill. The 1913 income tax bill was passed as Section 11 of the "Act to Reduce Duties and to Provide Revenue for the Government, and for Other Purposes."

Income taxation, as presently known, was developed during the 19th century and was an economic by-product of the Industrial Revolution. It provided a badly needed source of revenue for the growing fiscal needs of the modern industrial state, and it helped ameliorate the gross economic inequalities of income distribution under laissez-faire capitalism. It was consistent with the prevailing labor theory of value, according to which labor was entitled to all it produced. It was considered the best fiscal tool available to the government at that time for diverting resources from the private market sector of the economy, which before the income tax law controlled over 97 per cent of the gross national product, to the starved government or public sector, which was powerless to control recurrent and disastrous periods of panic and depressions in the United States.

The income tax was fought on economic and ethical grounds by the conservative economists and politicians of England and the United States. The conservative position was that the income tax was tantamount to confiscation of private property. It took property from one citizen or one class to give it to another. Disraeli castigated the taking of wealth from one class of taxpayers to give to another class as "plunder." James Stuart Mill called the income tax "a mild form of robbery."

Under an economic system based on the absolute rights of private ownership to property, the graduated individual income tax cannot be defended. The income tax presupposes a higher right than the private right of ownership to property. Madison, the chief architect of the Constitution, had denied the existence of any such higher right. The "natural rights of man" to life, liberty, and property were considered the highest rights under the law at the time of the American and French revolutions. These two revolutions were fought to establish the rights of private ownership to property against the right of feudal tenure and to protect the individual citizen in his property against the claims of the state. Locke, the intellectual father of the American and French revolutions, put it bluntly: "Government has no other end but the preservation of property."

A number of distinguished economists such as J. S. Mill, Alfred Marshall, A. C. Pigou, and Irving Fisher opposed the income tax on the grounds that it discriminated against savings and favored spending. Said Mill: "No income tax is really just from which savings are not exempted. ... Unless ... savings are exempted from income tax, the contributions are twice taxed on what they save, and only once on what they spend."[12] This argument, although sound, was academic, for the proponents of the income tax were not deterred by considerations of equity in the narrow sense of individual property rights. They were influenced by what they termed "social and humanitarian objectives." In this context all income should be taxed "for the benefit of society as a whole," and the criterion is "ability to pay," not source or use of income. This view was summed up by the Rowell-Sirois Commission in its tax report to the Canadian parliament in 1937:

"The personal income tax is the most highly developed modern instrument of taxation. It can be more delicately adjusted to individual circumstances, and thus made fairer in its incidence, than any other tax. It adjusts itself automatically to economic fluctuations. It can raise a given revenue with less burden on the national economy than any other tax because it is drawn from surplus income rather than made a burden on costs. That is, no income tax need be exacted from an individual unless he has an income above that necessary for subsistence. No obstacle is thus put in the employment at wages and salaries not exceeding the subsistence level, and it is probably in these marginal fields of employment that the major solution of our unemployment problem lies. The income tax is collected directly and relatively cheaply, with no hidden costs and waste. And it has become an integral part of modern economic, political and social policy. It is the most effective method yet devised, within the framework of the capitalist economy, for achieving the social and humanitarian objectives of our civilization; for applying wealth which is made possible only by organized society for the benefit of society as a whole; for preserving the freedom of individual initiative and at the same time making possible the financing of those services which can be most economically provided by the community as a whole."[13]

Today the income tax is considered by most economists as the tax system that best equalizes the tax burden and that best serves the desirable political objectives of (1) reducing income inequality, (2) stabilizing economic equilibrium, and (3) maintaining high consumption levels. The judgment stated by the House Ways and Means Committee in 1913 that "the individual income tax is the fairest of all taxes" is still widely believed. "No other tax accords as well with ability to pay or serves better to moderate economic inequality," according to economist Richard Goode, a leading authority on the income tax.[14] Most economists agree with Goode that the main justification for the personal income tax must be based on the principle of ability to pay. This is the "progressive" principle of taxation under which taxes are levied and paid according to the financial ability of the taxpayer, with the heavier burden falling on the wealthy. Ability to pay, as a guiding principle, is certainly one that accords with the highest sense of justice and fair play. It almost ranks with the Socialist creed. "To each according to his needs, from each according to his ability to pay" could be called the capitalist creed of the income tax system.

Despite the general accord among economists that the income tax system is the best tax system available, the governments of the United States and of other industrial countries are faced today with the dilemma of insufficient tax revenues, increasing welfare costs, and mounting taxpayer resistance. From the experts' viewpoint the income tax theoretically is the best of all possible taxes; the only problem is that it does not seem to be working.

Professor Richard A. Musgrave of Harvard made a study of the development of the tax structure in the United Kingdom, the United States, and Germany over the period 1880-1960 and noted: "The rise in the income tax share tapers off notably toward the end of our period and may experience a future decline." The reason for the decline of the income tax, according to Musgrave, is this:

> Whereas only a few decades ago it was a tax on the rich, based on only a small percentage of income earnings, it then became a mass tax, including practically all earners. Per dollar of revenue, the distributive impact of today's income tax, therefore, differs much less from that of a sales tax than it did in the earlier phases of its modern history. The income tax share has thus lost much of its attraction as a redistributive device and bids to become the major object of taxpayer resistance.[15]

The causes of dissatisfaction with the income tax are both political and economic. From the political side, the income tax has been attacked since its inception as undemocratic, inquisitorial, a violation of property rights, a violation of constitutional rights, and a threat to the privacy and dignity of the individual. From the economic side, the income tax has been accused of destroying the will to work, of financing a huge and growing welfare class, of misallocating economic resources, and of other socially harmful and economically wasteful effects.

Personal taxation is not inherently more pernicious or oppressive than other forms of taxation. Taxpayers, in general, will pay taxes willingly when they consider them fair or when the tax revenues are used for purposes they approve. This seems to be true regardless of the type of taxes or the size of the tax levy. On the other hand, taxpayers resent payment of taxes, no matter how light, when they regard them as unfair, when they feel tax monies are being wasted or misused, or when payment of taxes becomes personally demeaning or inconvenient.

It is sometimes said that all taxes are personal since they are ultimately paid by a person, whether he be a consumer, a wageearner, or a stockholder. But a personal tax, as more commonly known, is a direct tax that is paid by the person taxed on his income, and the tax may be paid either in money or in kind. In contrast, a commodity tax is an impersonal or indirect tax and is collected from the consumer at the time of sale, and for that reason is called a consumption tax. Both forms of taxation have been known since social life was first organized, for taxes are the price we pay not only for civilized society, as Justice Holmes said, but for social order itself.

The amount of coercion used in collecting taxes is a major factor determining taxpayer acceptance or resistance to a tax system. While personal taxes are more subject to coercive measures than commodity or consumption taxes, this is not true in all cases. A personal tax can be levied with payment on a voluntary basis. A tithe is a 10 per cent tax for the support of the church or church government, but this may be a voluntary tax, with no effort made to enforce compliance. A commodity tax on salt and bread, which are prime necessities of life, is a coercive tax since the consumer cannot avoid payment. A threat of starvation is as strong a threat as physical force.

Nevertheless, coercion is usually associated with personal taxes. Under the Roman empire all persons who were not citizens of Rome were subject to the payment of a tribute or tax. The payment of direct taxes became associated with an inferior political status. "The Romans always regarded direct taxation of their citizens as humiliating and undignified. . . . Direct taxation in those days was an extraordinary measure and the assessment, called *tributum*, levied upon the property of the citizen was a kind of War Loan which was in some cases repaid when the war was over."[16] After 167 B.C., direct taxes were levied only on subject people, never on Romans. Said Cicero, "The taxes which we exact, along with our provinces, constitute, as it were, the landed property of the Roman people."[17]

When collection is enforced against the person of the taxpayer, the result is a naked and unequal confrontation between the power of the government and the citizen. In ancient and feudal times the methods of collection were cruel and barbarous. The taxpayer was sometimes starved, beaten, killed, or sold into slavery, along with his family, for nonpayment of taxes. The threat of confrontation is always present in personal taxes. With respect to commodity taxes collected at the time of sale or consumption, the taxpayer has the option of refusing to pay the tax by refusing to buy. This option is not normally available in personal or income taxes. For these and other reasons direct personal taxes have in the past tended to be "vexatious" and "odious," according to early students of taxation. The recent history of income tax litigation leaves no doubt that this type of personal tax poses a threat to the individual's dignity and privacy and renders him subject to the coercive power of the state, in a direct and inquisitorial fashion.

The income tax law established the legal principle that the claims of the state to ownership of property are superior to the claims of the individual. After 1913 the right of the state to tax and distribute wealth and income in accordance with its financial needs and ethical judgment could not be challenged. This was a major breakthrough in social legislation.

The constitutional doctrine of individual ownership rights as being absolute and immune from state ownership claims was invalidated by the 16th Amendment. Locke's concept of the state as the protector of property rights was replaced by the Progressive concept of the state as the protector of the poor and the agency for distribution of wealth to correct inequalities of income. The 16th Amendment, by altering the fundamental property law of the nation, made possible a revolution by taxation. Within the lifetime of an American taxpayer the tax levy on personal income was to rise from zero to over $100 billion! Despite the enormous revenues it has raised, or perhaps because of it, the income tax is not popular.

3. It Violates Personal Rights

The basic *economic* problem inherent in the income tax law is the difficulty of defining income. The 16th Amendment refers to income "from whatever source derived," and the Internal Revenue Code lists items that are classified as income from certain sources for taxable purposes, but taxable income is "not limited to" the enumerated items. This leaves the definition of income up to judicial interpretation, but the courts in the United States have never promulgated a precise interpretation of income. In general, the courts have become much more liberal in their interpretation of what constitutes income compared to former times, when the constitutionality of income taxation itself was a matter of dispute.

Economists have wrestled with the problem of income definition without coming to an agreement. Richard Goode sums up the problem in his study, *The Individual Income Tax*, for the Brookings Institution:

> Many American students have accepted as an ideal starting point for tax purposes an income definition usually associated in the United States with the names of Haig and Simons but which was anticipated by Schanz in Germany and

apparently also by Davidson in Sweden. In Haig's language, income is "the increase or accretion in one's power to satisfy his wants in a given period in so far as that power consists of (a) money itself, or (b) anything susceptible of valuation in terms of money."

Simons equates personal income with the algebraic sum of consumption and change in net worth. Most experts believe, however, that it is not feasible to take into account all accrued changes in the value of assets and liabilities and that the income tax should be limited to realized income as reflected in transactions or conventional accounting statements.[18]

The problems of defining income in terms of either (1) consumption or power to command consumption of goods and services or (2) increase or decrease in individual net worth seem to defy exact quantitative measurement. Nicholas Kaldor, who favors consumption as a basis of measurement, decries the inequities of a tax law based on income: "Taxation according to 'income' introduces a bias in favor of property owners whose taxable capacity is underrated relatively to those who derive their income from work. Moreover since taxable income from property can be converted into capital gains in numerous ways 'income' is not only a defective measure of taxable capacity but one whose relation to taxable capacity can be manipulated by certain classes of tax payers." Kaldor concludes that "the problem of *defining* individual income, quite apart from any problem of practical measurement, appears in principle insoluble. There is no 'ideal' definition of income (at least none that could be objectively defined and measured) which, if adopted, would measure the amount of 'net accretion of economic power' of an individual (Haig) or the amount which each individual could spend in any particular year and 'still be as well off at the end of the period as he was at the beginning' (Hicks). The search for the 'true' measure of the spending capacity or the true 'increment of economic power' is a chase of a will-o'-the-wisp."[19]

Although Simons favored a definition of income as gain in individual net worth and "the market value of rights exercised in consumption," he was forced to admit that consumption "presents insuperable difficulties to achievement of a rigorous conception of personal income." Simons concludes:

Tax laws do not really define income but merely set up rules as to what must be included and what may be deducted; and such rules by no means define income because they are neither exhaustive nor logically coherent. That rules of this kind work out at all well is due to the cooperation of taxpayers, the paucity of ingenious lies, and to the availability of checks, in market prices, in information derived from third parties and in the mass of business records and accounts.[20]

The problem of defining income remains a crucial stumbling block in the way of achieving a fair and equitable law and in all probability is a problem that is incapable of solution. In the meantime the intense dissatisfaction the income tax is generating among taxpayers is making their cooperation increasingly involuntary and subject to coercive measures.

It is not only the small taxpayer who must stand before the inquisitorial bar of judgment of the Internal Revenue Service to answer as to what is or is not taxable income. President Richard M. Nixon himself has been accused of error in declaration of income and has agreed to pay a heavy back tax and interest. The IRS has also accused the International Telephone & Telegraph Company of undervaluing income by several million dollars for 1972. If the largest corporations and the highest officials of the government have difficulty evaluating income for tax purposes, the average taxpayer may be forgiven for assuming that the subject is (1) beyond understanding or (2) a fertile field for legal skullduggery.

Perhaps the chief political cause for dissatisfaction with the personal income tax is that it is inquisitorial and, as such, undemocratic. This is not to say that a tax designed to reduce inequalities of income is undemocratic in principle. At one time it would have been so considered, but in a consumer society, where individual consumption is not quantitatively related to individual production, a democratic government can establish, legally and morally, any income policy it wishes. In a consumer society the income tax, as presently established, is undemocratic because it violates the principle of individual privacy or encroaches unduly on the private domain of the citizen.

In a democracy a citizen's right to privacy is considered, by many authorities, as probably the most basic of all individual rights. Supreme Court Justice Brandeis in *Olmstead v. U.S.* (1928) stated: "The makers of our Constitution . . . recognized the significance of man's spiritual nature, of his feelings and of his intellect. They knew that only a part of the pain, pleasure and satisfaction of life are to be found in material things. They sought to protect Americans in their beliefs, their thoughts, their emotions and their sensations. They conferred, as against the government, the right to be let alone — the most comprehensive of rights and the right most valued by civilized men."

In the 18th century a person's rights to privacy within his own private property were regarded by enlightened politicians as one of the "natural" or inalienable rights of man. This right was recognized, not only in revolutionary America and France, but in royalist England. The elder Pitt, before his son passed the first income tax law, could say with pardonable pride that in England, "The poorest man may in his cottage bid defiance to all the forces of the Crown. It may be frail — its roof may shake — the wind may blow through it — the storm may enter, the rain may enter — but the King of England cannot enter — all his forces dare not cross the threshold."

Adam Smith reported that the first attempt to tax English farmers according to income or profits met with violent opposition: "An inquisition into every man's private circumstances, and an inquisition which, in order to accommodate the tax to them, watched all the fluctuations of his fortune, would be a source of such continual and endless vexation as no people could support."[21] The English character has become considerably more tame, and Englishmen no longer consider it vexatious to be visited by a tax appraiser or object to an inquisition into the fluctuations of their private fortunes by income tax collectors.

All political systems employ coercion to enforce compliance with laws. The amount of coercion in a system is an index of the liberty and privacy enjoyed by the individual citizen. A well-known political scientist, Professor D. E. Apter, evaluated the significance of privacy in these words: "The two most useful general indicators of coercion (when we wish to evaluate it in connection with government) are as follows: (1) The amount of privacy in the system; and (2) the amount of centralized governmental application of coercive measures." Apter then goes on to state that in autocracies "privacy is regarded as virtually subversive. As an idea, it runs counter to the view of politics in which the collectivity takes precedence over the individual, and the individual's personality is regarded as dependent upon the state. . . . In order to protect privacy, there must be a check on the arbitrary use of state power against the individual."[22]

In countries where the rights of the individual to personal freedom are disregarded or unknown, the rights of privacy are also unknown. There are no words in Russian for the Western concept of "personal privacy." The following report on privacy in Russia was made by reporter Georgie Ann Geyer: "In the woods between Moscow and the nearby village of Uspenakoye is privacy — but only for the privileged elite of Moscow. Here, protected by trees that turn black in the heavy shade and protected by roads that are tightly closed to all except those with special passes, live the elite party, intellectual and scientific community of the Soviet Union . . . In a country that has made an ideological fetish of grouping everyone together in huge, anonymous apartment complexes, in a country where collectivism and not one's personal life is supposed to be the arbiter of human rights, in a country where the holy tenet is 'to each according to his needs' members of the Soviet elite more and more are living like rampant individualists, alone and apart from the masses."[23] In countries with an undemocratic tradition, the rights of man to privacy are regarded, not as one of the inalienable rights of the individual, but as the exclusive right of the privileged élite.

The Magna Charta, the Declaration of Independence, the Bill of Rights, and other basic doctrines reflect a Western tradition of individual liberty that is absent in Communist countries. It is a tradition that clearly and sharply limits the right of government to interfere with or violate the privacy of the individual in his personal life and property. This tradition was reinforced by the pioneer life of colonial America. The American pioneer was necessarily the most independent of men. He developed a strong tradition of self-reliance. The American pioneer considered government interference in his personal life and property an intolerable affront. The democratic ideal of limited government and individual liberty blended with a pioneer environment to produce the American character. In its defiance of government interference and its glorification of personal rights it was much more extreme than the European. In most European countries, even in such democratic countries as England and France, the ideals of individual freedom and the rights of the individual are not built into the national character. The power of the sovereign state has always come first in Europe, and custom, if not law, has made men there more amenable to authority.

The individual income tax violates, in the opinion of many experts, the spirit, if not the letter, of the original Bill of Rights, specifically the 4th and

5th Amendments. The income tax law violates the rights of privacy of the individual and forces him, under pain of severe reprisals, to reveal to a government official the most intimate and detailed accounting of his personal and private affairs. This same official has the authority to subpoena him and his records and to subject him and them to the most minute examination. If not satisfied that the taxpayer has complied with all the tax regulations, the official can take the taxpayer to court and subject him to all the humiliation and expense of a trial. The official can use informers to testify against the taxpayer. He can produce, from government files, the past personal financial records of the taxpayer. All the powers of government are marshaled against the taxpayer, who must bear the cost of his own defense.

The subjection of the citizen of a free democratic country to the process of fiscal surveillance, to the extraction of confessions of a private and personal nature, to the subpoenaing of his records and person, to the compilation of personal dossiers for possible use against him — these are acts usually associated with totalitarian states, not with democratic countries.

Taxpayers who default on their taxes or evade them have always been dealt with harshly, even in democracies. This is understandable. Punishment for nonpayment of taxes is one thing. What is new under the income tax law and is undemocratic is the introduction of an inquisitorial system for prying into people's lives and homes and personal affairs to "check," "audit," "judge," and "investigate" the everyday private life of the taxpayer. It is this inquisitorial system, which is inherent in the administration of the personal income tax, that makes it contrary to the Anglo-American tradition of personal rights and a violation of the citizen's rights to privacy.[24]

On January 9, 1973 the Supreme Court ruled that the IRS can compel an accountant to surrender to the government personal records of clients whose income tax returns he has prepared. Justice William O. Douglas, in dissent, stated that such government seizure of personal records could be construed as infringing on the 5th Amendment guarantees and as a violation of the 4th Amendment prohibiting unreasonable searches and seizures. Said Justice Douglas: "One's privacy...has a very meaningful relationship....The decision today sanctions yet another tool of the ever-widening government invasion and oversight of our private lives."

The objection will be raised that the citizen has no right to privacy where financial matters that affect the public welfare are concerned. The maintenance of complete financial records on each citizen is a matter of administrative efficiency to insure fair play rather than a sinister plan by Washington to keep an eye on the taxpayer. Besides, claim these apologists, the income tax law was passed by Congress; Congress controls the operation of the law; and the citizens control Congress. This is technically correct, but the Congress has no direct day-to-day control over the operation of the income tax law, and there is no need for such Congressional control or supervision. The IRS, which collects the income tax, is a vast autonomous bureaucracy operating as a bureau of the executive branch of the government. The lines of control from the average citizen to the IRS are so long and tenuous that, rightly or wrongly, the average taxpayer fears the

IRS as an all-powerful, all-knowing, all-seeing "big brother" in whose computer memory are stored the most private and personal details of his life and those of his family. The need for the protection of individual privacy against government intervention is always present because the relationship between the citizen and the state is a fluid one.

When the Olmstead opinion was written by Louis D. Brandeis in 1928, the power of the government to invade the "private sector" of the individual citizen had not reached the Orwellian proportions it has today. In those days the individual was relatively immune from government controls over his private property and personal affairs, unless he committed a fraud, trespass, theft, or some other violation of the civil or criminal code. The law at that time conferred on the individual certain rights to control property within his private sector that were inviolate. Undoubtedly, the growth and arrogance of private power at that time called for corrective measures. The power of the government was dwarfed by the concentration of power in the private sector of the economy. Economic policy was dominated by such giants in the private sector as Morgan, Mellon, DuPont, and Rockefeller.

The legal impregnability of private property was breached by the 16th Amendment. The income tax law has been the chief means by which the government has progressively deprived the private sector of its power and importance, reduced its size, and brought it under the domination and control of the government or the public sector. As that sector of the economy grows larger, the bureaucracy increases, and a new dominant class emerges as the director of government programs and the controller of government funds. These funds are, of course, tax funds, but there is no direct control over their use by the taxpayer; neither must the government program director account to the taxpayer, not does he feel that the relationship of the beneficiary to the state is anything more or less than that of a ward. Under this new relationship the right of privacy becomes an executive privilege.

Commenting on the national scandal that erupted over the Watergate wiretapping incident during the Nixon presidential election former Supreme Court Justice Arthur J. Goldberg said: "Wiretapping strikes at the panoply of protections which our Constitution erects around privacy. Privacy — the ability to be confident of security in our homes and our conversations — is not only the bedrock of individual freedom; privacy of communications is the essence of democracy."[25]

As a threat to individual freedom, the Watergate incident involving the tapping of telephone wires in one office for the purpose of obtaining political information is relatively insignificant compared to the massive organized invasion of privacy carried on by the IRS, the FBI, and the Treasury Department under the authority of the income tax law.

4. It Is Complex

Another reason for the alienation of the taxpayer under the income tax system is the unbelievable complexity of the Internal Revenue Code. The income tax law is a lengthy and complex statute with many involved and detailed regulations that even a tax attorney has difficulty in understanding. The Internal Revenue Code and pertinent official regulations occupy many bulky volumes, and these do not give final answers to many income tax questions, which must be sought in court decisions, Congressional committee reports, legal journals, and other sources. One tax expert, Stanley S. Surrey, in a paper presented before the House Ways and Means Committee (1959) stated flatly: "The income tax provisions of the 1954 Internal Revenue Code represent probably the most complex revenue law ever enacted in the fiscal history of any country," and added that attempts to clarify some of its more difficult provisions presented obstacles "formidable almost beyond belief."[26]

If tax economists and tax attorneys have difficulty understanding the income tax law, what must be the feeling of the ordinary taxpayer when he is faced with the problem of filing his income tax report? In most cases the feeling is one of utter frustration and helplessness. The manual that the government provides the taxpayer to guide him through the labyrinth of rules and regulations only adds to the confusion. The 1969 Tax Reform Act was supposed to clear up some ambiguities and complexities of the 1954 income tax law, but it has not been successful. The new law, as passed by Congress, contains 368 pages of dense legal prose, accompanied by a 346-page conference report. The bill contains involved passages, such as: "For purposes of paragraph 3, an organization described in paragraph 2 shall be deemed to include an organization as described in Section 501 C4, 5, or 6, which could be described in paragraph 2 if it were an organization described in Section 501 D3." Or the following: "For purposes of paragraph (1) the amount taken into account to any element shall be the sum of (a) the amount (if any) determined by multiplying (1) the amount which bears the same ratio to the lower of the amounts specified in sub-paragraph (a) or (b) of sub-section (a) (1) for the section 1250 property as the additional depreciation for such element attributable to periods after December 31, 1969, bears to the sum of the additional depreciation for all elements attributable to period after December 31, 1969, by (11) the applicable percentage for such element, and (b) the amount (if any) determined..." etc.

The well-known humorist Art Buchwald in his syndicated column of April 7, 1972, wrote this satiric version of the Lord's prayer as spoken by the harassed taxpayer:

Heavenly Father, we beseech you in our hour of need to look down kindly on your humble taxpaying servants who have given all we possess to the almighty Internal Revenue Service. Grant us that we have completed our Form 1040 correctly so no power will find fault with it. We pray to God that we have added lines 12, 13, 14 and 15 accurately, and that we have subtracted line 17 from line 16 so our adjusted gross income is computed to their divine satisfaction. We ask you, O Lord, to protect our exemptions and bless our deductions as outlined in Schedule A (Form 1040) (see Chapters 10 and 11). Have mercy on those of us who failed to wisely estimate our payments during the year, and must now borrow from Peter to pay Paul. Blessed are they who spent more than they earned and contributed so much to the economy. Give us the strength, Lord, so that we may dwell in a lower tax bracket forever and ever (as outlined in Publication 17, the Revised 1972 Edition)... Yea though we walk through the valley of the shadow of bankruptcy (see tax rate schedule X, Y, Z, or if applicable Schedule D or Schedule G or maximum tax form 4726) there is no one to comfort us. [27]

It is small wonder that the average American taxpayer throws up his hands and turns his tax report over to an accountant. This, of course, was always done by persons of wealth, but even the small taxpayer now uses the services of tax "experts." There are great numbers of firms with offices throughout the nation that specialize in handling the income tax reports of small taxpayers. The annual ritual of filing the personal income tax report is now largely in the hands of a professional class of tax experts who are supposed to understand the occult mysteries of the Internal Revenue Code. These mysteries awe and frighten the ordinary taxpayer, and he seeks the assurance of the professional tax expert, who can allay his fears, take advantage of all legal deductions, and guarantee him immunity from the dreaded IRS. Under the income tax law the citizen feels no sense of participation or representation. The tyranny of the income tax system is not caused by the illegality or impropriety of the law. It is the most "legal" and most "fair" of all tax laws, according to lawyers and economists. The tyranny of the income tax, to the average taxpayer, is attributable to the fact that he does not understand it and cannot escape it, and people naturally fear what they do not understand and cannot control.

Legal complexity makes the income tax law fraught with peril to the unwary taxpayer or layman, but it has provided the tax attorneys with a stimulating intellectual challenge and a new and important status in the business community. In a symposium conducted by the Tax Institute of America on November 20-21, 1969, the president of the Institute, Mr. Victor E. Ferrall, who was also General Tax Attorney for the American Telephone and Telegraph Company, said that in "the period from the middle of the 1930s to the late 1940s... able young lawyers took into court tax questions that resulted in a series of notable Supreme Court decisions which are still basic to our tax learning. One of the most notable was *Gregory v. Helvering*, in which the Supreme Court announced that, in deciding tax issues, it would look through form to substance. These decisions introduced an intellectual challenge that had not been there before."

The complexity of the income tax law may be of minor concern to modern economists who are more concerned with social equity, resources allocation, and revenue, but to the taxpayer the famous tax principle of Adam Smith that a tax should be "certain, and not arbitrary... clear and plain to the contributor, and to every other person," still seems a reasonable expectation. A taxpayer is entitled to know his tax liability with a fair degree of certainty so that he can plan his personal affairs and business transactions. No tax attorney can vouchsafe him that certainty. A ruling by a tax court is not a legal guarantee; a decision by an appellate court is not a firm assurance. To be final, the decision must come from the Supreme Court, which looks to the substance of the case and not the legal form to arrive at its decision.

35

Lawyers may argue that simplicity per se is not a virtue, but a complex tax law undoubtedly places a heavy burden of uncertainty on the taxpayer that frustrates his ability to plan ahead. The uncertainty and complexity of the personal income tax is in sharp contrast to that of an impersonal commodity tax, such as a sales tax or excise tax, where the tax payment is automatic and uncomplicated and the tax liability is definite and known to all.

Because of its complexity and inquisitorial method of enforcement, the personal income tax is expensive to administer. This statement may sound strange, as tax experts have said that the enormous revenues collected through that tax could not be collected otherwise without much greater expense and effort. This is not true. While it is a fact that voluntary payroll tax deductions and voluntary tax payments throw the burden on the private citizen and his employer, the burden is there, nevertheless. It costs the government nothing, but this effort is paid for by society in numberless man-hours spent in calculating and reporting and paying the income tax. Society also pays for the hordes of tax consultants who advise and guide and protect the interests of their clients. The money, time, and effort spent in .tax matters by these consultants is enormous.

In California alone the state conservatively places the number of nonprofessional tax practitioners at about 25,000. This is in addition to about 11,000 certified public accountants and another 13,000 public accountants, most of whom also do tax work. The IRS estimates that about half of the 75.4 million individual tax forms filed in 1971 were prepared by a tax expert and paid for by the taxpayers. A House subcommittee investigating this subject has set a figure of $500 million as the amount paid by the taxpayers in 1970 to have their tax returns prepared by tax professionals. The head of the IRS, J. M. Walters, commented ruefully in an interview in 1972, "Our laws are too complicated, and, as a result, our tax forms are too complicated. The IRS can't promise everyone a simple return under a complex law."[28]

The Internal Revenue Service is one of the most efficient and incorruptible tax agencies in the world. Certainly, no other tax agency has a task of equal magnitude. The IRS, on the whole, has performed creditably and with efficiency and fairness, considering the size and scope of its activities. No scandal has besmirched its reputation, and the fear its name invokes among taxpayers is more the result of guilty feelings of apprehension than of any cruelty or abuse or disregard of personal rights on the part of the agency.

Nevertheless, efficient as it may be, the colossal task of the IRS necessarily requires a tremendous bureaucracy, complete with all the necessary equipment and specialists to deal with such a huge and complicated task. There is the usual civil service hierarchy, from chiefs of departments to file clerks. There are commissioners, deputy commissioners, lawyers, accountants, administrators, office managers, investigators, auditors, and prosecutors adding up to a total work force of about 72,000 people in 1972. This is not a large number when compared to the total Federal payroll of about 5 million workers and $64 billion (1972), but it undoubtedly serves to augment the already huge bureaucracy. The Commissioner of Internal Revenue draws an annual salary of $40,000, plus fringe benefits. Average salaries in the Federal Civil Service in grades 9 through 15 range from $11,614 to $30,018, plus normal fringe benefits worth 28 per cent of salary. Data-processing machinery of the latest type is installed to cope with the mass of paperwork. The IRS has offices all over the world, wherever Americans work, for the privilege of paying the income tax is one that follows the American citizen wherever he goes.

Silent, efficient, ubiquitous, the IRS is also huge, expensive, and bureaucratic. The cost to the government (i.e., to the taxpayers) of maintaining the IRS is enormous and represents only one of the costs of administering the income tax. Another is the enormous cost to the government and to the taxpayers involved in settling tax suits.

Court administration costs are not puny. A justice of the United States Court of Claims earns $42,500 annually, plus generous pensions and other benefits. The Assistant Executive Director of the United States Tax Court draws a salary of $34,323. The compensation of private tax attorneys and accountants is perhaps even higher on the average. All these costs directly or indirectly rest on the backs of the taxpayer.

The tax burden on the taxpayer is estimated at $336 billion dollars, or 36 per cent of the national income in 1972. The tax levy has multiplied 11 times in three decades, skyrocketing from a total in 1942 of $31 billion. Viewing the burden another way, the average American will put in 2 hours and 39 minutes of a regular working day to pay his tax bill — longer than he does to pay for his food, clothing, and shelter. According to the Tax Foundation, the average American will work for the government from January 1 to May 1. Every cent he earns during that period will go to the government for taxes. Only on May 2 will he start earning money for himself. Since the "average" American includes the unemployed and the underpaid, the tax burden carried by the middle-class American must approach or pass the dangerous point where he works longer for the government than he does for himself.

5. It Encourages Evasion

Another serious charge against the personal income tax is that it encourages tax evasion and thereby may be said to have a corrupting influence on public morals. Gladstone said of the income tax, "I believe it does more than any other tax to demoralize and corrupt the people." There is a widespread belief among the poor that "smart" people and "very rich" people somehow escape the "bite" of the individual income tax. This belief is encouraged by reports in the press of millionaires who pay no income tax. The poor do not understand the fine legal points of the tax laws, and they cannot hire tax lawyers, but they read and hear of the more common methods used by wealthy people legally to avoid the high rates of the individual income tax. The papers carry advertisements urging people to take advantage of "tax shelters" in investment and real estate situations. This is all very legal and proper and understandable. Everyone, even the poor man, tries his best to minimize his tax liability. However, the taxpayer in the lower brackets, who is locked into the tax-deduction payroll system, cannot but envy and perhaps resent the affluent citizen who can take advantage of the many legal tax shelters that are available to him: tax-exempt securities, foreign-based-corporations, real estate depreciation, oil depletion, and many others.

The Los Angeles Times on April 7, 1972 reported the results of an investigation made by the IRS in the two California districts. IRS employees posing as clients were sent to the offices of "tax experts" to have their income tax returns prepared. Of 330 returns checked in a survey of 318 income tax preparers in Northern California, 49 per cent were fraudulent, according to the IRS. In the Southern California survey, 35 per cent of the 220 experts checked had committed possible fraud. Of the 220 tax experts checked, only one prepared correct returns, according to Robert McKeever, Assistant District Director of the IRS for the Los Angeles area. Said McKeever, "This was not an effort to entrap, but an effort to determine who was trying to cheat the government." According to McKeever, the IRS investigators made no effort to influence the tax experts to falsify the returns in their favor. They did this on their own volition based, no doubt, on the tacit assumption that the taxpayer wanted to get as much as he could in the way of deductions. Among the 35 per cent who may have committed fraud, some tripled medical expenses, inflated church contributions, increased the number of dependents, entered false casualty losses, and omitted certain earnings, according to McKeever. One wonders how much more the experts would have done for their clients if they has been prodded. Undoubtedly the harried taxpayer, after reading of millionaires who do not pay income taxes, feels no moral obligation to pay his tax liability in full and considers any deduction he can take morally, if not legally, justified.

The situation in England is no different from that prevailing in the United States, according to Coffield:

> The direct income tax has always been associated with fraud on the part of the taxpayer even when the rate of tax was at its lowest. The reason, I think, is that the citizen is aware that the sanction behind the demand for income tax is the power of the state. It is a kind of naked confrontation of state and citizen. And when the demand is accompanied, as it often is, by an inquisition into the taxpayer's affairs, sometimes into his personal life, and the way in which he runs his business, he is apt to regard the exposure as both humiliating and oppressive. This fundamental objection has always existed. But when the rates of tax become progressive to the point of confiscation the taxpayer has no doubt that he is being robbed, albeit by due process of law.[29]

The viability of the income tax system rests on the voluntary cooperation of the taxpayer, and this cooperation can be expected only when the majority of taxpayers believe that the system is fair. Should a point be reached where the average taxpayer feels that the income tax is unfair and that he is being victimized by a system that discriminates in favor of the rich and powerful, at that point the income tax system would be endangered because it probably could not work without the voluntary cooperation of the taxpayer. This dire possibility is a spectre that haunts the government; according to the IRS, it can be exorcised only by massive increases in bureaucracy and surveillance and data processing. Said the head of the IRS in 1972:

> What we most need in the Revenue Service is a massive increase in manpower to have better audit coverage. We need it because our voluntary self-assessment tax system is in danger. There are indications of increasing noncompliance. The number of fraudulent returns from tax preparers is just one sign. There are others. We can't afford to have our tax system fall into disrepair. If it goes down the drain, so does our whole system of government.

That the income tax can, somehow, be made fair and equitable by government decree or by the closing of loopholes or by stricter enforcement has not been proved by American experience or indeed by the experience of any nation at any time. The difficulty of the problem was recognized by Pitt, who fathered the first income tax. He complained bitterly about "shameful evasion." Almost every president since 1913 has tried to solve this problem without apparent success. President Roosevelt, in a message to Congress on June 1, 1937, asked for a law to make the "present tax structure evasion-proof." Tax evasion, he said was "widespread" and violators were "amazing both in their boldness and their ingenuity." Roosevelt may or may not have been aware that his Senate floor leader Alben W. Barkley, who later became vice president under Truman, evaded payment of income taxes; only after his death was the government able to collect $343,444 in settlement of income tax claims.

When the taxpayer is involved in a suit over his income tax, the problems he faces are formidable. To begin with, there is very likely to be no clear-cut legal ruling applicable to his case. Regulations issued by the Treasury are his most reliable guides. The latest income tax regulations run to over 1500 pages, but these do not furnish legal guidance to the meaning of the statute in a specific application. The taxpayer or his attorney must consult *Cumulative Bulletins*, published in over 50 volumes, which contain rulings of a less formal character than regulations.

The problem is not solved by consulting these and other sources. The Internal Revenue Code is not only what the regulations say it is; it is also, to apply Chief Justice Hughes' dictum about the Constitution, what the judges say it is. Tax cases constitute a large proportion of the litigation in Federal courts; in fact, courts try more tax cases than any other type. Tax cases also contribute a sizable proportion of cases tried before the Supreme Court.

Tax laws enacted by Congress ust be interpreted. This duty falls upon the Federal courts; they decide each case, and their decisions become precedents. The courts, as presently constituted, are not ideal agencies for administering tax laws, which is, in effect, what they are doing. It is not that Federal judges are incompetent or unwise, but that the judicial process is a slow one and the outcome always doubtful.

The court calendars are usually crowded, and there is no assurance as to when a specific case will be heard. Some tax cases on record have taken 16 years to go from the lower courts, through the appellate courts, to the Supreme Court, and these cases involved individuals, not corporations. Tax cases taken to the Supreme Court may not be decided for as long as five years. According to Randolph E. Paul, "In the cases decided by the Supreme Court in the calendar year 1943, it was on the average at least ten years from the time the point was first raised until it was finally authoritatively decided."

Not infrequently, in estate and income tax cases, one or more of the defendants will die before the case is finally settled. Once caught in the legal machinery of tax litigation the taxpayer is faced with a long, costly, and frustrating experience.

The individual income tax in its present form is a nightmare to the taxpayers; it is incomprehensible to the voter; it is a trap to the wage earner; it supports an army of tax lawyers and tax accountants, whose avowed purpose is to circumvent it and render it painless to their clients. It maintains a huge and growing bureaucracy that is determined to enforce compliance and eventually will have a personal dossier on all individual taxpayers in its computers as detailed as those available to the secret police of a totalitarian state.

Almost all states have signed agreements with the IRS that provide for a sharing of taxpayer data. The only exceptions are Alabama, Connecticut, Louisiana, Nevada, Rhode Island, and Texas. These agreements provide for sharing of enforcement, personnel training, mutual assistance, and the sharing of such confidential information as taxpayer lists and personal data on computer tapes.

Despite the growth of surveillance, evasion continues and increases.

6. It Teaches A New Work Ethic

The effect of the personal income tax on work incentives is a subject of much controversy; in general, however, most observers agree that the effect has not been socially desirable or wholesome. The progressive rates of the income tax table penalize the enterprising newcomer and the successful innovator and protect the hereditary rich. It is true that means of circumventing the full effect of the income tax rates have been found, and that many new millionaires are made, as well as born, every year. But millionaires are not typical. It has also been observed by apologists for the income tax that monetary reward, per se, is not the mainspring of the successful business executive. The personal drive to achieve and excel in a given field appears to be as strong a motive — perhaps stronger — than pecuniary gain; psychologists hold that personal ambition may be directed toward power and prestige, as well as toward money.

This may very well be true, but such psychological evidence does not necessarily prove that the effects of the income tax on work incentives are socially desirable. It is true that ambitious men will rise to the top in almost any type of society. However, the industrial discipline of a society, its work habits, its attitude toward work, its capacity to make physical sacrifices and endure hardships, its energy and drive in practical enterprises, and all the other factors involved in the morals of the work force of a society are complex forces that are not fully understood today and probably never can be. All that can reasonably be assumed is that every society has a different industrial morale factor, that no two are alike, and that they differ even between different historical periods in the same country.

The English today are not what they were when Emerson visited them in 1848, and reported: "The English, at the present day, have great vigor of body and endurance. Other countrymen look slight and undersized beside them... They have the taste for toil, a distaste for pleasure or repose... An Englishman, while he eats and drinks no more or not much more than another man, labors three times as many hours in the course of a year as another European; or his life as a workman is three lives. He works fast. Everything in England is at a quick pace."[30] If Emerson were to visit England today, he would find a considerable change in industrial morale and work attitudes.

Eric Hoffer, the labor philosopher, made this comment on the English work force on October 5, 1969: "To produce the same piece of machinery, Britain needs twice as many men as Sweden, and four times as many men as the United States. Nothing the brilliant British economists, planners, and managers can think up has any effect. The readiness to work has become the great mystery of our time. Everywhere we look we can see how the health and vigor of a society are determined not by the quality of the elite, but by the temper and the habits of the common people."[31]

The ideals of the welfare state have permeated the thinking of the English working class so that there is a much more relaxed and hedonistic attitude toward work than formerly. Morally, this change may represent an improvement, but it may also explain why the English are no longer the leaders in industrial productivity.

The personal income tax may be partly responsible for the change in work habits and industrial morale that is noticeable in the United States today, as compared with, say, 50 or 100 years ago. There has been a decided change in the American worker's attitude toward his job. Some contend that the personal income tax has undermined the American work ethic, the incentive to sustained and exceptional effort. It has introduced the negative incentive of a tax penalty as a reward for exceptional effort. This negative work incentive tends to make leisure a socially acceptable substitute for work. "An income tax is in effect an excise tax on work," according to Professor Mark Blaug, which "alters the marginal rate of substitution between work and leisure."

The income tax, however, cannot be blamed as the only cause for the general decline in industrial discipline and morale in England and America. The growth of social legislation and the political power of labor have removed the spur of dire necessity that once drove some men to work against their natural inclinations. There is more job security, more unemployment insurance, greater pensions, less fear of deprivation, and less insecurity. As a result, the attitude toward work is now more casual, less fear-ridden, less

41

compulsive. This attitude is not necessarily detrimental to society, for men driven by fear, hunger, or insecurity may work hard, but the social tensions and repressed discontent existing in such a society may result in social and economic instability. Men should not, and need not, be driven to work against their will or be motivated by fear. A strong belief in work as a way of life provides a much more powerful motivation.

From colonial times the American worker was motivated by the so-called Protestant ethic, which glorified work and made it honorable and dignified in the eyes of the Lord. This ethic not only set a high social value on labor; it comdemned sloth or leisure as sinful. The Protestant ethic had its start here in the Puritan Commonwealth of Massachusetts, where the zealous asceticism of the Puritans was reinforced by the need to work hard to survive in a hostile environment. The concept of labor as honorable and worthy in the eyes of society and God was in marked contrast to the feudal and scholastic concept of labor as degrading and unworthy of anyone except a peasant, serf, or slave. The scholastic or aristocratic attitude toward labor prevailed longer in Latin, Arab, and Slav countries; according to many sociologists, this antiwork bias resulted in a marked inferiority in their industrial morale and efficiency as compared with countries in which the Protestant ethic and Locke's concept of property rights prevailed.

A healthy economy requires a healthy industrial morale based on a positive attitude toward work. Work should not be regarded by society as inferior, degrading, or less worthy than leisure or scholastic activity. On the contrary, labor should incorporate social values of the highest order if it is to be productive and innovative. Perhaps personal salvation can no longer be achieved by work alone, according to the Protestant ethic, but the ideal of personal achievement, and social accomplishment through work should not be denied or derided. The youth especially need to have a positive, healthy attitude toward work. In America the young have a superior, if not disdainful, attitude toward labor. The aphorisms of Franklin, the Puritan tradition, the Horatio Alger myth, the labor theory of value underlying the economic system (to labor belong the fruits of labor) — all these are out of favor with the modern generation. Unlike earlier generations, modern youth is isolated from the economy, prohibited by law from working, and maintained in scholastic institutions until past the age of puberty. Its training is oriented toward scholastic, not labor, values.

In addition, youth is exposed to the value concept inherent in the income tax system which, as they see it, apparently punishes, rather than rewards, exceptional effort. Why work hard if the government is going to take most of the extra income in taxes? The negative incentive of the income tax is accepted by youth as a dominant social value and weakens the will to work among those who, by nature or education, are inclined to a hedonistic or antiwork attitude. The rebellion of present-day youth against the "Establishment" or "Big Business" or "Technology" is also a rebellion against the concept of work as a way of life or of personal fulfillment. To an idealistic and scholastic youth, work seems an intolerable and stultifying drudgery. He wants no part of it. Nevertheless, to a nation work is a matter of survival; negative work incentives can cause a weakening of industrial morale and discipline and can retard industrial progress vis-à-vis other nations with more positive work incentives. Looked at in the light of international economic competition, the income tax appears as a deterrent tending to weaken industrial morale and to slow down economic growth.

The question is now being asked: Why more economic growth? Growth for growth's sake has come under increasing criticism as a national goal. It is being attacked from two sides. On one side are the ecologists, who wish to restore "nature," or at least to discontinue acts that harm the environment. On the other side are the prophets of synergism as the wave of the future. They envisage a completely automated production system that will render human labor obsolete. It is doubtful if such a society will ever become a reality, at least in the foreseeable future. If automated affluence becomes a reality, the mental attitude of workers must be changed to that of the ancient aristocrats and feudal lords, to whom the idea of labor was repellent and personally degrading. Until such a synergistic society is a reality or until the United States is ready to build a wall around itself, it is safer to cultivate the habit of work in what is still a very competitive world. In America, however, this habit is losing popularity.

In December 1972 the Department of Health, Education, and Welfare released a massive study, *Work in America*, on the problem of American workers' attitude toward work. It claims that a statistically large section of the American work force is bored on the job, as evidenced by rising absenteeism and a desire for more leisure rather than for more money. The report recommends many remedies, including a massive effort to "redesign" boring jobs and replace industrial efficiency with "social" efficiency. The nexus between work and reward is not regarded as primary, and so the income tax is not even considered as one of the factors in lowering industrial morale. The workers' malaise therefore appears as a mysterious social ailment, requiring a psychological rather than an economic remedy. Senator Edward Kennedy and 17 of his colleagues introduced legislation in February 1973, authorizing $20 million to study worker alienation and study possibilities for "job enrichment." Yet the University of Michigan had just then completed a study that might have provided the Senators with the answer, or part of it. The study was conducted to find out why women work. Was it to get out of the house? To prove equality with men? For personal fulfillment? Nine of ten women gave their basic reason: money. Had times changed women's reason for working? No. The same question was asked 15 years earlier, and exactly the same response was recorded then. That canny Scotsman, Adam Smith, may not have been too far off when he said that self-interest provides the greatest incentive to work.

Persons who are in more direct contact with workers think that worker dissatisfaction is neither as puzzling nor as surprising as most intellectuals or politicians believe. Writing in the February 1973 issue of *The Federationist*, the organ of the American Federation of Labor, William W. Winpisinger, a vice-president of the International Association of Machinists, laid the blame for worker dissatisfaction squarely on the gap between effort and reward. Said

Mr. Winpisingar, "The gap between what the average worker earns and what his family needs for a decent standard of living has been growing. So it should come as no surprise to anyone that worker dissatisfaction is also growing." He suggested a sure formula for "job enrichment": "If you want to enrich the job, enrich the paycheck." As for alienation, he suggested, "Reevaluate the snobbery that makes it noble to possess a college degree and shameful to learn skills that involve a little bit of grease under the fingernails."

Malcolm W. Warren, a director of organization and management development for Questor Corporation, stated in the October 1972 issue of *Management Review*:

> Perhaps the biggest discovery that Questor has made is the effect of 'positive reinforcement'; that is, when there is a desirable consequence for performing well, people continue to perform well. The five 'reinforcers' that Questor has found to be the most effective are money, but only when it is a consequence of a specific performance and the relation to the performance is known; praise or recognition; freedom to choose one's own activities; opportunities to see one's self become better, more important or more useful; and power to influence both co-workers and management.

Management's solution to work alienation is less simplistic than labor's, but it also puts money first as the most positive "reinforcer" of worker morale, provided it is given as a reward for accomplishment and not as a gift or a bribe. Both management and labor are keenly aware that the nexus between work and reward has been weakened and should be strengthened. Unfortunately, this is not always possible under the present progressive income tax law, which teaches the new ethic that greater effort is rewarded with progressively less income.

7. It Raises Problems of Compliance

Although considerable reduction in income inequality may have been accomplished by the income tax, the statistical data available do not offer conclusive proof.

There are statistics available to prove that the income tax has almost prevented the concentration of wealth; other statistics prove that the income tax has had little or no effect on equalizing income. An eminent economist, Joseph A. Schumpeter, declared in 1947: "To an extent which is not generally appreciated, the New Deal was able to expropriate the upper income brackets even before the war...a tremendous transfer of wealth has actually been effected; a transfer that quantitatively is comparable with that effected by Lenin." However, economist Irving B. Kravis, who has specialized in income tax data, states, "Progressivity of the tax structure has played little, if any, part in making the income distribution more equal."

Since statistics of income do not measure capital accumulation or capital gains, they are not a true or even very reliable indicator of shifts in the concentration of wealth. Robert J. Lampman made a study of wealth concentration for the National Bureau of Economic Research based on estate tax data that indicate that the share of personal wealth held by the wealthiest 1 per cent of the population fell from 36.8 per cent in 1929 to 20.8 per cent in 1949, but had climbed to 26.0 per cent by 1956. Lampman's study does not confirm the popular belief that high income taxes keep individuals from amassing personal fortunes. Lampman reveals that the number of millionaires increased from 13,297 in 1944 to 27,502 in 1953. According to Lampman, the millionaire class grew by over 30 per cent, while the population grew by 15 per cent and per capita income grew by 4½ per cent.

One of the best studies of the income tax was made by Richard Goode for the Brookings Institution in 1964. Goode concludes his study with these words:

This extended review of the statistics neither corroborates the opinion that the income tax is a Draconian measure for re-distribution, nor justifies writing off its equalizing effects as inconsequential. Although the difference between the before-tax and after-tax distribution of income, in recent years, is not striking, neither is it trivial. There is no evidence that the re-distribution impact of the income tax has been offset by changes in before-tax income shares. Income before tax has become less unequal, and there is reason for believing that the tax has contributed, to a minor extent, to this change.[32]

This is certainly a far cry from the prophecies of those who expected the income tax to become a means for confiscating wealth or a tool for redistributing income on an egalitarian basis. Most authorities agree that the income tax has had some effect, although not a drastic one, on reducing inequalities of income in the United States. Although it is impossible to prove, there is ground for belief that the income tax has a very strong corrective effect on *preventing* greater inequality of income. Had the progressive income tax not been passed, there is every likelihood that inequality of income would be greater than it is. Of course, this cannot certainly be known, for it pre-supposes the absence of other corrective measures by the government and by the private economy.

According to Goode, government actions and developments in the private economy have had more impact on reducing the inequality of disposable income than the income tax. Among these developments may be listed: government programs for public health and education, for transportation and mobility, and for lessening racial discrimination. Other factors include labor political power; the shorter work week; minimum wage laws; financial assistance programs for the farmer, the home owner, and the small business man; private and government insured pension programs; unemployment insurance; and the official recognition by the government of the desirability of maintaining full employment by subsidising consumption when necessary. It is the combined effect of all economic and political developments of this type that has done more than the income tax to raise the level of the low income groups and reduce the gross inequalities of income.

Income taxes are justified on the ethical ground that they reduce inequality of income — equality is equated with social justice, otherwise the income tax is legalized robbery. Therefore, tax avoidance is considered by the state as an ethical as well as a legal question. Those who take advantage of tax "loopholes" are considered to be "cheating" on the "honest" taxpayers. J. P. Morgan, the great Wall Street financier, once berated a Congressional committee that tried to imply that tax avoidance was unethical. Said Morgan: "If the government objects to tax [avoidance], it should change the law." Complying with tax regulations was then considered a legal, not a moral, problem, and Judge Learned Hand declared, "There is nothing sinister in so arranging one's affairs as to keep taxes as low as possible."[33]

Official attitudes have changed. In countries where the income tax is the prime source of revenue, income tax violations are now considered the "premier crime against the state." In the United States we may not have reached this point as yet, but penalties now in effect are severe and are enforced with a dispatch that is not noticeable in other types of litigation.

In England the income tax law has from its inception been enforced with a gentlemanly regard for the privacy of the individual taxpayers, and government enforcement was based more on the honor system than on punitive measures. However, the situation is changing. "In recent years, and especially since 1951, the inquisitorial powers of the Revenue have been widely extended with the result that investigations of taxpayers' affairs have increased by leaps and bounds. The harvest to the Exchequer has been very considerable while the misery inflicted on hundreds of thousands of taxpayers, both innocent and guilty, is beyond description. It is very difficult for officials, even with the best will in the world, to administer an inquisitorial law with humanity."[34]

In other countries the income tax is reducing the private sector to a small role in the economy and enlarging the public sector to a point roughly comparable to that found in Communist countries. When economic policy approaches the Socialist ideal, as in Sweden, there is a significant change in the relationship of the citizens to the state. The democratic belief in the liberty of the individual places the interest of the citizens at the top and makes the state his servant. In Sweden, however, the citizen is now subordinate to the state. This collectivist social attitude is expressed in official policy declarations of the Swedish Social Democrat government. The permanent Secretary of State to the Swedish Ministry of Justice, Ove Rainier, made this declaration in a talk to a conference of judges in 1971: "Crimes against the state must now be regarded as more serious than crimes against the individual." *The London Observer* reported the meeting in these words: "Rainier was using almost precisely the words invoked by the Soviet Union and other Communist countries to define the function of the law. It is the language of many dictatorships of the left and of the right, where the doctrine of collectivism, in its widest sense, holds sway . . . Rainier said that offenses against the individual, such as assault, fraud, and theft would be treated more leniently, and prosecution might be dropped whenever possible, even if the evidence were available. On the other hand, tax evasion — as a premier crime against the state — would be treated much more severely; more prosecution would be brought, so that its heinousness would be raised in the public estimation. It transpired that tax evasion would be considered to be more serious than burglary or assault. Moreover, the police would be given specific instructions to concentrate more on crimes against the state at the expense of crimes against the individual." This follows Communist legal doctrine, which punishes political offenses much more severely than personal crimes. Russia probably has 100 times more persons in prisons for "unfriendly" political activities than for criminal activity.[35]

The United States is noted for its permissive attitude toward dope peddlers, sex offenders, thieves, embezzlers, and even murderers. However, punishment for violation of the income tax law is swift and sure. Labor racketeers and criminal gangsters seem able to escape the retribution of the criminal law, but when they are caught in an income tax evasion, they are promptly incarcerated. Probably more American gangsters since the notorious Al Capone have been jailed for income tax evasion than for the murders and other criminal acts they committed.

The income tax is becoming, and in some countries has already become, the supreme law, the violation of which is the "premier crime against the state."[1] As the income tax diverts more and more money into the public sector for government use, the government's dependence on income tax revenues becomes more complete, so that it feels threatened whenever a citizen violates the income tax law. Such violation endangers its very existence. Any independent action by the individual that is contrary to offical tax policy becomes completely unacceptable to the government and generates a conflict of interest that the government cannot tolerate. Commenting on the public attitude toward the income tax system, the head of the IRS made this observation in 1972:

> One thing is the growing lack of confidence among taxpayers that all are being treated equally. Another is what seems to be increased public tolerance of tax cheating. This is mot disturbing, because when a taxpayer willfully cheats on his taxes he is stealing. And this, in my opinion, is worse than just stealing from an individual or a merchant, because it is stealing from the public — from all 200 million Americans. We can never afford to let that sort of philosophy become acceptable.[36]

Since the days of Hammurabi, offenses against state property or the royal domain have always been the most severely punished. Modern social welfare governments are no different from Babylonian empires in wishing to protect their tax revenues. Where the public sector, or royal domain, is limited and clearly defined, the citizen is able to stay away from it and move freely within his own private sector. But where the public sector, or the royal domain, takes over the entire country, or most of the economy, the citizen is in the precarious position of becoming a ward or client of the state.

8.   It Creates Class Antagonisms

Under the tariff system the import tax served a dual purpose: it raised revenue to pay the operating expenses of the government; this may be called its economic function. It also served, by the use of differential rates, to subsidize the particular government goal the party in power had chosen: the protection of infant industries, economic growth, and protection of high wages and agriculture. This may be called its political function. The ability of the tariff to perform this dual function was never spelled out. Nevertheless, political leaders clearly understood the importance of the political function. All the great debates over the tariff in Congress were over its political, rather than its economic, functions — its effect on manufacturers, consumers, farmers, labor, and national, regional, or class interests. The ability of the tariff to pass out subsidies to favored or "protected" groups was regarded by its enemies as discriminatory and cruel to those groups that were left out. That archenemy of the tariff, Cordell Hull, went so far as to declare that the tariff was an "infamous system of class legislation."

In retrospect, this criticism of the tariff seems rather naïve. However, at the time that the income tax law was being debated, nobody anticipated that it would become a political instrument for the redistribution of income and produce class antagonisms much more serious and deep-seated than the tariff had created.

The individual income tax law causes shifts in consumer buying power that are socially harmful and contribute to class antagonisms. These socially undesirable effects are produced whether the income tax equalizes income, as in Sweden, or does not, as in the United States. Whenever there is a general increase in income taxes, there is a corresponding reduction of after-tax or disposable individual income. Those in the lower income brackets invariably are hurt most, for they have the smaller reserves, or the least "fat." In the United States, these lower income groups drop out of the income tax group altogether and become welfare aid cases. The consumer market then exhibits those sharp and vivid contrasts that are characteristic of a classic capitalist society where there is a great inequality of income, hunger in the midst of plenty, and pockets of poverty in the midst of affluence.

In the United States these striking inequalities are always present, even in times of general prosperity. When taxes are reduced in favor of the lower income groups or welfare or subsidy payments are granted to them, their behavior as consumers is unpredictable and sometimes irrational. The influence of consumer advertising and exposure to luxury consumer goods has an overpowering effect on simple minds. Poor families will often sacrifice food and essential items for themselves; their children will be neglected and deprived so that they can buy a late model car or a color TV or some other luxury item. This is a form of "conspicuous consumption" the poor can ill afford, but that is almost inescapable under the pressure of the mass consumer market.

That market responds to aggregate demand pressures. These pressures give rise to patterns of mass consumption and mass production. It is difficult to say which omes first or which causes the other. The consumer is caught in these mass movements, and he buys what other consumers are buying, without knowing exactly why, but for vague reasons that have to do with keeping up with the latest styles, or buying what the others are buying, or "keeping up with the Joneses." The income tax heightens the effect of these mass consumer movements by reducing the amount of consumer discretionary purchasing power. With his purchasing power limited *at the source* by the income tax, the consumer's ability to choose is narrowed. If his after-tax income is low, it may cover only his essential needs, leaving him no option for free selection. In other words, with a reduced after-tax income, the average consumer may be able to do no more than buy what he feels he must purchase to maintain his standard of living — he has no discretionary buying power. This, in effect, is the actual condition of many, if not most, consumers in the American mass consumer society.

In the private free-market sector of the economy the income tax acts like a volume control in an amplifier. Such a control can perform only one function — it raises or lowers the volume of sound. It cannot, like the market price mechanism, perform the function of a conductor in a live orchestra, raise the volume of one instrument and lower the volume of another, vary the tempo, or orchestrate the entire ensemble of musicians so that each performs according to his best ability and in harmony with the others. The income tax is not a tool for economic "fine tuning"; it is a crude, one-dimensional, or volumetric tax. Even its progressive or multiple rate schedule has one main objective — reducing the total income to a lower uniform level and shifting a greater portion of the production from the private to the public sector. As the volume of disposable income is reduced by the income tax, the unpleasant side effects on society become more pronounced. The poor and unemployed are squeezed out of the consumer market; the worker loses morale and incentive to work; the rich find that uneconomic and unproductive measures are desirable because they reduce tax liabilities; and the citizen finds his income tax liability onerous, his privacy invaded, and his relationship to the government that of a ward.

The income tax has funded the growth of the public sector bureaucracy which, because it derives its income from taxes that were not related to commodities and prices, is insulated from the price competition of the market and can afford to spend hundreds of billions of dollars in the public sector of the economy without being directly involved in the private sector of the market economy. The income tax helped to create the illusion of a public sector as being something independent of the private sector in having an independent source of income of its own. In commodity taxation this duality does not exist. For that reason Congressional debates over the tariff were always directly connected with internal and external trade, commodity prices, industrial price policy, farm price policy, and other market-connected economic problems. By contrast, in debates over the income tax the Congressional leaders are concerned only with income redistribution and other nonmarket problems.

The income tax divides the nation into two warring camps: on one side the taxpayers, who resent paying for the support of those they consider lazy, improvident, and shiftless, and on the other side a large welfare class, supported by a welfare bureaucracy and an army of welfare lawyers, who are convinced that the poor on welfare are the victims of a system that exploits them and denies them equal opportunity and an equitable share of the national income. A decrease in welfare payments would almost certainly cause ugly riots and violent unrest in the urban ghettos. An increase in income taxes would almost certainly bring violent protests, or perhaps a taxpayers' revolt.

The income tax system has been tried and found wanting; the heavy load of social welfare is more than it can cope with. The new technological environment has destroyed the labor theory of value on which the income tax was based. The theory of distributive justice — the rich shall pay for the support of the poor — has been outmoded by the growth of a powerful middle class and the cancerous growth of a large welfare class, growing far beyond the help of wealthy philanthropists or rich taxpayers. Even if all taxable income above $100,000 were confiscated by the income tax, the total collected would not run the government for three weeks.

9. It Is Obsolete

The early champions of the income tax were social reformers who sought to establish a better world in which the wealth of the rich was to be taxed for the uplift of the poor. Poverty was considered a problem in distribution, and the income tax was considered the ideal economic instrument to solve that problem. Today economists and politicians are not quite so certain. The income tax has released a whole new Pandora's box of economic woes. Critics claim that the income tax has made Americans lose faith in the Puritan ethic, the central ethos of which was the pursuit of happiness through hard work and capital savings. In its place the income tax has helped create the brave new world of the welfare state, with its share-the-wealth ideology and the false affluence of the mass consumer market. This, in turn, has created new political and tax problems.

Legislators in the welfare state are caught between the pressures for more social services and for tax relief. They have looked to economists in vain to help them out of this dilemma. The economists have been very helpful in developing and implementing social welfare programs. They have left it to the harassed and perplexed legislators to find the new tax sources needed to fund these programs. The progressive income tax has been their one and only solution to tax problems. Now that the bottom of that barrel is exposed, the legislators know not where to turn. Most legislators are intelligent enough to realize that social welfare programs not backed up by adequate tax revenues cannot succeed. But how can additional taxes be laid on the backs of taxpayers who are already overburdened by heavy personal income taxes?

The answer to this dilemma may be to take a new fresh look at the income tax system, not with the idea of "reforming" it, but of replacing it with a new system based on a different principle — consumption. In May 1933, when

50

President Roosevelt took office, the Bureau of the Budget proposed a Federal sales tax of 1-1/8 per cent. It was defeated by Congress 265 to 137. Since then, the Congress has relied almost exclusively on the income tax for its revenues. However, consumption taxes are making a comeback. Sales taxes have become the main support of local and state governments. European countries depend more and more on such consumption taxes as value-added and turn-over taxes. In almost all countries there is a general feeling that the income tax has reached the end of its useful life and that new forms of taxation that are better adapted to modern economic conditions are needed.

The income tax was once acclaimed by the working people as the best of all taxes, since it threw the burden of taxation on the rich, who were in the best position to bear it. Progressive income taxation was regarded by liberal politicians as the most enlightened form of taxation, the one that best accorded with the principles of ability to pay and equal sacrifice.

Today there is a growing dissatisfaction with the income tax among the very people it is supposed to benefit. In recent years a hostile attitude toward the income tax has grown among the wage earners and salaried workers, the very classes that formerly were its strongest supporters. As salaried employees, these classes are locked into a tax-withholding system that they cannot escape. They feel helpless and betrayed by a tax system that was originally meant to ease their tax burden and shift it to the shoulders of the wealthy. They see the wealthy taking advantage of loopholes and tax shelters not available to salaried workers; increasingly, the latter have come to suspect that the progressive income tax is not as progressive as they have been told by the economists. Neither are politicians today completely happy with it. As rates of income taxation approach confiscatory levels, they become subject to the law of diminishing returns. The politicians are finding that there are limits beyond which income tax rates become counterproductive and encounter mounting resentment and evasion. As a result, most political leaders today are looking for new forms of taxation: sales taxes, turn-over taxes, value-added taxes, and other types of consumption taxes.

In the United States, the income tax replaced the tariff as the main source of revenue during the 1930's. In arguing for the increased reliance on personal income taxes, Henry C. Simons in 1938 wrote: "The transition to a fiscal system, in which every tax would have some substantial justification, would appear, therefore, to require increasing the contribution of the personal income tax many fold; indeed, to a point where it would cover considerably more than half of total Government expenditures. A personal income tax yielding, say, eight billions annually would represent a most difficult achievement; but it is, by no means, utopian."[37]

Little did Professor Simons realize that his prediction was not only not utopian, but modest to the point of timidity for an economist of his stature. What would he have said if he had been told that the personal income tax receipts for 1972 would amount to over $100 billion? Yet, strangely enough, the fantastic increase in total receipts was more than matched by the increase in total government outlays. As a result, despite the increased revenue from the personal income tax, it still is not sufficient to cover the "more than half of the

51

total Government expenditures" that Professor Simons hoped for when he dreamed of $8 billion in revenues.

The jump from $8 billion to $100 billion is not a simple linear progression — it is a quantum jump. It takes the income tax out of the classification in which it was originally placed by its proponents and gives it a new dimension. The income tax is no longer an extra revenue tax designed primarily to siphon off part of the surplus income of the wealthy for the benefit of a small minority of the unemployed and the destitute. The personal income tax provides about half of all government revenues. The other tax revenues come from corporation income taxes (about 20 per cent) and excise taxes (about 9 per cent). Customs duties, which once were the main support of the Government, now provide less than 2 per cent of the total tax revenues. From these figures it can be seen that the personal income tax has become a "mass" tax levied on the entire population, not on a rich minority, and is called upon to finance *all* government programs — not alone those that benefit the destitute. The personal income tax is called upon to finance the costs of ordinary government expenditures and to assume the extraordinary burden of funding the health, education, and welfare of all citizens. The income tax is trying to carry a revenue load far beyond the wildest estimates of its early advocates. In 1972 American taxpayers voluntarily paid their government approximately $105 billion in personal income taxes, or almost one-half of all government revenues. This represented over 25 per cent of total personal income. The voluntary self-assessment and payment of personal income taxes on this scale has never been seen before. It is a tribute to the spirit of discipline and social responsibility of the American people and to the fundamental justice and equity of the income tax system, or so say its defenders.

To its critics, the individual income tax in the United States is the most serious attack on the rights of personal liberty and of private ownership of property since King George III tried to tax the American colonists without their consent, and the most serious invasion of the rights to personal privacy since the Inquisition. It is also, they claim, the greatest fraud ever perpetrated on a supine and gullible population. Under the pretext of "soaking the rich," the income tax actually permits the wealthy to escape payment of taxes. According to IRS figures on tax returns for 1969, 56 families with incomes of $1 million or more paid no income tax. Some people consider this situation a scandal, but the critics of the income tax complain that the real scandal is the sight of millions of Americans being led, like sheep, to their annual shearing.

An income tax law was passed by the Congress in 1894, but the Supreme Court declared it unconstitutional in 1895. The present income tax law was passed, as the 16th Amendment to the Constitution, on February 25, 1913. Congress set an initial rate of 1 per cent on taxable net income and a surtax rate of 1 per cent on incomes of $20,000 to $50,000; 2 per cent on incomes of $50,000 to $75,000; 3 per cent on incomes of $75,000 to $100,000; 4 percent on incomes of $100,000 to $250,000; 5 per cent on incomes of $250,000 to $500,000, and 6 per cent on incomes of over $500,000. Corporations paid a flat 1 per cent. In 1916 the rate was raised to 2 per cent for both individuals and corporations. It was at this time considered an extra revenue measure designed to shift some of the burden of government expenses on to the shoulders of those best able to pay. In 1941 the tax yielded only $70 million.

It is difficult for today's Americans, who work from four to six months of the year to pay taxes to support their government, to realize that prior to 1913 the American people paid no direct taxes for the support of the national government. The Federal government was financed chiefly by receipts from customs duties. A little revenue was received from the sale of public lands and from a few excise taxes, mostly on liquor and tobacco. There were no personal income or direct taxes then, and none seemed to be needed. The nation made considerable progress between 1791 and 1913. The Treasury enjoyed a surplus during much of the time, and the government's main economic problem was finding ways to dispose of excess tax revenues. The people were financially independent and self-sufficient, asked no favors of the government, and received none. The hands-off nonintervention economic policy of the government was dictated by both economic and ideological considerations. The Federal government was too weak financially to intervene directly in the private economy. Until 1930 the Federal government's share of the gross national product was only 4 per cent. The New Deal started a new pattern of Federal spending. By 1936, the final year of F.D.R.'s first term, Federal spending took 13 per cent. By 1960 it reached 22 per cent. In 1972 it approached 26 per cent, and total government spending reached about 40 per cent. In the same period, between 1940 and 1972, the Federal government's revenues rose from $7 billion to $202.5 billion, largely from income and personal taxes. The growth of the Federal bureaucracy and income tax revenues was not coincidental. Big government was one of many unwelcome consequences of the income tax, a consequence completely unforeseen in the early days of the income tax. No one could have anticipated that Federal revenues would expand 2,790 per cent in three decades or that government civilian employment would ever reach the astronomical figure of 14,000,000, or one out of five American workers. In the days of the tariff, when the tax base was dutiable imports with an annual value of under $3 billion dollars, such figures would have been considered pure fantasy.

Political conditions in the United States today are vastly changed from those that existed during the 19th century. The private market sector of the economy is no longer dominant. It is controlled and directed by the government; further, the public sector of the economy has grown from 3 to about 33 per cent of the economy, and it is still growing. The labor theory of value, under which labor and capital contended for the rights to the fruits of production, is no longer relevant. The labor content of production has shrunk from about 80 per cent to less than 1 per cent in terms of energy. The laws governing the relationship of man to property have changed drastically since the 16th Amendment was passed. The legal concept of private rights to property embodied in the Bill of Rights as being inalienable and inviolate and beyond government usurpation has changed to a new legal concept of property as primarily community property, with the government owning an undivided interest and all citizens having a right to a share of the gross national product. This new legal concept of property was anticipated by

Henry C. Simons in 1938 when he said, in *Individual Income Taxation*: "The whole return from property is, in a sense, a gift from the community."[38]

It would be very unusual if a tax law designed to fit economic conditions of the 19th century remained untouched by these radical economic changes of the 20th century. It is true, of course, that the income tax law has also changed since its origin, but the changes have been dimensional, not structural. The income tax today is a bloated version of the original law, but its structure is still recognizable as basically unchanged from that of Addington's law of 1803.

It is possible that the individual income tax in a modified form may be retained as part of a new national income policy, for example, as a flat surtax on incomes over $40,000. The corporate income tax is merely a hidden personal tax. As Professor Musgrave explained, "It is silly to say that corporations really pay taxes. In the end it is the shareholder, the consumer or the wage earner who pays those taxes indirectly, depending on whether and how the corporation shifts its tax burden. Taxes are paid by individuals, period."[39]

Total dependence on the income tax for government revenues and as a tool for economic planning has led to serious political and economic problems that cannot be fully resolved without a major shift of the tax system to a new base other than income. A tax based on consumption need not be "regressive" or discriminate against the poor, as is customarily believed. As Professor Musgrave has pointed out: "A system of commodity taxes on luxury items (defined relative to living standards) in particular may prove a more effective means of progressive taxation, and one more in line with the objectives of development, than an ineffective attempt at progressive income taxation."[40]

Since taxation is an integral part of the political economic system, it cannot contradict or subvert the ethical-legal basis of that system. An arbitrary, inquisitorial tax of any kind is manifestly incompatible with democratic ideals of personal liberty. Unfortunately, there are no objective criteria for evaluating taxes; whether an act of Congress is liberal or reactionary, democratic or antidemocratic is a matter of personal opinion. The final judgment rests ultimately on public opinion and the verdict of history. But in the heat of political battle, where all tax laws must be hammered out, the lawmaker is forced to fall back on his own judgment of what is just, fair, equitable, practicable, and in harmony with public opinion and with established institutions.

In a democratic society a new tax system cannot be imposed by fiat. New taxes cannot be legislated without the consent of a majority of the taxpayers. As voters, the taxpayers, must approve the plans the government proposes for the use of the tax revenues. This cannot be accomplished overnight or by executive order. It is a gradual process during which one kind of taxes is phased out and new taxes are adopted in their place. The replacement of consumption taxes by income taxes as the main source of revenue took considerable time after the income tax act was passed in 1913. As late as 1938, the revenues from individual income taxes were less than $1 billion. Any new system of consumption taxes enacted to replace the present income tax system would probably require considerable time before the change could be completed.

Before a new tax system is enacted, the inertia in the old system must be overcome and the people must be convinced that the new system is more fair and equitable than the old. This is not an easy task. Vested interests do not voluntarily relinquish their privileges; neither is the general public interested or knowledgeable enough in tax matters to vote for a new tax system on the strength of economic arguments. The average taxpayer does not take an interest in tax matters until he feels the pinch in the pocketbook. Although the American taxpayer has been squeezed hard by the income tax, the crisis point has not yet been reached.

The present tax system has some very powerful vested interests: a huge bureaucracy in the executive branch with plenary powers over the economy; a new class of welfare recipients financed by the income tax; a huge sector of the private economy living off expense accounts, tax loopholes, capital gains, advertising and promotion budgets, and from the production and distribution of frivolous, wasteful, and socially harmful products, all made possible by the effect of the income tax on the market system. Backing these vested interests is the prestige and authority of the academic community speaking through the professional economists, who are just as much in love with the income tax today as they were opposed when Pitt first introduced it.

American politicians, while no longer happy with the income tax, see no feasible substitute that can match it as a revenue producer and as a redistributive agency for equalizing income. The view of most politicians is that the income tax, although not perfect, is a successful tax and perhaps only minor reforms, such as closing loopholes, are needed to make it more acceptable to the taxpayer.

The existing personal income tax no longer has the universal support of the American people. Hostility is growing toward it among the working classes locked into a tax-withholding system they cannot escape and do not understand. This growing resentment could become a powerful factor in the battle for tax reform. There is also the growing fear and distrust of executive power by the legislative branch. Executive power is based on a large tax-supported bureaucracy. When Congress passes such laws as the income tax that transfer wealth from the private market sector to the public sector it is, unwittingly perhaps, forcing the growth of the executive bureaucracy and asking it to undertake the functions formerly performed by the citizen, the family, private associations, and the market. This tendency will continue until a point is reached where such transfers of income will make the executive bureaucracy a Leviathan that will, to all intents and purposes, be the *de facto* government, on which the citizen is dependent, from the cradle to the grave, for such matters as income, health, and education. The legislature will become a subsidiary branch, a legislative mill to grind out enabling legislation and appropriation bills for the bureaucracy. The executive will be in a position to castigate the Congress if it does not provide it with all the income it demands in the name of its dependent and grateful citizens. The Congress can, of course, outbid the executive in granting higher income allowances and more

Social Security benefits, but these will only serve to increase the power and size of the bureaucracy.

Individual rights to property, considered inalienable in Jefferson's time, have been eroded by the growth of a custodial bureaucracy that has been given the legal right to distribute income according to need. The rights of labor to the fruits of labor — ownership — have been eroded by the growth of automation based on inanimate energy. Modern governments have been unable to resolve the dilemma caused by these changes in property and labor values. In particular, the question of labor costs and labor values in relation to nonlabor costs and environmental values has become one of crucial importance. It is impossible to formulate, or even to understand, tax policy unless these radical changes in economic values are taken into consideration.

Chapter

II

LABOR RIGHTS

1. Labor Values Under Capitalism

The origins of the labor theory of value go back to John Locke, who laid its theoretical foundation; to Adam Smith, who gave it economic prominence; to Malthus and Ricardo, who refined it; and to Marx, who borrowed it for his own use. To modern man, the labor theory of value appears as a simple and self-evident truth; all property values are derived from human labor. In both capitalist and Socialist societies the theory that labor is the source of all value is widely believed; to labor belongs the produce of labor.

In ancient times the labor theory of value was unknown. It was not applicable to the classic agrarian society that existed from ancient Babylonian days to the breakdown of feudalism and serfdom in Western Europe. In the classic agrarian society labor had no social standing. Labor was considered degrading and a mark of social, if not biological, inferiority. The laborer was a beast of burden, an untouchable, of no more value than an animal, and in some cases not as valuable. The laborer could not own land, he could not marry into the landowners' class, and he could not inherit land. As a slave he was the property of his master, a chattel.

Farmers could not provide for their own security, but were forced to seek the protection of a lord, who could give them the protection of his castle or his armed knights. When that protection was withdrawn, workers could be plundered unmercifully by any marauding band of armed vandals. Their labor was of no value unless it was protected and made secure. In the agrarian society this security was provided by the armed guardians of the landlord. This protection was not without its risks to the landlord. It has been estimated that, as late as the period 1330-1479, 46 per cent of the sons of English dukes died violent deaths; as a class, their life expectancy was only 24 years.

In addition to providing security, the landlord also performed the management functions involved in directing the labor of the workers and assumed responsibility for production and distribution. The management and security provided by the landlord were the decisive factors in agricultural production.

The protection of the land was, in ancient times, a matter of highest priority and, since wars were frequent, a matter of grave and continuous concern. The cultivation of the land, on the other hand, was a matter of no great concern. The productivity of labor and of the soil, once established, could not be materially increased. It was subject to the vicissitudes of weather, insect plagues, and soil chemistry, none of which was then under human control. The labor of a man, like that of an ox or a horse, was set by certain physical limitations; it was hopeless to try to extend them. The concept of progress or economic growth by increase in productivity was totally unknown and outside the realm of possibilities. In the classic agrarian society a cultivator was defenseless and of no value to himself or to society unless he had the protection of the landlord. Therefore, his labor, although necessary, was not decisive to the survival of the state. Only military valor was decisive, for only warfare created economic growth.

Wars for the acquisition of land were endemic in the classic agrarian society. In a sense, war was the "business" of the titled landowners. It was their only means of acquiring capital assets. Wars of conquest were gigantic real estate acquisitions. Their objective was to capture titles to lands that belonged to others. There was, in those days, no other method available to acquire titles to new land. They were not sold in the marketplace. Aristotle states in *Politics* that "The art of war is in some sense a natural mode of acquisition."[41]

In the agrarian society land, as a general rule the most valuable property, could not be acquired except by war or inheritance. Therefore, the relative standing of an individual or a nation depended in great measure on the ability to defend or acquire land. Personal and national wealth and power also depended on this ability. Small wonder, therefore, that military valor was so highly valued. A conquering soldier was a hero because he brought wealth to his family or to his nation. Pompey acquired for Rome parcels of real estate larger than Italy itself; Scipio Africanus gave Rome all of North Africa; Caesar acquired most of France and Britain. Compared to these real estate operations, commercial operations in the town and country markets were of minor importance.

In the classic agrarian society, the city markets were surplus commodity exchanges where the landlord or his agent exchanged the surplus produce of his land for some foreign or city-made trinket or luxury. The worker did not participate in the market. Since he owned nothing, he had nothing to exchange. He had no purchasing power. Apart from nations that specialized in sea commerce — Phoenicia, Crete, Athens, and Carthage — ancient agrarian society was based on land ownership, and land was acquired by inheritance and conquest, not bought in the marketplace. The market was a

58

peripheral activity in classic agrarian societies, outside the mainstream of agrarian life. The Romans were not interested in commerce and left it in the hands of subject races — Greeks, Syrians, and Jews. The Romans knew there was much more profit in real estate than in commerce. From their conquered lands Rome extracted tribute in the form of slaves, gold, and food.

During the Renaissance the values of the ancient world began to be called into question. Men such as Copernicus, Newton, and Galileo developed new theories to explain the physical world. At the same time thinkers on political and economic subjects such as Hobbes, Bodin, Grotius, and Locke tried to develop new theories to explain the changing relationship of man to property.

Laws, written and unwritten, governing the relationship of man to property have been in existence since the beginning of social life. The concept of "mine" and "thine" (*meuum* and *teuum*) has been well established since earliest times and was elaborated in codes of conduct, carrying moral and legal sanctions, long before it was written into the Mosaic law or the code of Hammurabi.

Today, the relationship of man to property is defined in very minute detail in laws that spell out the property rights of individuals, corporate entities, and social bodies and define the nature or "legal description" of property. Everyone today is familiar, from personal experience, with the laws of property as they affect his daily life, particularly those laws that govern the sale, transfer, conveyance, and inheritance of property; laws that cover the taxation of property or its encumbrance by liens, easements, assessments, and attachments; laws that apply to the possession, loss, and repossession of property; and laws governing distribution of income from property. Modern society is encased in a solid framework of laws covering every aspect of property in its most minute detail. No other subject in law is protected, classified, analyzed, or codified as much as property. Nevertheless, despite the vast amount of minute and specific detail written about property, it remains an abstract legal concept that defies exact definition.

Blackstone, in his *Commentaries,* defined property as an "absolute right which consists in the free use, enjoyment and disposal of all acquisitions without any control or diminution, save only the laws of the land." This concept of property, as an unlimited private right, was derived from the theories of John Locke.

Locke believed God had given the wealth of the world to mankind in common. This view was held by many scholars and saints in medieval times, but Locke proceeded from this premise to establish a revolutionary new theory of unlimited individual property rights. Locke claimed that every man had the same right to draw from God's or nature's storehouse whatever he could *by his own labor;* once acquired, it was his private property, which he alone was entitled to own. Property, therefore, was the product of labor, and the individual's right to his property was based on his labor in making it or acquiring it. This was contrary to the accepted law and custom of the times. In ancient and medieval society real property rights were generally considered exclusive, acquired by conquest or through noble birth and confirmed by the sacramental rite of inheritance, ranging from a simple parental blessing, such as Jacob received from Isaac, to the elaborate ritual of title transfer and investiture in cases of large properties, such as a duchy or a kingdom. Against this traditional belief Locke affirmed that every man had the right to own property, provided it had been acquired by his own labor. Locke's concept has endured and was restated by Murray D. Rothbard as late as 1962 in the following words: "The origin of all property is ultimately traceable to the appropriation of an unused nature-given factor by a man and his 'mixing' his labor with this natural factor to produce a capital good or a consumers' good."[42]

Locke's theory had some revolutionary implications, which were fully realized only by the American and French revolutions. Locke was a philosopher; in his day (1632-1704) his theories were of interest only to a small group of scholars. They could not be implemented until workers were free from servitude. The worker could not claim as his property what he produced as long as he was a slave or a serf. The theories of Locke anticipated a new and changed relationship of men to property and particularly to landed property, a change that was already taking place in his day.

In England after the 14th century, the system of agriculture based on serfdom or villeinage was replaced by a system based on contracts between free tenants and landlords. Under the early English law of copyhold the villein held land "at the will of the Lord according to the custom of the Manor." The courts in feudal times considered the "will of the Lord" as paramount and denied protection to the villein. In the 15th century judges began to interpret the law in favor of the villeins, and "the custom of the Manor" was interpreted to mean that that the "will of the Lord" could not prevail when the villein had rights of tenure based on long family possession. Without formally emancipating the serfs, English law by many apparently minor judicial decisions changed the law of tenure by custom to tenure by contract and thereby relieved the serf or villein of his bondage. Of course, the landlord played a significant role in this change. The landlord was more than happy to receive rents in money rather than in service. Serfdom was to be abolished in France and other nations by revolution and radical legislative reform, but in England it was phased out by the new courts of equity, gradually and without bloodshed, a tribute to the pragmatic political genius of the English people.

Cromwell is reputed to have called the English property system "an ungodly jumble;" undoubtedly, however, its complexity contributed to its power and flexibility. The English concept of juristic possession or an abstract estate rather than land itself as the substance of ownership was a breakthrough in legal theory and made possible orderly economic progress through legal reform. By contrast, in countries where the law of possession or *dominium* still governed, there was no way to reform the economy except by violent dispossession of the titleholders.

As soon as titles to land became, not inalienable and hereditary, but negotiable, the economic base of the agrarian society was vulnerable to destruction. Not at once, of course, for the process was long and continuous. The replacement of agrarian values by monetary standards was a slow process, which still continues in some parts of the world. In England the titled landowners, after the 14th century, began to see the economic advantages of money. They started to replace their tenants with wage laborers or leased their land to tenants on a money-rent basis. Money became essential to large-scale agriculture. This was a revolutionary development, for money in times past had been primarily a medium of exchange in commerce. The increase in trade made it profitable to grow crops for the market for money, rather than for use or for local consumption. In England, the economy was gradually transformed during the 16th and 17th centuries from an agrarian to a market structure. Land titles were challenged by a new property symbol - money. Money values replaced land values. Contractual obligations based on trust and good faith and payable in money replaced feudal obligations based on kinship and valor and payable in military service.

The values of the agrarian society were based on the military code: valor, fealty, honor, chivalry, loyalty, homage to superiors, refinement in dress and manners, skill in the arts of war and government, contempt for both labor and commerce, and status based on family title. The warrior, the priest, and the noble were the elite of the agrarian society. Work of any type was associated with serfs and slaves and was therefore degrading and without social value. Trade was reserved for inferior or subject people. Money-lenders — the original bankers — were looked upon as outcasts because the lending of money at interest was illegal and sinful in the eyes of the Christian church.

The new market economy set up its own system of values: labor as the highest social value and the moral basis of property; contempt for idleness; respect for thrift; contracts based on mutual trust between independent parties; and status based on individual net worth rather than on family name or title. In this new economic environment the labor theory of value was ready to become a powerful political weapon, but first the military code of value must be destroyed.

The destruction of feudal property values is described by Adam Smith in *The Wealth of Nations:*

> But what all the violence of the feudal institutions could never have effected, the silent and insensible operation of foreign commerce and manufacturers gradually brought about. These gradually furnished the great proprietors with something for which they could consume themselves without sharing it either with tenants or retainers. All for ourselves, and nothing for other people, seems, in every age of the world, to have been the vile maxim of the masters of mankind. As soon, therefore, as they could find a method of consuming the whole value of their rents themselves, they had no disposition to share them with any other persons. For a pair of diamond buckles perhaps, or for something as frivolous and useless, they exchanged the maintenance of a thousand men for a year, and with it the whole weight and authority which it could give them . . . and thus, for the gratification of the most childish, the meanest and the most sordid of all vanities, they gradually bartered their whole power and authority.[43]

Since Smith was a professor of morals, this view of feudal decline betrays a moral judgment based on his labor theory of value. To him, all economic values were based on labor. Said Smith: "Labor alone, therefore, never varying in its own value, is alone the ultimate and real standard by which the value of

61

all commodities can at all times and places be estimated and compared. It is their real price; money is their nominal price." This labor theory of value was refined by Ricardo and became the basis of the capitalist system of values. Marx adopted the Smith-Ricardo theory and made labor the source of all value in the Communist system. Like Smith, Marx believed that the whole produce of labor belonged to the laborer.

2. Labor Values Under Marxism

Marx studied all the classic capitalist economists, particularly Smith and Ricardo. The Socialist or Marxist theories of labor as the source of all value are derived from Smith, Ricardo, and Malthus. The theoretical ammunition for Socialism was, strangely enough, supplied by the economists of the free market economy. Marx did not need to invent the labor theory of value or the theory that rents and profits are unearned income taken from the produce of labor. Smith and Ricardo had already worked out these theories in a convincing and logical manner.

The labor theory of value appears today as a basic contradiction in capitalist doctrine. If Smith and Ricardo believed that labor was entitled to all the produce of labor why did they not also advocate, like Marx, that labor take over the means of production? This appears a logical corollary; on the surface, the labor theory of value seems to fit the Socialist doctrine of Marx much better than the capitalist theories of Smith and Ricardo. The one who reaps the fruit of the tree should, it seems, be the owner of the tree.

The contradiction was not apparent at the time because, in Smith's free market doctrine, owners and workers were considered in theory as one and the same. Smith, in 1776, was describing a preindustrial economy made up of individual production units: the small farmer, the small shopkeeper, the small craft shop, the small merchant. The corporate structure had not yet become significant. The one-man one-owner enterprise was still the norm. It was on the independent farmer that Jefferson based his policies and all his hopes for the future of democracy in America.

The labor theory of value, under 18th century economic conditions, was not incompatible with Jeffersonian democracy and the theory of unrestricted private ownership rights to property. On the contrary, it reinforced the political theory of democracy that every man was entitled to own his own land and be the sole owner of what he grew or made by his own efforts. This was the revolutionary capitalist or bourgeois doctrine of the 18th century.

In the 19th century, when socialized production in factories operated by large corporations turned independent producers into corporate employees, the labor theory of value began to lose its appeal to capitalists. The capitalist as an independent owner or petit bourgeois could believe wholeheartedly in the labor theory of value; the capitalist as a corporate owner could not. He was compelled to operate on the theory that the corporation, not labor, owned the production of the factory. Thus, the conflict between labor and capital evolved.

Corporate capital began to emphasize the right of ownership as paramount and based all economic values on ownership. The rights of labor to production were considered paid by wages whose value was based on work produced and the market price of labor. Labor, while not denying the rights of private ownership — except in Marxist labor movements — continued to emphasize its rights to production, based on the labor theory of value. Under corporate capitalism, labor modified its claims to *total* production, but retained its claim to *prior* rights over production, and, in particular, its right to *control* production by voluntary withdrawals (strikes) or slowdowns.

Had Marx followed John Stuart Mill instead of Smith and Ricardo, the course of history might have been changed. Mill was a morals philosopher, like Smith, and a contemporary of Marx. In 1848 Marx brought out his *Communist Manifesto* exhorting the workers of the world to revolt, crush their capitalist exploiters, and take over the "means of production." Only by so doing, he said, could they ever hope to obtain their rightful share of the goods they produced. Marx was convinced that only by the overthrow of the capitalist systems and the "liquidation" of the capitalists could the workers acquire a just share of the national income.

Yet Mill, in a book published that same year *(Principles of Political Economy,* 1848) stated calmly and logically that income distribution had nothing to do with production and that it was quite feasible to have capitalist production and yet make whatever arrangements for distribution of income that are best suited to the general welfare of the people: "The laws and conditions of the production of wealth partake of the character of physical truths ... It is not so with the distribution of wealth. That is a matter of human institutions only. The things once there, mankind individually or collectively can do with them what they like ... the distribution of wealth, therefore, depends on the laws and customs of the society. The rules by which it is determined are very different if mankind so choose."

Upon this new and revolutionary concept Mill, if he had been a political reformer like Marx, might have erected a political system based on the socialization of consumption. But Mill viewed the problem of income distribution as primarily a matter of morals: "Poverty in any sense implying suffering, may be completely extinguished by the wisdom of society, combined with the good sense and providence of individuals ... As for vicissitudes of fortune, and other disappointments connected with wordly circumstances, these are principally the effect either of gross imprudence, of ill-regulated desires, or of bad or imperfect social institutions."[44]

Mill's idea for improving society was not through political reform, but through individual self-improvement in a free society and through the doctrine of utilitarianism. Where Marx thundered with the fury of an Old Testament prophet, Mill spoke with the sweet reasonableness of a Christian convert: "In the golden rule of Jesus of Nazareth, we read the complete spirit of the ethics of utility. To do as you would be done by, and to love your neighbor as yourself, constitute the ideal perfection of Utilitarian morality. As the means of making the nearest approach to his idea, utility would enjoin, first, that laws and social arrangements should place the happiness or (as speaking practically, it may be called) the interest, of every individual, as nearly as possible with the interest of the whole." This was as close as Mill came to a new theory of value. Marx called it "an insipid, brainless syncretism."

Marx took the Smith-Ricardo labor theory of value, applied it to an industrial society, and made it the cornerstone of Communist social value. However, the Ricardian labor theory of value had applied to a market economy based on free exchange and on individual production. How could such a theory be applied to an industrial economy based on mechanized socialized production?

The original labor theory of value had never been completely satisfactory. Aside from the rather questionable dictum classifying all nonagricultural workers as nonproductive consumers whose income was "unearned", there was the baffling question of differential labor rates. Why was the labor of one person more valuable than that of another? How could the labor of a ship's captain be equated with that of a seaman? Why did certain things that incorporated relatively little labor — a diamond in the rough, a share in a growing enterprise, a cargo of spices — have high value, whereas some things that incorporate a large expenditure of labor — a crop of wheat, bread, homespun cloth, pottery — have little or no market value? Another troublesome problem was the question of accounting for the three classic factors of cost: labor, rent, and interest. If only labor created value, what logical or *legitimate* value could be assigned to the other two factors? These questions, with their ominous implications, were left hanging because Smith and Ricardo did not have the time or inclination to work them out, or perhaps could not. To them, the labor theory of value was a useful explanation of certain market phenomena and not an article of faith.

Marx regarded the labor theory of value as fundamental to Communist economics. He tried to work out answers to the questions left open by the classic economists. However, in trying to fit the classic labor theory of value to the new industrial society, Marx was forced to stretch it considerably, much farther than it was designed to extend.

The classic labor theory of value cannot, by any stretch of logic, cover mechanized socialized production. This becomes obvious when both types of production are compared. A shoemaker, who makes shoes by hand without outside help, may be taken as an example of individual production by manual labor. He presumably has already paid the rancher for the leather he uses and has incorporated the labor value of the leather in his cost of production. He adds his own labor cost, and the two add up to the total labor cost. His production is one pair of shoes a day. They belong to him. No one questions his right of ownership to the shoes. His labor produced them.

In a shoe factory, with the latest automated equipment, a single worker turns out 1000 pairs of shoes a day. What is the labor value of the 1000 pairs of shoes? According to Marx, the labor value is the same as if the worker made them by hand. Said Marx, "Machinery, like any other component of constant capital, creates no new value, but yields up its own value to the product that it serves to beget... Given the rate at which machinery transfers its value to the product, the amount of value so transferred depends on the total value of the machinery. The less labor it contains, the less value it imparts to the product."[45] Marx completely ignores nonhuman energy factors. Why did Marx fall into such an obvious error?

It appears that Marx was caught in a trap of his own making. The labor theory of value was fundamental to the Communist dogma. According to Lenin, "The doctrine of surplus value is the keystone to the economic theory of Marx." This surplus value is created by labor. Said Lenin, "One part of the working day he spends in order to meet the cost of supporting himself and his family (wages), but another part of the day he spends working for nothing, creating for the capitalist surplus value, the source of profits, the source of the wealth of the class of capitalists."[46]

The entire theoretical edifice of Communism was based on the labor theory of value. Labor and only labor was the source of all value. Said Marx,

A use-value, or a useful article, therefore, has value only because human labour in the abstract has been embodied or materialized in it. How, then, is the magnitude of this value to be measured? Plainly, by the quantity of the value-creating substance, the labour, contained in the article... The value of one commodity is to the value of any other, as the labour-time necessary for the production of the one is to that necessary for the production of the other.[47]

From this follows the Communist dogma that to labor belongs the whole produce of labor. If it could be shown that the worker was not entitled to *all* he produced, if under the new technology it could be proved that human labor was, in reality, only a minor one of the total energy factors expended in production, then the whole elaborate Marxist value system would be fundamentally endangered.

Marx used his labor theory of surplus value as a political weapon to discredit and destroy the capitalist system, and it should be judged more as an instrument of political strategy than as an economic theory. On this basis it served its purpose well, and Communists care little whether professional economists believe it true or false. But if the labor theory of surplus value was only a revolutionary weapon, what was the heart of Marx's theory? Marx gave it in one sentence in *The Communist Manifesto*: "The theory of the Communists may be summed up in the single sentence: Abolition of private property."

The classic problem in economics revolves around the relationship of man to property, and the question it poses is: what is property and who is to own or control it? Classic agrarian society had established land as property and restricted the right of ownership to a class of hereditary owners. The American and French revolutions established the rights of private individuals to ownership of property on an unrestricted and equal basis. Marx's property laws were a *reaction* against the property laws established by the French and American revolutions, which Marx labeled as "bourgeois" revolutions. Marx established a new property law: property belonged to the working class and ultimately to the state. The final triumph of Communism would establish the perfect state in which all property, as such, would be abolished. From this follows the Marxist myth or vision of the future workers' paradise in which all property, all classes, all laws, all political institutions, and all money "wither away." A "free association" of workers and consumers, a commune, with each working according to his abilities and each receiving according to his needs, is the Socialist ideal.

The ideal may be a myth, but the Marxist relationship of men to property, once established, becomes law and cannot be changed except by overthrow of the legal Communist government. The law is fundamental: private property rights are abolished. No individual can own property. Only society, i.e., the state, can own property. Marxists, of course, cannot abolish property by decree. Marxism can abolish *private* property or *capitalist* property, but this is not the same as abolishing *property*. It is merely changing the legal relationship of man to property by making illegal the individual rights of control and ownership. The legal rights of control and ownership are *transferred* to the state, not abolished. Control of all property gives the state complete economic power; the individual, to gain economic power, cannot acquire property himself, but must become a part of the state power structure. Marxism thus reestablished the principle of absolutism in government by depriving the individual of economic power or ownership rights. The labor theory of value, or as Marx restyled it, the "Theory of surplus labor value," was the ideological weapon with which he attacked the property system of capitalism. It still serves as the ideological or moral basis of the Communist state which, in theory, is the workers' state in which only labor values count.

Jeremy Bentham introduced the concept of utility as a moral principle, and his disciple J. S. Mill prepared the way for its use in economics. A number of economists developed the concept of utility as an economic theory of value during Mill's lifetime. The German economist, Hermann Heinrich Gossen, published the first work on the subject in 1854, but it went unnoticed. By 1870, however, Carl Menger and Bohm-Bawerk in Austria, Leon Walras in Switzerland, and Jevons and Marshall in England, all working independently, brought out their versions of the new theory of value, called *the marginal utility theory of value*. This theory may be described in the words of one of its authors, William Stanley Jevons:

Repeated reflection and inquiry have led me to the somewhat novel opinion, that *value depends entirely upon utility*. Prevailing opinions make labour rather than utility the origin of value, and there are even those who distinctly assert that labour is the *cause* of value. I show, on the contrary, that we have only to trace out carefully the natural laws of the variation of utility, as depending upon the quantity of commodity in our possession, in order to arrive at a satisfactory theory of exchange, of which the ordinary laws of supply and demand are a necessary consequence. This theory is in harmony with the facts; and, whenever there is any apparent reason for the belief that labour is the cause of value, we obtain an explanation of the reason. Labour is found often to determine value, but only in an indirect manner, by varying the degree of utility of the commodity through an increase or limitation of the supply.[48]

The statement that a commodity must be useful to have value seems redundant. All classic and Socialist economists appreciated the function of utility. Marx had stated: "Nothing can have value without being an object of utility. If it be useless, the labour contained in it is useless, cannot be reckoned as labour, and cannot therefore create value." And Adam Smith had also mentioned that "The word VALUE, it is to be observed, has two different meanings... The one may be called 'value in use', the other, 'value in exchange'".[49] Utility was recognized, but it was recognized only as a derivative value, derived, that is, from the labor content of the commodity.

The labor theory of value is a "cost-of-production" theory based on *production* as the source of value. The marginal utility theory of value is a "cost-of-sale" theory based on *consumption* as the source of value. Both Marx and Smith made a distinction between "exchange" value and what Marx called "social" value and Smith called "value in use." This was to account for the paradox that such commodities as diamonds had little utility, but great value, while other commodities such as water had great utility, but little value. However, the labor theory of value never *completely* explained market value or commodity prices because labor value itself was a variable; that is, there was a great difference between labor costs in various commodities based on different wage and productivity rates. Both classic and Socialist economists tried to reconcile these differences, but could not do so because they were unwilling or unable to deviate from their basic premise that human labor was the source of *all* value.

The marginal utility theory of value shifted the basis of value from production to consumption. By the middle of the 19th century Mill, Marx, and others had recognized the separation of the production and consumption functions. In London, Paris, Hamburg, and other centers of commerce it was obvious that consumption was no longer tied directly to production. Production was for the market, not for the consumption of the producers. Consumption was not regulated or controlled by production, as had been the case in simple agrarian economies. It was based on such complex factors as wage levels, currency values, employment levels, interest rates, savings and investment trends, import duties, export bounties, taxes, population growth or decline, and a host of other factors. The labor theory of value was unable adequately to explain the complex factors that influenced value and price fluctuations in modern markets.

The marginal theory of value was able to explain the market price system in a much more complete and satisfactory manner because it attacked the problem of value from a consumption viewpoint: the utility of an item was judged solely on its value to the consumer *at the time of sale* or consumption. This is what is meant by the concept of *marginal* utility. It is not utility judged as a value for any quantity of a given commodity, but only for the value of the last unit of quantity of that commodity being purchased, the "final utility," as Marshall called it.

The marginal utility value theory explained the buying habits of consumers and what caused them to buy one item in preference to another. It also explained the old problem, which had bothered both Ricardo and Marx, of different qualities of labor or differential labor costs. A seamstress is paid $2 an hour and a fashion designer $20 an hour. Why? The labor theory of value could not give a satisfactory explanation, but the marginal utility value theory could show that the reason was that the designer produced work that had a higher utility value. Therefore, the utility value determined the labor value of the commodity unless political or legal or other abnormal influences intervened.

As Jevons pointed out, the marginal utility value theory was a "satisfactory theory of exchange of which the ordinary laws of supply and demand are a necessary consequence." It explained the operations of the market and the factor of consumer preference. However, to say with Jevons that "value depends entirely upon utility" is obviously wrong. Prices and market values do not depend entirely on the marginal utility values of commodities or consumer preference. Market values and prices are also determined by fixed labor costs, fixed overhead costs, tax rates, and other expenses that are not likely to be changed by considerations of utility. However, the principle of marginal utility was an important contribution toward a more complete theory of value; once established, it enabled economists to work out more complete and precise formulas for solving problems of supply and demand.

The concept of marginal utility was simple, yet so broad that it covered all market relationships and, for the first time, introduced the element of *time*. Supply and demand ratios were studied as forces in equilibrium for a given period of time under specific conditions of production and consumption. This concept of general equilibrium, developed by Marshall, Walras, Pareto, and Keynes, among others, is usually expressed in mathematical terms, in a system of simultaneous equations by which, in theory, all unknown prices and quantities in a hypothetical regime of pure competition can be determined. This theory of general equilibrium expressed in price ratios and ratios of marginal utilities, or "marginal rates of substitution," is still widely used by modern economists and has proved a valuable analytical tool under certain controlled conditions.

Despite its value to theoretical economists, the utilitarian theory of value was not received with great favor by many social philosophers. It was rejected in its entirety by Marx and his followers. In the United States and England the utilitarian theory was rejected by John Dewey, Bertrand Russell, Thorstein Veblen, and others who turned away from a value system based on market utility as basically shallow, hedonistic, and socially degrading. Nevertheless, the utilitarian theory of value influenced the development of the mass consumer market and the rise of consumer-dominated economies.

Thorstein Veblen, an iconoclast among economists, was one of the first to question the utility value theory. Veblen did not believe that man's behavior as a consumer could be mathematically calculated or predicted. Veblen was not convinced that man acted always in accordance with the principle of maximum utility. Man, he said, is not "a lightning calculator of pleasures and pains, who oscillates like a homogeneous globule of desire of happiness under the impulse of stimuli that shift him about the area, but leave him intact."

To Veblen the "price system" was based on "pecuniary" values that were not true values, but led to "conspicuous consumption" and other "pecuniary canons of taste" that were false and misleading, if not socially harmful. Veblen was deeply conscious of the social and political realities of economic life. He did not see economics as a watertight compartment separate from politics. He did not see workers and capitalists and consumers as aggregates reduced to algebraic symbols. He viewed political life as a battle between the "pecuniary interests" and scientific technology, between the engineer and the business man. Like Saint-Simon, whom he resembled in many ways, Veblen visualized science and technology as the ultimate salvation of mankind. He believed that a form of technocracy, or rule by engineers or a scientific élite, would be the next historic phase after the collapse of the inefficient and wasteful "price system."

Although he never stated it in a theory of value, Veblen believed that the "machine process", or technology, was the basic economic reality of modern society. It was on this base that the technocratic political structure was to be built, but how the scientific élite was to govern or what values were to guide them was not explained. Veblen's genius for critical analysis was not matched by an equal talent for constructive synthesis. The value system inherent in his concept of a technocracy could certainly be neither the labor theory of value nor the utilitarian theory of value. A society organized on a scientific basis and run by engineers and scientists would be concerned with *total* energy resources and their allocation. The problem of allocation of resources is a political question involving a system of values and priorities, to which Veblen offered no solution.

The traditional theories of value still exert a powerful influence on modern society, but technology continues to mold society into a new form in which these old theories of value seem inconsistent, irrelevant, illogical, and contradictory. The labor theory of value is still regarded as sacred in Communist and capitalist regimes, in theory, if not in practice.

The Communist economic system is based on the theory that labor — the working class — owns the means of production and its output. The Ricardian-Marxist labor concept of value still forms the theoretical keystone of the Communist economic system. It gives Communist life its moral legitimacy and political ethos. Everything the government undertakes is done in the name of labor or "for the working class." The Communist government itself is merely the representative of "labor" and has no reason for being except as the voice and arm of the working class. The dominant values of society are derived from labor. The Socialist hero is the worker. The artist or writer who departs from the strictly proletarian labor virtues is "decadent" or a revisionist or unpatriotic.

In China industrial managers, civil servants, professionals, teachers, writers, intellectuals — all highly trained classes — must leave their occupations for periods of several months to several years to go to the countryside and work with their hands at farming and construction. The purpose, it is said, is to lessen the danger of their slipping back into a "leisure class" mentality and to identify the class consciousness of the intellectuals with that of the peasants and workers, from which all values are derived.

In the everyday operation of the Soviet economic system, the labor theory of value has little practical significance and is as casually disregarded as Christian ethical values are disregarded by Christians in the market place and on the battlefield. Absolute control enables Communist leaders to follow strategic plans that allow little consideration for the beneficial rights of labor to the produce of labor. The produce of labor may be turned into armaments which, in the case of the Soviet Union, are used to build up the Red Army and the Red Fleet for the destruction of the "enemies of labor" and the protection of the *workers'* state. Thus, the labor theory of value retains its ideological content and serves to give credence and moral justification to a régime based on the dominance of military and political values.

Marx regarded the use of production for profit or war as one of the greatest evils of capitalism. The Communist system was based on production for use, that is, for consumption, by the workers. In the Soviet Union, however, the worker has no sovereign rights, as a consumer, against the rights of the state. Production is planned neither for the use of the worker nor for consumption. Production is planned by the state for state purposes, which may or may not coincide with the vital interests of the worker as a citizen, but certainly do not coincide with his beneficial interests as a consumer. In any case, the labor theory of value is no longer of any practical utility to Soviet economists, although it is still useful for purposes of political propaganda and public morale.

According to Russian legal doctrine, the Soviet government is the organic political arm of Russian labor. A neutral observer, however, is forced to classify the Russian government as a political ruling apparatus like any other government and as probably less inclined to favor labor as a producer and as a consumer than most governments. The consumer market in Russia has no power to set wage levels. All economic values are set by political authority.

In capitalist countries, the labor theory of value was replaced by the marginal utility theory of value. This utilitarian theory, however, is applicable only within the market place under a system of perfect competition. It has little or no application to problems of wages, income, dividends, interest, depreciation, taxes, advertising, or insurance in a welfare state. In the capitalist society the labor theory of value is still sacrosanct. Labor political parties and organized labor unions base their whole existence on the labor theory of value. Labor values, in their eyes, take priority over the rights of any other group or even of society as a whole. The labor theory of value gives labor the priority rights — or even exclusive rights — to production. The rights of consumers are not morally justified under the classic labor theory; neither are the rights of government, captalists, entrepreneurs, shareholders, or proprietors. Theirs are residual rights. Labor has produced the goods, and it is this that gives labor its preemptive rights to production.

The labor theory of value has long ceased to be of any value to economists, but it still exerts a strong hold on the loyalties or prejudices of the general public. Human labor at one time may have been the chief source of energy or the chief factor in production. It no longer is. The industrial revolution has displaced human energy with mechanical or electrical energy. Manpower now contributes less than 1 per cent of the energy input of industry. The age of automation, now just beginning, will decrease the value of labor even further.[50]

3. Labor Values Under Automation.

The fundamental problem in economics is political rather than economic. It consists in the establishment of a legal framework within which the production and consumption of goods may be carried out for the greatest good of the greatest number. Economic science *per se* is unable to provide this framework.

However, within this political framework, economics can provide valuable theoretical data on the most efficient — not necessarily the best — methods to achieve the goals of production and consumption set by political consensus or legal authority. Since energy is required to make and distribute goods, one of the basic problems of economics is to evaluate and allocate energy resources for maximum utilization.

In the agrarian society, the energy base was animate human and animal energy applied to the production and distribution of food and to manufactures and other services in the form of hand labor.

The chief energy input in the industrial production process comes, not from human energy, but from inanimate or mechanical energy. To use a trite phrase, man has been replaced by the machine. The machine both uses and creates energy. Energy sources are limited, and energy output is also circumscribed by natural reserves and by the pollution tolerances of nature. The world is a limited and closed energy system, and each country is a smaller and even more limited energy unit. Within each national energy system human energy represents a small and increasingly unimportant fraction.

Manpower has long since ceased to have any quantitative relationship to total production. Under these circumstances, the labor theory of value ceases to have any meaning. This is obvious even to a casual observer who sees a great city like New York or London paralyzed by the acts of a handful of workers in a strategic industry such as transportation, coal, oil, or electric energy. It is not that there is anything illegal or unethical in the act of workers striking for more pay or other benefits. The strike, however, may have far-reaching destructive effects to the general public, which is not concerned with the stoppage. There is generated a feeling of alarm and dismay that a handful of workers can cause such large-scale paralysis of the economy. In actuality, the workers have no economic importance, and they could, in most cases, be easily replaced so long as the machines are left intact, for it is the machines that do most of the work.[51]

In 1863 Lincoln signed the Emancipation Proclamation and freed the black slaves. The year 1863 was also the year that the horsepower generated by steam engines in the United States exceeded the biological horsepower of horses and men, thereby freeing all workers from certain types of backbreaking farm labor. The farm workers moved to the cities and became factory workers operating machines run, not by human labor, but by energy from coal and oil.

In a technological society the energy base has shifted to inanimate electric or chemical energy working through machinery and automatic devices. The energy input needed to operate the machinery on an American farm may exceed the food energy available from the crops raised thereon. Formerly the farmer and his family and his draft animals provided the energy required for food production. In large-scale plantation-type farming, energy was increased by the use of slave labor, an almost universal practice up to the 12th century and not ended in the United States until 1865 and in Russia until 1861. But even at the height of Roman power, when cultivation by slave labor in the plantation *(latifundia)* economy was at its height, the cultivator could support only one city family. Today the American farmer supports 51 city dwellers. Industrial production derived from human energy in the economy of the United States and other technological societies today is very small, about 1 per cent; 99 per cent is derived from nonhuman energy sources.

Contemporary economic theories of value do not take this fact into account. "Cost-of-production" value theories base value, not on *total* energy factors, but almost solely on human labor factors, which are insignificant and difficult to evaluate, since labor input is no longer quantitatively related to production. The marginal utility theory of value is very useful for determining market prices and activity based on consumer preferences and given aggregate levels of supply and demand. However, it is not useful or relevant under conditions where prices are set by government boards or by a combination of powers composed of labor, management, and government and where nonhuman energy factors are disregarded in the price system.

A basic assumption of economists in both the labor theory of value and the marginal utility theory is that natural energy resources are a "free" gift of nature or of God. Land itself has no value until labor has made it productive. But this theory could not explain the function of the landlord: if labor alone made the land productive, the landlord had no ethical right to charge rent. This was pointed out, not only by Marx and Proudhon, but by such bourgeois economists as Smith, Say, Senior, and Ricardo.

Proudhon asked, "Who has the right to charge for the use of the soil, for the wealth that was not made by man? To whom is due the rent of the land? To the producer of the land, of course. Who made it? God. In that case, landlord, you may withdraw."

The noted English economist Senior argued: "Those who have appropriated the resources of Nature receive compensation in the form of rent without having made any sacrifices. Their role consists merely of holding out their hands for contributions from the rest of the community." This view was shared by Smith and Ricardo and other contemporary English economists. The charitable view was that rent was unearned income; the more radical view was that it was a form of robbery. Since man did not create the resources of nature, it was neither *right* nor *fair*, according to this system of values, for some men to charge for their use. From this it was only a simple step to the

Marxist argument that nature's bounty — land and natural resources — should be free to all. The Marxists translated this idea of free goods into the economic concept of "public property", which is not the same thing. But the idea of free goods distributed according to need rather than price had a powerful appeal. Marxists made political capital out of it. The bourgeois or capitalist economists, finding that the theory of labor made land and natural resources a gratuitous gift of nature and realizing that this was a politically subversive idea, decided to place natural resources outside the realm of economics. Said Say: "The blessings available to all which all may enjoy as they will, without the necessity of procuring them, without fear of exhausting them, such as air, water, sunlight, etc., having been given us gratis by Nature, may be called *natural wealth*. Since they cannot be produced or distributed or consumed, *they do not fall within the scope of political economy."*

This theory could be held only by economists who lived in the world as it existed before the space age. The accepted view, then, was that the natural resources of the world were infinite. Land, air, and water were regarded as inexhaustible gifts of nature or of God.

Today, the view of the world held by most literate persons is that of a small globe hurtling through space, only 8,000 miles in diameter and enveloped in a thin film of air perhaps three miles thick, a rather small and fragile spaceship with limited life-supporting capabilities. In the economic sphere it is now generally recognized that almost all natural resources are severely limited in supply and that, unless drastic measures are taken to conserve them, their ultimate pollution or exhaustion, or both, is only a matter of time, and not too much time at that.

The Bureau of Mines stated in 1970 that, in the last 30 years, the United States had consumed more minerals than had the entire world in all the centuries before. It had dug 2.8 billion tons of ore out of the Mesabi range in Minnesota since 1892, exhausting the richest vein of iron ore in the world, and leaving a residue of low-iron taconite. American steel companies now must go to Venezuela, Canada, and Liberia for their iron ore. This is only one of many natural resources that have been depleted. The great copper deposits of the Keweenaw peninsula in Michigan have been cleaned out; the softwood forests of the East and around the Great Lakes have been logged off. The United States no longer has a big edge over other nations in raw materials and fuels. It is becoming increasingly dependent on foreign sources for its material and energy resources. World reserves of natural resources are being depleted while the energy demands of the United States and other industrial countries continue to rise. The United States has been consuming a disproportionate share of the world's energy resources — about 36 percent, with a population of 6 percent. As other countries seek to expand their share of the world's resources and as these resources continue to shrink and disappear, a new and potentially explosive rivalry may develop among the consuming nations and between the consuming nations and those still possessing raw materials.

Under the radically changed economic environment of today, the value concept of natural energy resources as a free gift without limitation as to use or potential seems irrational. Every economist and scientist who speaks on the subject warns of the perils of the present profligate use of natural resources. Nevertheless, the values inherent in the labor theory of value and the marginal utility theory continue to place economic stress on labor and market utility factors in the pricing and tax system and to disregard, with catastrophic consequences, the value of energy factors derived from natural sources. The situation is analogous to a spendthrift who uses up his capital in riotous consumption without regard to its limitations or to a firm that places no value on its assets and makes no allowance for depreciation. The result of such an irrational policy is that, the faster the gross national product rises, the faster available resources are depleted. The richer the nation grows, the poorer it becomes in natural resources.

According to the environmentalists, infinite growth cannot be sustained by finite resources. Many studies have been published in recent years, some by reputable scientists, to prove that the limits to growth will be reached sometime within the next 100 years. By that time energy resources will have been exhausted, overuse of the land will bring soil erosion and a decline in food production, and the atmosphere and the hydrosphere will have become so contaminated by wastes from overproduction and overpopulation that human life will be impossible. These "doomsday" predictions may be exaggerated or even hysterical, according to some observers, but they serve the useful purpose of alerting mankind to the urgency of the problem.

Philip H. Abelson, editor of *Science* magazine, has stated that present low prices, which do not reflect all social costs, tend to encourage overconsumption of energy and promote wasteful and frivolous expenditure of scarce energy resources:

> Our economy has been geared to profligate expenditure of energy and resources. Much of our pollution problem would disappear if we drove 1-ton instead of 2-ton automobiles. Demand for space heat and cooling could be reduced if buildings were properly insulated. Examples of needless use of electricity are everywhere ... A major factor in the burgeoning use of energy is its low price — one that does not take into account all the costs to society. In the generation of electric power from coal and oil, millions of tons of sulfur dioxide are released, which causes billions of dollars worth of damage to health and property. We are consuming rapidly, at ridiculously low prices, natural gas reserves that accumulated during millions of years. Prices of energy should reflect their full cost to society.[52]

The internal-combustion engine is a major source of pollution. Do petroleum prices reflect the billions of dollars' worth of damage caused by the spewing of 66 million tons of carbon monoxide into the air every year in the United States? Do the prices of automobiles reflect the billions of dollars' worth of damage to society done by the annual killing of over 50,000 people and the maiming of over 3 million people in car accidents?

Conventional bookkeeping methods do not take these costs into account. Damage to the environment does not appear on the balance sheet of industrial firms. The exclusive interest of every firm is to increase the output of its product, whether that be automobiles, electric energy, petroleum, or any other manufacture. The goal is always maximum profit and growth. In a profit-

and-loss statement, the bottom line is the only one that counts. Profit maximization is an appropriate goal for a commercial firm, but not for the government. The goal of the national government, according to the Constitution, is to promote the "national welfare" and peace. Practices that are contrary to the national goal should be discouraged by the government. It is now generally agreed that waste and extravagance in the uses of natural energy resources are contrary to the national interest. It is also generally agreed that pollution should be controlled to a point where it does not seriously damage the environment.

The problem remaining is one of means to achieve these desirable national objectives. It is here that conflicts arise. There are many who wish to have their cake and eat it, too. They want conservation and a high rate of production growth; pollution control and automobiles; cheap gas and a limitation on oil drilling. The American people must decide which comes first. This involves a value judgment. Once that is made, the setting of national priorities involves the relatively simple mechanics of budget-making and tax policy. The values, involving a decision or judgment regarding what is most desirable, must come first. Indications seem to point to a growing interest in a social value concept that includes all energy factors in environmental balance and to a decreasing popular support for strictly market utility or labor values.

The need for a concept of social value based on total energy — a total energy concept — has been recognized by those who are concerned with the rapid depletion of the world's natural resources and the deterioration of the environment. On January 30, 1970 John N. Nassikas, Chairman of the Federal Power Commission, in testimony before the Subcommittee on Energy, Natural Resources, and the Environment, Committee on Commerce, United States Senate, pleaded for the recognition of a total energy concept: "I recommended the establishment of a National Energy Resources Council with the primary purpose of examining the nation's energy resources in relation to long-term requirements under a *total energy* concept recognizing the need to balance economic and environmental concerns." It was not until the economy literally began to run out of gas in 1973 that the need became a matter of grave concern to all.

The failure of the market to account for total energy costs may be attributed to the fact that existing economic values are derived from the preindustrial age. Both the labor theory of value and the market utility theory of value assume that natural resources are a "free" good or a boundless "gift" of nature or of God. This assumption is no longer tenable. The concept of human labor as the exclusive or the primary economic standard of value according to which all goods must be measured is no longer valid. Man is not "the measure of all things"; legal property is no longer acquired by possession or by appropriation of natural resources by human labor; the energy obtained from nonhuman resources can no longer be regarded as "free" and therefore worthless until "mixed" with human labor. Man is entering a new economic phase that has been variously described as "the planetary economy", "the spaceship economy", or "the natural ecosystem." In this new economy the role of man is no longer that of a supreme being, the source of all value, the lord of creation who can appropriate for his own ends the resources of nature without payment.

Since 1970 it has become increasingly and painfully clear that man is not supreme; that his dominion over nature is not absolute; that he can consume natural resources, but cannot create them; that he must learn to value natural resources, not only as items for human consumption, but as irreplaceable elements in his terrestrial home; that, in truth, he is a prisoner in a closed planetary energy system with finite resources that he cannot destroy without simultaneously destroying his habitat for himself and for his posterity. Man's dependence on his limited natural resources is now generally recognized and puts a definite limit or price on his capacity to consume, to pollute, and to waste. It is a price he cannot evade paying, whether or not it is included in his taxes or in his price system.

The general public, as well as the government, is becoming painfully aware of the inadequacy of the present tax and price system that does not take into account all energy costs. Taxes in the form of fines or penalties for noncompliance with pollution control laws are becoming more common and more severe. They are an effort to shift more of the social costs of environmental deterioration back to the producer. They are certainly necessary, but they are a stopgap measure. Punitive taxation is not the answer; neither is a system of mandatory allocations for material in short supply. Such a mandatory system brings with it, of course, another heavy layer of bureaucracy supported by tax revenues and all the evils and inequities associated with government rationing. A better system would be to have prices of commodities reflect true energy and social costs so that allocation is handled through the price system. So long as labor and market utility factors remain the basic cost factors in prices, the price system will not reflect true social value. Only when a total energy concept is used as a criterion of value will prices reflect true social costs. This criterion of value must take into account the central fact of modern life: that the earth is a limited self-contained energy system and that, to prevent pollution of the environment and exhaustion of energy resources, a value must be placed on all energy consumed. It is no longer economic, in the highest sense of the word, to disregard all values that are not market utility values or labor values. The values must be social values, in the most all-inclusive sense.

Chapter
III

CONSUMER RIGHTS

1.   What is a Consumer?

The market, when free from external controls, sets prices according to economic costs or factors of production: labor costs, material costs, rents, overhead, and other "standard" production costs. The free market is a remarkably efficient mechanism for the relative allocation of goods and services within the framework of its own value system. The value system of the classic free market is oriented toward labor and market utility values. It is blind to social and moral values. Here a product is judged, not on its moral, social, or aesthetic value, but on its price and utility. The market will sell Shakespeare or pornography, food or poison with equal efficiency. It will sell drugs to addicts or to doctors. It will sell dynamite to anarchists or to roadbuilders. The blindness of the market to social values has been recognized, and laws are enacted to protect buyers and sellers against unethical practices and to protect consumers against hazardous or unsafe products.

Within the limitations set by laws to protect consumers, the market is free to set prices according to its own system of values. Because prices are set by competition between producers, it is often assumed that the market price necessarily represents the best value to the consumer and, by inference, to society in general. This was, of course, the doctrine of Adam Smith and Jeremy Bentham and of their followers. The invisible hand of the market directed the distribution of goods and services in the most efficient and impartial manner possible; and the enlightened self-interest of both the consumer and the producer kept the system honest and weeded out the

77

inefficient, the lazy, and the unethical and automatically provided for "the greatest good of the greatest number."

Early critics of the market economy, such as Sismondi, Ruskin, and Marx, pointed out that human values and social costs were not included in market prices, and this they regarded as a serious omission. The theory of Socialism was designed to correct this omission, that is, to establish the rights to consumption for all. Under Socialism, production was to be for public consumption, not private profit. The Marxists believed that the only way to socialize consumption was to socialize production, as well.

Economists in the West regarded Marxism as too radical a solution to the problem of social values being excluded from market prices. Rather than destroy the existing market price system and build a substitute for which there was no blueprint — Marx never bothered to give the vaguest outline of a Socialist economy — they preferred to work within the market system and sought to soften the effect of market price competition on the poor or unemployed consumer by progressive taxes and social welfare legislation.

The market price system of the 19th century caused considerable hardship to those classes of consumers who were frozen out of the market by prices they could not afford. This hardship was concentrated in the industrial cities of Europe and America. Away from those cities, the world economy was still largely an agrarian economy dominated by the farm family, which was not dependent on the market for its food supplies and was relatively self-sufficient.

Economists in the agrarian society did not recognize the consumer as having a separate economic function. The consumption function was considered inherent in the production function. This was stated clearly by Ricardo: "No man produces but with a view to consume or sell and he never sells but with an intention to produce some other commodity, which may be immediately useful to him or which may contribute to future production. By producing, then, he necessarily becomes either the consumer of his own goods or the purchaser and consumer of the goods of some other person."

The growth of technology and mass production in the 19th century resulted in the gradual differentiation of the production and consumption functions. This had the effect of distorting or nullifying the "laws" of classic economics. There were times of economic crisis in industrial societies when the law of supply and demand did not seem to work and when supply and demand could not be brought into equilibrium. Consumption was unable to absorb all the production despite Say's Law that production was always equal to demand. Classic economists could not satisfactorily explain these periods of crisis except as aberrations or deviations from the normal, caused by human error or greed or both.

The periodic depressions caused severe hardships and shook the people's faith in the free market system. However, the 19th century was a period of worldwide industrial expansion. Depressions were relatively short and soon gave way to new booms as new industries were founded, new sources of energy discovered, new products invented, and new markets discovered and exploited. The fact that depressions were always followed by recovery and that most depressions were confined to local or national markets and struck only industrialized economies made these periods of crisis bearable.

However, in the 1930's a worldwide depression of catastrophic proportions forced politicians and economists to realize that the market system had collapsed and that, to bring consumption and production into equilibrium, basic structural changes must be made in the market economy. In the United States alone, during the 1930's one of every four workers and their families was without work.

The power of producers to control production threw the burden of balancing supply and demand upon the consumers, who were also, in most cases, the workers. It was they who suffered from unemployment when the producers closed the factories and it was they who suffered from the "over-production" of goods they could not afford to buy — in other words, they suffered from underconsumption.

The monopolistic power of producers was the result of the socialization of industry, that is, the growth of production units from small independent craft shops to large industrial corporations and the transfer of economic power from the independent craftsman to the corporate managers and owners. The worker now has no control over his work or over the production of his factory. The factory worker, employed or unemployed, does not have the economic power to restore the balance between production and consumption. As a corporate employee, he has no power to increase production, and as a consumer he has little or no power to lower market prices.

The unemployed industrial worker posed a special problem to society — the problem of the unproductive consumer. The unemployed workers were not producers. Could they, for that reason, be denied rights as consumers? For the first time, economists had seriously to study the function of consumption in the economy and the role of the consumer apart from that of the producer. As surplus goods accumulated and depressed the markets of the world, it began to dawn on the public consciousness that the consumer had a very important function in the economy. People began to ask, "What is a consumer?" Despite the gravity of the times *Punch,* the English weekly of humor and satire, had its own Puckish version of the consumer as a new economic figure to be reckoned with. The following appeared in the April 25, 1934 issue:

> "And what do you mean to be?"
> The kind old Bishop said
> As he took the boy on his ample knee
> And patted his curly head.
> "We should all of us choose a calling
> To help Society's plan;
> Then what do you mean to be, my boy
> When you grow to be a man?"
>
> "I want to be a Consumer,"
> The bright-haired lad replied
> As he gazed up into the Bishop's face
> In innocence open-eyed.

> "I've never had aims of a selfish sort,
>> For that, as I know, is wrong.
> I want to be a Consumer, Sir,
>> And help the world along."

> "But what do you want to be?'
>> The Bishop said again,
> "For we all of us have to work", said he
>> "As must, I think, be plain.
> "Are you thinking of studying medicine
>> Or taking a Bar exam?"

> "Why, no!" the bright-haired lad replied
>> As he helped himself to jam.
> "I want to be a Consumer
>> And live in a useful way;
> For that is the thing that's needed most,
>> I've heard Economists say.
> There are too many people working
>> And too many things are made,
> I want to be a Consumer, Sir,
>> And help to further Trade."*

A consumer in the sense the word is used today is a person who consumes what he does not produce. A consumer need not be a producer in the economic sense. He may be an unemployed worker, a child, an invalid, a soldier, a housewife, an artist, or a pensioner. To be a consumer, it is necessary only to have appetites and the money to satisfy them. The best consumer is the one who consumes the most. The best consumers in the United States economy are the soldier, sailor and airman who together consumed over 30 per cent of the total government budget or over $70 billion of goods in 1970. The soldier produces nothing in an economic sense, but he has tremendous importance as a consumer, and many giant industries and many millions of workers are dependent on his capacity to consume.

In the modern technological society the consumer may be a producer, but his economic function as a consumer has little or nothing to do with his function as a producer. He seldom, if ever, consumes what he produces. A factory worker may produce motor vehicles, armaments, airplanes, appliances, submarines, chemicals, or metal products, none of which he may consume directly. He may consume Brazilian coffee, English woolens, Japanese cameras, Iranian oil, Italian cars, or Panama bananas, none of which he produced. The modern consumer does not live off the surplus produce of the farm worker. The total production of society, not the surplus only, is thrown on the consumer market.

In industrialized economies no reserve is kept by the workers for their own consumption. In a technological society, such as the American, farming has

*Reprinted by permission of the publisher.

been industrialized, and the farm family shops in the supermarket along with other consumers. Farm production is sold on the market for money and is not consumed within the farm household except, of course, in small old-fashioned family farms that are relics of the agrarian age. In the technological society the consumption function has been completely differentiated from the production function.

The rise of the consumer has been neither a natural nor spontaneous process. It has been necessary to acquire or implant consumer habits. Early traders contended with resistance from savage peoples who did not understand the principle of peaceful exchange and regarded it with suspicion as a form of trickery. They were accustomed to taking what they wanted by force, not by trade. As a rule, primitive peoples were not interested in the consumption of alien or artificial commodities not essential to their mode of life. German traders in Africa used to complain of the natives' "verdammte Badürfnislösigkeit" (accursed wantlessness). Anthropologists have noted that among primitive peoples the creation of an agricultural surplus and leisure time does not automatically create a desire for more goods or for a higher standard of living. This *desire for more* must be learned or taught.

Even today, in the United States, over $20 billion are spent annually on advertising to teach the consumer to want and demand goods he may not know he needs. Some economists contend that the mass consumer market is largely a creation of advertising, which builds up an artificial demand for products the producer wants to sell and without which the consumer was happy. Others say that the creation of a mass consumer market, rather than mass production techniques, made America rich and powerful. Henry Ford, they say, did not originate assembly line production methods. They were known and applied by Eli Whitney and by the boat-builders of 14th century Venice. Ford would not have been able to mass-produce cars if the mass market had not been there to buy them.

Whether mass production or mass consumption came first, the fact is that the mass consumer market is an historic phenomenon less than 100 years old. It came into its own at the start of the 20th century. It has created a great abundance, but also great problems.

2. Growth of the Consumer Market

For the past 100 years there has been an apparently irreversible growth of the public sector in all modern nations. Adolf Wagner regarded the growth of the public sector as a necessary consequence of industrialization, a theory that became known among economists as Wagner's law. What was not generally recognized was the equally striking growth of the consumer market in the private sector during the same period. Up to the 20th century, only the *surplus* world production went to market to be exchanged or sold. The great bulk of world production was consumed by the producers within their households.

The private economy of most nations during the 19th century was dominated by what Alfred Marshall called the "representative firm" family-owned farms, shops, and stores. The basic production and consumption unit was the family. It was only after the turn of the century that production techniques perfected by Ford and others displaced the household economy with a new corporate economy based on mass production and mass consumption. A result of this shift was the growth of a mass consumer market that absorbed the entire gross national product; replaced household distribution with market distribution; and brought the family and other nonmarket institutions within the commercial control of the market.

According to the labor theory of value, only manual workers could be classified as productive workers, and persons who consumed what they did not themselves produce were considered economic parasites, exploiters, or nonproductive consumers. The latter lived off the surplus food voluntarily or involuntarily contributed by the workers.

When a person consumes what he does not produce, or can consume what is produced by others, or need not produce the exchange equivalent of what he consumes, there is no economic limitation on his appetites. He is freed from the restraints or limitations imposed by his own productive capacities. His only restraints are those imposed by law or by his own physical capacity to consume and his own sense of restraint, proportion, and equity. Against the virtues of self-denial are arrayed man's innate ambition, pride, and cupidity. Although there are many examples in history of members of the leisure class who, as consumers, were personally abstemious or frugal, there were many more who were wasteful, extravagant, and hedonistic consumers.

The problem of consumer rights was first analyzed in depth by two economists, Thorstein Veblen and J. A. Hobson. Both were denigrated by fellow economists as mavericks because they strayed from the orthodox marginal utility school of economics that regarded the consumer as an automaton who responded only to market stimuli. Veblen and Hobson looked beneath economic factors to grapple with the complex human and social factors that caused the consumer to act in ways that defied strictly economic or market utility values.

Veblen devoted most of his analysis to the "leisure class" of nonproductive consumers. In analyzing the appetites of the members of this class, in a striking passage he illuminates the compulsions that drive the consumer to an ever-higher level of consumption:

> But as fast as a person makes new acquisitions, and becomes accustomed to the resulting new standard of wealth, the new standard forthwith ceases to afford appreciably greater satisfaction than the earlier standard did. The tendency in any case in constantly to make the present pecuniary standard the point of departure for a fresh increase of wealth; and this in turn gives rise to a new standard of sufficiency and a new pecuniary classification of one's self as compared to one's neighbors . . . the end sought by accumulation is to rank high in comparison with the rest of the community in point of pecuniary strength. So long as the comparison is distinctly unfavorable to himself, the normal, average individual will live in chronic dissatisfaction with his present lot; and when he has reached what may be called the normal pecuniary standard of the community, or his class

in the community, this chronic dissatisfaction will give place to a restless straining to place a wider and ever-widening pecuniary interval between himself and this average standard...However widely, or equally or "fairly" it may be distributed, no general increase of the community's wealth can make any approach to saturating this need, the ground of which is the desire of everyone to excel every one else in the accumulation of goods.[53]

To Veblen, "pecuniary emulation", the desire to achieve or surpass the standard of living of one's neighbors, is the driving force that motivates the consumer. This desire is visible at all levels of consumption and, as the levels become higher, the articles of consumption become more luxurious and are purchased more for ostentation or "conspicuous consumption" than for utility, for, "In order to effectively mend the consumer's good fame it must be an expenditure of superfluities. In order to be reputable it must be wasteful. No merit would accrue from the consumption of the bare necessities of life, except by comparison with the abjectly poor who fall short even of the subsistence minimum; and no standard of expenditure could result from such a comparison...the standard of expenditure which commonly guides our efforts is not the average, ordinary expenditure already achieved. It is an ideal of consumption that lies just beyond our reach, or to reach which requires some strain. The motive is emulation — the stimulus of an invidious comparison which prompts us to out-do those with whom we are in the habit of classing ourselves."[54]

When Veblen wrote *The Theory of the Leisure Class* in 1899, the class of consumers that were engaged in "conspicuous consumption" could still be referred to as a "leisure" or a minority class and were not included in the majority of a population consisting of farmers and industrial workers. Since they were living at a low subsistence level, the masses of workers were not members of the class of hedonistic consumers. Their participation in the market was not total — many households were wholly or partially self-sufficient.

In the seven decades since Veblen wrote his book, Americans have seen the final separation of consumption and production. The consumer is no longer a member of a minority class. Today everyone in America is a consumer. Consumer dependence on the market is total. Only in very rare atypical cases can an American be found who, like his pioneer forbears, is consuming what he produces in the basic necessities of life as well as luxuries.

The American as a producer works for a large organization whose end-product he seldom uses. As a consumer he strives to maintain or surpass his level of consumption or standard of living or, to put it in the vernacular, to "keep up with the Joneses." He is chronically dissatisfied with his present economic position and strives always to better it by all possible means. The standard that once was considered the highest goal becomes, after it is reached, the point of departure for a still higher goal. There is no end to man's desires for material things, as long as the spirit of emulation and competition are part of human nature and are directed into materialistic channels or are expressed in property symbols.

When separated from his production function, the consumer is reduced to a bundle of appetites for which there is, in a consumer society, no saturation point or point of complete satisfaction. The consumer is constantly exposed to new goods and services in a materialistic culture; in the absence of a counterculture such as Puritanism, Monasticism, Spartan or Communist austerity, or Ghandian agrarianism, the consumer's appetites are constantly being whetted by temptation. This constant expansion of desire without limitations set by individual productive capacity or an austere moral code eventually leads the consumer to regard consumption as the end-all of life and to reject any restriction on his rights as a consumer.

Consumer psychology then takes on the "two fundamental traits" that Ortega y Gasset described as part of the psychology of the "mass man:"

> The free expansion of his vital desires, and therefore, of his personality; and his radical ingratitude toward all that has made possible the ease of his existence. These traits together make up the well-known psychology of the spoilt child... They are only concerned with their own well-being, and at the same time they remain alien to the cause of that well-being. As they do not see, behind the benefits of civilization, marvels of invention and construction which can only be maintained by great effort and foresight, they imagine that their role is limited to demanding these benefits peremptorily, as if they were natural rights.[55]

But Hobson claimed that consumer standards were set, not by the consumers, but by the producers:

> Where the production of an economic society has grown so far as to yield a considerable and a growing surplus beyond that required for survival purposes, this surplus is liable to several abuses. Instead of being applied as food and stimulus to the physical and spiritual growth of individual and social life, it may be squandered, either upon excessive satisfaction of existing routine wants in any class or classes, or in the stimulation and satisfaction of more routine wants and the evolution of a complex conventional standard of consumption, containing in its new factors a diminishing amount of human utility or even an increasing amount of human costs. If the industrial structure is such that particular groups of business men can make private gains by stimulating new wasteful modes of conventional consumption, this process, as we have seen, is greatly facilitated.[56]

This argument that producers stimulate or create artificial wants for their own private gain has become familiar to readers of Galbraith and other modern economists.

There existed in the agrarian society a direct relationship between production and consumption that could never be completely denied, so that consumption or claims on consumption were forced to remain within narrow limits fixed by the available production. Because the agrarian economy was one of scarcity, the gross national product was barely sufficient to keep the workers on a subsistence level, with only a small surplus left over to support the leisure classes. The monetary standard was a commodity — gold or silver — so that it, too, was not subject to extension. Neither of these two limiting factors operates in modern economies. Consumption has been divorced from production, and so wages and other claims on consumption are not subject to the limiting control factor of individual productive capacity. The monetary supply has been separated from the gold standard; consequently, prices are not subject to the limiting control factor fixed by the availability of gold.

The capacity to consume or the appetites of the consumer are insatiable and, when freed from the restraints of physical limitations, the "sky is the limit." Veblen referred to this consumer appetite as "cupidity" and said that, "Being in no way related quantitatively to a person's workmanlike powers or to his tangible performance, it has 'no saturation point.'" The insatiable appetite of the consumer had a saturation point in the agrarian society based on the physical limitations of production and the quantitative limitations of the monetary metal, gold, but these limitations no longer exist to restrain the consumer.

Again quoting from Veblen and referring to the Romans:

> The Latin phrase is *auri sacra fames*, which goes to show the point along the road to civilization reached by that people. They had reached a realization of the essentially sacramental virtue of this indefinitely extensible need of more; but the *aurum* in terms of which they visualized the object of their passion is after all a tangible object, with physical limitations of weight and space, such as to impose a mechanical 'saturation point' on the appetite for its accumulation. But the civilized people of Christendom at large, and more particularly America, the most civilized and most Christian of them all, have in recent times removed this limitation. The object of this higher want of man is no longer specie, but some form of credit instrument which conveys title to a run of free income; and it can accordingly have no 'saturation point' even in fancy, inasmuch as credit is also indefinitely extensible and stands in no quantitative relation to tangible fact.[57]

The American people, like the Romans, have reached a point in their civilization at which the insatiable appetite for material goods is considered a sacramental virtue that must be encouraged and subsidized at all costs. Consumption becomes a cult, and in this cult every consumer is a king. However, like most kings, his sovereignty has limitations. He is all-powerful in the aggregate, but individually the consumer may be poor and lack purchasing power. He exercises the veto power of life and death over a product by buying or not buying it. However, in certain lines he finds that he cannot control prices as he once did. The prices stay high, whether or not he buys. Prices no longer drop according to the demand or lack of demand of the sovereign consumer. Producers show a distressing tendency to ignore consumer demand and instead spend money on advertising to educate him to buy what they have already produced.

Despite these limitations, the power of the consumer is enormous, and the business world in America revolves around him. Consumer sovereignty is a fact that producers cannot afford to ignore except at their peril. Even Ford could not force the consumer to buy the Edsel; neither could General Motors keep him from buying foreign minicars. The consumer made Ford eat the Edsel and a half-billion dollar loss and forced General Motors to go into the minicar business against its will.

In the United States the most important market is still the consumer's market. In the second half of 1972 private consumption was running at an annual rate of $737 billion, compared to government spending of $257 billion. In the United States the consumer is king. Consumer sovereignty dominates the entire society, not only the private sector. Industrial and farm production revolves around the dominant position of the consumer. The economic welfare of the consumer is the chief concern of the government. The health of the economy is measured in terms of the consumption level or the standard of living of the average consumer. A strong or rising consumption level is regarded as an index to economic health. A declining or weak consumption level is regarded as an index of economic distress, usually accompanied by unemployment and other negative symptoms.

The consumers' market in the technological society is not like the free market of the agrarian society. In the free market, production, distribution, and consumption were relatively free and uncontrolled. Production and consumption were equalized by the law of supply and demand, and economic priorities and prices were set by the market. In the agrarian society the market was a surplus commodity exchange. Only the farm surplus was brought to the market to be traded. The bulk of the food was consumed by the families that produced it. As independent farmers and artisans turned into corporate employees and as private proprietors turned into corporate shareholders, the market became less and less a place for the exchange of surplus goods made by independent producers and more and more a mass retail outlet for mechanized factories controlled by giant corporations.

The mass consumer market of today is characterized by (1) the complete separation of the functions of production and consumption; (2) the importance of nonmarket factors in setting priorities and prices; (3) the absorption by the market of all production, not surplus production alone; and (4) the concept of consumer sovereignty as the guiding principle of the market.

3. Consumer Sovereignty

In a technological society the claims of workers to consumption are not apparent or self-evident. The worker is very seldom able to consume what he produces. He does not, in most cases, make a complete product. He may perform only a single specialized operation in the production process. It is difficult for the worker, therefore, to feel that he "owns" or has a legal claim over the product that rolls off the final assembly line. Such a claim may be established through an organization of workers or a corporate entity, but it then becomes a collective or social claim and not a direct and personal claim such as a farmer or a shoemaker had over the product he grew or made himself.

The worker and the consumer are separated by function. As a worker, he receives wages that are claims against the goods available in the consumer market. If he does not work, his rights as a consumer are terminated. Presumably he can then starve or be denied any consumer goods. This logical

86

result of the separation of the production and consumption functions resulted in tragedy for the unemployed in the first depressions. In those days, the political and economic leaders were still under the influence of Say's Law and the labor theory of value. The claims to consumption by the unemployed were denied on the ground that they were not producers.

Today the rights of the consumer have been established on both humanitarian and economic grounds. The humanitarian grounds are those of the concern of man for his fellow-man. They are ethical and religious in nature. The economic grounds were established first by the Socialists and later by economists of the welfare state. The Socialists have established as a basic principle of their economic system the fact that production should be for consumption by all on an equal basis. Under "pure" Socialism, everything is "free," and no one may be deprived of any goods that are available to all. "To each according to his needs" is a basic doctrine of Socialism. It is this broad and humanitarian principle of consumer rights that has helped make Socialism popular.

In a democratic society the government is forced to take some action to control consumption levels, not only from humanitarian motives, but also because the level of consumption is a decisive factor in determining the level of production. John Maynard Keynes first introduced the theory of consumption as the decisive factor in determining levels of production and employment. Keynes pointed out that "consumption — to repeat the obvious — is the sole end and object of all economic activity. Opportunities for employment are necessarily limited by the extent of aggregate demand. Aggregate demand can be derived only from present consumption or from present provision for future consumption." Keynes attempted to prove, by rather involved mathematical reasoning, that employment was a function of consumption and that there was a direct causal relationship between "aggregate demand" (demand for goods by consumers) and employment levels (or production levels, since production and employment levels are comparable).

Keynes also attempted to prove "that men are disposed, as a rule and on the average, to increase their consumption as their income increases, but not by as much as the increase in their income." Alvin H. Hansen, in *A Guide to Keynes,* states that "Keynes' most notable contribution was his consumption function" and that it was Keynes who first noticed that "the behavior patterns of the community are such that a gap exists (which gap widens *absolutely* as real income increases) between the amount the community wishes to consume and that output the community is capable of producing." This gap is the basic cause of unemployment; the wider the gap, the larger the unemployment, according to Keynes. During periods of unemployment, therefore, Keynes recommended government subsidies to bolster consumer "aggregate demand."

Some of Keynes' theories were adopted as official policy during Roosevelt's New Deal and by Labor and Social Democrat régimes in Europe. They were considered quite radical then because, according to the orthodox ethics and economics of the times, only the producer had earned rights to consumption. Keynes' theory that consumption should be subsidized seemed to conservative politicians and laymen both bad economics and unethical and detrimental to the worker. If goods were not to be earned by work or given as a reward for effort, how could the worker be induced to take hard or unpleasant jobs? Keynes' theories seemed contrary, not only to the doctrines of Adam Smith and J. P. Say, but to the "Protestant ethic" as well. According to the labor theory of value, the producers alone were entitled, on moral and economic grounds, to the rewards of their labors, and these rewards were to be commensurate, insofar as possible, with the quality and the magnitude of the labor.

To take from those who labored to give to those who consumed, but did not labor, was contrary to accepted economic and moral doctrine, both capitalist and Communist. The morality of the law, "Whosoever does not work, neither can he eat," may have been justified in a society in which the worker could eat what he produced. It could not be justified in a mass consumer market economy in which the laborer could not consume what he produced.

If the production and consumption functions are now separate and distinct, what guidelines, if any, can be established for the rights to consumption? The Socialist doctrine of equal and indiscriminate distribution of goods has been found unworkable. In Socialist societies as presently organized, consumer rights are severely abridged, and consumer sovereignty is never allowed to challenge state dominance. The Keynesian doctrine of consumer rights guaranteed by the government has left the problem hanging in midair. If some consumers are subsidized by the government, other consumers, who must work for what they get, are likely to feel cheated or conclude that labor, per se, is no longer the indispensable virtue, the only moral basis for claiming the fruits of labor.

It is now generally agreed that consumers have rights that cannot be denied them even if they are unable to work or pay for them. Among these may be included the rights to sufficient food to maintain life; to minimum housing or shelter; to basic household amenities to support family life; to education; to medical care; and to a minimum income.

There is, however, no general agreement on how these rights are to be secured and benefits provided. In a two-sector economy, the most common method is to tax the private sector and to provide the benefits through government agencies in the public sector. This system is far from perfect. The imbalance in the private sector that caused the maldistribution of consumption rights is not corrected. Instead, the public sector takes over some of the functions of the market economy and provides products and services that the market has failed, or is unable, to provide. Consumer sovereignty is not dethroned; it is only circumscribed. Within the reduced private sector the same struggle for consumer goods is carried on under the same rules: goods must be sold, preferably at a profit, and the consumer must buy them, even if he does not need them. Sometimes goods pile up in unmanageable surpluses and every trick of psychology and creative advertising is used to dispose of them. The consumer is cajoled, bribed, threatened, serenaded, shamed, reviled, insulted, screamed at, flattered, scared, and admonished to buy something he neither needs nor wants. His automobile may be transporting him well enough, but the ads tell him that, unless he buys a new Cadillac, he will not be socially acceptable. Her clothes are not worn, but the ads tell her that she must buy the new Paris styles or face social embarrassment. Variety is the spice of life and innovation in consumer goods is no doubt desirable. However, it cannot be denied that consumer goods are often designed for a short life and that rapid style changes are often made for the purpose of accelerating sales.

The consumer is guided and educated by advertising. This education is thorough and inescapable. Day and night, in the privacy of his home or in his car, from every radio and TV channel, from every newspaper and magazine, from every poster and billboard, the consumer is incessantly bombarded with the commercial message of the huckster, the vendor, the pitchman. The messages vary from the factual and the inane to the nauseating and the mendacious.

Advertising thus contributes to the expansion of consumer appetites that, according to some, should be restrained rather than expanded. But how can consumer appetites be restrained? Aristotle suggested an answer: "It is the nature of desire to be infinite; and the mass of men live for the satisfaction of desire. The source from which a remedy for such evils may be expected is not the equalization of property, but rather a method of training, which makes the better sort of natures unwilling, and the poorer sort, unable, to indulge in covetousness."[58]

Unfortunately, consumer training effected by advertising is done expressly for the purpose of arousing covetousness by invidious comparisons, prurient allusions, fear, pride, and other factors. Advertising creates the standard of affluence that the consumer strives to emulate in his life style. Failure to live up to the accepted or advertised standard of affluence for his group causes the consumer to feel socially inferior, alienated, and deprived. False priorities of consumer affluence in the private sector set up by advertising make it difficult for the government to set up national priorities based on social values that conflict with consumer sovereignty.

Consumer sovereignty does not guarantee the fair distribution of goods to *all* consumers. Under present market rules of consumer sovereignty there is, in fact, a very unfair distribution, with families in the upper income brackets enjoying privileged consumer rights and families in the lower income brackets suffering from lack of basic necessities. Although these are often assumed to be the result of a free market, consumer inequalities cannot be attributed solely to the exchange function of the market. The market operates under many rules, legal and extralegal, of which consumer sovereignty is only one.

4. Employment As A Function Of Consumption

Consumer sovereignty goes deeper than market dominance — it structures the entire economic system and makes the system dependent on the consumer.

The consumer's tastes are fickle, and he is easily swayed by new and novel products. Producers must stay on their toes to please him. They know that, in the next 25 years, more than half of the products now on the market will be replaced by new ones. This dependence on the consumer is not altogether healthy because (1) it causes business and employment to fluctuate according to consumer demand which, 40 years after Keynes, is still not completely understood or predictable, and (2) it causes production and employment to be subsidized for the sake of consumption.

Since New Deal days the government has assumed responsibility for solving the first problem, and considerable progress has been made, although no complete cure has yet been discovered for unemployment.

The second problem calls into question the legitimacy or *raison d'être* of consumer sovereignty, the sacred cow of the American economy. For that reason, perhaps, it is not recognized as a social problem, although it is perceived as an economic difficulty, the major one, according to Keynesian economists.

During both World War II and the Korean war a great many people were concerned about the coming of peace and fearful that it would bring another major depression. This anxiety was especially prevalent among workers in the defense industries, of which there were many. To them it seemed that only under war conditions could there be full employment, and peace was regarded with mixed emotions. Socialist writers, of course, charge that wars are waged by profiteers and capitalists to boost production, reduce unemployment, and increase profits and contend that, without the artificial stimulant of "imperialist" wars, the capitalist system would collapse. This is the extreme view that any production — even war production — is justified on the grounds that it provides employment and thereby maintains or subsidizes consumption.

Less extreme cases are those involving labor unions' efforts to maintain jobs in the face of technological unemployment. This practice is commonly referred to as "featherbedding." When a worker is displaced by a machine, he is kept on the payroll to avoid further unemployment or added loss of purchasing power. This practice is common in industries under strong unions such as the Longshoreman's Union, the Railroad Brotherhood, and the Carpenters' Union. Another aspect of this problem is the so-called slowdown or the stretch-out or make-work practices of some unions.

Unions make work for their members by forbidding them to touch work not covered by their job classification. This practice is sometimes carried to ridiculous lengths. A plumber may call an electrician just to insert a plug into a wall receptacle; a painter will call the repair man for minor adjustments on his spray equipment that he could do himself; a machinist will not move a tool or machine one inch because that is the job of the maintenance man. This practice is common in American industry, particularly in craft union shops. Although it is meant to create jobs and subsidize consumption, it has some other less commendable side effects.

War production and featherbedding are only two extreme examples of work condoned for the sake of maintaining employment and consumption. There are many more commonplace examples of make-work for the sake of preventing unemployment. Defense Secretary Laird in 1971 refused to close superfluous military and naval installations on the ground that it would create unemployment. These examples indicate that the consumer has become a tyrant who demands that work be done, not because it is necessary or useful, but simply because it is required to maintain consumption.

In a two-sector economy the problem of unemployment is confined to the private sector. Government workers lose jobs, but this is a minor problem, and government jobs can be found at any time if funds are made available. Overproduction of goods, which necessitates a reduction of the work force in business, is never a problem in government. According to Parkinson's law, the volume of work to be done by a government bureau always expands in proportion to the number of people employed. There is no need to restrict the number of workers employed to conform to the level of output, as in a private enterprise.

The absolute limit to the number of public employees is set by the budget and the tax revenues. In a two-sector economy, the public sector tries to maintain full employment in the private sector. When unemployment is severe, the public sector tries to absorb the unemployed as (1) dependents without work obligations, (2) workers in public works projects, and (3) workers in government-owned industries or services. The government becomes the employer of last resort. Where the public sector is dominant, as in most European social democracies, the government often takes over private industries when they fail and operates them, not with the prime objective of making profits, but of providing employment. Where the public sector is the only sector, as in Communist countries, unemployment presents no problem, as everyone is classified as a state employee.

The American economy is dominated by consumer sovereignty. The consumer can perform economic miracles, for he controls two-thirds of the gross national product. By spending he can lower unemployment, reduce Federal budget deficits, and increase corporate profits. By saving he creates investment opportunities for builders of houses and producers of capital goods. How critical the relationship of consumer spending and consumer savings is to the economy was illustrated in two Wells Fargo Bank forecasts of the 1972 economy made in November 1971. One forecast was based on an econometric model that assumed the savings rate would average 8 per cent of after-tax income. In the second forecast the rate was dropped to 7 per cent. The bank estimates that lowering the savings rate 1 per cent, that is, spending the money instead of saving it, would create one million jobs, reduce unemployment by six-tenths of a percentage point, increase personal income by $13 billion, increase pretax corporate profits by $8 billion, and reduce the Federal deficit by $7 billion. It would appear that the bank was trying to talk its customers into taking out their savings and spending them. But when that is done, certain unpleasant side effects can manifest themselves — the rate of interest may go up, investments may be curtailed, and economic growth through capital expansion may suffer.

The consumer is damned if he spends and damned if he doesn't, although most economists are Keynesians, that is, in favor of spending. Dr. Sidney L. Jones, Assistant Secretary of Commerce for Economic Affairs, agrees that consumer spending is the key to economic growth:

> The American consumer is somewhat unpredictable even in the best of times, and rapid increases in prices and frequent changes in wage and price control programs have added a new dimension of doubt to forecasts of consumer spending. There is no question, however, about the importance of consumer expenditures in the overall economic outlook. Purchases of goods and services comprise about two-thirds of Gross National Product, and to a large extent they will determine the economy's growth pattern in the near future...[59]

The absence of a consensus among authorities on consumer behavior has caused many economists to turn from equations and econometric models to peer into the consumer's psyche and to develop psychological explanations of consumer behavior. According to these analysts, the key to consumer behavior is "confidence." Confidence has become the *deus ex machina* of the modern economist. If he can't explain why things are better than expected, he notes with satisfaction that confidence has improved. If things are going worse than he expected, he blames it on lack of confidence and is automatically absolved of any professional shortcomings.

Arthur F. Burns, chief of the Federal Reserve System, appeared before the Joint Economic Committee of Congress on July 23, 1971 and gave three reasons for concern regarding the nation's economy. "First," he said, "there is little evidence as yet of any material strengthening in consumer or business confidence." The second reason was the deterioration of the competitive position of the United States in world trade. The third reason was lack of new orders for capital equipment. It is illuminating to see how such an intangible factor as consumer confidence has become the prime mover in the economy.

Like most sovereigns, the consumer is unpredictable, and his behavior continually confounds the best economic forecasters. He refuses to be pigeonholed or to follow the course programmed for him. The President's Council of Economic Advisers laments: "Consumer behavior has been especially difficult to predict in recent years, and may be more complex than had been thought previously."[60]

The consumer, of course, has no idea that he is a sovereign or that his behavior causes economists to feel insecure and inadequate. On the contrary, the consumer feels harassed and vulnerable to economic pressures he cannot control. He is dependent on his job to maintain his consumer standard of living. Without a job, he is a pariah living off welfare or charity. What the job is may be important to him as a person, but the job is more than personal satisfaction — it represents his livelihood, his claim to consumption. In the final analysis, what the job is or what it means to him is immaterial. He must have it to maintain his standard of living as a consumer. Hence the final irrationality of the consumer market: human energy and natural resources are expended to satisfy consumer appetites without regard to the social value or human need of the work performed.

To work on socially useless projects or to "make work" merely to create a job to maintain consumption is an incredible waste of human and material resources. It leads to such economic absurdities as the digging of holes by manual labor and then filling them again, recommended by Keynes during the Great Depression as an alternative for Americans too proud to copy the English dole.

In a consumer-dominated economy the consumer may absorb so much of the gross national product that there may be little left over for investment in the new or better production facilities. In the United States the ratio of gross national product devoted to consumer goods is probably already too high relative to capital goods. It is much higher than that of Japan or West Germany. This is one of the main reasons why those countries have a higher productivity growth rate than the United States. Most economists agree that gross national product growth is proportional to the amount of national income that is withheld from consumption and invested in plant capacity. In 1972 investment in plant equipment in the United States was 13 per cent, compared to 27 per cent in Japan and 20 per cent in Germany.

Unemployment is a by-product of the system of consumer-supported production. The factors involved in consumer spending, being psychological as well as statistical, political as well as economic, are unpredictable. Undoubtedly such economic stabilizers, unemployment insurance, Social Security transfer payments, and farm subsidies have done much to flatten out unemployment curves and relieve human suffering, but the problem of unemployment still defies solution 40 years after Keynes demonstrated mathematically that *unemployment was a function of consumption* and therefore subject to control by fiscal policy.

Employment in the public sector is not a function of consumption. It is determined by budget requirements. As the government budget increases, the public payroll increases also. In 1900 only 3 per cent of the labor force was on the public payroll, which corresponded to the government's share of the gross national product. Today 33 per cent or more of the working force owes its employment to public expenditures, which again corresponds to the government's share of the gross national product.

In such nonmarket economies as those of the Soviet Union or China, employment is not determined by aggregate consumption levels; it is directed into areas and occupations predetermined by political decision. There is never any fear that unemployment will result from the cutback of any specific economic activity because the state always has unlimited projects into which employment may be directed. The consumption levels have been set at a low level and are not subject to revision by consumers. No pressure need be feared from consumer demand for more goods than planned. On the other hand, care is taken that no consumer is deprived of the necessities that are available to all, so basic consumer wants are not left unfilled. The state, freed from consumer pressures, allocates manpower where it best serves its *political* purposes.

5. Earned And Unearned Consumer Rights

Organized labor believes that the standard of living can be raised by demanding more for doing less. The government income tax policy penalizes the successful producer for creating "surplus" production or "surplus" profits. The government farm policy has been to pay producers not to produce. Obviously, there is need to reestablish a more rational correlation between effort and reward, work and income.

If rewards are not tied to effort, there may be a significant loss of productivity. Government policy in the future will, no doubt, try to maintain by price and income policy correlations between production and consumption and between work done and monetary rewards that, in effect, are claims against consumption. In such authoritarian countries as Russia this problem has been solved by government decree, which arbitrarily sets production and consumption quotas for all the population. "The Soviets have adopted the concept that earnings should be tied closely and immediately to production. For workers the piece-rate system of payment reigns supreme. For managers, monthly bonuses make up a major part of income and are tied to operations *during the very same month* of the production unit for which the executive is responsible."[61]

It is not likely that authoritarian solutions will be adopted by democratic countries. However, democracies cannot evade the problem of controls over income and wages that represent claims on consumer goods. Since such claims are not quantitatively related to output, there is no longer a limiting economic factor. There is nothing, for example, to stop the unemployed or those on welfare from organizing and demanding benefits equal to the compensation of those gainfully employed. A craftsman, farmer, or artisan could, in the agrarian society, count on his own efforts for his economic reward; the correlation was direct and proportional. In a technological society this direct correlation no longer exists.

Since wages and income are claims against the consumer market and since they are no longer quantitatively related to production, there is no anchor or ballast to keep wages and income in line with existing production levels. Income and wage levels can be pushed as high as the bargaining or coercive power of employees and unions can raise them. The employer today has little countervailing power against labor.

In a statement before the Joint Economic Committee of Congress on July 23, 1971, Arthur F. Burns, Chairman of the Federal Reserve System, made this observation:

Labor seems to have become more insistent, more vigorous, and more confident in pursuing its demands, while resistance of businessmen to their demands appears to have weakened — perhaps because they fear the loss of market position that would be caused by a long strike or because they believe that their competition will give in to similar wage demands. More recently, the balance of power — so important to the outcome of wage bargaining — may have been influenced by expansion in the public welfare programs which can be called upon to help sustain a striking employee and his family, valid though these programs may be on social grounds. And the hand of labor may have been strengthened also by the evident success that public sector employees have had in recent years in winning large wage increases, frequently with the use of illegal strikes against the government. In my judgment, and in the judgment of the Board as a whole, the present inflation in the midst of substantial unemployment poses a problem that traditional monetary and fiscal remedies cannot solve as quickly as the national interests demand.

In most cases, the union is restrained in its demands by the danger of pricing the industry and itself out of the market. This restraint is not so compelling in industrywide bargaining. Here labor is in a monopoly position and can ignore the domestic market with impunity. Only the international market remains as a check on its demands. Steel and auto unions in the United States, for example, are nationwide labor monopolies, and they can raise wages to any limit they wish without pricing themselves out of the domestic market; the consumer may not buy as many cars when prices are higher, but he will not stop buying cars. However, since labor monopolies are not, as yet, international, excessive domestic wage rates will price goods out of the international market and cause foreign cars, in this example, to invade the domestic market.

Labor, capital, and government intervene in the market process to protect their interests. Labor seeks higher wages. Capital seeks to pass on higher labor costs in higher prices. Government seeks to control inflation, which is politically unpopular. Nixon was the first American peacetime president to impose wage and price controls on the economy in an attempt to control the inflationary spiral of wages and prices. The theory behind President Nixon's policy was to try to restore some semblance of orderly rational relationship between wages and prices. Two boards were set up in 1971, the Price Board and the Pay Board. Except for the rules of moderation and productivity, there was no yardstick or value system to judge wages and prices. The boards were to prohibit any wage or price increases that were "excessive" or "inflationary," and the top limit of allowable wage increases was put at 5.5 per cent. The results were far from satisfactory; according to one expert, the reason is: "Our government is trying to control prices in markets of the American economy that are really only subsectors of the world economy. As differentials between world export prices and controlled domestic prices become more wide-spread, black market transactions and other extraordinary devices can be expected to increase. Maintaining price controls in our economy within an environment of worldwide demand-pull inflation can have the perverse effect of producing more domestic shortages than would otherwise be the case."[62]

The separation of the production function from the consumption function has all but destroyed the old direct nexus between work output and pecuniary reward. To restore it by government decree is difficult in the face of labor pressure. Union leaders are driven by pressures from the membership to demand equal or higher wage raises than those obtained by rival unions. The teamsters watch the carpenters, the carpenters watch the electricians, the teachers watch the plumbers, and the auto workers watch the steel workers, all following with avid interest the reports of the latest wage raises gained by one or another, blazoned in headlines across the nation's newspapers and on T.V. and radio networks.

National interest is focused on wage negotiations when they involve a serious threat to the economy such as happens when longshoremen, electrical workers, teamsters, or railroad workers go on strike. When the settlement is finally reached, everyone learns the exact amount of the wage increase, and this adds fuel to the fire of other union demands. All labor leaders naturally feel that they must obtain equal or better wage raises for their members. All workers resent any insinuation that their work is less deserving than any other. A plumber feels, and perhaps correctly so, that his work is just as important as that of a teacher or an attorney. A garbage collector also feels that he performs an economic function as crucial to society as that of the plumber. Who is to establish the standards of value between these conflicting claims?

The unions themselves have no criterion of value except the standard, if it can be called that, of maximum benefits for their members. The father of organized labor, Samuel Gompers, laid down the classic labor formula for wage standards: "More, when we get that more we shall insist upon again more, and more, and even more." This formula has been followed by American union leaders ever since. Wage gains in one industry affect the expectations of workers in other industries, setting off a "leapfrog" contest, with each union trying to catch up or pass the other. The race for higher wages develops a momentum of its own that cannot be stopped by the conventional economic remedies of fiscal and monetary policy and appears immune even to the effects of recession, unemployment, and trade deficits. Direct government price and wage controls are imposed as a last resort.

Labor critics of the market system have called for basic changes in the power structure of the economy, toward greater "economic freedom" or more "worker democracy." Irving Bluestone, Vice President of the United Auto Workers, recently restated that viewpoint: "In a society which prides itself on its democratic system of freedom for the individual and rejection of dictatorial rule, the work place stands as an island of authoritarianism. The work place is probably the most authoritarian environment in which the adult finds himself." Bluestone said that the success of companies is still measured "not by the quality of life in the plant but by the extra bit of profit that flows into the treasury."[63]

The ultimate aim of all critics of the market system is the replacement of the profit motive by a more "humane" and "social" motive — love, social justice, social welfare, social cooperation, or communal freedom.

In actual practice, where the market system has been replaced by another system, the result has not been an increase in worker freedom, but a more authoritarian system of control. The coercion exercised by the market through price competition and the profit motive is replaced by a paternalistic state that considers itself the benign protector of the poor, but does not tolerate any opposition to its authority. The condition of the workers in the "workers' democracies" such as now exist in Russia and China is certainly far less "free" in any real sense than that of workers in a market economy.

The dilemma of those who demand freedom for workers is that, when they attain power or assume responsibility for production, they are faced with the problem of enforcing discipline and exercising authority. Replacing a corporate executive with a Commissar of Industry does not solve the problem of production or necessarily make the economy more humane or democratic.

The question of establishing a better relationship between private or public workers and employers is a political problem, the perennial conflict between freedom and authority. Freedom from all authority leads to anarchy; absolute authority leads to despotism. The cry for more democracy in the economy is based on the false premise that democracy is the equivalent of "freedom." In actual practice, where democratic governments have been established the longest, one finds that freedom is always balanced with authority. In the American government the executive authority is established by the Constitution and is given the power required to enforce laws, fight wars, maintain peace, and dispense justice.

Like the new American army, the new American economy may be undergoing a radical process of greater "democratization." How far this process can be carried without seriously impairing its primary function — the production of goods and services — only the future can tell. Complete and total authority in the hands of the producers achieves industrial efficiency, but at a cost of lower labor morale. Complete and total authority in the hands of the workers would lead to serious losses in production and quality control. The worker is also a consumer. In working for a more "democratic economy," the consumer interest must not be disregarded. Suppression or disregard of consumer rights by labor through production stoppages, featherbedding, and archaic work rules is, in its way, as authoritarian and antidemocratic as suppression of labor rights by the producers.

Suppression of ownership rights and interests by labor is also not in the best interests of all consumers and is likely to injure the worker in the long run, since the worker is also a consumer. Inadequate profit margins and excessive expansion of income devoted to consumption can lead to a lower rate of productivity compared to that of other nations that invest a larger share of their national income in new or better production facilities. In the United States during 1965-1971, while the gross national product rose 53 per cent, corporate profits after taxes increased 2 per cent, and employees' compensation rose 63 per cent. A continuation of this trend would lead ultimately to technological obsolescence. According to official estimates, about 40 per cent of American industry's equipment is already more than ten years old.

If they outrun productivity and if they weaken profit margins, pay raises will impose a severe strain on the economy. "This is not to say that we have to give up the hope of pay raises," said Arthur Burns. "Productivity in the American economy — the output per man-hour — has tended to go up at a rate of 3 per cent a year, and with good economic management we can hold it at that rate or even increase it. In any event, that is all we have to distribute, and wage increases of 10 per cent a year are simply a monetary illusion. The

97

average of incomes cannot increase faster than the increase in the nation's productivity."[64]

Responsible labor leaders are aware of this problem. I. W. Abel, President, United Steelworkers of America, said in November 1973: "I believe we are standing at a pivotal point in our history. If we adopt a don't-give-a-damn attitude, we risk becoming a second-class economic power....I call upon every American to enlist in the crucial battle to improve our lagging productivity. Nothing less is at stake than our jobs, the prices we pay, the very quality of our lives. Ominous signs have appeared that all is not well. Between 1960 and 1972, the average annual productivity rise in the U.S. was 3.1 per cent. In comparison, the growth rate in a number of foreign countries was double, in some cases even higher."[65]

Until the rights and interests of all three elements in the market economy — labor, management, and consumers — are balanced to achieve maximum social benefits — high labor morale, high productivity, and a high standard of living — unilateral demands by any one element for special privileges must necessarily weaken the other elements and the total economy.

In a free market economy everyone is free to claim his share of consumer goods. Since each consumer strives to acquire as much as his abilities, political influence, or union power enable him to, and since this is not directly related to his output, there is generated a strong and continuous inflationary pressure on the economy. Government wage and price controls have been tried by various nations to check these pressures, but such measures have not been successful in the long term, except in authoritarian countries where the total economy is controlled by the government. Nevertheless, some controls must be maintained unless the economy is to become subject to destructive inflationary pressures and a prey to raids by organized pressure groups, each trying to outdo the other in demanding for themselves higher wages, bigger tax exemptions, larger capital gains, and other special concessions and benefits. The unorganized, the unemployed, the unschooled, the aged, the mentally and physically handicapped, and the meek and the timid at the bottom of the social pyramid find their levels of consumption, or standard of living, shrinking vis-à-vis the more aggressive and better organized groups. The families of the poor are especially hard pressed for the average American family or household unit is no longer able to survive on its own resources.

6.   The Family as a Consumption Unit

In primitive agrarian societies the family functioned as a self-sufficient economic unit. In the most perfect agrarian society, the Chinese, the family unit was maintained for thousands of years, and authority within the family was controlled by the head of the family group. Ancestor worship was a form of family religion. Filial piety was the cornerstone of all morality. Attachment to the family group and to the ancestral land was so strong that exile was regarded as worse than death.

In Greece during the Homeric period, in Rome before the Twelve Tables, in Israel during the days of the patriarchs, and in North Europe in the feudal era, the family was an autarchic and independent politicoeconomic unit. Social justice was administered within the family and between families by the family head or the family council. There was little or no market influence on consumption or production. In America, the isolated pioneer family reverted to this archaic status both in economic autarchy and in the dispensing of social justice by the family or clan. The blood feuds of the Hatfield-McCoy type are reminiscent of the Homeric family feuds, albeit on a less epic scale.

As Homeric families grew into tribes and tribes into cities, the family began to decompose and lose some of its political functions to the city-state and some of its economic functions to the city market; tribal and folk deities replaced household gods; public law replaced private law; and the market economy supplemented or replaced the household economy. This development took place in Greece after the commercial era beginning in the 8th century; in Rome during the commercial expansion following the Punic Wars; and in Western Europe after the revival of trade during the Renaissance. The market economy was dominant in only a few commercial centers such as Athens, Rome, Carthage, Venice, and London. In these cities, however, the effect of the market was to dissolve family bonds, undermine the economic independence and self-sufficiency of the family, and make the individual, rather than the family, the responsible and the effective party, both legally and commercially.

The family as the center of economic, political, and religious life was too small a unit to assume the functions of a commercial or political empire. It was necessarily sacrified for the sake of the larger economy. This was the view of Plato — the guardians in the Republic had no family life — and of Epicurus, among others. In both Athens and Rome the family as a functioning social institution was almost completely discarded about the third century in Greece and during the first century after Christ in Rome. This was evidenced by the collapse of parental authority, the popularity of easy divorces and marriages of convenience, the liberation of women, the rebellion of children against parents, homosexuality, childlessness, and laws giving individuals, including women and children, the right to own property in their own names.

The authority of the *pater familias,* the reverence for the household gods, the devotion of the Roman matron to the family, and the unquestioning acceptance by children of family duties and obligations seemed to make the Roman family indestructible, yet it succumbed to the social effects of political and economic imperialism. The stoic Roman family of the *dignitas* household became the dissolute Roman family of the *concubinatus* ménage. The individual became dependent upon the state, rather than upon his family, for economic welfare, guidance, and discipline.

In the West the process of family decline set in with the start of the commercial era. The medieval family was severely attacked by many social theorists including Locke, Bodin, and Rousseau, culminating in the abolition of the marriage sacrament by the French revolutionists. Marx and the Socialist intellectuals considered marriage a bourgeois institution based on private property. The family as a politicolegal entity was abolished in the Russian revolution; it has since been reestablished, but without political or economic power.

It is easy to exaggerate the atomization of the family by the state and the market because the centers of commerce were also centers of culture. The writers and philosophers lived in such centers as Athens, Rome, London, and Paris, and the books they wrote are about city life or have an urban bias. Since peasants did not write books, it is easy to forget that, apart from these urban centers, the people of the world — including those in China, India, in the primitive village economies of South America, and Africa, and in the peasant villages of Europe — were relatively untouched by commercialism until the 20th century. In these undeveloped areas the family was still the basic economic unit. It produced and consumed what it needed and was almost completely self-sufficient.

The expansion of the market economy and the separation of the production and consumption function has made the American family obsolete as an economic unit, according to one eminent authority, who states that it has entered a period of decay and demoralization comparable to that of the Greek and Roman family:

> Scores of books are written on marriage and the family. Almost without exception they view marriage and the family as a private affair... Marriage is taken more lightly in our society than the purchase of an animal. If one purchases an animal he comes under the supervision of the town dogcatcher, the Society for the Prevention of Cruelty to Animals, an agricultural agency, or some public health agency interested in tuberculosis, animal diseases, fever tick eradication, or undulant fever. In the family, however, the steady movement is toward the inviolability of private right and private agreement.
>
> It is true that we have many family laws, volumes of them. Some of them try to mold the family into the semblance of a public institution. But all of society, from the writers of family books on down, have ideas which fundamentally place the individual rampantly above the family and are openly skeptical, even derisive, of any suggestion of familism. It is a fact well known, and associated with these changes, that the western world has entered a period of demoralization comparable to the periods when both Greece and Rome turned from growth to decay.[66]

At first, in order to establish its authority over the family, the state was forced to enact severe laws to curb interfamily blood feuds that often wiped out entire blood lines. The laws of Draco and Solon, the first written codes, were an attempt to suppress the power of the old Greek families, the *genos,* and to bring them within a peaceful framework of public law. The Twelve Tables was a similar effort to curb the power of the Roman *gentes.*

Eventually the state became all-powerful, and the family was reduced to a voluntary association without political or economic bonds. When this happened, the old family *mores* disappeared and were replaced by an epicurean code of ethics. Family demoralization shocked and alarmed the more thoughtful rulers, and the state stepped in to restore family unity and morality.

Augustus passed laws against adultery and prostitution and ordinances to penalize celibacy and to encourage marriages and children: Unfortunately, the emperors who succeeded him undid all his good work by their dissolute and immoral conduct. In those days the effect of economics on family life was not understood. It is better comprehended today, but whether it is possible to alter the course of family decay is difficult to say, nor is there agreement that such efforts are desirable. Assuming that urban life and a market economy are the basic causes of family decay, is it to the best interests of society to wipe out commerce, close the markets and the cities, and return to the archaic agrarian family with its eye-for-an-eye system of justice?

Thomas Jefferson faced this question squarely and opted for the agrarian economy. He disliked and feared urban centers and believed that city people were not capable of self-government. He was willing to sacrifice industrial growth and city markets for an agrarian economy and rural family life. So, of course, was Thoreau. This extreme ' dedication to rural values and uncompromising opposition to urban values has been regarded with some embarrassment by admirers of Jefferson as one of those quirks of personality to which all geniuses are prone. In later years Jefferson modified his views somewhat. It took 200 years to make Jefferson's attitude more understandable to Americans, many of whom now realize that urbanization and technology are not unmixed blessings. However, unlike many modern rebels against technology, Jefferson embodied no individual nihilism in his makeup, and his philosophy of agrarian democracy was based entirely on the traditional domestic virtues of the farm family, which he correctly perceived would be destroyed by city life. The history of the United States has fulfilled Jefferson's direst forebodings. The country is now completely commercialized and urbanized. Family farming and the rural household economy that Jefferson knew have disappeared. The family is atomized. The husband and wife have separate economic functions and separate incomes. The children are state-educated and free of parental control and authority. The older family relations are supported by the state or have their own income. The state has taken over the educational and economic support functions of the family. Complete independence of all family members is recognized by law. Parental authority is not backed by legal authority. In some cases the state appears to be deliberately following a policy of undermining the family. Women are being encouraged to work and to leave childrearing to public nurseries. Programs to aid mothers with dependent children discourage mothers from marrying and families from having male heads. In his sociological study of the Negro family, Moynihan comes to the conclusion that Negro dependency and crime are the result of the breakdown of the Negro family. But the breakdown of the Negro family was itself the result of the largest internal migration in American history which brought the Negro from the South to the North and from the country to the city. In the process, the Negro family was destroyed. Uprooted from its rural environment, it was no more immune to the corrosive

101

effects of city life than the white family. State welfare aid in many ways is doing more to complete this process of family atomization than to reverse it.

The breakdown of the American family, white and black, has reached a point where only some massive structural change in the economy will reverse the present process of disintegration. Today only 35 per cent of families in the United States are united — husband, wife, and children. Three-fifths of the people on welfare are mothers without husbands. There are 16 million divorced people in the United States. Divorce is now accepted as normal or even fashionable, where formerly it was considered a social stigma. The Women's Lib movement advocates women's emancipation from family duties. Women now often refuse to take single responsibility for raising children. As a result, the number of children living with fathers is on the increase. Abdication of parental duties by both parents is also increasing rapidly, according to Chief Judge John R. Evans of the Juvenile Court of Denver. Extralegal cohabitation, birth control, abortion, and a rootless nomad life make domestic life and childrearing an anachronism and a hindrance.

According to Hobson:

> There is an economy of consumption in the family standard of life as important for social welfare as the economy of production in the business . . . Distribution of income according to needs, or ability to use it, does not, indeed, depend for its practical validity upon the application of exact and direct measurement of need. The limits of any sort of direct measurement even of material needs appear in any discussion of the science of dietetics. But inexact though such a science is, it can furnish certain valid reasons for different standards of food in different occupations . . . What holds of food will also hold of housing, leisure, modes of recreation and intellectual consumption. Nor must it be forgotten that, for expenditure, the family is the true unit. The size and age of the family is certainly a relevant factor in estimating need, and in any distribution on a need basis must be taken into account.[67]

The restoration of family rights to consumption based on family allowances would help keep the family together as a unit. Since consumption and production are separate functions, a system of awarding consumption claims on a family basis rather than on an individual basis is not economically any more illogical or unsound than methods presently used.

As it grows, the market economy absorbs the household economy and acts as a liberating or demoralizing influence, depending on the point of view. It undermines the traditional family structure and leaves the problem of individual social adjustment up to society and to the individual. The market provides no income support for such family activities as cooking, housework, child care, character training, or social education. The market rewards such activities only when they are performed away from the family, in a restaurant, school, hospital, or other public institution, or when the wife becomes a teacher, a nurse, a cook, or a maid. A mother who successfully raises a large family and gives society citizens who are healthy, productive, well adjusted, of good moral character is not paid by the market and is unrecognized by society. After a few years spent in college, a young lady is honored by society with a

Ph.D. in family sociology and is rewarded with a well-paying job. This value system does not build family solidarity; neither is it necessarily good economics. When household chores — feeding, child training, health care, education, clothing, housing, and entertainment — are done outside the home, the result is not always an improvement in quality or in economic efficiency. Billions of dollars are spent in education and penal institutions, in the food-service, health-care, beauty-care, child-care, clothing, and other industries, and the results are often disappointing and inferior to those obtained "free" in the family or household economy.

The government can try to build up family solidarity by family support programs. President Nixon tried to pass Moynihan's Family Assistance Plan in 1969, but failed. Many governments such as France and Sweden have extensive systems of family allowances. They are not altogether successful. The social process of liberation or demoralization is hard to reverse. Once a "liberated" woman gets out of the kitchen and becomes an attorney or a secretary or a physician, it is difficult to get her back to doing housework. Other governments have tried to replace the family with new social structures where children are treated as wards of the state and parents are divested of family duties and have duties only to the state. The Chinese commune and the kibbutzim of Israel are examples. Modern sociologists are inclined to agree that the family as an economic and social unit for education, production, and capital accumulation is no longer needed. They view with skepticism any attempt to legislate marital harmony or family regeneration.

In his historical study of the family, Carl Zimmerman points out that the family is not only an economic and social unit, but also the basic biological unit. The family has adapted to all past social conditions; even when completely atomized, it remains as the nuclear or basic social unit that can survive when all other larger social and economic units have disintegrated. Any attempt to write off the family unit as obsolete runs into this biological fact. There is also considerable historical evidence, according to Zimmerman, to indicate that periods of family atomization are periods of great social instability and moral confusion. Regeneration of social life, from within or without, has in the past come with the regeneration of family life based on strong blood ties and an integrated family ethos. European immigration to the United States during the 19th and 20th centuries may somewhat have arrested the process of family atomization in America. The barbarian invasions arrested the process of family disintegration in the Roman empire. Such external forces are not likely to be a factor in family history now that the world is "colonized". The problem must be solved by internal forces, planned or unplanned.

To arrest family atomization in America calls for a national plan of family support; but no comprehensive national policy for family support has been debated and established. Moynihan's Family Assistance Plan, rejected by Congress in 1971, was the first serious effort by the American government to attack the problem of American family breakdown. In the meantime the policy of income equality for individuals by the government and by the market wage system and the lack of income support for nonmarket family activities quicken the process of family atomization.

Whether man can, by political action, halt or reverse the trend toward family atomization or whether it is subject to forces beyond his control is a question only the future can answer. The current political programs being actively implemented to establish free day care centers where working mothers may leave their children undoubtedly will contribute to further family disintegration. The next step is state care from the cradle to the grave for all on a purely individual basis.

One of the most original and far-reaching ideas for reestablishing the American family on a stronger economic base came from a businessman, H. Ross Perot, in a statement given to the House Ways and Means Committee on March 21, 1973:

> America's working families need a government policy which encourages and permits them to accumulate a stake — to accumulate capital — so that they can enjoy, as others, a meaningful share in the growth and gain of their economy...
>
> Therefore, I propose that every American be given the opportunity to accumulate $100,000 in capital gains — tax free, in other words, up to a lifetime total of that amount. This is meant only for the average working American who is trying to accumulate a stake in life which all American families want and need.

It is extraordinary that such a revolutionary proposal should be made, not by a Socialist politician, but by a self-made millionaire and corporate executive. The idea of giving American workers a proprietary right in industry was first suggested by a famous economist, Henry Carter Adams, in 1886 while he was teaching at Cornell. He contended that the family must have a secure property base. Since the industrial system and the market have destroyed the family "stake" — the family-owned farm or shop — Adams believed that a new theory of property rights must be devised to give the worker a stake in industry. Adams believed that such a proprietary property right could be established through collective bargaining. Perot suggested working through the income tax and capital gains tax laws.

Neither method appears to be practicable from a political viewpoint; for that reason, perhaps, the proposals did not arouse the interest they deserved, although in Adam's case it was enough to have him dismissed from Cornell. Undoubtedly, there is a very strong interest in restoring family economic stability or at least in halting further erosion of the family economic base.

Despite such erosion as has occurred, the family institution in America still has a potent economic base. According to data compiled by the National Bureau of Economic Research for 1968, the private household sector of the American economy had total assets of over $3 trillion as against total assets of $1.46 trillion for all private financial institutions. Private household assets include real property and other tangible goods, of course, but the family also had more financial assets than institutions — $2.3 trillion versus $1.4 trillion — and more corporate stocks as well — $828 billion versus $253 billion. Of course, part of the assets listed under the family or household sector are held by individuals, but in general the financial strength of the American family is not as feeble as some reports would indicate. Nevertheless, the trend toward atomization and loss of economic power, particularly in the lower income brackets, is undeniable. This trend is neither natural nor inevitable.

Market values that penalize the household economy can be corrected if such a policy is approved by the people. There is really no logical reason why a woman who cooks, nurses, or teaches should not receive the same reward, whether she does the work at home or in a commercial or public place.

Working through the income tax system and through state subsidies offers one approach that, to date, has not proved completely satisfactory. One other approach to restore family solidarity would be through a system of commodity taxes added to market prices to ensure an adequate family standard of living.

If family solidarity has a social value, it should be reflected in the price system; to put it in another way, the price system should reflect the social costs of broken homes and fatherless children.

7.   Taxes on Consumption

The Tax Foundation, a private research organization, made a study in 1953 of the number of taxes incorporated in common consumer items and discovered that a loaf of bread carried 151 taxes, included in the price; an egg 100 taxes; a man's suit 116 taxes; and a house 600 taxes. Not all taxes were counted.

In the case of bread the only taxes counted were Federal and state taxes paid by the grocer, and baker, the companies making the ingredients that went into the bread, and the railroads that hauled the ingredients. The grocer paid four Federal taxes — individual income tax, telephone tax, tax on transportation, and tax on safety deposit box. The baker, a company in Indianapolis, paid eight Federal taxes — corporation income tax, stamp tax on its security transfers, telephone tax, telegram tax, transportation tax for its salesmen and product, safe deposit tax, and Social Security tax. The grocer and baker also paid 15 state taxes, including state income taxes. A Kansas City flour mill that supplied the flour paid seven Federal taxes and eight Missouri state taxes. The railroad that hauled the flour paid five Federal taxes and an assortment of taxes to Missouri, Illinois, and Indiana. The sugar supplier from New Orleans paid eight Federal and six Louisiana taxes. Additional taxes were paid by the railroad that hauled the sugar and by the other suppliers of salt, malt, shortening, milk solids, and yeast. Undoubtedly, the number of taxes has increased substantially since 1953.

Taxes in the United States today are not generally levied for the specific purpose of incorporating social costs in the commodity or service. Tariffs and selective excises are unpopular; only in the extreme cases of alcohol and tobacco are taxes levied according to the principle of social value. In all other instances, social costs are completely disregarded as criteria insofar as taxes are concerned. For that reason the prices of commodities and services do not reflect true social costs. The disregard of social costs in the price structure causes severe misallocations of material and manpower resources.

Professor Kenneth E. Boulding has pointed out that the failure of the price system to include social costs has contributed to the environmental problem: "Many of the immediate problems of pollution of the atmosphere or of the bodies of water arise because of the failure of the price system, and many of them could be solved by corrective taxation."[68]

In cases where a commodity or service has harmful effects on public health, safety, morals or the environment, a tax should be imposed to neutralize the social costs as a minimum correction. Beyond that, the principle of relative social value should determine if a higher tax rate is called for.

Twentieth-century economists have tried to develop a theory of social costs or maximum social utility based on the equalization of marginal private costs and marginal social costs of all resources. A. C. Pigou in *The Economics of Welfare* (1920) discussed the divergence between private costs and social costs and gave numerous examples of social costs that were not reflected in prices — for instance, the loss of real estate values when factories are built in residential areas or the cost of police protection when liquor prices are lowered. Pigou suggested that, when private and social costs diverge, the government may have to make up the difference by tax subsidies or tax credits to compensate for the cost borne by society. In 1923 John Maurice Clark in his *Economics of Overhead Costs* pointed out that standard business costs excluded many social costs such as health hazards.

Veblen attacked the market price system as unfair, unjust, based on distorted values, and run by incompetent absentee owners, who operated it for personal commercial gain instead of for the public good. These corporate owners or capitalists are "incapable of anything like an effectual insight into the uses of resources or the needs and aims of productive industry, in any other terms than those of commercial profit and loss. Their units and standards of valuation are units and standards of price, and of private gain in terms of price; whereas for any scheme of productive industry which runs, not on salesmanship and earnings, but on tangible performances and tangible benefit to the community at large, the valuation and accountancy of salesmanship and earnings are misleading." J. A. Hobson also wrote extensively on the omission of "human" or "vital" costs from the market price system. Modern economists are conscious of the problem and of its relation to the current energy and environmental crisis.

The difficulty encountered by economists is that they are unable to establish a formula for combining market and social costs. How can the social costs of slum clearance or unemployment or water pollution be expressed in market prices?

"The basic environmental problem, for example, is that some resources, like air, are common property and consequently the private economic system does not put a price on their use. The result is over-use or mis-use — such as the dumping of excess pollutants into the air. Similarly, much of the knowledge that can be created by research and development becomes a free good, so that private people do not have an adequate incentive to produce it. A

106

part of the health problem is the difficulty of finding a pricing system for medical care which gives an incentive to economy in its use but at the same time assures adequate service for all. In the field of energy we see that a shortage and high price of fuels may be caused by regulation intended to hold down the price of fuel." These comments on the failure of the market pricing system to set prices according to true social value were made by the Council of Economic Advisers in their annual report to the President, dated January 24, 1972. What is the lesson to be derived from these facts? "The lesson of all this is *not laissez-faire.* There are conditions where a functioning price system does not naturally exist and has to be created or simulated. But the lesson is of the great and cumulative losses likely to result from continued suppression of the price system where it is functioning in anything like a normal manner." The learned council proclaims the need to "create" or "simulate" a new price system, but at the same time fears the risks of suppressing the pricing system of the market. This respect for the market is well founded.

The market is an ancient and durable institution. In one form or another, it has survived since the earliest village economies. When the public sector was growing under the welfare policies of the modern state, it was assumed that it was at the expense of the market. But the market was growing also, and took over the large and vital private sector, which had been dominated by the private household, the family farm, and other nonmarket institutions. The market collapse of the 1930's was not the death knell of the market, as Socialists so confidently assumed. The market was merely undergoing a radical change, as it has been doing for thousands of years. The market has confounded its critics by remaining a vital force in the world economy. The market economies of Japan, West Germany, Taiwan, France, and the United States have shown economic vigor greater than the Communist economies of China, Russia, and Cuba, which thought they had found in planned rationing a substitute superior to market competition. Within the Communist orbit the more progressive countries — East Germany, Czechoslovakia, Rumania, Poland, Hungary, and Yugoslavia — are straining to recapture some of the vitality of the market economy and to replace bureaucratic regulation and technocratic regimentation with market competition, economic incentives, and free choice. The market has arisen like a phoenix from the great depression and is demonstrating that it has great powers of survival and adaptation. The market mechanism will endure in some form as long as man values free choice. However, the market of tomorrow will not be like the market of today, just as today's mass consumer market is not like the surplus commodity market of the agrarian society. The market of the future will have to grapple with the problem of pricing environmental resources now regarded as free goods, and social costs now excluded from market prices will necessarily be brought back into the price system.

This problem was explained to the Joint Economic Committee of Congress by Professor Robert Haveman, according to a report by the Committee chairman, Senator William Proxmire:

> "Haveman pointed out that numerous reasons have been given to explain why we have an environmental problem. Some say it is because we have too affluent a

107

society. Because we produce so much, we must dispose of so much. Others say it is because we produce the wrong things — too many automobiles, not enough mass transit; too much primary paper, not enough recycled paper; and too many tin cans, beer bottles, and plastic containers.

But Haveman insists that while each of these provides some explanation, the basic cause of the environmental problem is economic. He charges that the problem exists because the market economy fails to place a price on the use of environmental resources...They are treated by everyone as free goods...Haveman argues that a way must be found to price environmental resources. They have to be brought back into the economic system.[69]

Just as classic economists avoided the problem of natural resources by leaving them out of their system, so neoclassic economists avoided the problem of social costs by calling them "externalities" and omitting them from the economic system. Both problems remained submerged for a long time, but they have surfaced now, and the energy crisis and the environmental crisis have become the major social and economic problems of the times. Social costs can no longer be ignored. The question now is, how are they to be charged? Are they to be included in the price of things produced and, if so, by what cost criteria? Are they to be assessed against offending industries as punitive taxes? What costs, if any, should be borne by society and paid from general tax revenues? The market price system has been found inadequate — not because it has robbed the worker of "surplus labor value," as Socialists claimed a century ago — but because market prices do not reflect the costs of pollution, waste of energy resources, environmental deterioration, and other social costs. By ignoring social costs, the market price system has brought the national economy to a critical stage where increasing growth of the gross national product indicates that the country is growing richer while, in reality, it is becoming poorer in natural resources.

It is clear that incorporating social costs in the price of a commodity or service in the form of a tax places a truer value on such a commodity or service than where social costs are disregarded. Where social costs are ignored, the price is false and incomplete since it does not take *all* costs into account. Social costs that are ignored in prices eventually are paid for by society in exhaustion and pollution of natural resources and the degradation of the environment.

Is it possible to devise a "price formula" that would incorporate all predictable social costs? What, for example, is the social cost of smog and how can it be charged to the known sources of air pollution? Air is "free," so it has been utilized for industrial production without cost to the producer, but pure air has a social value also, for society cannot get along without it. A process or product that pollutes the air should be (1) regulated by air pollution control regulations and/or (2) charged with a tax sufficient to pay for neutralizing the toxic effects. This has not been done to date. As a result, the air is fouled with pollutants freely and indiscriminately released from industrial and other sources. The cost of air pollution runs into many billions of dollars. This cost is borne by society under the present tax and price system, neither of which incorporate the social cost of air pollution.

The story is the same with regard to water pollution. Many American rivers have been turned into open sewers. Chemical wastes flowing into the oceans will turn them into dead seas within a century at present rates of pollution, according to marine scientist Jacques Cousteau. Ecologists state that, unless present trends are reversed, human life itself may be endangered by air and water pollution. Unfortunately, the price system sets no value on the depreciation of natural resources or on such intangible social values as public safety, health, ethics, and aesthetics. The price system is concerned only with market values. As a result, the more affluent society becomes, the more the environment is impoverished.

The United States Congress passed an antipollution bill in 1972 that authorized $25 billion for this purpose, the largest single appropriation in American history for nondefense needs. These and other remedial measures are necessary, no doubt, but a permanent program for maintaining a healthy economy in a healthy environment requires a systematic means for introducing social costs into the price system. By so doing, the economy will operate on a basis of price competition within environmental limits set by the government. The need has been recognized by the United States Government. On January 15, 1971 the Chairman of the Council on Environmental Quality said:

> We think that significant reductions in waste discharges might be more quickly and inexpensively effected if, in addition to regulatory restrictions, changes were made in the costs facing polluters. For example, a system of effluent and emission charges requiring payment for the amount of specific pollutants added to the environment would, it seems to me, help harness the normal competitive prices of our economy to work with us rather than against us in achieving our pollution abatement goals.

The other alternative is to politicize the economy and control pollution by bureaucratic regulation and mandatory allocation. Taxation will not eliminate the need for all regulatory restrictions, antipollution laws, and safety and health standards. However, to leave the private sector to operate on a maximum profit value basis and impose on it a dual standard of social value enforced by a vast government bureaucracy is not an effective solution.

This was the opinion of a study published by the Brookings Institution entitled *Setting National Priorities — The 1972 Budget:*

> The enforcement of standards through judicial procedures entails a lengthy, tedious, and often ineffective process of negotiations with states and individual pollutors. The opportunities for delay and for the erosion of standards by pollutors are numerous. As a result, enforcement efforts are subject to long delays and are usually concentrated on only a limited number of conspicuous violators. The primary incentive under an enforcement approach is for industrial pollutors to hire lawyers to delay administrative and court actions.

The Brookings Institution study comes to this conclusion:

> What is needed is some mechanism to weigh the social costs of pollution against the economic costs of eliminating it — economic costs that ultimately are reflected in a slower rise in consumption as we ordinarily measure it. Fundamentally, the

nation has to balance its desire for an increased supply of the usual kind of consumer goods — automobiles, television sets, clothing, and the like — against its desire for a cleaner environment. Charging pollutors a tax on every unit of pollution they discharge into rivers or streams is one way of providing such a balance. The tax would be calculated to reflect society's evaluation of the damage from pollution and could be set as high or as low as that evaluation demanded. Pollutors would have powerful incentives, in their own interest, to do what society wanted — namely, to find the most efficient and effective means for reducing their output of pollutants in order to reduce the tax. In cases where no economical means for reducing pollution could be found, the tax would cause the price of the product to rise, and thus less of it would be bought and less produced. Sales and production would shift toward less polluting activities.

The choice is between political regulation and mandatory controls and allocations, on the one hand, and the use of the market price mechanism, on the other. The market price system is the most effective method yet devised for handling the incredibly complex problem of how to take care of a trillion daily individual orders from over 200 million customers for over a million different commodities and services. Provided market prices correctly reflect the cost of all scarce resources, including clean air and water, and of all social costs, they provide the best mechanism for making rational choices in a free society, far superior to any government rationing system.

The introduction of social costs into the price system sounds unorthodox to modern ears and appears to be a flagrant violation of the "law" of supply and demand and other economic so-called laws that operate apart or "free" from social or political value judgments. But the concept of prices as being determined by "natural laws" of the market is a modern idea, less than 300 years old. Prior to the 17th century, laws regulating prices were more often based on political or social than on market values. Sumptuary laws regulated prices on food, drink, dress, and household and personal property, usually to discourage extravagance or for religious or moral reasons. Distribution was done by family, tribal, or state authority, not by a price system. Since marketable commodities were rare and money was seldom used, most ancient laws relied on direct prohibitions rather than on prohibitive taxes. In ancient Sparta all luxuries were prohibited by law. Sumptuary laws against luxuries were also in effect in early Rome. They restricted expenditures on funerals, entertainment, dress, food, and other personal goods. During the Middle Ages, English and French kings imposed sumptuary laws prohibiting or restricting the consumption of luxury goods in dress, shoes, gold and silver embroidery, silk goods, and fine linens. Edward III in 1336 attempted to restrict the consumption of luxuries and decreed that consumption of meat or fish be restricted to one meal a day. The upper classes were exempt from many of these sumptuary laws or could afford to ignore them. In the Far East, and especially in Japan, sumptuary laws regulated and restricted the consumption of personal goods to a degree and in minute detail unknown in the West. After the establishment of market capitalism and a money economy, sumptuary laws designed to restrict consumption of selected goods that had a low or negative social value were framed as excise taxes. Alcoholic beverages, tobacco products, and jewelry have been the commodities most often taxed by excises to artificially raise prices above true market value.

The antitrust laws of the United States are designed to keep the market price level free from monopolistic pressures or nonmarket values. They have not been completely successful, but the philosophy behind them is that market competition alone should determine price. In its extreme form, market value appears contrary to the principle of social value. When a commodity is placed on the market, and the market is free or places no restraints on competition, the commodity will be sold at the lowest competitive price. Whether the commodity has social value or not — that is, whether it is actually or potentially unsafe, unsanitary, unhealthy, immoral, indecent, offensive, unclean, obscene, noxious, wasteful, or environmentally harmful — is a question involving social value to which the market is blind. In extreme cases such as guns, explosives, drugs, alcohol, and tobacco, the toxic or lethal consequences are so fraught with social peril that laws are framed to restrict their consumption, distribution, or production.

For that reason consumption taxes have never been completely discarded. They have been extremely useful in times of war to discourage production of luxury goods, as well as to raise revenue. To finance the war of 1812, excises were levied on sugar, liquor, carriages, and other "luxury" goods. Similar taxes were levied during the Civil War. They were repealed in 1870, except for taxes on alcohol and tobacco, which have remained in effect ever since. During World War II consumption taxes or excises were levied on a list of "nonessential" goods and services such as furs, jewelry, cosmetics, luggage, automobiles, and theater admissions.

In times of national emergency, consumption taxes have been found useful for a number of reasons. 1. They can be highly selective in their application; that is, they can pinpoint the specific commodity that is to be taxed. 2. The rate structure can be varied with relative ease and within a wide range of values. Property taxes and income taxes are structurally rigid; once rate schedules are set and published, it is difficult and inconvenient to change them. A tax on a specific commodity, however, can be changed by fractional amounts or by large increments without administrative problems. 3. They can be extremely versatile and offer practically unlimited possibilities for the incorporation of social value in all commodities and services, in any range or combination of tax rates, as demonstrated in the tariff schedule.

To those living under the income tax system, the tariff principle of differential tax rates on items of consumption may appear as arbitrary, presumptuous, or even tyrannical, but the principle is an old one and is no different from that applied to income taxes with progressive or differential rates. According to the "fairness" principle or "ability to pay" principle, a poor man should not be taxed at the same rate as a rich man. This principle may be applied to consumption as well as to income.

8. Socialization of Consumption

In a two-sector economy, failure of the market to generate tax revenue has a serious effect on the public sector. The public sector returns goods and resources to the public, sometimes directly in the form of welfare benefits, pensions, grants, and in the form of interest payments and also through the market in the form of government contracts, procurement programs, and market purchases generated by the Federal payroll. The totals generated by the public sector are not negligible. Between 1940 and 1972 the Federal government's gross annual revenue rose by 2,790 per cent, from $7 billion to $202.5 billion. Total Federal expenditures rose by 2,140 per cent, from $10.1 billion to $226.2 billion. It is estimated that one third of the working force now owes its employment to public expenditures.

According to some economists, the effect of public-sector spending stimulates or stabilizes the economy; according to others, it diminishes and weakens the market. The two viewpoints are not necessarily contradictory; it is possible both to stimulate and stabilize an economy by nonmarket government policies, control, and regulations. The problem is that government policies that increase the public sector tend to weaken the market and reduce its effectiveness as a distributive agency. The public-sector bureaucracy replaces the market distributive function with its own redistributive system, which is regulated by executive orders.

As the income tax diverts more and more income into the public sector; as the function of the market for setting rewards for production declines; as the government is forced to assume the market function to set wages and prices; as the economy becomes susceptible to pressure from organized power blocs — in all these circumstances, the rewards of production in the form of profits and wages and other income (claims on consumption) becomes prizes in a naked political struggle. The organized and the powerful grab the biggest prizes; the unorganized and the weak are pushed into the lowest income brackets. The organized are not only the old-line labor unions. The teachers, the airline pilots, the doctors, the policemen, the gas station operators, the firemen, the engineers, the journalists, the actors, the independent truckers, the teamsters, and even the writers are forced by the pressure of bloc interests to organize and fight with political weapons for their share of the consumer market. Even those on welfare organize and wage a political battle for more free income.

When the market loses its function as the mechanism for economic guidance and price control and is replaced by direct political controls, business — especially big business — ceases to be guided by the market and relies more heavily on subsidies, on tax credits, and on government guidelines and policies. The worker looks to the government for free income or consumption rights when he is without employment.

When a government subsidizes its citizens, the market need for earned income is bypassed. As a result, the traditional market controls over business and labor are eroded. Robert L. Heilbroner touches on this problem in his book, *The Future as History*:

What is crucial in the loosening of the market mechanism is the gradual disappearance of the traditional means of *social control* over business . . . We are as yet only in the initial stages of this breaking down of the traditional mechanisms of control. No doubt for some time the accustomed market pressures will serve their purpose well enough. But it is already clear in respect to both labor and business that the drive toward abundance is creating a vacuum in the established means of socio-economic control...the measures which may be needed to re-establish social control over business, the degree of compulsion which may be required to allocate labor, the range of economic freedom, as we know it, permissible in a society which lacks an invisible hand — these are all questions of great moment but unanswerable complexity. It may be that in the end the loss will outweigh the gain, and that we shall acquire economic abundance only at the cost of crushing social restrictions. Yet there can be no turning back from a prospect whose material allurements far exceed these premonitions of future constraint. Nor, perhaps, should there be. The important thing, rather is to realize that the road to abundance leads subtly but surely into the society of control.[70]

The replacement of market controls by political controls that involve "rigid controls over business" and a "degree of compulsion which may be required to allocate labor" is seen as an acceptable risk by those who see no market alternative except more government supervision. Needless to say, this solution calls for a political power structure with broad executive powers and a bureaucracy of gargantuan proportions. The executive bureaucracy may, when all-powerful, absorb the private market sector entirely, as in Communist dictatorships, or it may force the private sector to work for the government without confiscating private property, as in advanced welfare states or in military dictatorships. In either case, the bureaucracy replaces the market, and the nation is ruled by administrative orders rather than by legislative process.

A bureaucracy is a necessary adjunct of executive power. Officials trained to exercise their special duties and to obey orders as well as to enforce them, are necessary for the administration of justice, the collection of taxes, the defense of the nation, and whatever other tasks are required by the government. Government officials are, by law, required to enforce and execute, not only statutes, but court orders, executive orders, and administrative decisions of government regulatory agencies.

There is nothing inherently evil about a bureaucracy. It is authoritarian, but that is the function of a bureaucracy — to enforce authority, not to question it. A bureaucracy may be corrupt or incorruptible, efficient or inefficient, animated by esprit de corps or demoralized, hard-working or indolent, arrogant or servile. Bureaucracy is normally concentrated in the executive branch of government. Even when the executive is subordinate to the legislative, the executive function remains a separate and authoritarian role. Making the executive ministers or the army generals subordinate to the legislature does not make the executive bureaucracy or the army democratic institutions.

When animated by high ideals of public service or dedicated to some lofty mission or inspired by a great political leader, a bureaucracy can achieve miracles. Great moments in the history of the Chinese, Turkish, and British empires may be attributed to the dedicated bureaucrats of the British Civil

113

Service, the Janissaries, and the Mandarinate. A bureaucracy acts as the executive body of the government, through which the legislature imposes its will on society. Without it, a legislature is a futile debating society.

The risks inherent in bureaucracy are those intrinsic in any institution: inertia, patronage, corruption, and too much power. History abounds with examples of bureaucracy under some bloated, powerful, and corrupt executive, who crushes the liberty of the people, usurps its legislative power, and bleeds it white with taxation. The bureaucracies of the Roman emperors, the French Bourbons, and the Russian tsars are well-known examples.

The Constitution wisely separated the legislative, executive, and judicial powers and sought to devise a system of checks and balances that would keep any one of the three branches from becoming all-powerful. Since New Deal days the executive branch has become disproportionately larger and more powerful than the other arms. This development has been aided and abetted by a legislature that, reluctantly perhaps, passed the enabling legislation to foster the growth of the executive bureaucracy. The legislators have been compelled by the voters to increase government services, and this in turn has led to the increased power and size of the executive branch. Power tends to corrupt. The normal processes of democracy that are designed to prevent corruption — short tenure in office and recurrent elections — are not applicable to a bureaucracy. Protected by civil service laws that virtually assure their tenure, bureaucrats sometimes let authority go to their heads and become petty tyrants. They may control and dispense large sums and decide what private groups are to receive public funds, what guidelines are to be applied, and how regulations are to be enforced. The power of the bureaucracy is now so great because of the growth of the public sector that no member of Congress can be aware of, let alone exert, any significant influence, over the activity of the bureaus that come under his committee responsibility.

A bureaucracy not only grows with the development of the public sector and the executive power; it also generates its own growth from within. Attempts to cut back established bureaus usually fail. President Nixon tried to cut back some Great Society programs that had been conspicuous failures, but found himself hamstrung by powerful bureaucratic inertia. The defeat of the Nixon move and the triumph of the bureaucrats was approvingly described by Peter Wall and Rochelle Jones in *The Nation*:

> The bureaucracy ... has frequently been able to resist and ignore presidential commands ... bureaucratic frustration of White House policies is a fact of life. Furthermore, the bureaucracy often carries out its own policies that are at the time the exact opposite of White House directives ... the bureaucracy has become a fourth branch of government, separate and independent of the President, Congress and the Courts.
>
> Ultimately the bureaucracy curbs the President because it has independent sources of political power. Nixon's attempt to cut back governmental programs and reduce spending conflicts with vested interests of powerful groups in and out of government. Because the bureaucracy depends on the political support of these allies for its continued existence, and because this alliance survives the four or eight years a President is in office, the bureaucracy is apt to prefer its interests over the wishes of the President.

The "allies" referred to were liberals in Congress who favored the Great Society programs and private groups that benefited from funds and privileges controlled by the bureaucracy, which is primarily motivated by the instinct for survival. Ideology is secondary, as was proved in the battle for Moynihan's Family Allowance Plan. The Defense Department bureaucracy fights for military expansion as much as the Health, Education, and Welfare bureaucracy fights for welfare programs.

It is futile to call for a decrease in bureaucracy while there is a concurrent demand for public services. In a complex society a large bureaucracy is probably inevitable. The Congress, if it wishes to keep bureaucracy within reasonable bounds, must restrain its legislative compulsion to create executive agencies and pass laws that substitute government functions for functions formerly carried out by the individual, the family, the neighborhood, or the market. In passing laws that expand the public sector and the executive department, the legislature is creating a bureaucratic Leviathan that may ultimately devour it. When all economic power is in the public sector, society will be governed by bureaucratic regulations, and the function of the legislature will be to pass on executive plans, approve economic controls, and budget appropriations. If a crisis arises where the elected legislators are opposed to the wishes of the bureaucracy, the latter would undoubtedly back a strong executive who would suppress the legislative process. This is a familiar historical drama.

An authoritarian society dominated by an executive bureaucracy, or a "society of control," as Heilbronner calls it, does not seem a fitting substitute for the political ideals of Jefferson, Lincoln, and Theodore Roosevelt, all rugged individualists in theory and practice. Nor is there assurance, so casually assumed by Heilbronner, that "The road to abundance leads subtly but surely into the society of control." Nevertheless, it is a fact that such theories have become accepted almost as a matter of course by many, if not most, economists. Very few give the market the major decision-making power in the economy of the future.

However, the market has never been popular with social theorists. Professor H. B. Acton, in his study *The Morals of the Market,* has noted that from Plato to the present day there has been a "continuing chorus of disapprobation" of the market economy. The defense of the market by Adams and Bentham and their followers was "only a brief interlude."[71] Some of the bitterest critics of the market have been economists: Marx, Veblen, Keynes, Heilbronner, and Galbraith. Professor Acton lists the five major criticisms of the market as follows:

1. The profit motive is inherently immoral and rewards selfishness and greed (the Marxist theory).

2. Competition, survival of the fittest, is the law of the jungle, and cooperation and public service will better promote the general welfare (the Fabian theory of G. B. Shaw, H. G. Wells, and Sidney Webb).

3. Market competition ultimately is replaced by market control and oligopoly (the monopoly theory of Progressives, Populists, New Dealers, and

of economists R. T. Ely, H. C. Adams, A. A. Berle, Jr., G. C. Means, J. Robinson, and E. H. Chamberlin).

4. In the production for the consumer market, the satisfaction of human and social needs is neglected (the social neglect theories of T. Veblen, J. A. Hobson, and J. K. Galbraith).

5. Competition is necessarily chaotic and unjust, and a planned economy is more efficient and fair (the Stalinist theory or, in milder form, the Keynesian theory).

In most cases market critics endorse all five theories, but some more than others. All these theories are, of course, true in some degree.

The market may be immoral in the sense that it may be used to make exorbitant profits for private gain, but the market is not really concerned with making profits, only with exchange. Exchange can be a simple barter, or it can involve public or semipublic bodies where the profit, if any, is used mostly for the payment of wages, depreciation of machinery, and taxes.

The market may encourage competition of the cutthroat type, but it may be regulated by laws that put limits on such factors as child labor, hours of work, and minimum wages.

The market may be subject to control by monopolists, but it can be subject also to antitrust laws.

The market may neglect consumer needs, but laws for the protection of consumers may be enacted to provide whatever safeguard is desired.

Market competition may be chaotic but, to restore its order and direction, it is not necessary to kill it and replace it with a mandatory system of allocations according to executive decree or plan.

Is there not, however, a "perfect" market model such as described by classic economists where the equilibrium between supply and demand is always in balance?

The market is not a perfect institution. Like all social institutions, it is fallible and subject to manipulation by organized groups and to historic changes, particularly those wrought by technological innovation and the development of new energy sources. The market exists within a framework of laws enacted by the political authority and cannot be understood or evaluated apart from this framework. The economic model of a "free" market as a system of simultaneous mathematical equations of supply and demand in perfect equilibrium is found only in textbooks and applies only to a market within a specific legal framework in a given time and place, in this case a market operating under the laws of private property rights. Seriously weaken or remove those laws, and the free market model collapses.

Gunnar Myrdal says that the welfare state has "socialized" consumption and by so doing has made itself more prosperous and less dependent on private consumption and the private free market:

> What is actually happening in most advanced welfare states is a stress on the 'socialization of consumption' as distinct from the old socialist policy proposals for socialization of large scale industry and high finance . . . It is true that with the progressive system of taxation the burden of paying for social reforms falls more heavily on people in the higher income brackets. This is part of the

redistributional effect of the reforms. More generally, it is also true that aggregate public consumption, particularly when, as often, it assumes heavy initial investment, cannot be increased without lowering the rate of increase of private consumption — otherwise there will be inflation, which means that it is paid for by forced saving. The two choices have to be made.[72]

Myrdal holds up Sweden as the model of the welfare state and argues that increased "public" consumption — financed by progressive taxation that diverts private income into the public sector — while it diminishes private consumption, actually appears to increase overall economic growth, so that in the end the consumer benefits even more than in countries where consumer sovereignty is unrestrained. This argument may or may not be true.

However, Myrdal has again demonstrated that, by socializing consumption, the state need not socialize production. The redistribution of consumption rights (income) can be done through progressive taxation. In a Socialist state, socialized consumption is regulated through coercion and confiscation of private property. In the welfare state with a public and private sector, the people make the choice: higher taxes and more public goods or lower taxes and more private goods. Not a very satisfying choice, but better than no choice at all!

The theory that consumption can be socialized without interfering with private property rights or market operations is feasible, as Mill pointed out in 1848. However, the type of tax system used for socializing consumption need not be the income tax. A tax system based on consumption would be more effective and democratic. An income tax system leaves the problem of unemployment in the private sector unresolved; it leaves the public consumption dependent on the voters, but it provides no mechanism, such as the market price system, that the voters can use to choose the specific goods and services they want or do not desire. Instead, they are presented with a broad choice to transfer more or less tax revenues to the public sector. The bureaucracy then spends the tax revenues for public goods and services in ways that may or may not coincide with the individual wishes of the voter-consumer-taxpayer. Under a commodity tax system using progressive rates, the individual voter-consumer-taxpayer would have the power to make individual choices on *all* goods and services and not be limited to the either-or choice of which Myrdal speaks.

The current intellectual climate is definitely hostile to the market and to consumerism as a way of life. The minds of consumers are, in a mysterious way, being prepared for a nonmaterial culture, or at least a culture in which consumer values will not be dominant. The mass consumer market that made consumerism possible is facing a new crisis. This crisis is not only economic, it is ecological. Increasing pressure is being brought on the American government to direct the market away from consumerism and to make it more subservient to the needs of social services and for fresh air and fresh water, as well as for consumer gadgets.

Henry C. Simons once asked whether the United States was "quite safely removed from the predicament of that hypothetical society which employed every increase in its income for the purposes of further increase, and so on

117

until the end of time."[73] The belief in perpetual growth in the gross national product is no longer unquestioned; the ideal of materialist success no longer commands the loyalty of youth. Like King Midas, the world's most affluent society finds that it cannot eat the gold of its marvelous technology. The gold has turned to dross; the very air and water and food have become poisoned. The rich are bored with consumerism; the middle class groans under its burden; the youth are in revolt against it; the poor are exiled from it.

As Professor Kenneth E. Boulding has pointed out, there is a danger "in a predominantly commercial society, that people will take economic behavior as the measure of all things and will confine their relationship to those which can be conducted on the level of the commercial abstraction. To do this is to lose almost all richness or purpose in human life. . . . If the market is to be a stable and fruitful institution in society it must be hedged around with other institutions of a non-market character in the home and the school and the church."[74]

Market value per se is likely to be a false index of social value or at best an unreliable indicator of what is best for society as a whole. However, the alternative to market pricing as a method of setting value leads to even more serious problems, if the alternatives are government price-fixing or planned distribution by rationing or mandatory allocation. The setting of priorities in the public sector according to the budget principle rather than the market principle has, to date, not achieved the social utopia that had been anticipated by the Saint-Simonians, the Marxists, the Fabians, the Keynesians, the Socialists, the National Socialists, the Communists, and all the other social reformers who are enemies of the market.

In a market economy the private individual has a free choice. He is not forced to take what he does not want or does not like or does not need. It is this freedom of choice that the public sector bureaucracy cannot provide. The market can provide it, but not automatically. The market can be controlled or monopolized by powerful groups that exclude and discriminate against other groups. The market is also subject to changes in the economy that render its rules obsolete. The socialization or industrialization of the means of production in the 19th century radically changed the ground rules of the agrarian market and made it an easy game for the industrial barons. It became necessary to devise new rules of the game to protect the poorer players and to equalize the conditions of the contestants. The legal or political framework under which the market operates is constantly changing and must do so to keep up with economical growth.

Despite its shortcomings and despite the massive intellectual and political assault of its enemies, the market has survived even under the most regimented planned economies and has astounded its critics with its vigor and regenerative powers. The market has a long history and has undergone many radical changes; it will undoubtedly undergo many more. That it can be liquidated and replaced by a "better" system of state controls is a theory that must yet be proved. Nevertheless, today the market sector is losing power and prestige, and it is in the public sector that the important economic decisions are made and that the national economic priorities are set.

Chapter
IV

SETTING PRIORITIES IN THE PUBLIC SECTOR

1. Private and Public Priorities

Every nation sets certain goals toward which it marches or drifts. These goals are set by a political consensus that may be broadly based, as in a democracy, or articulated by a small élite group organized as a political party. The goals, when accepted by the people, largely determine the economic priorities or the allocation of energy, material, and manpower resources. National priorities are not always set in a state budget, as in the Soviet Gosplan. The national goal may be in favor of individual freedom and permit private individuals to accumulate economic power singly or in combinations and to control the allocation of significant material and energy resources.

This does not mean that the government is abdicating control of the economy; on the contrary. In a democratic society with diffused economic power spread over many private organizations, the legal framework the government must create to allow the economy to operate efficiently is much more complex and minutely detailed than in centrally planned economies. There are many more lawyers in the United States who deal with private, corporate, and public property law than there are in the USSR; the laws of contract and equity are more involved with historic precedent and more subtle and comprehensive in the former than in the latter. The fact that the political framework permits freedom of economic action does not mean that it does not exist. It is less visible and less heavy-handed, but it is just as pervasive and legally binding. A laissez-faire economist may believe that the free market economy operates best when it is completely free of political controls, but in reality the free market operates within a tight political framework of laws based on contract and property rights, without which it could not survive. Free competition does not exist in a social vacuum. "In reality, free competition neither exists, nor has ever existed," according to Myrdal. "It cannot even be clearly conceived, for freedom of contract presupposes rules and regulations about the conditions under which contracts are to be made. These rules and regulations substantially affect price formation."[75]

National goals are, of course, limited by economic resources. A nation such as Peru, for example, could not set as a national goal the landing of a man on the moon. Within the limitations imposed by its economic resources, each nation sets priorities to reach its social and political goals. The need for priorities is obvious. There are never enough resources or energy to do everything.

The United States government in recent years has, to a large extent, usurped the function of the market in allocating resources and in so doing has reduced market efficiency by about 40 per cent. This means that 40 per cent of the income that otherwise would be spent in the market by consumers is now turned over to the government. It is true, of course, that the government uses the money to buy goods and services in the market, but the government's buying decision is not a market decision. It is a political action. The allocation of resources has been determined, in advance, between the private and the public sectors, and this allocation has been made by tax law, not by the market. The function of the market has been preempted by tax policy. According to economist J. K. Galbraith, the present allocation is less than just to the public sector. According to economist Milton Friedman, it is more than just. It is obvious that, the greater the income drawn from the consumer by taxes, the less he will have to spend. The annual gross national product is a pie that can be cut only into so many pieces and can go just so far.

In Communist countries, the private sector has been expropriated and reduced to a small and unimportant segment. In capitalist countries, such as the United States and Japan, the private market sector is still the larger sector. However, the public sector is growing in importance, and in many ways is the dominant partner. In Sweden, Austria, France, and West Germany, both sectors appear evenly balanced — both having about an equal share of the gross national product — but, of course, the public sector wields the greatest political and economic power. Whether this 50/50 balance in the economy is a state of healthy equilibrium or whether it is a case of arrested development on the way to full public or Socialist control remains to be seen.

Until recently it was assumed by many economists that full public control of the economy was inevitable. The only question was the timetable and the exact methods to be employed to achieve this end. However, complete liquidation of the private sector appears to carry with it certain economic hazards that were not anticipated by Socialist theorists. On the other hand, a reduction of the public sector to the pre-World War I level (3 per cent of the gross national product) would mean complete liquidation of social welfare services to which modern man has become accustomed.

Despite the gargantuan growth of the public sector in the United States, despite the proliferation of government agencies and departments to regulate and direct the private sector, the planning of industrial production in 1973 is still largely in the hands of private industry, dominated by giant corporations.

Some multinational American corporations have more economic power, greater income, and larger assets than many countries. The income generated by General Motors or IBM, for example, is greater than the national income of Austria, Spain, Portugal, Colombia, Peru, Cuba, Yugoslavia, Greece, Turkey, Denmark, or many other countries. The need for planning by these giant corporations is dictated by their size. Huge production organizations require a plan of operation and development just to keep them from disintegrating. The larger a corporation is, the more it needs to plan its activities and make projections into the future. The "lead-time" for a product to be made on a very large scale may run into years. It involves preliminary planning; market research and testing; financing and amortization plans; advertising programs to arouse consumer interest; engineering; making prototypes; field testing; layout of production lines and production schedules; development of new machines and material-handling techniques for the new product; training of personnel; new packaging; and, finally, introduction of the new product in selected markets according to a sales plan that may involve one city, one state, or one or more countries. Production of this type naturally calls for long-term planning. Only a very small business can operate on a day-to-day basis in the United States.

The giant corporation usually has a large department for corporate planning, staffed with economists to forecast trends, analyze potential areas of growth, recommend investment opportunities, and suggest what lines to cut back or eliminate. Very sophisticated techniques are used by the large corporations to make growth projections. There is extensive use of computers, econometric models, input-output analysis, market sampling, linear programming, and all the latest analytical tools of economics.

Corporate planning has one overriding objective: to maximize profits. All other objectives are subordinate to this. How is this objective to be achieved? In a manufacturing industrial corporation there are two recognized means: (1) increase production and (2) increase productivity or productive efficiency. A corporation is a productive organization whose planning is centered on the production function. Its only interest in consumption or in the interests of the consumer is limited to the specific act, the time and place, when the corporation's product is purchased by the consumer. Apart from the act of consumption, the corporation has no further interest in the consumer. Corporate planning has no place for the consumer except as a customer for its products. It is not concerned with the consumer's personal problems or his relation to other producers. It is, of course, directly concerned with its own labor force, since labor is a key factor in production. Corporate planning tries to minimize labor costs by the introduction of labor-saving machines and efficient organization. In this it would seem to be working against its best interests, for the workers are consumers, and the more money they earn the more they can buy. This theory may be accepted by labor unions as valid, but the corporation cannot accept it or apply it. To survive in competition with other producers, the industrial corporation must cut costs to a minimum. This is a matter of survival. All other questions, of labor's right to a job or to higher wages, of the rights of the consumer, or of social value are secondary.

The industrial corporation is a production organization, pure and simple, and any other activity it engages in must, of necessity, remain a peripheral one. Corporate planning is basically production planning. It is chiefly concerned with making a product for profit. The American industrial corporation is a remarkably efficient engine of production. When it tries, or is forced to try, to become an agency for the betterment of the worker or the consumer or the environment, it becomes less efficient. But a corporate structure is a versatile edifice capable of housing many different functions, profit and nonprofit. Corporations can be formed to carry out mixed private-public functions along the lines of public utilities or COMSAT or AMTRAK or the Ford Foundation. Unlimited combinations may be developed outside the stereotyped concept of the conventional profit-oriented private corporation and the conventional government-owned nonprofit corporation.

The American government accepts the fact of private planning in the production of goods and services and even acknowledges its superiority in efficiency. However, since the government now has the ultimate responsibility for economic welfare, it cannot permit production planning to proceed without regard to major economic policies set by Washington. The tendency under the policy of *dirigisme* initiated by Franklin Roosevelt in the New Deal is for the government increasingly to take over direct responsibility for the planning of industrial production, at least in broad policy objectives.

Projects such as mass transportation and space exploration are too big for even giant American corporations. For that reason, companies such as Boeing, Lockheed, and the Pennsylvania Railroad have sought government financial assistance and have welcomed close government support and participation in planning. The American government, protesting that it is running a "free economy," has seldom in the past taken an aggressive or cannibalistic attitude toward private industry. Private enterprise has, in most cases, sought government financial support and protection. The whale is not swallowing Jonah; Jonah is walking into the whale's mouth! President Kennedy and President Johnson initially set up "guidelines" for the economy, a sort of gentlemanly *dirigisme* without teeth. Both labor and management refused to be guided. When U.S. Steel raised its prices after yielding to union demands for higher wages, President Kennedy called the President of U.S. Steel to the White House and read him the riot act. The President of U.S. Steel was shocked. Wasn't America the country of free enterprise? If the government started to dictate prices, what would happen to the free market? Eight years later in 1971 President Nixon put some teeth in *dirigisme* and imposed "temporary" price and wage controls on the economy. To such a degree had *dirigisme* progressed in the United States in one decade. The American public is no longer surprised at the right of a president to dictate price and wage policy to labor and management; corporate presidents are no longer outraged at violation of the sacred principles of free enterprise. *Dirigisme* is no longer seriously contested by private industry; the only argument is over the question, in what direction is government guiding the economy, to the left or to the right?

Production and distribution of public goods and services are not affected by market demand or price competition. They are determined largely by government budget decisions; these in turn are decided by government political policy. It is not the market that decides whether public roads, new schools, new weapons systems, or new social welfare programs are to be provided. In the free market the private buyer votes with dollars, and his vote largely determines the production volume. In the government sector the total supply of public goods remains unaffected by the participation of the end-user; everyone uses public roads, whether he pays taxes or not. The public goods sector of the economy is governed by political, not market, decisions. The decision to increase Social Security payments, to build new intercontinental ballistic missles, or to provide free medical service is determined by political considerations, not by market demand.

In countries where a government planning committee or budget office has taken over the function of the market in setting values and priorities and where government decisions rather than market decisions are crucial, the price system is not used as a primary mechanism for determining the production and distribution of goods and services. Instead the government, or the executive branch of the government, uses investment credits for directing and controlling the economy, bypassing the regulatory function of the market price system.

The use of government credits, loans, and grants is an effective and popular method of controlling expansion of industrial production along a predetermined plan. It is a method used by the United States in financing production of airplanes, tanks, rockets, submarines, space satellites, and other public goods used by the government. The use of government grants and investment credits may be a logical and practical method. However, government investment credits are by their nature authoritarian and difficult to administer in a democratic manner.

In the United States investment capital is controlled by capital markets, private bankers, private capitalists, and government bureaus. Credit is extended by bank loans, bond and stock issues, and government contracts and grants. Private capital is still widely diffused, and the stock exchanges serve as a medium for directing credit and capital where it is needed or can be used to the most profitable advantage. The criterion of value in the extension of private credit is profitability. Social value is a secondary consideration.

A great many economists have sided with Keynes in his criticism of the control of investments by private capitalists and capital exchanges, which he likened to gambling casinos. According to these critics, the profit motive is not a good guideline for the economy and is incapable of planning for the long-term public interest, since it is concerned with short-term private gain.

In countries that have advanced the farthest along the road of *dirigisme*, such as West Germany and France, control of investments and credit is in the hands of the central government bank and is extended according to a plan worked out with the collaboration of the heads of labor, management, and the ruling political party. In Communist countries, investment credits are under the control of the state and are paid out according to the state budget and master economic plan. R. W. Davies in *The Soviet Budgetary System* states flatly that "what primarily distinguishes the Soviet planning system from other economic systems is that capital investment is planned centrally by the state."[76]

Government control over capital investments represents an authoritarian solution to the problem of setting economic priorities. It relegates the function of the market to a subordinate rank and deprives the consumer of power in making buying decisions. The extension of credits is very difficult, if not impossible, to control and direct in a democratic manner, once it is removed from a capital market and placed in the hands of government credit managers. The allocation of credits easily becomes involved with party politics, bureaucratic prestige, official favoritism, and other drawbacks of an authoritarian or bureaucratic system.

Centralized investment planning may be feasible under the Soviet state monopoly, but in a competitive economy a sharp conflict of interest is generated. In the Soviet economy there is only one commissariat for each industry. If the Soviet government wishes to increase the production of vacuum cleaners, it extends additional credits to the commissar responsible for vacuum cleaners, which the comrade commissar uses for developing more plant capacity. If the United States government wishes to increase production of vacuum cleaners, it can extend assistance to the industry in the form of credits, subsidies, or direct loans. In a competitive economy, however, who is to determine who gets how much? Despite the most stringent safeguards there is bound to be nepotism, favoritism, lobbyism, influence peddling, graft, bribery, and all the other evils of a politicized economy.

Absolute monarchies and empires in ancient and medieval times frequently fixed the price of staple commodities such as grain, bread, and salt. The reason given: to protect the poor and prevent hoarding by the rich or profiteering by greedy merchants. In some cases, but not all, the government that set the prices reserved for itself a margin that it collected directly or indirectly as the king's share or tax. Where the government had a monopoly, as it often had, the tax was hidden in the fixed price. This is a common practice in state-controlled economies from ancient Egypt to modern Russia. In Egypt in the age of the Ptolemies (323-30 B.C.) the government controlled all production and forced farmers to sell grain at fixed prices to the royal monopolies.

In discussions of price theory, two extremes are usually debated: exchange value set by a free market under the law of supply and demand and arbitrary price controls set by government decree. In modern industrial states these extremes are seldom seen, and the pricing controls used are more complex than either pure market or government pricing. The price paid in the mass consumer market is more likely to be a negotiated one, with the market playing an important but perhaps not a decisive part. Increasingly, the role of the market in setting prices has been taken over by the government and by quasi-public bodies that are not part of the government, but that wield political power. Before 1971, the most common form of government intervention in the price system was through tax policy in the form of duties, excises, and sales taxes.

Tax policy tends to distort market values because the addition of taxes to the price necessarily raises it above true market value. If the taxes are uniform and open, the distortion is less significant. If the taxes are selective or progressive or both, the distortion may be severe. Economists are no longer concerned lest tax policy distort market values. Their main concern is with equity fairness and ability to pay. If taxes cause price distortions that favor the poor or reduce inequality of income, the tax policy is called *progressive*. A uniform tax that does not disturb market values, but favors the rich is called *regressive*. The ideal tax system, therefore, is not one that preserves pure market values in the price system or one that leaves the market price undisturbed; *the ideal tax system, by common consent, is one that distorts market prices by the addition of social values considered desirable by modern society — equity, fairness, and ability to pay.*

The increment between market price under theoretical conditions of pure market competition and the actual price paid by the ultimate consumer may be called the "X" or unknown factor of social cost that has been added to the true market price. The government is not the only agency that intervenes in the market to alter prices. The X factor included in the price system is a variable that is affected by the intervention of powerful quasi-public bodies such as guilds, labor unions, consumer unions, employer organizations, corporate bodies, and professional societies. These bodies may exercise as much influence on market prices as the government. A labor union, for example, can raise labor costs above market costs. When the market price drops, the labor content of the price does not drop. The labor contract provides a price support for labor. Labor costs today are not generally regulated by market competition. In most large production organizations labor costs are fixed by a labor contract or a government law that effectively bypasses the market function to regulate the labor cost factor in prices by the law of supply and demand.

Collective bargaining is a form of price-fixing. Dr. Arthur M. Okun, Chairman of the Council of Economic Advisers in the Eisenhower administration, described it in these terms: "Collective bargaining had become an exercise in agreeing how much to take out of the consumer's pocket. In making their wage settlements in '70 and '71, business and labor were really determining how much business would go ahead and raise its prices to make up for inordinate wage increases."[77]

The consumer pays for the raise in higher prices. Since the worker is also a consumer, the process seems self-defeating. In reality, it is not. The union demand is generally higher than the general rise in inflation caused by the raise. The union workers who do not win raises, the nonunion workers, the pensioners, and others with fixed income are those who bear the brunt of the added cost.

Producers as well as labor unions can exert a powerful influence on market prices. In simple market economies producers attempted to maintain prices above the market level by withholding goods. Farmers with perishable goods and weak producers with limited capital were at the mercy of strong producers of durable goods because the former were unable to control supply. As a result, farm prices exchanged at lower than "parity" or "fair" exchange value with industrial goods. In extreme cases, where industrial producers were in an oligopoly or monopoly position, the profit margins included in prices would be above competitive profit margins and would be reflected in abnormally high prices. Marx categorized *all* profit margins included in prices as "surplus value." In his system of economics, only labor costs were legitimate; all other costs were unfair, unnecessary, and arbitrary; profits were based on exploitation of labor; and the capitalist was a parasite who lived off the labor of the workers.

Modern society accepts the idea of profits as a legitimate cost to be included in prices. It is regarded as a reward for the contribution of capital and management skills. The lack of profits is not considered a social blessing, even in Soviet economics; rather, it is considered a symptom of business inefficiency or bad planning. The profit margin in a private economy is still regulated by market competition, but not altogether so. Profits are set by corporate price policy, as well as by the market.

Where prices are set by corporate price policy rather than the market, the profit margin is distorted, and this distortion is reflected in prices. The profit margin is insulated from the market supply-and-demand pressures. Once the price has been fixed by corporate policy, the tendency is to maintain it regardless of market pressures. If market demand slackens, prices are not lowered. Instead, production is decreased, and goods are withheld from the market by the producer until the consumer is ready to buy at the producer's price.

Corporate pricing policy takes into account, not only standard production costs, but the tax liability that absorbs as much as 50 per cent of its profits. In general, large corporations follow a price formula geared to their own needs. However, the formula worked out by Donaldson Brown for General Motors has been widely copied. In essence, a corporation determines prices by a formula that compensates it for all estimated costs of production, including research and development and all marketing costs, plus a fixed return on capital to cover taxes, profits, and dividends. The "target" price must be set high enough to ensure against loss and yet be low enough to discourage competition.

Setting a target price low enough to discourage competition involves a complicated formula based on costs of research and development, average unit production costs, sales and advertising costs, and many other costs, some predictable, some not. The agrarian markets dealt with commodities that were basic staples of commerce: grains, wool, meat, hides, spices. The market alone set the price. In the industrial society new products are the lifeblood of commerce, and their prices are generally calculated before they reach the market.

General Motors was the first large corporation whose very size forced it to confront and solve the difficult and complex problem of pricing for a mass consumer market. In its pricing formula General Motors solved or attempted to solve the unknown variables that governed consumption of their product; age groups of potential buyers, their disposable income, replacement factor for used cars, effect of competition by other auto makers, types and models preferred by different classes of buyers, and loss or gain in sales from urbanization and highway construction. These variables were first put in mathematical price formulas by the auto industry because it was necessary to know, two years or more before the new model came on the market, the optimum price the model would sell for. Market price and market volume must be anticipated far in advance, if mass production runs are to be planned and organized properly.

The pricing policies of large corporations are further complicated by their size. A corporation such as U.S. Steel must set prices on about 50,000 items, which is a medium figure. International Harvester must establish prices for about 250,000 items. These firms are manufacturers, not retailers such as Sears Roebuck or Montgomery Ward, whose pricing problems are of even greater magnitude. Obviously, the pricing policy of such large "collective enterprises", to borrow a phrase from Gardiner C. Means, is difficult if not impossible to administer on a day-to-day open market basis. The price turmoil of such an open-market pricing policy would bring chaos to the market as well as to the sales, accounting, purchasing, and planning departments of the corporation. It is absolutely necessary that large corporations have stable prices or prices with a minimum of instability, and this can be achieved only by a pricing policy that follows an approved corporate formula that must take into account, not only market conditions, but also government tax and price policy.

Government tax policy introduces price distortions that vary according to the social welfare goals of the ruling political party. Commodity taxes obviously distort prices, but income taxes are supposed to have a neutral effect on the price structure. Since all taxes must be paid eventually by the consumer, it is obvious that prices must include provisions for taxes. However, it is claimed that personal income taxes are deducted from wages, not added to prices. This is technically correct. However, the price system still carries the burden of taxation, albeit in hidden taxes. When $100 is deducted from wages by the income tax, the $100 is transferred to the public sector as tax revenues, which are used to buy public goods instead of private goods. The overall price structure must reflect the effective demand for *all* goods, public and private. If part of this demand is paid for by tax dollars, the price system must absorb the tax cost. The price system does so by incorporating provisions for anticipated taxes in prices and by inflation, which soaks up the tax dollars in higher prices. Inflation may also be caused by such other factors as inflated labor costs and inflated profits, for example, but government tax policy can also be highly inflationary. In some ways the income tax is the most serious inflationary threat because it is insidious, that is, it does not seem to be related to prices, and the consumer cannot see how income taxes cause high prices, except in a general way. An increase in price caused by an increase in a commodity tax is immediately perceived; the connection is obvious and direct. In income taxes the connection is less obvious, but equally inescapable. "Taxes must in the long run be derived from net annual production. Individuals may acquire goods through gambling, speculation, gifts, and bequests; but these individual gains contribute nothing to that reservoir from which all taxes must be drawn."[78]

The market price mechanism is affected by numerous nonmarket pressures, which distort prices in varying degrees. The market in any given time and place operates under the prevailing legal "rules" of the political authority and the value system existing in the society. The consumer market today reflects the values inherited from a market system that was based on labor and utility values. Under the labor theory of value, the "free" market is supposed to bring value in exchange or price down to a reasonably fair level — that level being expressed in labor factors of production and such other factors as capital and machinery, which also represent residual or "congealed" labor value. Marginal utility theory achieves the same ethical objectives as the labor theory, assuming a system of perfect competition, but it does not account for natural energy factors, that is, the energy inherent in wind, soil, sun, water, and air. They are assumed to be a *free* gift of nature and enter into the value or price structure only as marginal costs, that is, the costs involved in bringing them to market. Economists spend a great deal of time identifying the various costs of production so as to determine the marginal cost of the finished product. They have analyzed and quantified raw material costs, machinery costs, labor costs, depreciation, administration, taxes, and sales costs, but they have not identified or calculated the social costs of production, that is, the costs to society for the depletion of natural resources and the degradation of the environment. These costs are not included in the concept of marginal cost pricing or corporate cost accounting. This omission has had far-reaching and socially harmful consequences.

2.   Planning Under The Executive

The setting of priorities in a two-sector economy suffers from a duality of purpose, as well as from a conflict of interest between the legislative and executive branches of government. Planning in the private sector is directed toward profit maximization; in the public sector, it is directed toward social welfare. Within the public sector the planning function is conceived and directed by the executive branch, but the financing is controlled by the legislative branch through the traditional "legislative control of the purse."

These conflicts of purpose and interest in a two-sector economy are particularly severe in the United States, where the executive branch is a coequal partner with, rather than a subordinate arm of, the legislative, as in parliamentary régimes. In parliamentary governments, the conflict within the planning process is between an entrenched bureaucracy in the executive branch, protected by civil service laws, tenure, inertia, and technical expertise, and an elected lawmaking body that has power, but lacks technical competence and manpower. The executive bureaucracy has a powerful influence on policy-making by its capabilities, size, political influence, and legal privileges. The bureaucracy or civil service in country A may be more efficient, better organized, larger, and more incorruptible than in country B. This, of course, has a direct effect on the economic plans government can make and explains why they are carried out more successfully in country A than in country B. In almost all countries the bureaucracy is above politics or practically immune from direct control by the legislators. Once they are established, government bureaus never die; in most countries, once an employee gets on the government payroll, it is practically impossible to get him off. In Italy, for example, state employment is considered a sinecure, and many civil servants collect pay checks, although the government has no knowledge of what they do, if anything. The Italian colonial office still existed in 1972 with a large staff, although Italy had lost all her colonies in World War II. In some countries the military, which is the highest form of executive bureaucracy, dominates the legislative branch.

In the United States, the government bureaucracy is headed by a President, who represents an autonomous executive power. The executive department, being coequal with the legislative, is more powerful than in parliamentary governments, and the conflict between the executive and legislative branches extends to the policymaking level. The "battle of the budget" and the struggle over tax policy and economic priorities is more bitter and drawn out between the President and the Congress in the United States than between a European parliament and the heads of the bureaus or ministries who are themselves members of parliament.

The executive branch of government is, by its very nature, authoritarian. It does not matter whether it is military, paramilitary, or civilian. The executive branch gives and obeys orders. It executes the laws. It does not debate them; that is the function of the legislative branch. It does not question them; that is the function of the judicial branch.

Economic planning by the executive branch is, therefore, authoritarian in nature. It gives orders to the private sector. It treats its welfare beneficiaries as dependents or wards, although the tax funds it uses are provided by the taxpayers. Leaders from the private sector are consulted during some phases of economic planning, but the main responsibility rests on the executive ministers, department heads, cabinet secretaries, or bureau chiefs for formulating budget policy and economic plans and for implementing them. In a two-sector economy, the legislature receives the economic plan from the executive branch and approves it with minor changes. The legislature is not equipped to pass on the technical aspects of the budget or economic plan, which is detailed, complex, and largely incomprehensible, except in its broad outlines. Few legislators have the time, patience, or interest to check out the millions of details of a technical and fiscal nature that go to make up a national budget or economic plan. All budget plans have such worthwhile objectives as national security, public roads, social security, unemployment benefits, health and pension benefits, and education. There is never any question of the *need* for these desirable objectives.Therefore, most national economic plans are automatically approved by legislators. The question of limitations imposed by the available tax funds is faced later when appropriation bills are introduced.

It is natural to think of taxes as an economic problem; they are also a political problem. Taxes are levied by law, and tax laws are the result of a political process involving, in the United States, the executive, legislative, and judicial branches of the government.

Article I, Section 8, of the United States Constitution stipulates that "Congress shall have power to lay and collect taxes." This power, the so-called power of the purse, has always been jealously guarded by Congress. Ultimate economic power rests with Congress. The executive may propose economic priorities, but only Congress has the power to implement them through tax and appropriation bills. The tax power has been given to the legislative branch as a guarantee against the abuse of this power by the executive, which is less amenable to popular control. Hamilton in *The Federalist*, No. 35, explains the reasoning: "There can be no doubt that in order to a judicious exercise of the power of taxation it is necessary that the person in whose hands it is should be acquainted with the general genius, habits and modes of thinking of the people at large and with the resources of the country." This power, said Hamilton, may be safely entrusted to the legislator, who is dependent on his constituents:

> "Is it not natural that a man who is a candidate for the favour of the people and who is dependent on the suffrages of his fellow-citizens should take care to inform himself of their disposition and inclinations and should be willing to allow them their proper degree of influence upon his conduct? This dependence, and the necessity of being bound himself and his posterity by the laws to which he gives his assent are the true, and they are the strong chords of sympathy between the representative and the constituent."

Since the New Deal, the initiative in tax legislation has passed to the executive. In his State of the Union message and other special messages to Congress the President recommends and initiates economic policies and programs and the tax measures to fund them. It is true that every major presidential tax proposal is thoroughly revised by Congress and that many are rejected outright. Nevertheless, the initiative in tax legislation has passed to the executive. The President proposes, the Congress disposes. The relatively recent growth of economic power in the executive branch has been brought about by two developments:

1. A Federal bureaucracy with enormous tax revenues under its control that has grown as a result of New Deal policies of *dirigisme*. Federal budget outlays have grown from $9.5 billion in 1940 to $250 billion in 1973! The growth of Federal bureaucracy under executive control poses a challenge to the historic role of Congress as the dominant economic partner in the Federal government. The Congress still has the tax power and is still the watchdog of the Federal treasury, but the very size and complexity of the Federal budget

130

and the inscrutable and largely uncontrollable workings of the Federal budget-making process make the economic power of Congress far less important than envisaged by the makers of the Constitution.

2. The transfer of the tax base from consumption to income by the 16th Amendment has radically changed the role of the Congress in relation to the economy. Prior to 1913, the Congress had an active role in setting economic goals; in relation to the executive, the Congress was the dominant partner in terms of economic power and initiative. Economic guidance was provided by Congress in its tariff bills, which set economic priorities on imported commodities and indirectly subsidized or penalized domestic producers. The great economic questions were debated in Congress and dealt with the regulation of foreign and domestic trade. The executive was concerned primarily with foreign relations, the enforcement of laws, and the preservation of peace. There was no Federal budget as such during the tariff period. Prior to 1913, the main fiscal problem was what to do with the "fiscal dividend," the recurrent surplus revenues that accumulated in the Federal treasury. But times have changed, as the noted economist Milton Friedman pointed out in June 1973: "For 150 years, from the birth of the Republic of the United States to 1932, or '33, we had governmental spending kept down to relatively small levels. In the past 40 years, we've had a revolution. The New Deal ushered in a period in which government spending has been growing by leaps and bounds and has now reached 43 per cent. Something historic needs to be done to stop that process."[79]

In the pre-New Deal days, the gold standard and the need to balance the budget set limits beyond which politicians could not overspend. Keynesian theories have liberated politicians from these artificial limitations. Dollars are freed from convertibility to gold, and deficit spending is not only acceptable, but fashionable. In the year 1972 President Nixon sent to the Congress a budget of $246 billion, nearly 2½ times the total for President Johnson's first budget just 9 years before. The 1973 budget includes a deficit forecast of $25 billion. If that is accurate, the cumulative deficit for fiscal years 1971, 1972 and 1973 will be about $88 billion dollars — this on top of a $58 billion deficit accumulated during the previous ten years!

Politicians are notoriously generous and free-handed with tax moneys and seem constitutionally incapable of saying no to their constituents when their need and their clamor are strong enough. After all, the money is not coming out of their pockets, and it is not difficult for politicians to justify the claims for more tax funds when they are to be spent for schools, medical care, new roads or street maintenance, national defense, parks and playgrounds for the poor, and old-age pensions. The need is genuine and the pressure, therefore, is irresistible. Only a cold-blooded, analytical, unemotional type of person could resist such pressures, and such types do not make successful politicians.

3.   The Tax Legislative Process

In reaching a decision on tax policy the President is dependent on his economic advisors, of whom the most important are the members of the Council of Economic Advisors, the Director of the Office of Management and Budget, the Secretary of the Treasury, the head of the Federal Reserve System, and other key members of his official family. The decision made, the work of preparing the tax proposal for Congress is turned over to the Assistant Secretary of the Treasury for tax policy. He is aided by the Office of Tax Analysis and the Office of the Tax Legislative Counsil, which make a comprehensive analysis of the tax proposal. Lawyers, accountants, economists, statisticians, business and professional consultants, and labor and consumer representatives are called upon during this initial phase of research and analysis, which may last several months for a major tax recommendation. From these deliberations a draft is completed and submitted to the President.

The President reviews the draft proposal and goes over it again with his economic advisers. A final draft is prepared, or the proposal is revised and returned to the Treasury for further study and redrafting, with instructions to resubmit the finished draft by a certain date.

Important tax recommendations are usually included in the State of the Union message or in the budget message, which must be transmitted 15 days after Congress convenes. This means that the tax proposal must be in finished form by the middle of December. Work on it may have started in the preceding year.

Announcement of the tax proposal by the President is the beginning of a new phase — the public phase. Newspapers, radio, television, and periodicals take up the proposals and debate them pro and con. Organizations representing business, farmers, labor, and consumers discuss the proposals and form opinions corresponding to their interests or what they believe to be the national interest. These opinions are transmitted to their Congressmen or are expressed in the public hearings called by the House Committee on Ways and Means. This is the most powerful committee in Congress and the one that must pass on all tax proposals. The committee's public hearings on pending tax bills are long and sometimes exhausting. The first witness is the Secretary of the Treasury, who presents the administrations case for the tax bill. This presentation may take one or two days and may include over 1000 pages of printed material, statistical data, graphs, analysis, and technical explanation. The committee may call other officials, such as the secretaries of Commerce and Labor and official representatives of interested groups — the AFL and CIO, chambers of commerce, the National Association of Manufacturers, and private associations. The public hearings may take several weeks or even months. Hearings on the Tax Reform Act of 1969 lasted about seven weeks.

When the public hearings are concluded, the committee goes into executive session. In this session the Chairman of the Ways and Means Committee acts as presiding officer and moderator. He is assisted on technical matters by the Joint Internal Revenue Committee — taxation is one of the five major policy areas that warrant a joint Congressional committee — staffed by tax economists, statisticians, analysts, attorneys, and research assistants. The members of the committee discuss all aspects of the bill, listen to their economic advisors, and reach their decisions, which are incorporated in the committee's report. The report is usually a lengthy one running to several hundred pages and incorporates both the majority view and the dissenting views of the minority.

Article 1, Section 7 of the Constitution states that "All bills for raising revenue shall originate in the House of Representatives." Revenue or tax legislation is "privileged" and has priority over other business, but in practice tax legislation is debated under a "closed rule," which requires prior approval by the Rules Committee. Under the closed rule, debate is restricted in the House of Representatives to a motion to accept or reject the entire bill as it emerges from the Ways and Means Committee. At the close of the debate, the bill is approved or sent back to the Ways and Means Committee for amendment. A major tax bill that has been passed by the Ways and Means Committee is seldom rejected by the House.

After the bill passes the House, it is sent to the Senate and referred to the Committee on Finance. There it goes through substantially the same process as in the House. Public hearings are held, and most of the witnesses repeat their testimony before the Finance Committee, both in the public hearing and executive sessions. The Senate Finance Committee is no rubber stamp for the House and usually makes significant changes in the bill. The Senate Finance Committee made over 40 major amendments to the House 1969 tax bill. The Finance Committee report, covering the same ground as the House committee report and explaining reasons for the amendments it has made, is prepared and sent to the Senate.

Senate debate on the tax bill is open and unrestricted and normally longer than the House debate. Amendments may be offered from the floor, some relating to the bill, some unrelated or intended to thwart the purpose of the bill. Amendments not approved by the Finance Committee or administration spokesmen are usually defeated, but not all amendments are opposed. During the Senate debate on the Tax Reform Act of 1969, over 110 amendments were proposed; of these, over 70 were incorporated in the Senate version of the bill. After Senate debate the two versions of the tax bill are sent to the Committee of Conference, composed of the senior members of the tax committees of the House and the Senate. The Committee on Conference reconciles the two versions of the bill and rejects or approves the Senate amendments.

After the Committee on Conference agrees on a final draft of the bill, it is voted on by both houses and is sent to the President for signature or veto. The President rarely vetoes a tax bill. In the past 30 years only two important tax bills were vetoed: the Revenue Act of 1943 and the Revenue Act of 1948, and Congress passed both bills over the President's veto. The President makes every effort to modify the tax bill to suit him before it reaches his desk. After it is passed by Congress there is little he can do except show his displeasure.

The President's signature makes the tax bill a law, and it is turned over to the Treasury Department for implementation, administration, and enforcement. This is not a simple process. Detailed regulations must be issued, and the IRS must prepare new tax forms and new instructions and train personnel to interpret and enforce the new law. This involved process may be so lengthy that, by the time it is completed, a new tax proposal may already have started its course in the legislative mill, repeating the same cycle.

The tax legislative process has been criticized on the grounds that (1) it is unduly influenced by special interest groups, (2) it does not set economic priorities according to the national interest, (3) it is too slow to be effective in times of economic crisis, (4) it does not give Congress a clear picture of how revenues are tied to expenditures, and (5) it does not provide for allocating all resources in an optimal manner, but only for their diversion from the private to the public sector.

Joseph A. Pechman, author of *Federal Tax Policy,* made these comments on the lack of representation of the public interest in tax hearings:

> Individuals who appear before the two tax committees hardly represent a cross section of opinion on tax matters. The committees generally permit anyone to testify and rarely invite expert testimony, except from government officials. The result is that, day after day, the committees are subject to a drumfire of complaints against the tax system, arguments why special tax advantages should not be eliminated, and reasons why additional preferences are needed.
>
> In such an atmosphere, the Secretary of the Treasury assumes the role of defender of the national interest. He spends much of his time fighting off new tax advantages and is only moderately successful in eliminating old ones. Whether taxes are to be raised or lowered, most of the witnesses find good reasons for favoring the groups or individuals they represent. The secretary takes a broader, national view and tries to strike a balance among competing claims. Since the stakes are high and there are no generally accepted criteria for evaluating questions of tax policy, his decisions may be regarded as arbitrary or contrary to the public interest by some groups and be vigorously opposed in open hearings or in behind-the-scenes lobbying.[80]

Pechman favors reform of the tax process and suggests as the first step "to give better representation to the public interest in the open hearings conducted by the Ways and Means Committee and the Finance Committee." This is certainly a worthwhile objective, but not one easy to achieve. The "public interest" is, as Pechman himself states, subject to individual interpretation. All taxpayers, as individuals, cannot appear before the committees; it would be a physical impossibility. They must be represented. But by whom? Private associations? But are these not the very lobbies that represent the "private" as against the "public" interest? Are not Congressmen the people's true representatives? Why, therefore, look elsewhere for representation of the people's interest? The problem is not that the Congress does not represent the people or the public interest; it is rather that, under the present income tax system, the people are not directly involved in the legislative tax process because the very nature of the process excludes them.

The slowness of the legislative tax process is a serious drawback, particularly in times of recession or inflation when quick action is needed. Many attempts have been made to give the President authority to make temporary changes in tax rates. But Congress, jealous of its tax power and fearing further executive encroachment on its constitutional privileges, has shown no interest in modifying the present system. As a result, when tax changes are badly needed to control inflation, there is no remedy available, and the administration must fall back on expenditure changes, which are comparatively inefficient and ineffectual.

The tax process does not present Congress with an opportunity to deal with the revenue problem in relation to total expenditures. The tax committees pass on revenue bills. When expenditures are to be approved, they are turned over to an appropriations committee. This fragmentation or division of the taxing-expenditure legislative process leads to serious deficiencies in overall planning and sometimes causes the committees to work at cross-purposes. The appropriation committees have numerous subcommittees handling a multitude of individual appropriations; they regard themselves as cost controllers or fiscal watchdogs, but take no responsibility for the general tax policy that provides the revenues. The appropriation committees are not directly concerned with tax policy; the tax policy committees are not directly concerned with expenditures and budget appropriations. The cost-benefit relationship is not tied directly to the legislative tax process. Attempts by Wicksell and others to remedy this problem have not been successful.

The most serious drawback of the legislative tax process is its failure to allocate resources in an optimal manner. It provides, by the income tax, for the diversion of resources from the private to the public sector, but in so doing it fails to utilize resources in the private sector in a manner consistent with national economic objectives. In the private sector, resources are wasted by unemployment, unused capacity, underproduction of socially necessary goods, overproduction of nonessential superfluous goods, pollution of air and water, and profligate waste of natural resources. In the public sector, resources are wasted in cost overruns, uncontrollable bureaucratic empire-building, grants and subsidies without cost controls, domestic and foreign give-away programs, and other expenditures that, in general, are not tied to national needs or priorities. The result is a rampant consumerism that encourages both superfluities and waste in the private sector and an unrestrained growth of bureaucracy in the public sector.

4. Setting Priorities Through the Budget

The tax legislature procedure is only one of the processes used by the Federal government for setting priorities through tax policy. The other is the Federal budget, which allocates tax funds according to priorities set by the executive and legislative branches. It is not an inspirational document. As Senator Proxmire puts it, "Unfortunately, the primary instrument by which great decisions are made, priorities determined, and goals carried out is the dull, boring, opaque, obtuse and ponderous document called 'The Budget of the United States Government'."[81]

The Federal budget for the fiscal year 1972-1973 is a formidable document in size and scope, consisting of 4 volumes and over 2000 pages. The United

135

States government is the world's biggest business. The Federal budget takes in only about 20 per cent of the gross national product, but the total is still sufficiently large — $246 billion in fiscal 1973 — to be impressive.

The Federal budget finances and subsidizes an almost countless number of social welfare programs, national defense needs, highway construction, cancer research, nuclear energy research, Indian reservations, foreign aid programs, urban renewal, shipbuilding, airline and farm subsidy programs, oil exploration, crime detection, public health and sanitation, food and drug inspection, unemployment benefits, veterans benefits, aid to dependent children and so on, ad infinitum. The 1971 *Catalog of Federal Domestic Assistance Programs* lists over 1000 different Federal programs covering everything from Adult Vocational Training for American Indians to Water Resources Development. The *Encyclopedia of U.S. Government Benefits* is 1013 pages long and offers everything from aerial photographs from the Department of Agriculture to the Zoological Park in Washington D.C.

The Federal budget was not always so important. Prior to the New Deal, the Federal budget was relatively unimportant. It was a simple housekeeping tool used to keep government expenses in line with tax receipts. New Deal economists, applying Keynes' theories, transformed the Federal budget into an instrument for national economic planning. If the economy was stagnant, the budget poured more money into the economy than it took in, thus stimulating demand and putting people and plants to work. It was no longer nesessary to wait and suffer until deflation had run its course and people and business began to buy and invest. The Federal budget could put money immediately into people's pockets by reducing taxes, by spending on government projects, or by subsidizing certain activities such as farming. Of course, all this spending might create a budget deficit, but that in itself was a plus, for it acted like a stimulant in times of depression, just as a budget surplus acted as a depressant in times of inflation.

To balance current expenses with current revenues is no longer the chief function of the Federal budget, which is balanced at a hypothetical level of full employment; that is; the level of production is *assumed* to be that which it would attain under conditions of full employment. If the economy is operating at less than full employment, a deficit will be incurred in an amount/determined by calculations of potential gross national product and a compromise between acceptable levels of unemployment and price inflation.

The use of budget deficits and surpluses to stabilize the economy has been given major credit for the long uninterrupted period of economic growth since 1940 and the absence of major depressions. On the debit side, budget policy has been indicted as the chief cause of inflation, the weakness of the dollar, and the continued growth of government control over the economy and the resulting loss of market freedom. The budget policy was not successful during the great depression. There were 13 consecutive deficits in 13 years; unemployment remained at 10 per cent or more and did not end until the beginning of World War II. Since the war, unemployment has continued to elude the best efforts of the budget planners. The growth of the public sector has brought with it the need for larger budgets and a larger bureaucracy. In a way, bureaucracy itself may be considered a palliative, if not a cure of umemployment. There were more employees on the government payroll in 1973 than the total umemployed in 1933. The Socialist remedy for unemployment is to put everyone on the government payroll. In a two-sector economy, the public sector may be regarded as an elastic reservoir capable of absorbing all the unemployed in the private sector.

A bureaucracy feeds and grows on paper; the extent of paper work or red tape, whether measured by the ream or by the ton, is an accurate index of its size and vigor. The Federal government finds it necessary to print about 4.5 million cubic feet of forms to carry on its operations. It has 377,000 tons of paper work in storage and, according to one senator's estimate, spends over $18 billion dollars a year to print and store its records. The same senator estimates that it costs businessmen another $18 billion a year to fill out and return government forms. The activities that generate this fantastic flood are bureaus, agencies, commissions, secretariats, departments, missions, divisions, and subdivisions of the Federal bureaucracy, all fed and nurtured by the Federal budget.

Warren G. Harding submitted the first Federal budget in 1922. It listed total expenditures of $3.5 billion and projected a deficit of $168 million. Both figures were viewed with alarm by Vice President Coolidge and Secretary of Commerce Hoover. The thought that national economic priorities would be set in a government budget seemed incompatible with the American doctrine of free enterprise.

Prior to 1922 and throughout the 19th century the Federal government operated without a budget. The cabinet officers sent requests for needed funds to the Treasury, and the Treasury simply stapled those requests together and forwarded them to the Appropriations Committee of the House without comment. There were no budget estimates of revenues and of expenditures projected for years ahead. The public never knew whether the government was in the black or in the red until years later, yet four wars were thus financed. During most of its history the Treasury's greatest problem was what to do with the surplus tax revenues that continued to grow. In every year from 1866 to 1893 the Federal government had surplus revenues. In 1887 the Federal government was forced to go into the open market to buy bonds as the only way of releasing for the use of business its large surplus revenues.

In European countries budget procedures were developed in the struggle between kings and parliaments over the control of tax revenues and government expenditures. By the 19th century/parliaments in England and in other democratic countries had won the right to control government expenditures and had discovered that through this power they effectively controlled the government, since all government operations need money. The king, like the American President, was obliged to obtain the approval of Parliament before he could spend government funds. Budgetary control was lodged in the legislative branch in both European and American democracies, and this was considered one of the basic principles of democratic government.

But this legislative control of the purse was far from being completely effective. Government bureaus had a bad habit of running out of money and coming to Congress or Parliament for supplementary appropriations. The legislators were not in a position to pass on costs of administration and generally felt constrained to grant the requests. As the bureaucracy increased in size and complexity, the costs of administration were more difficult to control, and deficits became a chronic problem that annoyed and frustrated the legislators. The demands for supplementary appropriations from the various bureaus and departments were generally backed by such pressure groups as farmers, oil men, and veterans. Out of frustration, the legislators would sometimes attach "riders" to the appropriation bills to try to restrain or punish the bureaucracy, but seldom succeeded. In modern times in the United States, Congress has come to rely less on restraints for effective control and more on analysis and legislative revision of the budget at the time it is submitted for approval, and the bureaucracy has countered this move by making deficit financing an integral part of budget policy.

The function of the budget in a modern state was explained by Gerhard Colm in 1952:

> The budget, so to speak, is the nerve center of the public economy. Its role can be compared with that played by the market place in the private sector of the economy. In the private sector of the economy decisions about what goods and services are to be produced, what factors of production are to be utilized, and who will receive the goods and services are determined by the actions of the people in their capacity as consumers, workers, entrepeneurs and financiers. These actions in turn are guided through the interplay of incomes, prices and costs, that is, the mechanism that equates supply and demand on the market for goods, labor and money. We therefore characterize the private sector of the economy as the *market economy*.
>
> In the public sphere, decisions about what goods and services are to be produced, who will receive the benefits, and who will pay for the goods and services are largely made by the political mechanism, that is, the interplay of parliamentary bodies, executive officials and public servants in accord with what happens to be the constitutional procedure in a particular country . . . The budget serves as an instrument in the reaching of these decisions. It reflects the outcome of the political struggles and is the tool through which political decisions are translated into specific programs. Therefore we may properly speak of the *budget economy* as characteristic of the basic mechanism in the public economic sphere.[82]

Colm did not mean to imply that the market economy (the private sector) and the budget economy (the public sector) were two separate and distinct worlds. Although organized on two different principles (the market principle and the budget principle), both sectors are part of the same national economy, and each reacts to the other in both a direct and an indirect manner. A depression in the private market sector would inevitably have a direct visible effect on the public sector and the Federal budget. An increase in budget allocations for defense or highway construction would have immediate and direct effects on industries in the private sector.

The Federal budget is formulated with the market economy in mind, and three of the major objectives of the budget are market-oriented: full employment, economic growth, and price stabilization. Among the major objectives not *directly* related to the market economy may be mentioned national defense, public education, public safety, and public health. Obviously, however, government spending in these fields has very significant, if indirect, effects on the market economy.

The Federal budget in the United States is not an economic plan on the Soviet model. The Russian budget is essentially a plan for government operation of the national economy and is enforced by compulsion. The Federal budget in the American system is essentially a statement of economic policy by the President, indicating the major economic objectives of his administration and the financial means at his disposal with which he hopes to achieve them. In the Federal budget the general social goals of the President are reduced to specific programs and expressed in dollars and cents. The relative budget estimates for national defense, housing, education, public health, farm price supports, social welfare, pollution, and transportation indicate in unmistakable quantitative terms the priorities that the President attaches to each of these social programs.

The effect the Federal budget will have on the market economy of the private sector is subject to many economic and noneconomic factors that are beyond the control of the government: the behavior of consumers and investors, wars, natural disasters, international competition, and other forces. The President is forced to revise his economic priorities to fit realities unforeseen in his budget estimates. Fortunately or unfortunately, only a small portion of the Federal budget is available to the President for new programs. The giant Federal bureaucracy that eats up most of the budget has a momentum that cannot be stopped or even slowed down. A study by the Brookings Institution reveals that, in the 1972 Federal budget of $229 billion, only $14 billion was available to the President for his discretionary use. The $215 billion was already committed to ongoing programs that were uncancellable. Included in this category were $70 billions for Social Security pensions; $43 billions for contracts made in prior years; $21.6 billions for interest on the national debt; $38 billion for such assorted programs as those for veterans' benefits; medical aid; food stamps; farm-price supports; postal service; and state grants under revenue-sharing. Apart from these programs, about $52 billion had been budgeted for defense. The balance of the budget had to be spread out to cover funding of schools and colleges, antipoverty agencies, space explorations, housing, transportation, and conservation of natural resources, all of which feel they deserve much more than they get. All programs have their champions in and out of Congress who resist fiercely any attempt to reduce their budget funds.

The relative immobility of the Federal budget is the result of the time lag in Federal economic planning. Budget decisions to commit resources may not have an immediate effect on the economy. A decision to start a new highway system, a new space program, a new class of nuclear submarines, a new health program, or to increase Social Secutiry benefits may not show up in the current budget as a very large item. However, the commitment will affect the budget for subsequent years and freeze revenues over a long period of time. The cumulative result is that the current budget reflects not so much the decisions of the current administration as the consequences, some planned and some unplanned, of decisions made by prior administrations. In this respect, the Federal budget acts as a conservative influence on an incoming administration. A new President is not given, a blank check. His revenues have already been committed to a considerable extent by prior administrations.

The Comptroller General of the United States, commenting on President Nixon's budget for 1972, said: "Nearly three-fourths of the budget is beyond his control — locked in by previous legislation or earlier decisions that cause money to flow out for Veterans pensions, Medicare and other programs."[83]

The President's budget serves three important functions:

1. It establishes priorities in the public sector consistent with the general economic goals of the administration. This function may be called budget planning. There are always more government programs than available resources, so the planning phase must select and grade them according to the priorities established. This is largely a political process, with ultimate goals decided by the President, guided by his Council of Economic Advisors.

2. The budget by its very nature must reduce political decisions to economic realities; this is done by economists in the Office of Management and Budget. A financial plan is worked out based on estimates of cash flow to see if tax revenues will be sufficient to fund existing and proposed programs. This financial plan will be used as a basis for decisions on whether to eliminate or reduce some programs or to ask for additional taxes or to increase the public debt by borrowing.

3. The Federal budget has a strong impact on the private sector, both short-term and long-term; this impact, although not measured in budget figures, must be taken into account. Both tax levies and government expenditures affect levels of income, prices, employment, production, and consumption. These effects may be inflationary or deflationary, designed to stimulate, subsidize, or dampen production and growth in certain segments of the private sector of the economy. The fiscal authorities of the government take these effects into consideration and try to adjust fiscal and monetary policy to conform to budget estimates and to anticipate economic trends foreshadowed by the budget policies.

Through the budget, therefore, the government sets economic priorities within the public sector, allocates tax resources, and influences the private sector through its fiscal policy. The three aspects are necessarily interdependent. It is probable that sustained noninflationary growth of income and employment and rational allocation of resources in the national economy cannot be achieved by budget planning alone. Too many economic and noneconomic factors that go to make up a healthy economy are beyond the control of the government. However, the combination of budget planning and fiscal policy can go a long way toward achieving national economic objectives and toward stabilizing the economy at high employment levels. When the private economy shows symptoms of serious inflation or deflation, the government is now required to take both remedial fiscal and nonfiscal measures to restore market equilibrium. These procedures can include price and wage controls, Social Security policies, tax investment credits, subsidies, monetary credit controls, and tax reforms. Unfortunately, the budget process is not sufficiently flexible to be useful as a means to correct or counteract sudden or unexpected economic crisis situations. Fiscal policy acting in conjunction with the Federal budget was not able to overcome the unemployment and inflation crisis of the Nixon administration, and the President resorted to direct controls over wages and prices in August 1971. Fiscal and budgetary policy alone cannot correct structural imbalances caused by an unsound tax structure, according to Professor Neil Jacoby, one of the President's economic advisers in 1964:

> So many forces, such as monetary actions, determine the growth of output — most of them beyond the scope of Federal fiscal policy — that it is impossible to weigh the influence of fiscal policy *per se* ... It appears clear, however, that a radical overhauling of the Federal income tax structure in the direction of the lower, less progressive rates applied to a broader segment of personal income would have a much more powerful influence upon economic growth than any fiscal actions during 1961-1963.[84]

Nevertheless, the Federal budget remains a powerful instrument for guiding the economy, and this instrument is firmly in the hands of the President, according to one Congressional observer, Senator William Proxmire:

> Not only are matters like tax expenditures outside the budget and therefore entirely outside an annual Congressional scrutiny, but Congress does little more than give a perfunctory examination to those items that are in the budget. This means that the instrument by which priorities are determined or reexamined — the budget — is essentially outside the purview of the Congress ... The essential fact remains that the budget document and hence American priorities are essentially what the President says they should be in his annual budget. Congress needs both a method by which the budget can be examined properly and the means to make its judgment effective.[85]

The budget process does not seem amenable to Congressional control, and every effort to reform budget procedures ends in failure because the budget process is essentially an executive one. Congress can regain its function of setting national economic priorities, but not through the budget process. For Congress to regain control and direction over economic and tax policy, it must exercise this control and direction through a legislative process.

5. Total Planning

In the public sector the element of social value is the paramount factor in reaching a budget decision; that is, the relative social value of a public good or service will determine whether it will be budgeted. The priority of a public good or service is not determined by economic costs although, of course, these costs are a limiting factor. The budget appropriation for a new aircraft carrier will not be denied on the basis of high cost if the Navy can show it is essential to national defense. In a democracy, the government will always provide whatever goods and services the public needs and votes for, and this is determined by the scale of social values by which it measures those needs, as well as by the amount of tax revenues that can be squeezed out of the private sector.

From the beginning of the republic until 1930, Federal revenues were spent mostly on defense needs and for veterans' benefits. From 1879 to 1929 the nondefense spending of the government accounted for less than 1 per cent of the gross national product, and total expenditure in the public sector, including defense spending, was less than 3 per cent. At that time the United States was almost a pure market economy. During that period the government had a very strong influence on the private market economy, but that influence was exercised through legislative statute, a tariff tax policy, and a system of laws that enforced free market decision and upheld the inviolability of private property.

The free market did not exist in a political vacuum. It was based directly and solidly on the political concept of unlimited individual rights to ownership of property that was thoroughly defined by laws governing the individual's rights to the ownership, use, transfer, possession, sale, barter, lease, and inheritance of property; by laws defining such classes of property as real property and chattels; by laws defining exchange of property through sales, mortgages, or deeds; by laws governing the use of legal tender to facilitate exchanges; by laws governing the relationship of man to property as slave, debtor, creditor, owner, renter, or landlord; and by laws restraining individual activities with respect to property such as trespass, theft, robbery, fraud, misappropriation, embezzlement, and confiscation.

Since a bureaucracy is usually a part of the executive branch, it appears historically during a period in which a strong executive establishes hegemony over a weak legislature or popular assembly. The growth of the public sector in the United States started under the leadership of President F. D. Roosevelt and was precipitated by an economic crisis that neither the legislature nor the private market economy was able to control.

Under Bismarck, Germany was the first modern industrial nation to develop a large public sector. By 1929 the government sector of the German economy was 30.6 per cent of the gross national product, about what the United States public sector was 40 years later. This rapid growth slowed down considerably as it approached 40 per cent of the gross national product. It has been the position of economists that a private market economy cannot function effectively when it must "support" a public economy larger than itself; that is, a market economy cannot function at less than 50 per cent of the gross national product. It is believed that, at that point, taxes would become confiscatory, private property would have no value, and market values in prices, wages, and contracts would break down completely. The government would be forced to assume complete control of the economy, and all functions previously carried on in the private market sector would necessarily be transferred to the public sector and incorporated into the state budget. The head of the office of Management and Budget in the Nixon administration, Caspar W. Weinberger, made this comment in an interview on February 3, 1973:

> The share of the gross national product that's devoted to government is now over 34%; and it just seems to me that when you get a third of the whole national effort to supporting government, it becomes increasingly difficult to maintain a viable, effective private sector. It isn't the increase in the number of dollars that worries me. It is the increase in the amount of authority and power in government that those dollars represent. My worry is that as government gets bigger, individual human freedom gets smaller, and I think that's not really consistent with the premises that went into the founding of the country.[86]

The head of the budget and planning bureau of a Socialist state has the opposite reaction to the growth of the private sector. Socialist economists assume that a growth of the private sector to 50 per cent of total gross national product would probably destroy the state budget planning system now used in Socialist countries and make the public economy dependent on the private consumer or private sector. For that reason, growth of the private market sector beyond a certain minimum point is totally unacceptable to Soviet leaders; where it exists in satellite countries, it is closely watched and repressed by discriminatory laws and taxes or military coercion.

The percentage of all public expenditures as part of the gross national product increased only very slightly prior to 1929; as a result of New Deal policies, however, the percentage increased from 9.8 in 1929 to 22.9 in 1941 and reached a peak of 49.0 in 1944 under full war mobilization of the economy. After the war, public expenditures declined to 18.7 per cent in 1947, but have increased to almost 36.0 per cent in 1973. The increase is slightly higher in Western European countries, where it ranges from 35 to 45 per cent.

The continued growth of the public sector of the economy presents a serious threat to individual economic power and personal liberty, as explained in Chapter I. The citizen becomes a ward of the state when the government takes over the function of the market and of private associations. According to one outstanding authority on social problems:

> Every piece of social policy substitutes for some traditional arrangement, whether good or bad, a new arrangement in which public authorities take over, at least in part, the role of the family, of the ethnic and neighborhood group, or the voluntary association. In doing so, social policy weakens the priorities of these traditional agents and further encourages needy people to depend on that government rather than on traditional structures for help. Perhaps this is the basic force behind the ever-increasing demand for social policy, and its frequent failure to satisfy the demand.[87]

In November 1973 the former head of President Nixon's Price Commission, the price control board, expressed a pessimistic opinion regarding the government's ability to control the economy:

For almost 15 months during Phase II of the Economic Stabilization Program I served as the Chairman of the Price Commission. I saw the complex, capitalist economy from a most unusual observation post.

From this experience and from what has happened since, I am personally convinced that our economic system is steadily shifting from a private enterprise free-market economy to one that is centrally directed and under public control.

Price and wage controls such as we have experienced in Phase I through IV have helped to extend the degree of public control and to accelerate the rate of change. At some point — and I predict that, at the present rate, this point may be reached in about 15 to 20 years — the essential characteristics of a competitive, private enterprise system (non-regulated prices, profit motive, risk taking, collective bargaining) will no longer make up the economic engine that drives our system.[88]

Although the general public may be temporarily in favor of price and wage controls, this attitude may change as the people discover that centralized control of the economy does not lead to an economy of abundance, but to shortages, black markets, corruption, and rationing.

Where the public sector is all-powerful, as in Russia, the market function is virtually liquidated and replaced by executive planning that sets prices and controls production through investment credits. The state is not dependent on the citizen, either as a consumer or as a taxpayer. The consumer market and personal tax revenues are not a major factor in Soviet economic planning.

In a society in which the public sector has absorbed the private sector, wages and prices and production levels are determined by budget decisions rather than market decisions. In the Soviet budget the basic decisions are those of the Central Committee of the Communist Party. The central planning bureau, the GOSPLAN, incorporates these decisions into the annual budget and the five-year economic plan.

In democracies, the congress or parliament has the ultimate authority to approve the executive budget, but in Communist countries there is no independent legislative power. The executive power is supreme and can make economic plans without legislative interference and, of course, without interference from the private consumer market. For that reason Soviet planning approaches the goal of total planning and approximates the ideal of those who believe in a planned society. Engels expressed this ideal in a much-quoted passage. After Communism has been established, said Engels:

The objective, external forces which have hitherto dominated history will then pass under the control of men themselves. It is only from this point that men, with full consciousness, will fashion their own history; it is only at this point that the social causes set in motion by men will have, predominantly and in constantly increasing measure, the effects willed by men.[89]

The theory that, in a scientific age, the scientist is the person best qualified to govern society has had wide acceptance, and not only among scientists. The erratic genius Henri de Saint-Simon gained international fame in 1814 with his then-revolutionary concept of an industrial society managed by a scientific élite. It was inevitable that Saint-Simon should have found his disciples in the world's first great technological institute, the École Polytechnique of Paris.

The doctrine of Saint-Simon that science alone could save the world from poverty and superstition and that scientists were eminently fitted for the task of saviors seemed like a revelation to the budding young scientists of the École. But neither Saint-Simon nor his disciples were able to translate the theory of scientific Socialism into a practical political program. The fanatic zeal of the student disciples turned the theories of Saint-Simon into a new and absurd religious cult, but Saint-Simon's idea of rule by a scientific élite did not die.

It was continued in France by his most gifted disciple Auguste Comte, who founded the new science of sociology. Comte elaborated Saint-Simon's scientific Socialism and Condorcet's revolutionary concept of "progress" into a complete science of social control. The success of Comte and his followers is attested by the almost universal belief in the idea of social change as "progress" when generated and directed by science. Before Comte, philosophers from Plato and Cicero to Rousseau had associated social change with decay, corruption, and degeneration. Their golden ages were in the past. They urged men to regain the lost virtues of their heroic ancestors who lived in a society that was perfect and unchanging. Comte, flushed with the prospect of man playing God and controlling his own destiny, advocated a secular religion with sociologists as the new priesthood and the planning of a perfect society as their mission.

In England H. G. Wells picked up the theme and in *The Shape of Things to Come* described the coming of an élite group of scientists, engineers, and technicians who could create a new and more efficient society after the old one had been ruined by capitalists and politicians.

H. G. Wells was a member of the influential Fabian society, an élite group formed to impose a scientific Socialist order on what they considered the unjust, disordered, market economy and the disorganized social order. This élite group sought to capture the state for the promotion of Socialist ideas by "legal" rather than by revolutionary Marxist means, but they naturally regarded the existing legal order with contempt. This contempt is shared by the British Labour Party, the heir of the Fabian Society, which is less inhibited about the use of violence.

William Graham Sumner, who despised Socialism as a European "metaphysical" dogma, stated the pragmatic 19th-century American concept of liberty in these words:

> Civil liberty, the only real liberty which is possible or conceivable on earth, is a matter of law and institutions. It is not metaphysical at all. Civil liberty is really a great induction from all the experience of mankind in the use of civil institutions; it must be defined, not in systems drawn from metaphysics, but in terms drawn from history and law. It is not an arbitrary conception; it is a series of concrete facts. These facts go to constitute a status — the status of a free man in a modern jural state.[90]

Sumner was the most influential American economist of the post-Civil War era. He was an apostle of Spencerian individualism and social Darwinism, that is, the theory of unrestricted market competition and the doctrine of "survival of the fittest."

At the end of the 19th century the Progressive movement started a trend away from individualism and laissez-faire and toward greater government concern with and involvement in the private economy. American economists began to criticize the classic market doctrine of Sumner. Among the most outspoken critics were T. Veblen, R. T. Ely, H. C. Adams, S. N. Patten, J. B. Clark, and E. R. A. Seligman. Although opposed to Marxist ideas of complete state ownership and control, they advocated the use of government power to alter or modify economic conditions for the general welfare. Said Ely, "I condemn alike that individualism which would allow the state no room for industrial activity and that socialism which would absorb in the state the functions of the individual."

Seligman pointed out that laissez-faire was not the final economic system based on natural unchangeable laws, as Sumner believed, but rather the natural reaction against the excessive restrictions of the mercantilist era by farmers, merchants, and artisans who were economically self-sufficient and independent. The industrial revolution, said Seligman, had made society more complex, and laissez-faire as a government policy was no longer realistic or desirable. It was obsolete.

Simon Nelson Patten is today little known to the general public, yet in the 1880's he was giving expression to economic ideas so far ahead of his time that only now can they be fully appreciated. Very early in his career and in collaboration with Edmund James, Patten advocated state planning for the general welfare — 40 years before Stalin and the Russian GOSPLAN. Patten realized the futility of his efforts and in 1888 took a professorship at the University of Pennsylvania, where he taught until 1917.[91]

In his classroom Patten always set up one standard; the public welfare. The laissez-faire system did not promote the public welfare. Patten claimed that mass production had reduced the opportunity of the common worker to become an independent owner. At the same time it had created surplus revenues that were appropriated by the corporate owner. These owners, as a class, did not use these surplus funds for the public welfare. The state, said Patten, should appropriate these surplus funds by taxation and use them to provide badly needed social services — public parks, public roads, public health and sanitation, and public education. So far Patten seems to be writing the blueprint for the economic policies of the New Deal and other forms of *dirigisme*. However, Patten was no mere welfare economist, born 50 years ahead of his time. He also had very original ideas about the environment, social psychology, consumption, and economic growth. The economic environment, said Patten, is not a mere physical inventory of resources and assets. It reflects also the psychological makeup of the people who occupy it. Their abilities, energy, and knowledge mold the economic environment. The changes created in the environment by the people in turn change the standard of living and affect the psychology of the population, weakening or strengthening their incentive to work and heightening or lessening their enjoyment of material goods.

Whereas Marx believed that material conditions alone determined economic and political institutions, Petten saw economic growth as a dynamic evolutionary interaction between subjective psychological factors in

146

the population and objective material factors in the environment. Patten was convinced, although he could not document his conviction, that as the economy grew, the individual would become more interested in the public welfare than in his individual well-being. One reason for this change in consumer psychology, said Patten, was that some of the wants of an advanced technological society, such as public roads, education, health, communications, and electricity, are best served when operated in the public interest. Patten believed that, in time, the psychology of the consumer would be conditioned to accept increases in social benefits in preference to increases in consumer goods. Patten believed also that in a dynamic society there would be constantly changing consumer tastes and new industries that stimulated or satisfied new consumer wants and that the state should take an active part in bringing the habits of consumption into harmony with the environment. State economic controls would not be in the crude form of socialization of industry or controls over management. Patten advocated a much more refined and selective policy for the state. He recommended a policy of economic guidance based on the protective tariff and price control. Through these controls the state could encourage or inhibit the growth of any particular industry.

In general, American economists rejected Marx. This attitude could not be attributed to ignorance of Marxism or to any lack of radicalism on the part of American economists. The contrary appears to be true. There was a strong uninhibited strain of radicalism in American politics and economics; unlike Europe, where Marxism went underground and became a conspirational movement, in America Socialism was openly debated and freely championed. Edward Bellamy wrote a book about a Socialist utopia, *Looking Backward*, that sold over a million copies in 1889-1890 and caused a nationwide sensation. But Marxism did not take root. American political radicalism of the Progressive era had its grass roots in American soil — it was concerned with regional, not world, problems. William Jennings Bryan and Robert La Follette were the popular American radicals who were quite different in political philosophy from such European political radicals as Lasalle and Lenin.

However, the elitist ideology of Comte was transplanted to American universities by Lester Frank Ward, whose monumental *Dynamic Sociology*, published in 1883, attacked laissez-faire as a government policy and advocated rule by a scientific élite or legislators trained in sociology. "No legislator," said Ward "is qualified to affect the destinies of millions of social units until he masters all that is known of the science of society." To the "scientific control of the social forces by the collective mind of society" Ward gave the name of "sociocracy," which, he explained, "is the symbol of positive social action as against the negativism of the dominant *laissez faire* school of politico-economic *doctrinaires*."[92]

Ward offered no political program by which his élite group could attain power, but his theories gave theoretical support to the growing academic interest in sociology as the "science of society" that would ultimately enable the government to organize society in a scientific manner. According to a

147

contemporary historian, Ward was the American prophet of "all those movements looking to the reconstruction of society and economy through government intervention which is the most striking development in the political history of the last half-century in America."[93]

Ward's influence was carried on by Edward A. Ross, one of the greatest American sociologists. Said Ross, "In order to protect ourselves against the lawlessness, the insolence, and the rapacity of over-grown private interests we shall have to develop the state, especially on its administrative side." Nevertheless, before World War I American sociologists did not openly advocate Socialism. They were content to tear down the folklore of capitalism, individualism in politics, and laissez-faire in economics.[94] It was an economist, Thorstein Veblen, who proposed the most popular of all American plans for rule by a scientific élite. In *The Engineers and the Price System* and other books, Veblen urged the establishment of a "Technocracy" in place of the wasteful, inefficient, and disorderly market price system.

The doctrine of technocracy has been subverted by what James Burnham has called the "managerial revolution." Instead of science taking over business and scientists replacing businessmen, the trend now is for business to become a science and for businessmen to become scientists. Graduate schools of business administration are now on the same academic level as schools of medicine or law or engineering. The subjects taught as business management courses are as demanding and rigorous as those of other scientific disciplines. They require a thorough preparation in mathematics, psychology, law, economics, and other social and behavioral sciences. As MBA's from Harvard, Wharton, California, Columbia, Chicago, Michigan, Stanford, and other universities come more and more to occupy top management positions in business, the doctrine of Saint-Simon and Veblen that businessmen are by education untrained and unfit to manage business in a scientific manner becomes untrue and outdated. The creation of a business management science has created a new and separate specialty that speaks its own language, has its own scientific rules, and is as jealous of its prerogatives as any other discipline. To the school of business administration graduate the idea that a general scientific education qualifies a person to manage a business would seem preposterous. Scientists today must be specialists; a nuclear physicist, for example, would not be expected to know anything about entomology. Veblen prophesied that engineers eventually would take over the operation of business, but how could a chemical engineer, for example, solve problems of labor relations, physical distribution, training and motivating employees, pricing policy, market analysis, advertising, financial controls, cash flow, budgeting, and other business problems? These problems constitute a specialized field of study and make business management as complex and as broad as chemical engineering or any social science course. As business management becomes increasingly more scientific, Veblen's theory of the technocratic élite becomes a reality — except that the technocrats turn out to be businessmen, after all.

This development has not entirely invalidated the philosophy of rule by an intellectual élite — it has merely shifted the basis from scientific Socialism,

Saint-Simonian or Marxist, to a newer and more sophisticated élitism. Marxist Socialism has been established, and the reality has killed the dream. Stalin and his successors have kept intellectuals in a tight harness, and Mao puts them to work with manual laborers to teach them humility. The intellectuals in the West are disenchanted and confused. The evangelical fervor of those who sought the millenium through science has been tempered by the scientific triumph of Hiroshima; the fanaticism of the Communists has been cooled by Stalin and piecework. The intellectuals of the liberal Socialist tradition still speak of revolution in a cultured voice with traces of irony and melancholy. Disillusioned with their plans for the industrial society, they now look with renewed hopes toward the postindustrial society. Professor Daniel Bell in *The Coming of a Post-Industrial Society* sees the emergence of a ruling élite made up of scientists, economists, sociologists, and technologists who will plot "alternate futures" with the aid of computers. The choice of a future is too complex to be left to the individual decision of the uneducated voter or the lowly politician. In all scientific utopias the pragmatic, problem-solving legislator is never mentioned; the emphasis is on superior science or technical competence, an élite certified by credentials. The function of the politician, as the people's representative, in solving social problems is never seriously considered, unless, of course, he is acting to implement the plans of the scientific élite.

Professor Robert L. Heilbronner, whose felicity with words makes him one of the most popular of American economists, expresses the case for a society run by social scientists in which the economy would be run by economists. He asks: "Where can economics go?" and answers:

> There is one direction, I would suggest, that would enable it to retain the marvellous architecture of the scientific model while shedding the restrictions that rob that model of so much relevance. *This would be the conversion of economics into an instrument of social science whose purpose and justification was not so much the elucidation of the way society actually behaves, as the formulation of the way it should behave.* To put it differently, it would change the purpose of economics away from the discovery of consequences of presumably known behavioral tendencies to the specification of the necessary behavioral patterns to enable society to reach a postulated goal.[95]

J. K. Galbraith in *Economics and the Public Purpose* calls for a "new Socialism" that would set up "full organization under public ownership" of the areas in which the market has "failed", such as housing, medical care, and transportation; convert large "mature" corporations into government corporations such as the Tennessee Valley Authority; and superimpose a public authority to coordinate overall economic planning. Galbraith takes pot shots at the "technostructure" that exists in both big government and big business, but he is too loyal a Keynesian to opt for anything that could reduce the power and size of the public sector. In a statement quoted by *Business Week*, January 5, 1974, Galbraith said: "For government to get increasingly into economic planning and intervention is not necessarily the right direction. It's the inevitable direction." Galbraith and Bell represent the more

149

literate and popular advocates of the philosophy of social amelioration by the superior wisdom of dedicated scientists. Other intellectuals carry this philosophy to a more extreme point; B. F. Skinner would manipulate the environment to control personality development and John Rawls would impose a complete and total equality to make a "true" democracy.

Politicians must deal with facts, not theories, with people as individuals, not as disembodied abstractions. It is this daily contact with reality that makes most politicians realists or, as some claim, cynics. But political realism or cynicism is a necessary antidote to the intellectual arrogance of certain social scientists who consider mankind a proper subject for experimentation. The politician is, or should be, primarily concerned with the basic political problem of erecting a legal framework of laws under which people can work and live with a reasonable amount of happiness and freedom. The erection of such a political or legal framework is not a process that follows a rational or scientific process of logical deduction. It is an historical process developed over time by the slow but constant interaction of man and his environment. Justice Benjamin N. Cardozo has described this historical process as follows:

> No lawgiver meditating a code of laws conceived the system of feudal tenures. History built up the system and the law that went with it. Never by a process of logical deduction from the idea of abstract ownership could we distinguish the incidents of an estate in fee simple from those of an estate for life, or those of an estate for life from those of an estate for years.[96]

Justice Oliver Wendell Holmes was even more emphatic:

> If we consider the law of contract we find it full of history. The distinctions between debt, covenant and assumpsit are merely historical. The classification of certain obligations to pay money imposed by the law irrespective of any bargain or quasi-contract, is merely historical. The doctrine of consideration is merely historical. The effect given to a seal is to be explained by history alone.[97]

The culmination of this historic process is a body of laws that represent the accumulated social experience and political wisdom of a people. The validity of this historic process is denied by the followers of Comte, Marx, and Hegel, who would replace law and the legal-political system by one based on "Reason" or "Historic Materialism" or "Scientific Socialism" and replace the legislators by bureaucrats who would impose their ideal system on the people by executive decree.

Political decisions are based on political judgment, ethical values, legal precedents, history, and the logic of events. All are variables. A social scientist could feed all the variables into a computer, and the answer would merely reflect his own innate bias. Thus, any attempt at a solution imposed by a scientific élite in matters of politics must presuppose a bias against historic experience and individual political rights and a faith in some transcendental ideal that justifies the use of absolute power.

Critics may interject that democracy and liberty are ideals, too, and that demagogues can be as dangerous and impractical as a scientific élite. When politicians become demagogues and appeal to popular prejudices under the name of liberty, they are subverting democracy, not supporting it. Civil liberty under a government of laws is not an abstraction; it must inhere in some sensible object that can be defined by law. The object it defines, rather than the definition, is the essential element. The Constitution of the United States can be copied, and has been copied, by many other nations, but it has not brought them democracy American-style. Theories of liberty and democracy are easy to write, but they do not create the institutions of liberty and democracy. Liberty may be defined philosophically in many different ways, but in real life the liberty enjoyed by an American citizen is the liberty embodied in historic institutions that are the result of centuries of political struggle — a struggle reflected, not only in American political institutions, but in the system of Western jurisprudence that has evolved slowly and painfully since the codes of Justinian.

The average politician is likely to be skeptical of abstract social theories. At the same time he cannot afford to ignore the need for new social legislation to meet changes in the political and economic environment. He looks to the social scientist for guidance and advice, but he cannot evade the final responsibility which is his to sift and select from the available theories — there are always theories to support opposite views — those that are consistent with the political realities of his situation. The theories of Jefferson and Hamilton, Calhoun and Webster, Hoover and Roosevelt were dramatically antagonistic. In practice, that is, in the political arena, they were tested and accepted or rejected. In a democracy the legislative assembly is the forum in which all social theories are debated; the elected politician has the final responsibility to reject them or enact them into law[98]

The function of the politician realistically to appraise and sift social theories before enacting them into law was stated by a lawmaker who was also a political philosopher: "Whenever I speak against theory I means always a weak, erroneous, fallacious, unfounded or imperfect theory; and the way of discovering that it is a false theory is by comparing with practice. This is the true touchstone with all theories which regard man and the affairs of man — Does it suit his nature as modified by his habits?"[99]

Social theorists are sometimes prone to exaggerate their importance. Keynes once observed rather loftily that "the ideas of economists and political philosophers, both when they are right and when they are wrong, are more powerful than is commonly understood. Indeed the world is ruled by little else."

It is not unusual for social scientists to discuss capitalism without mentioning coal or oil and without naming Watt, Hargreaves, Eli Whitney, McCormack, Diesel, Marconi, and other innovators, without whose inventions modern industrial capitalism is unthinkable. It is possible that modern capitalism or modern industrial society could exist without Ricardo, Marshall, Walras, Comte, or even Keynes. But modern life is unthinkable without the steam engine, the internal-combustion engine, radio, T.V., the electric generator, the airplane, and other modern inventions and the coal and oil to make them work. Joseph Schumpeter may have come closer to the truth when he argued that progress is made by an innovate élite composed mainly of

151

inventors and entrepreneurs. To this élite group should be added the legislator whose function it is to devise political, legal, family, and social institutions that permit inventors and entrepreneurs to work on their inventions and their enterprises with maximum freedom and incentives.

The legislator is in the front line of political reform. Every day is a battle in which he fights the forces of action and reaction. Each day he lays his political life on the line. He cannot avoid the consequences of his acts; his enemies will see to that. He cannot afford to sponsor theories that do not work in practice; his constituents will see to that.

Politicians deal with human beings as individuals with all their frailties, strengths, and vices. On the other hand, economists sometimes become so entranced by mathematical solutions to economic problems that they tend to overlook the human or political element in the equation. This attitude was criticized by Myrdal in his *The Political Element in the Development of Economic Theory.* Only if economists are modest in their claims and renounce all pretensions to postulate universal laws and norms can they promote effectively their practical objectives, viz., to keep political arguments rational, that is to say, to base them on as complete and as correct a knowledge of the facts as possible.[100]

Any social system that tries to bypass the political process built on custom, law, and elected legislatures by a system of direct controls manipulated directly or indirectly by an élite class endowed with superior education, technical competence, or some transcendental mandate must be viewed with some misgivings by all those who believe in the democratic process. Rule by the élite is not without its pitfalls, as George Santayna pointed out: "It is better that we should blunder freely in love, in politics, and in religion, than that we should follow the prescriptions of external authorities, dubious authorities at best, which might save us a few knocks, only to lead us and the world, in their ponderous organized blindness, to the most hideous catastrophe."[101]

The blind faith of the followers of Comte and Marx in men's ability to control their social environment and "fashion their own history"; the Cartesian boast that men are the "masters and possessors of nature"; the supremely confident belief that man can, by his own labor and reason, remake the world in his image — all have brought man to a climactic confrontation with nature. It now seems likely that man's efforts to remake the world may either cause it to blow up in his face or make it unfit for human habitation. It is up to the political wisdom of the legislators to see that neither will happen. A tax law that incorporates social and environmental values in the price system would make a significant contribution toward a better balanced economy and one more in harmony with nature. It would give legislators a better guide for setting national priorities than the one-sided planning for growth of the national gross product that now represents the highest standard of value for national welfare and economic progress.

6. Planning For Growth In The Gross National Product

Since the 1940s the gross national product, commonly called the GNP, has been the sacred myth and the outward symbol of the modern society. The American public is fascinated by the economists' charts showing its growth year by year. When it reached the trillion dollar level, there was a national sigh of relief as if a new sound barrier had been passed and its growth could resume at supersonic speeds.

Before the 1940s the GNP concept was neither well known nor widely accepted. According to Professor Kenneth E. Boulding, the concept was basic to Keynesian economics: "The basic notions of the Keynesian theory are so simple that once they are grasped it is difficult to realize the desperate intellectual struggle by which they were evolved. The basic concept is that of the Gross National Product — the total value measured in constant prices; of all goods and services produced."[102] Simon Kuznets did pioneer work in this field in the United States, although some observers claim that a British White Paper prepared by James Meade and Richard Stone published in April 1941 was the first real exposition of the concept based on national product estimates at market prices. These GNP estimates and statistics were intended to help the British and American governments mobilize industrial capacity and resources for war production. After World War II the GNP concept was not abandoned; it grew in importance and became firmly established in all advanced nations. The GNP became associated with the idea of growth, for measuring a lifeless form is not very exciting.

The excitement of the GNP is based on watching it grow and associating national progress and individual welfare with that growth. The vital interests of the nation and the individual are reflected by the GNP; for that reason, it is watched as anxiously as a doctor watches the fever chart of his patient. Rapid growth of the GNP is hailed as the triumphant vindication of national progress and per-capita gain in welfare. In the United States a decline in the growth of GNP vis-à-vis that of Russia, Japan, or Germany plunges the nation into agonies of self-doubt and causes critics to attack the deficiencies of the American system compared to that of more "progressive" nations with faster growing GNP rates.

The postwar GNP myth largely replaced the Socialist myth of equal distribution of wealth that had such a powerful hold on the collective consciousness of the world before World War II. After the war people came to believe that growth was the answer to poverty; that the secret to a more abundant life was, not in cutting up the existing GNP pie in more even shares, but in making the pie bigger so that the shares could be bigger. Before World War II even Kuznets could not convince Roosevelt that there was such a thing as unlimited GNP growth. The New Dealers were more interested in correcting inequalities of income and breaking down the excessive concentration of wealth than in growth. Roosevelt was certain that the last American frontier has been reached. The task, he said, was to administer and distribute more equitably what was produced, not to try to expand industrial capacity that was already overbuilt and causing problems of overproduction. World War II demonstrated the fact that GNP planning produced miracles, and the lesson was not forgotten. The state moved in the direction of *dirigisme*, and the GNP became the symbol of state planning in peacetime.

The modern state, capitalist or Communist, watches its GNP growth chart with anxious concern. It will not willingly suffer it to decline. No effort or sacrifice is spared to make the GNP rise at the fastest possible rate. The GNP growth curves of all nations are watched; the world judges how they stand in the international race for economic power, which is equated with political and military power.

Some economists downgrade the GNP, but most accept it as a symbol of their cult, which confers on them a special status as arbiters of national policy. Said Galbraith: "St. Peter is assumed to ask applicants only what they have done to increase the GNP. There are good reasons for this insistence on the totality of economic goals. It arrests what otherwise would be a disconcerting obsolescence in the profession of economics. For so long as social achievement is coterminous with economic performance, economists are the highest arbiters of social policy. Otherwise not. Theirs is an eminence not to be sacrificed casually."[103]

The United States Government has not found economic problems so entirely amenable to solution by government fiscal monetary policy as Keynesian economists once so confidently predicted they would be. According to Keynes, the level of business activity is determined largely by monetary expenditures for products and services. Theoretically, at a given level of monetary spending, the economy would be fully employed, with no tendency to inflation or deflation. This ideal equilibrium could be reached, according to Keynes, by proper government fiscal-monetary policies. Thirty-six years after the publication of the *General Theory*, with government facing severe inflation and unemployment and monetary problems, Arthur M. Okun, former head of the Presidential Council of Economic Advisers, said wistfully: "Judged by its contribution to solving social welfare, to solving the big social problems, fiscal-monetary policy can be regarded as trivial and perhaps somewhat obsolete."[104]

Theories of economic growth or progress are not new, of course. Simon Kuznets noted that theories of growth have fascinated the general public and have challenged economists since the days of Adam Smith:

There are significant differences among the views of Adam Smith on the growth process as caused by the expansion of the market which results in increased division of labor and the competitive action of entrepreneurs watched over by the state to prevent the collusion to which they are prone; those of Malthus and Ricardo, who shared the conviction that pressure of population growth and exhaustion of land would make the entrepreneurs (profitmakers) helpless against a progressive reduction of their share in the nation's product and hence against the arrival (considered fairly imminent) of the stationary state; of Karl Marx, whose labor theory of value provides the basis for the theory of exploitation ... and of Schumpeter, who views the entrepreneurs as an elite group of innovators capable

154

of overcoming the resistance to change of the traditionalist and numerically preponderant groups in the economy.[105]

Economists have searched for a theory of growth that would be applicable under any and all historical conditions, for "the ultimate test of theoretical analysis is the extrapolative value of its conclusions," that is, the universal applicability of the theory, such as found in the laws of physics. However, such a theory is difficult to formulate because market prices are the basis for computing the gross national product and other national statistical indices of value, and most economists admit that value is difficult to define in quantitative terms.

Said Henry C. Simons: "Economy implies valuations; and valuation is peculiarly and essentially relative. The prices with which rigorous economics deal are pure relations; and relatives cannot be summated into meaningful totals. Market prices afford only the most meager clues (or none at all) to the 'value' of *all* goods produced and services rendered."[106]

A purely economic theory of growth, according to Kuznets, is an impossibility. "Much as one may regret leaving the shelters of an economic discipline, it does seem as if an economic theory of economic growth is an impossibility if by 'economic' we mean staying within the limits set by the tools of economic discipline proper, even within the broader limits of classical and Marxian economics and all the more within the much narrower limits that have prevailed since the middle of the last century." These passages were written by Kuznets at a time (1955) when economic growth was regarded by all as the highest desideratum, the ultimate goal of natural economic activity. Growth is now (1973) regarded in a different light. The need for a theory of "growth" is no longer pressing, since growth itself is not accepted as an unmixed blessing. What is wanted is a theory of economic health in which growth *under certain conditions* is one of the factors to be considered, but not the only or even the most important one. The people are finding that growth in the body economic can be malignant as well as benign, that it can lead to environmental destruction as well as to consumer affluence.

The theory of never-ending GNP growth, or perpetual progress, is regarded today by many economists as somewhat obsolete. Paul E. Samuelson — like Kuznets, a Nobel Prize winner in economics — made this observation in April 1973: "To many thoughtful people, the prospect of 'healthy' growth in the gross national product (GNP) is not unlike the spectacle of an arrogant young racer, barreling along in his Ferrari down a dead-end country road."[107] The GNP measures only market-connected and market-priced goods. Growth of the GNP is, therefore, growth of consumerism, which has been exposed as a hollow valueless system. The idea that growth of the GNP can be planned by government economists is also misleading, for it masks the problem of social growth as one of pure economic goals based on production targets, regardless of whether the product is guns, books, whiskey, bread, cars, toys, works of art, or shoddy goods. Even if the economic wizards could produce the economic miracle of perpetual GNP growth, it is doubtful that they could persuade the people to follow them to the end. The specter of ecological disaster is already visible not too far down *that* road.

There is considerable logic as well as merit in the ancient concept of nature as something sacred, to be respected, even revered, rather than something to be profaned, in Durkheim's definition, for "vulgar things that interest only our physical natures." In other words, desecration of nature by acts of pollution, waste, and destruction is a process that, even in a scientific age, could be considered taboo.

Ancient civilizations, such as the Egyptian, worshipped nature and deified the supreme source of energy, the sun. Modern rational man regards this belief as a superstition. However, modern scientific civilization is only a few centuries old and is already showing symptoms of possible eventual exhaustion or suicide. It may not last 3000 years, as the Egyptian did. Man's belief in eternal progress by GNP growth may, in time, be considered a superstitious belief in a god called materialism, more destructive than a belief in a sun god. It is neither possible nor desirable that social scientists should worship the sun god Ra or Rousseau's cult of nature, but it might be highly desirable for economists to bring nature and other "externalities" back into the economic system, so that a true value may be put on both human and nonhuman resources. Modern man cannot afford to ravage and plunder nature on the "rational" theory that only *his* labor and *his* consumption needs have any value. There is ample scientific evidence in the biological sciences to support the view that man is an important part, but only a part, of the natural environment, or of natural evolution, or of some unfathomable design, natural or supernatural.

7. Energy Stabilization

Economic growth is tied directly to the utilization of energy, whether animate, chemical, electric, solar, nuclear, or other.

In the agrarian society, stabilization of energy at about one horsepower-hour per day of mechanical energy per capita was reached in some areas by about 4000 B.C. By that time destructive practices of soil energy utilization (slash-and-burn agriculture) had been replaced by methods of soil energy conservation (the use of natural fertilizers, cover crops, fallow strips, and crop rotation) that made soil energy reusable indefinitely. In some areas of the world — China, India, Egypt, the Danube basin, for example — the fertility of the soil was preserved for thousands of years, and life continued uninterrupted on the same economic plane despite recurrent invasions and violent political upheavals.[108] It has been estimated that in ancient Sumeria the crop of wheat was nearly 32 bushels per acre, a yield not surpassed in fairly recent times. But soil fertility was lost in many areas for considerable periods of time. It is difficult to believe, for example, that North Africa was once the granary of the Roman Empire. There was a loss of population in Greece in the two centuries before Christ and in Italy during the 4th and 5th centuries A.D. It has been suggested that the loss of population and the decline of Greek and Roman power can be attributed to a decline in or exhaustion of soil fertility brought on by overcultivation. Undoubtedly, the failure of an agrarian nation properly to utilize and conserve its soil energy resources often led to national decline in population and power. On the other hand, it must be noted that dearth of national energy resources sometimes compelled nations to migrate and conquer more fertile lands. The migrations of the Turks from Central Asia, that of the Bedouins from the Arabian desert, and other mass migrations were probably caused by pressure of population and declining food energy resources.

Faced with known limits of energy resources or known limits of environmental tolerances to energy consumption, industrial society faces the same problems of energy stabilization as did the agrarian society, but on a much higher and more critical level. For the first time in history man is faced with potential natural and man-made catastrophes that threaten his biological survival. History has recorded the decline and fall of mighty empires but, looked at from a global perspective, such catastrophes appear as minor disasters that affected only a few members of the human race. The vast majority of people survived and continued living in their own isolated environment. The political and economic blunders of the Egyptians, the Greeks, the Romans, and the Mongols brought disaster on their own nations, and their neighbors suffered or prospered as a result. Nevertheless, large sections of the globe remained untouched and unaffected by their fate.

The world today faces a different situation. Atomic and chemical warfare poses the threat of annihilation for all mankind. Even if there were survivors of a nuclear holocaust, it is probable that they would be relatively few in number and perhaps biologically damaged by radiation.

If this peril can be averted, there remains the equally grave contingency of racial suicide by starvation or suffocation. It has been claimed by neo-Malthusians that, at the rate the population is multiplying and at the rate pollution is increasing and poisoning the biosphere, it will not be long before the world will run out of fresh air, fresh water, and/or food. The early destructive agricultural practice of "slash-and-burn" has been paralleled by the early industrial practices of "waste-and-consume." Such priceless, irreplaceable national resources as iron, oil, coal, copper, and tungsten have been consumed and wasted and are being consumed and wasted at a shocking rate. A few hundred years from now, future generations may inhabit a ravaged planet and will curse the 20th century as the age of industrial barbarism when men destroyed what had been, by comparison, an unspoiled garden of Eden. Unless science comes to the rescue with ersatz substitutes and new sources of energy — which the world confidently assumes it will — the planetary economy could run down and enter a new dark age of famine and destitution.

Scientists say that it is doubtful that the world's agricultural resources could support a population of more than 12 billion people. Before this ultimate population limit is reached — at whatever figure it is set — the strain on agriculture may produce a weakness that would make it vulnerable to some

157

infection, virus, blight, insect plague, drought, or other natural disaster. The agriculture of the United States and other nations that are following the lead of American scientists is based on a somewhat narrow and unstable foundation. It requires large inputs of energy. An American farmer may use up more energy in his farm machinery than the food energy contained in the crop he harvests. Modern agriculture, like any other industry, depends on energy in the form of electricity and gasoline. It could not operate without the roads, products, automatic food machinery, motorized transportation, capital investments, and other components of an industrial society. This dependence on large amounts of energy and technology is both a serious weakness and a great strength. Curtailment of energy would result in a serious loss of farm output. Another weakness is the overspecialization of plant culture. A natural environment such as a primitive wilderness is a complex ecosystem in which plant and animal life in great variety support one another. Because of its complexity, the natural environment is invulnerable to most natural calamities and may be said to be self-perpetuating, because all living things are kept in a natural balance.

Man upsets this natural balance by the artificial culture of plants. In a primitive agricultural society the damage may be slight and easily repairable, but under modern farming conditions the natural complex ecosystem is violently disrupted by machinery and chemical agents and artificial plant breeding. The result is a simplified artificial environment built around one plant, which is grown in huge quantities over an immense land area. Obviously, such a man-made environment is less stable and less immune to the destructive forces of nature than a more complex natural environment. There is historic proof that overspecialization carries with it the seeds of disaster. According to Toynbee:

> When Attica, on Solon's initiative, led the way from a regime of mixed farming to a regime of specialized agriculture for export, this technical advance was followed by an outburst of energy and growth in every sphere of Attic life. The next chapter of the story, however, takes a different and a sinister turn. The next stage of technical advance was an increase in the scale of operations through the organization of mass production based on slave labor ... the social consequence was the depopulating of the countryside and the creation of a parasitic urban proletariat in the cities, and more particularly in Rome itself. Not all the efforts of successive generations of Roman reformers, from the Gracchi onwards, could avail to rid the Roman World of this social blight which the last advance in agricultural techniques had brought upon it. The plantation-slave system persisted until it collapsed spontaneously in consequence of the breakdown of the money economy on which it was dependent for its profits.[109]

The parallel with modern conditions of agriculture in the United States is not too far-fetched if one substitutes corporate farms for *latifundia* and machine work for slave labor. The mass production and overspecialization for the world market; the creation of a parasitic urban proletariat; the depopulation of the countryside; the social blight brought about by the uprooting of rural families from farms and country towns — all these are visible on the American scene in a much more exaggerated form than in its Roman counterpart.

One is left to wonder how American society could survive a period of grave crisis in agriculture brought about by the collapse of the world money market; or by a serious loss of energy in the production or distribution process; or by a natural disaster such as a prolonged drought, insect infestations, and plant virus disease. This possibility seems rather remote today, and there is very little public apprehension on that score. The miraculous capacity of American agriculture is generally believed to be inexhaustible.

However, one observer believes that American agriculture is courting disaster in following a policy of mass production for the market and of "decreasing ecosystemic complexity and stability," that is, increasing specialization in cash crops:

> It must be remembered that man is an animal, that he survives biologically or not at all . . . We may ask, however, if the chances for human survival might not be enhanced by reversing the modern trend of successions in order to increase the diversity and stability of local, regional and national ecosystems. . . . It seems to me that the trend toward decreasing ecosystemic complexity and stability, rather than threats of pollution, overpopulation or energy famine, is the ultimate economic problem immediately confronting man. It may also be the most difficult to solve, since the solution cannot easily be reconciled with the value, goals, interest and political and economic institutions prevailing in industrialized and industrializing nations.[110]

The trend toward greater specialization and mass production in American agriculture is increasing and seems irreversible. The United States is losing ground vis-à-vis Japan, West Germany, Sweden, France, and other nations in technological innovation and production costs. The United States is also facing the necessity of importing huge quantities of foreign oil at a price estimated to reach as high as $20 billion a year. The government is depending on agriculture, not industry, to pay this bill for imported oil. In 1973 all controls on farm production were removed. The top earner of foreign exchange will be, according to experts, the soy bean, not the automobile; wheat and corn, not industrial products.

Professor Ernest R. May, director of the Institute of Politics at Harvard, has described this trend as a return to an earlier historic stage:

> The capacity of the Japanese in particular, and of other nations, to outdo us in technological innovation and production seems to me quite clear. So it is possible that we will revert by the next century to the kind of role that we were playing in the mid 19th century, with our great strength being agriculture rather than industry. That is certainly a place where we retain our comparative advantage . . . Look at the trend in the structure of the American economy. The percentage of the labor force in industrial production is steadily going down. Seventy per cent of the working people are engaged in providing services. . . . People just don't want to do the work, and there is a good question as to why they should. If we can grow corn, cattle, and hogs and do that very efficiently and sell them to the Japanese in return for automobiles and TV sets, why shouldn't we?[111]

Agricultural resources are basic; without them, life cannot be sustained unless food is imported, which is not a permanent solution. To depend entirely on market forces to guide and develop agriculture leads inevi-

159

tably to overspecialization in cash crops for the world market. The answer does not lie in a return to acreage or market controls by the government or price subsidies tied to world market prices. Food prices should not only reflect market priorities, but should also conserve and strengthen the agricultural resources of the nation; do the least possible damage to the local or regional ecosystem; and make food products available to the population on a need basis, as well as on a market demand basis. In other words, food prices should reflect social values and total energy values in addition to purely market utility values. But how can food prices — or prices in general — be made to include nonmarket values? The usual method is by government action in the form of taxes and price controls. The taxes most generally used for this purpose are consumption taxes or commodity taxes such as excises or those used in the tariff system.

But would not this use of the tax powers of the government to create a price structure incorporating social values call for a tremendous increase in bureaucracy in the public sector and the virtual elimination of the market in the private sector? This question would require a yes answer if the tax were an income tax. But under a tax on all commodities along the line of the tariff, the market would not require regulation or control by a government bureaucracy. The tax incorporating social value, added to the price, would not be assessed and collected by a government bureaucracy, but would be fixed by Federal statute law, that is, by Congress, and collections would be automatic, as in the case of sales or commodity taxes.

A system of commodity taxation comparable to the tariff system, but applied to the internal market — an internal tariff — would make possible the conservation and stabilization of energy at reasonable levels consistent with a comfortable economic rate of growth, as set by political consensus. But what is a comfortable energy rate of growth?

Russell E. Train, head of the Environmental Protection Agency, puts the target level of energy stabilization at 2 or 3 per cent annual growth: "Our demand is rising 5% a year and the U.S. already uses 30% of the world's energy. I don't think we can continue that sort of exponential growth. We ought to set a national policy of reaching a lower energy growth rate, and I've suggested 2% or 3% as a rough figure."[112]

The problem of energy stabilization is not a simple one, for it not only involves the setting of an arbitrary rate of energy consumption, but the establishment of priorities over all economic activities so that the reduced energy is utilized for maximum social benefit. The Nixon administration grappled with this problem in 1973 when it was faced with a serious oil shortage. It tried desperately to avoid rationing and to maintain market distribution:

> William E. Simon, the nation's new energy czar, has said he wants to see if more generous reliance on the classic market mechanism — price as means of equating demand with supply — would help solve the energy crisis. But there is evidence that the market response will not provide an acceptable answer to the problem of cutting gasoline use by 20% or 30%. ... The problem is the often-demonstrated reluctance of the motorists to change their driving habits. Auto commuters, for

example, are hesitant — and sometimes unable — to switch to mass transit, and cost does not seem to be a paramount in this decision, anyway. . . . Of course, there are other arguments against massive gasoline price increases, and those might effectively choke off this route as a conservation measure. If costs were allowed to seek a free market level, oil companies would get windfall profits, but supplies would not be appreciably increased during the crisis period. If an excise tax were imposed instead, low- and middle-income workers who rely on autos to commute would be penalized disproportionarely, which explains the proposal of various ways to rebate the tax to them. . . . All of which makes some economists think that rationing, now at the bottom of Simon's priorities list, may be the only answer. The administration is reluctant to take this route because it believes that rationing will lead to an active black market and create an unnecessary bureaucracy.[113]

Under the present tax and price system, it is impossible for the market to handle the allocation of energy resources, and the market failure may force the government to add another layer of bureaucracy to take over the market function and replace it with rationing. Rationing, however, is not an acceptable alternative to the market. Milton Friedman in colorful language stated the alternative thus: "Two hundred and ten million persons each with a separate incentive to economize; or 210 million persons dragooned by men with guns to cut down their use of oil — can there be any doubt which is the better system?"[114]

The need to restore a normal market in oil is obvious, but under the present price system, which places an artificial value on natural energy and which is influenced by the intervention of powerful nonmarket forces, it is difficult to see how the market price mechanism alone can solve the present energy crisis or provide a long-range solution to the problem of energy stabilization.

The market operates within a political framework of laws that define the function of market activities. In the 19th century an imposing legal structure was built to support the classic laissez-faire free market system in America. Added to the Constitutional guarantees of private property was the doctrine of the sanctity of contracts, patent protection, laws for the handling of negotiable instruments, tax laws that operated through the market price system, laws relating to currency, banking, and insurance, and laws relating to forms of association, especially the laws passed in the 1880s that declared the corporation a juristic or legal person. According to Robert Riggs:

> The great transformation that permitted men for the first time to escape from poverty rested on two fundamental bases: (1) the growth of markets, which in the United States had its origins in increasing foreign demand and in population growth under conditions of unlimited land; and (2) the evaluation of secure private property rights, including the private right to intellectual property. These developments, stretching back for centuries, have no precise dates of origin. But the Constitution was a major landmark, and in the first half of the nineteenth century, when private property rights became firmly established, several convergent influences finally culminated. By the post-Civil War era, self-sustaining growth had become the normal condition of the American economy. Of course, nothing guaranteed the continuation of these conditions. But in fact the rights of private property were consolidated and extended during the half century after the Civil War at the same time that markets were growing at unprecedented rates.[115]

161

The two developments were not entirely coincidental. According to Boorstin, "Without a general American legal system, technically defined and available in books, the free commerce among our states and the industrial unity of our nation might have been impossible."[116]

The erosion of private property rights since the passage of the 16th Amendment has undermined the legal framework that James Madison, Alexander Hamilton, John Marshall, Joseph Story, and many other statesmen and jurists had so patiently erected. The legal concept of private property has been attacked as inherently antisocial, and in its place there has developed a new concept of property that gives the state the right to share in the income and disposition of private property on a joint ownership basis. The law covering the sanctity of contracts has been modified to include the state as one of the parties to all contracts to protect the interest of the underprivileged. There is being erected a new legal structure in which property is defined as belonging to the community. The individual may have an equity in it, but his equity is always subject to the prior claim of the state. This claim is exercised by many legal means, but primarily by the tax powers of the government. No property is immune from tax assessment today.

The erosion of the legal framework built around the laissez-faire market of the 18th and 19th centuries is an historic process that Justice Cardozo has described in the words: "Liberty was conceived at first as something static and absolute. The Declaration of Independence had enshrined it. The blood of revolutions had sanctified it. The political philosophy of Rousseau and of Locke and later of Herbert Spencer and of the Manchester school of economists had dignified and rationalized it. Laissez-faire was not only a counsel of caution which statesmen would do well to heed. It was a categorical imperative which statesmen, as well as judges, must obey."[117] Justice Cardozo puts the turn of the century as the beginning of a new epoch and goes on to say: "It is the dissenting opinion of Justice Holmes, which men will turn to in the future as the beginning of an era. In the instance, it was the voice of a minority. In principle, it has become the voice of a new dispensation, which has written itself into law. 'The Fourteenth Amendment does not enact Mr. Herbert Spencer's *Social Statics!*' 'A Constitution is not intended to embody a particular economic theory, whether of paternalism and the organic relation of the citizens to the state, or of laissez-faire...' That is the conception of liberty which is dominant today."

The conception, in essence, is that private property rights are not sacred and that the "final cause of law is the welfare of society." This new legal conception was elaborated in the decisions of such later justices as Brandeis, Hughes, Frankfurter, and Warren. It is now, of course, a majority view.

The historic process that destroyed the laissez-faire or free market system cannot be reversed. To believe that former conditions can be restored is unrealistic. The market must operate under a new technological environment with a high energy base quite different from a simpler environment based on steam and manual labor. To do so, the market must have a political framework that permits it to carry out its functions for distribution of goods and allocations of resources in a manner compatible with this new environment.

A consumption tax, such as an internal tariff, set by the highest lawmaking body on all commodities and services in accordance with the traditional tariff principles of social value and national interest, would give Congress the opportunity to set national priorities through the market price system. Under the internal tariff, the market could serve as a means for carrying out an energy stabilization program in accordance with the goals of society; the energy stabilization program would be a Congressional program developed by legislative process, not an executive program imposed by decree or by rationing.

Congress is not unfamiliar with the operation of a commodity tax system. From the first days of the republic until 1932 the commodity tax system known as the protective tariff was the main source of revenue for the Federal government and the chief instrument of both foreign and domestic economic policy. The tariff covered every commodity that entered foreign commerce and almost every single commodity that moved in internal or domestic trade. The commodities that moved in the internal market were not taxed, but the tariff rate on the same commodities moving in foreign trade had a very direct effect on the internal market prices. Congressional tariff policy was, therefore, a means of regulating both internal and external market prices and conditions. This economic power was recognized and consciously used by the architects of tariff policy to achieve political and economic goals they considered desirable and for the national interest. The use Congress made of its tax powers under the tariff illustrates the great potential of a commodity tax system, its many inherent advantages, and the relative ease with which it was adapted to the legislative process and the market economy.

Chapter
V

TAXES ON CONSUMPTION

1. Hamilton's Tax Policy

Through taxation modern governments redistribute income, finance social welfare, and pursue other national economic and political goals. The importance of taxation as the main instrument of national economic policy is widely recognized. "There is almost universal agreement also among economists that by far the most powerful instrument of government stabilization is the system of public finance, and especially the tax system. Banking policy and other indirect controls have their place, but it is a secondary one. The shift from regarding the tax system simply as a method for raising money for government to spend to the view of taxes as an instrument for stabilizing the whole economy is perhaps the most fundamental change in policy outlook of this period."[118]

The "period" referred to by Professor Kenneth E. Boulding is the 1930's, when the Roosevelt revolution or the Keynesian revolution — one term is used by politicians, the other by economists — made the government the active director and partner of the private economy. However, the belief that the government has the responsibility, even the duty, to manage the economy for the public welfare is not a modern concept. In American politics it goes back to Alexander Hamilton and his theory of the protective tariff.

The protective tariff is now obsolete. It has been replaced by the income tax and other personal and payroll taxes as the main source of revenue for the government. The tariff, as conceived by Hamilton, was a comprehensive system of commodity taxation. The tax factor in prices was explicit and recognized in the tariff system, whereas in the income tax system the tax factor in prices is hidden and unrecognized. The tax factor in commodity prices under the tariff was identifiable as economic, for raising revenue to pay the expenses of government, or political, for promoting manufacturing, for protecting domestic labor against foreign labor, and for subsidizing farmers. Enemies of the tariff liked to point out that the political objectives were not always, if ever, achieved, but this was part of the Congressional and public debate.

In the 19th century the protective tariff was the most powerful instrument of national economic policy in America and Europe. The income tax was introduced and perfected in England, but the initial development of the protective tariff as an economic plan for promoting industrial growth was the achievement of American statemen, notably Alexander Hamilton and Henry Clay. Hamilton, in particular, may be said to be its father. In the 16th, 17th, and 18th centuries, the tariff was used as a means of accumulating gold reserves, creating a favorable balance of trade to finance the expansion of the national European state. It was used by the elder Pitt and Colbert to establish and finance British and French colonies. In the latter half of the 18th century the tariff system and the whole mercantile system came under attack by the rising bourgeois class and by such economists as Adam Smith who believed in free trade. But Hamilton, despite his admiration for Smith, was a political realist who realized that free trade, while suitable for England, could not serve the best interests of the infant American republic. He went back to the tariff and adapted it to the needs of the American economy, making it an instrument for transforming an "undeveloped" agrarian economy into a highly urbanized industrial nation.

Hamilton, like Franklin and Jefferson, was a versatile genius, merchant, lawyer, statesman, soldier, financier, linguist, and political philosopher. He shares with Madison chief credit for the *Federalist* papers, which embody the basic political and social doctrine underlying the Constitution. Although he had reservations about the final draft of the Constitution, he did as much as, or more than, any other person to win its ratification. When Washington became President he selected Hamilton, then only 34, to be his Secretary of the Treasury; in effect, however, Hamilton became the prime minister. Almost single-handedly, Hamilton gave the new republic its economic structure and mapped out an economic program for future national development that was followed with minor deviations by future national administrations until 1913.

Hamilton's program was denounced and attacked by Jefferson and Jackson. Jefferson threw out excise taxes in 1802, and Jackson killed the First Bank of the United States in 1836. Still, the economic structure that Hamilton had built remained basically untouched by partisan politics. Jefferson conceded that the "ideas of Hamilton" on the public debt and the tariff would be difficult to change: "We can pay off his debts in 15 years, but we can never get rid of his financial system."[119]

Not until Cleveland's term was there a frontal attack on the protective tariff policy by a President or a major party in office, Hamilton's economic reports still have a relevance to modern students of government finance, according to Louis Hacker, a professor of economics and one of Hamilton's biographers. Hamilton's ideas for government guidance of the economy and for the promotion of industry for the general welfare are common and generally accepted ideas today. Since the New Deal, the Democratic Party has been more Hamiltonian than Jeffersonian, but in his day Hamilton's economic policies were considered pernicious by classic economists and Jeffersonian liberals.

Paradoxically, neither the income tax nor the protective tariff was the work of economists. The leading economists of the day were either indifferent to or strongly opposed to both. The income tax was completely ignored by Ricardo in his study of English taxation, a glaring omission considering Ricardo's interest in taxation and the fact that he lived during the gestation period of income tax legislation. This fact has been noted by Professor Carl S. Shoup in his book, *Ricardo on Taxation*: "Oddly enough, Ricardo devotes no chapter, no paragraph even, to the income tax, although he had just lived through a period when it had played a leading role in the British wartime tax drama."[120]

This hostile or indifferent attitude was shared by the leading economists of the day, particularly those who belonged to the classic school. From Smith to Mill, the classic economists were in favor of free trade and free markets, that is, free of government interference. Both the income tax and the protective tariff were contrary to what they considered orthodox economic principles. These economists vehemently opposed both political controls over the market and government interventionist policies. They were not opposed to a *revenue* tariff with flat nondiscriminatory rates for raising revenue. They were opposed to a *protective* tariff, with discriminatory rates set to protect or favor some industries and trades and to inhibit or penalize others. This latter type they considered a regression to the hated economic policy of mercantilism or Colbertism, which they contended had stifled economic growth by the crushing burden of government bureaucracy and red tape.

The first United States tariff went into effect on July 4, 1789, three months before Hamilton was appointed Secretary of the Treasury. It was the first act passed by the first Congress. It was enacted as a revenue measure for the "support of the government" and to "discharge the debts of the United States," but its preamble stated that it was also for the "encouragement and protection of manufactures." This intent was not carried out in the rate structure. It levied specific duties on a few commodities ranging from 7.5 per cent to 15 per cent *ad valorem*, but the bulk of imported commodities were taxed at a flat 5 per cent. The protection, if any, was minimal.

Tariffs had been set previously by the individual states under the Articles of Confederation. These state tariffs were designed to raise revenue, but some imposed discriminatory duties against the goods of other states, as well as foreign goods. The tariffs of some Northern states set duty rates to protect their infant industries or to encourage new ones.

In the colonial period Americans had been exposed to the concept of protection in the form of British mercantilism, which, however, protected English rather than American interests. The Iron Act of 1750, for example, encouraged the exportation of raw American iron to England by low duties, but prohibited Americans from manufacturing steel, slit iron, tin plate, and finished or semifinished mill products. Similar restrictions prohibited or discouraged American producers of woolen goods, hats, and other products that might have competed with British producers. England encouraged, by subsidies or by reduced duties, the production of certain American raw materials such as lumber, furs, tobacco, hemp, and naval stores. The British imperial plan was to keep America as an undeveloped raw material supplier and a market for English finished goods. This plan was not wholly successful because colonial assemblies encouraged local manufacturers by overt or covert acts including land grants, lotteries, loans, military exemptions for factory workers, and subsidies.

The British Board of Trade and Plantations, the ministry in charge of American affairs, frequently ordered the royal governors of the colonies to suppress American manufacturing, but the governors found this task either politically unpopular or economically difficult. By the time of the Boston massacre, the colonies had built up an industrial base sufficient to carry on the war and provide American Soldiers with better rifles than those used by British soldiers.

After the American and French revolutions, public opinion in the leading Western countries swung sharply away from mercantilism or government regulation of the economy and toward a system of free trade, or laissez-faire. Adam Smith's *Wealth of Nations*, published in 1776, became the Bible of the new doctrine of free trade and free markets. It was widely read in England, America, and France. It was well known to both Jefferson and Hamilton, and each extracted from this seminal work the theories that suited his political philosophy. Smith was violently opposed in principle to government regulation. In his opinion, the protective tariff was not the best way for a nation to promote economic growth. These views found favor with Jefferson, but not with Hamilton. Said Smith:

> When a landed nation oppresses either by high duties or by prohibitions the trade of foreign nations, it necessarily hurts its own interest...though, by this oppressive policy, a landed nation should be able to raise up artificers, manufacturers and merchants of its own, somewhat sooner than it could do by freedom of trade; a matter, however, which is not a little doubtful; yet it would raise them up, if one may say, prematurely, and before it was perfectly ripe for them. By raising up too hastily one species of industry which only replaces the stock which employs it, together with the ordinary profit, it would depress a species of industry which, over and above replacing the stock with its profit, affords likewise a neat product [a net profit]...
>
> The best and the most liberal and generous system, therefore,...the most advantageous method in which a landed nation can raise up artificers, manufacturers and merchants of its own, is to grant the most perfect freedom of trade to the artificers, manufacturers and merchants of all other nations.[121]

Protective tariffs were anathema to Smith and the classic economists of the 19th century because:

1. They were a form of government control of the economy; a regression to the mercantilist policies of the 16th, 17th, and 18th centuries, and contrary to the new "revolutionary" policies of free trade, "laissez-faire" and inalienable individual rights to "life, liberty and property."

2. They subsidized certain industries at the expense of the consumer. They created monopolies that diverted resources and manpower from efficient to inefficient industries and raised the cost of living for the general public.

3. They invited trade retaliation by other nations; this sometimes led to military retaliation and war.

The new theory of free trade found favor with Americans and Frenchmen who had in their revolutions overthrown a "tyrannical" system of government taxation and were in favor of maximum individual freedom and a minimum of taxation and government controls. Most Americans agreed with Smith that government controls over the economy were unnecessary and pernicious:

> Every individual is continually exerting himself to find out the most advantageous employment for whatever capital he can command. It is his own advantage, indeed, and not that of the society, which he has in view. But the study of his own advantage naturally, or rather necessarily leads him to prefer that employment which is most advantageous to the society ... The statesman who would attempt to direct private people in what manner they ought to employ their capital, would assume an authority which could safely be trusted, not only to no single person, but to no council or senate whatever ... to give the monopoly of the home-market to the produce of domestic industry, in any particular art or manufacture is in some measure to direct private people in what manner they ought to employ their capitals, and must, in almost all cases, be either a useless or hurtful regulation. If the produce of domestic can be brought there as cheap as that of foreign industry, the regulation is evidently useless. If it cannot, it must generally be hurtful.[122]

The charge that protective tariffs lead to countermeasures, which in turn lead to trade wars and shooting wars, is borne out by the history of European nations, according to Smith, who cites the French-Dutch war of 1672 as an example. Colbert, the minister of France, "by the tariff of 1667, imposed very high duties upon a great number of foreign manufacturers. Upon his refusing to moderate them in favour of the Dutch, they in 1671 prohibited the importation of the wines, brandies and manufactures of France. The war of 1672 seems to have been in part occasioned by this commercial dispute. The peace of Nimeguen put an end to it in 1678, by moderating some of those duties in favour of the Dutch, who in consequence took off their prohibitions."[123]

Smith and his generation had suffered from the effects of the regulations of trade by government and the cruel, senseless, and arbitrary methods sometimes used to enforce tax laws. Smith cites as an example the fact that in the reign of Elizabeth I the export of sheep was prohibited and "The exporter of sheep, lambs or rams, was for the first offense to forfeit all his goods for ever, to suffer a year's imprisonment, and then to have his left hand cut off in a market town upon a market day, to be there nailed up; and for the second offense to be adjudged a felon, and to suffer death accordingly."[124] In the reign of Charles II the exportation of wool was made a felony. Smith hoped that, for the sake of "national humanity," neither of these statutes was ever enforced.

These severe tax laws explain the general revulsion during the 18th century against all types of government controls and the popularity of economic theories of limited government controls, laissez-faire, and free trade. Smith did not lay the entire blame on government, but accused the merchants and manufacturers of pressuring the legislature to set high duties to protect their own selfish interests. Smith, like Hamilton, has been called an apostle of capitalism and accused, by implication, of condoning all the selfish aspects of capitalism, yet neither man expressed sympathy, much less allegiance, to the interests of a particular class. Both men were dedicated to an economy in which the public interest would be paramount and consistently opposed special privileges to any group or class.

The woolen manufacturers, in particular, Smith accused of

persuading the legislature that the prosperity of the nation depended upon the success and extension of their particular business. They have not only obtained a monopoly against the consumers by an absolute prohibition of importing woolen cloth from any foreign country; but they have likewise obtained another monopoly against the sheep farmers and growers of wool, by a similar prohibition of the exportation of live sheep and wool. The severity of many of the laws which have been enacted for the security of the revenue is very justly complained of, as imposing heavy penalties upon actions which, antecedent to the statutes that declared them to be crimes, had always been understood to be innocent. But the cruelest of our revenue laws, I will venture to affirm, are mild and gentle, in comparison of some of those which the clamour of our merchants and manufacturers has extracted from the legislature, for the support of their own absurd and oppressive monopolies. Like the laws of Draco, these laws may be said to be all written in blood.[125]

The popular sentiment in France and America after the French and American revolutions was for democracy, liberty, and equality; an end to government controls; and unlimited freedom to buy, sell, and trade, limited only by the natural law of supply and demand, which impartially governed all free markets. It was widely believed that the price mechanism and market competition, rather than government decree, provided the best agency for the allocation of resources, capital, and labor. Hamilton was aware of this popular sentiment. However, when Washington appointed him the first Secretary of the Treasury, Hamilton sent to Congress his *Report on Manufactures,* which turned its back on free trade and instead advocated an external tariff with a variable rate schedule that not only could be used for raising revenue to pay the cost of government, but also be an economic tool for encouraging the growth of new industries. This economic tool was to be controlled by the government. It gave the government the power to influence prices. In effect, it replaced market decisions by political judgments. The power of the market to set prices was not abrogated. In some commodities, however, the power of Congress to raise or lower duties affected consumer prices in a decisive manner, which was, in fact, part of Hamilton's plan to influence the growth of certain trades and industries by commodity taxation.

Hamilton was primarily a statesman and a firm believer in the supremacy of political power. Although he was an able economist, he never let economic theory blur his political realism. The classic theory of the market as a suprapolitical institution supported by an "unseen hand," according to Smith, was not credible to Hamilton. He knew that the market was supported by a complex web of laws based on private property rights, without which it would not function. Neither did he accept the Benthamite theory of market utilitarianism as the medium to achieve the greatest good for the greatest number. He knew that the political power of a strong government was the protector of the market and had the ultimate power to control the distributing system.

Hamilton knew that somebody must pay the start-up costs of industrialization. It was necessary to institute a system of forced savings to divert income into capital investment in new factories rather than have such income lie idle in savings or find investment opportunities in such areas as farming, the shipping trade, and foreign ventures. The protective tariff was a hidden subsidy to manufactures, making them attractive to investors and giving them an added incentive to grow.

But it is important to note the difference between a protective tariff and a system of government investment credits and subsidies used for economic development. The tariff:

1. Does not distort market prices. The tax is added to the market price of all affected imported commodities. The original pretax market price is not distorted. Domestic prices are *all* affected equally by the import tax, within the commodity classification of the tax. By contrast, a system of government subsidies, or investment credits invariably favors some producers and discriminates against others. Power, prestige, and favoritism are always involved in government loans or subsidies.

2. Does not require a huge bureaucracy to collect taxes and administer government economic programs. The tariff was relatively easy to collect. A few collectors at ports of entry sufficed to collect duties. Management of the tariff was by legislative process. Congress debated the tax rates and set them by consensus. The redistributive effects of the tariff were worked out through the market price system. By contrast, the income tax sets up a nonmarket redistributive system in the public sector that collects the tax revenues and then uses them to finance and administer government investments, grants, subsidies, contracts, operating expenses, and foreign and domestic aid. The income tax is managed by an executive bureaucracy operating independently of the market and remote from the legislative process.

2. Jefferson's Farm Support Program

The Constitution gives Congress the power to collect taxes to pay the debts and provide for the common defense and general welfare of the United States (Article 1, Section 8, Clause 1). The law requires that no capitation or other direct taxes shall be laid unless in proportion to the census (Article 1, Section 9, Clause 4); that no tax or duty shall be laid on any article exported from any state (Article 1, Section 9, Clause 5); and that direct taxes must be apportioned, while indirect taxes must be uniform throughout the United States (Article 1, Section 2, Clause 3). Tax bills must originate in the House of Representatives (Article 1, Section 7, Clause 1). The 16th Amendment gives Congress the power to levy income taxes without apportionment, thereby voiding the major applicability of Article 1, Section 9, Clause 4.

Tax laws, like other statutes, were to be administered by the executive. In the executive department responsibility for administration of tax laws fell to the Secretary of the Treasury. Because of the dominant personality of the first Secretary of the Treasury, the Congress discovered, much to its surprise and chagrin, that the executive branch wielded an economic power in tax matters out of all proportion to what had been written into the Constitution and probably greater than had been intended by the founding fathers.

Congressional eyebrows were raised when the first Secretary of the Treasury proposed to levy taxes on imports, not only for raising revenue, but to subsidize new industries. Such radical tax programs initiated by the executive were to become an accepted part of Congressional life, but they were new then and resented by the Jeffersonians as an attempt by Hamilton to create an autocratic executive power.

When Alexander Hamilton took over as the first Secretary of the Treasury, the treasury was empty, the national government had no credit, and the currency was worthless. "Not worth a Continental" was a common saying. The new nation had a history of eight years of financial chaos under the Confederation, four under the revolutionary Congress. Prior to the revolution, the chief distinction of the American people had been their stubborn refusal to pay their share of taxes to support the mother country. Now (1974) that the United States budget shows the cost of national defense to be about $88 billion, or about one-third of the total Federal budget, the American people can be somewhat more tolerant of the British effort to impose some token taxes on the American colonies for their defense. Adam Smith, after analyzing the costs to England of administering and defending the American colonies, concluded that they were a heavy drain on the English economy and advised his government: "It is surely time that Great Britain should free herself from the expense of defending these provinces in time of war, and of supporting any part of their civil or military establishments in time of peace, and endeavor to accommodate her future views and designs to the real mediocrity of her circumstances."[126] England took his advice, but about 170 years later.

England's unresolved problem of trying to tax Americans for the support of the government was passed on to Hamilton. Fortunately for America, Hamilton was a financial genius who measured up to the task. He not only resolved the most critical fiscal problems and established the public credit of the United States on a sound basis, but he left the imprint of his economic doctrines permanently on the American government. Hamilton's protective tariff, although not immediately adopted by Congress, became the cornerstone of American national economic policy in the 19th century.

Hamilton's decision to finance the government by import duties was not unexpected. It was an obvious choice that had already been made by Congress. Direct taxes had been, in effect, ruled out by the Constitution, and internal commodity taxes such as excises were troublesome and unpopular. The Whiskey Rebellion of 1794, caused by the imposition of a 30-cents a gallon tax on whiskey, indicated that Americans were still uneasy about being taxed, even by their own government.

The external tariff, with duties collected at the ports of entry on imported commodities, far from the ultimate taxpayer, was the logical tax for a large sparsely settled country such as the United States. What made Hamilton's tariff approach extraordinary was the way in which he analyzed the economic state of the union and prescribed a policy that was contrary to the accepted economic doctrine of laissez-faire. Hamilton's theory of the tariff was not a simple revenue bill with flat rates; neither was it conceived, like the tariffs of the mercantile era, as a means of accumulating gold under a favorable balance of trade. The tariff proposed by Hamilton was to be an instrument of economic policy, wielded by the national government, for the explicit purpose of promoting the industrial growth of the United States. Although it came to be known as the protective tariff, its avowed purpose was not protection, but growth and what is equally significant, growth directed by political plan rather than market decision.

This daring economic policy was at variance with the popular doctrine of laissez-faire, and Hamilton had to contend with a powerful opponent who was the very embodiment of that doctrine — Thomas Jefferson. Although radical in his political outlook, Jefferson was reactionary in his economic views, if the word reactionary is used to denote a viewpoint favoring the status quo or in sympathy with an era that has passed rather than an era that is coming. Jefferson was completely devoted to the concept of agrarian democracy based on one-owner farms and one-owner shops. He feared and distrusted big industry and big cities. Where Hamilton wanted to use the tariff to encourage manufacturers, Jefferson opposed their introduction:

> The political economists of Europe have established it as a principle that every state should endeavor to manufacture for itself; and this principle, like many others, we transfer to America, without calculating the difference of circumstances which should often produce a difference of results. In Europe the lands are either cultivated, or locked up against the cultivator. Manufacture must therefore be resorted to of necessity, not of choice, to support the surplus of their people. But we have an immensity of land courting the industry of the husbandman. Is it best then, that all our citizens should be employed in its improvement, or that one half should be called off from that to exercise manufactures and handicraft arts for the other? Those who labor in the earth are the chosen people of God, if He ever had a chosen people, whose breasts He had made his peculiar deposit for substantial and genuine virtue. It is the focus in which He keeps alive that sacred fire, which

172

otherwise might escape from the face of the earth. Corruption of morals in the mass of cultivators is a phenomenon of which no age nor nation has furnished an example . . .

Generally speaking, the proportion which the aggregate of the other classes of citizens bears in any state to that of its husbandmen is the proportion of its unsound to its healthy parts, and is a good enough barometer whereby to measure its degree of corruption. While we have land to labor then let us never wish to see our citizens occupied at a workbench, or twirling a distaff. Carpenters, masons, smiths are wanting in husbandry; but, for the general operation of manufactures, let our workshops remain in Europe. It is better to carry provisions and materials to workmen there than to bring them their manners and principles. The loss by transportation of commodities across the Atlantic will be made up in happiness and permanence of government. The mobs of great cities add just so much to the support of pure government, as sores do to the strength of the human body. It is the manners and spirit of a people which preserve a republic in vigor.[127]

What Jefferson was recommending for America was a return to the colonial status, as England had originally planned, with the difference that the dependency would be only on the economic level. Coming from the author of the Declaration of Independence, this attitude may appear paradoxical. In reality it was not.

A society the government of which is weak and permissive must have citizens who are economically strong and self-supporting. Jefferson correctly perceived that such a society could function effectively only where the individual as sole owner of his farm or shop was economically self-sufficient and not dependent on government support. His observations in Paris made him keenly aware that the urban proletariat and the factory workers were not economically independent or self-sufficient, but propertyless and rootless masses that had no economic power and were not capable of self-government because of this powerlessness.

Jefferson feared for the future and predicted that the growth of great cities in America would doom the democratic system. Fortunately or unfortunately, the growth of manufactures and cities could not be arrested, and even Jefferson could not stop the mechanization and urbanization of America that was already in its incipient stages. Like the ancient Greek poets who cursed the ships that brought commerce and corruption to Arcadia, Jefferson and his followers cursed Hamilton for plotting to industrialize America and corrupt agrarian democracy.

Jefferson wrote Madison: "Hamilton is really a colossus to the anti-republican party. Without numbers he is a host within himself." Jefferson's awe and fear of Hamilton must have been intense, for his criticism of Hamilton lacks the philosophic detachment characteristic of him and veers toward the irrational. He accuses Hamilton of conspiring to make Washington a king and makes other extreme charges of corruption and bribery, although he concedes that Hamilton was personally honest: "Hamilton was indeed a singular character. Of acute understanding, disinterested, honest, and honorable in all private transactions, amiable in society, and duly valuing virtue in private life, yet so bewitched and perverted by the British example as to be under thorough conviction that corruption was essential to the government of a nation..."[128]

The political rivalry between the two titans was so bitter and intense that Jefferson may be excused for having let political animus pervert his usual calm and unbiased judgment. Hamilton certainly did not believe in corruption. Far more than any other American of his generation, Hamilton was aware of the need for establishing the public credit of the infant republic and he knew that, without good faith and scrupulous honesty, credit could not be established:

> If the maintenance of public credit, then, be truly so important, the next inquiry which suggests itself is: By what means is it to be effected? The ready answer to which question is by good faith; by a punctual performance of contract.... While the observance of that good faith which is the basis of public credit is recommended by the strongest inducements of political expediency, it is enforced by considerations of a greater authority. There are arguments for it, which rest in the immutable principles of moral obligation.[129]

Hamilton was not impressed by Jefferson's idyllic picture of agrarian democracy in America. Unlike the aristocratic Jefferson, Hamilton was a self-made man and had no illusions about cultivators being repositories of virtue or God's chosen people. He knew that, in Jefferson's South, most of the cultivators were abject slaves.

Hamilton was quite familiar with the economics of colonial trade. He had as a very young man managed a trading firm in the West Indies. He later came to New York, studied law, and entered politics. His commercial apprenticeship may have developed in him that ability to analyze financial problems and formulate economic policy, in which he was so far ahead of his contemporaries. With remarkable prescience he anticipated the future evolution of the American economy and, without forebodings or backward glances at an idyllic past, he boldly proposed a series of economic policies applicable to the needs of a rising industrial state. These policies were written and presented to Congress for legislative guidance under the titles of *Report on the Public Credit, Report on the National Bank,* and *Report on Manufactures.* Most but not all of Hamilton's proposals were enacted into law. The *Reports* represented the most advanced economic learning of the day, but they were no academic theories. Hamilton's genius lay in his ability to apply contemporary economic knowledge to the political realities and economic conditions facing an underdeveloped nation emerging from colonialism.

Hamilton's economic *Reports* were widely misunderstood then, and even today he is bitterly attacked by many as a "mercantilist," a "monarchist," and a "reactionary." Richard Hofstadter said Hamilton had no sympathy for the poor and advocated child labor because he said that manufactures would give employment to women and children, but Jefferson is admired for his compassion, although he was a slaveholder. Despite his detractors, history has vindicated Hamilton. He remains a dominant figure, with Washington, in the early days of the republic. Washington was personally closer to his fellow-Virginian, Jefferson, but in the contest between Hamilton and Jefferson, Washington backed Hamilton. He knew that Jefferson was not an organizer and had no knowledge of economics. Washington's judgment in this case, as in many others, was correct and reflected his knowledge of character and his ability to make the right decision. He knew that only Hamilton had the organizing executive ability to put the new government together and the financial genius to rescue it from bankruptcy and to make it work. When Jefferson, who was a greater political leader than Hamilton, came to power, the organizational work had been done. The government was a functioning solvent enterprise, no longer threatened with bankruptcy. For this Hamilton deserves the lion's share of the credit.

The *Report on Manufactures,* which Hamilton presented to Congress on December 5, 1791, was not received with favor and was largely ignored. However, it was this *Report* that contained the theory of protection for young industries that came to be associated with Hamilton's name and that had such a far-reaching influence on American political and economic development and, through Friedrich List, on the economic development of Germany.

3. A Tax Policy to Industialize America

Hamilton starts his *Report on Manufactures* by attacking the basic economic theory underlying Jeffersonian democracy: the concept that agriculture is the only or the chief source of the wealth of nations and that all other industries and occupations are essentially parasitic. This was a theory very popular in the latter part of the 18th century among the intellectuals who were exploring what was then a new frontier in science — economics. In fact, the word economists was probably first applied to a group of radical thinkers in France called the Physiocrats, whose leader Quesnay was greatly admired by Adam Smith.

The central thesis of the Physiocrats was that only agriculture fed or "supported" society in an economic sense and that all who did not work on the land were parasites who must be fed by the produce of the land. It was the surplus produce of the land — over and above what was needed to maintain the farm workers — that supported the leisure class of clergy, officials, and soldiers, as well as other nonfarm workers. Important as this leisure class was to society, it was completely dependent on the surplus farm produce, without which it would starve. The Physiocratic doctrine was summarized by Smith in *The Wealth of Nations:* "Artificers, and manufacturers in particular, whose industry, in the common apprehension of men, increases so much the rude produce of land, are in this system represented as a class of people altogether barren and unproductive. Their labour, it is said, replaces only the stock which employs them, together with its ordinary profits." Smith was in basic agreement with this view, although he did admit that manufacturers contributed to the division of labor and the expansion of the market for agricultural produce, but it was the "rude produce of the land" that determined the wealth of a nation.[130] Jefferson was familiar with the philosophy of the Physiocrats and, like Smith, was partial to the concept of agrarian preeminence in economics as well as in politics. Hamilton was skeptical of this claim:

> It ought readily to be conceded that the cultivation of the earth — as the primary and most certain source of national supply — as the immediate and chief source of subsistence to man — as the principal source of those materials which constitute the nutriment of other kinds of labor, as including a state most favorable to the freedom and independence of the human mind — one, perhaps, most conducive to the multiplication of the human species — has *intrinsically a strong claim to pre-eminence over every other kind of industry*. But, that it has a title to any thing like an exclusive predilection, in any country, ought to be admitted with great caution....It has been maintained that Agriculture is, not only the most productive, but the only productive species of industry. The reality of this suggestion in either aspect, has, however, not been verified by any accurate detail of facts and calculations... [131]

Hamilton, whose mind was like a steel trap, more concerned with "facts and calculations" than with nebulous theories, then subjected the Smith-Jefferson theory of agrarian supremacy to critical analysis and found it inapplicable to American economic conditions. Hamilton's policy was to encourage manufactures, although he made it clear that this policy was not detrimental to agriculture but, on the contrary, was meant to create a larger home market and "a more certain and steady demand for the surplus produce of the soil."

Hamilton summarized his policy of national aid to manufacturers by listing seven advantages that would accrue from such a policy:

1. The division of labor would be extended; this was, at that time, the cardinal principle of economic growth.

2. The use of machinery would be encouraged.

3. Additional employment would be given to classes of the community not ordinarily engaged in business.

4. The promotion of immigration to man the farms and factories.

5. The furnishing of greater opportunity for the diversity of talents and occupations.

6. The affording of a more ample and diversified field for enterprise.

7. The creation in a home market of a larger and a more certain and steady demand for the surplus produce of the soil.

"The foregoing considerations," said Hamilton, "seem sufficient to establish, as general propositions, that it is in the interest of nations to diversify the industrious pursuits of individuals who compose them — that the establishment of manufactures is calculated only not to increase the general stock of useful and productive labor; but even to improve the state of agriculture in particular... "[132]

It is noteworthy that Hamilton did not include in the list of benefits the one that formerly had been regarded as the chief benefit of the tariff — the accumulations of a gold reserve by a favorable balance of trade. Had Hamilton been a mercantilist, he would have used the tariff as a weapon to build up the national treasury and employed tax revenues to support a large Federal bureaucracy, to fund Federal programs, and to regulate the domestic economy as Colbert had done. Hamilton was more interested in promoting the industrial growth of the United States than in promoting the growth of a powerful and rich Federal bureaucracy. His theory that the tariff could be used as a means to develop new industry in an undeveloped agrarian society was not considered economically sound by Adam Smith: "Were Americans, either by combination or by any sort of violence, to stop the importation of European manufactures, and, by thus giving a monopoly to such of their own countrymen as would manufacture the like goods, divert any considerable part of their capital into the employment, they would retard instead of accelerating the further increase in the value of their annual produce, and would obstruct instead of promoting the progress of their country toward real wealth and greatness."[133]

Hamilton was willing to concede that, "If the system of perfect liberty to industry and commerce were the prevailing systems of nations, the agreements which dissuade a country, in the predicament of the United States, from the zealous pursuit of manufactures, would doubtless have great force." But Hamilton was too experienced a politician not to know that the system of perfect liberty "is far from characterising the general policy of Nations. The prevalent one has been regulated by an opposite spirit." Under such adverse conditions, economic considerations alone are not sufficient to guide the policy of a great nation. Said Hamilton:

> The regulations of several countries, with which we have the most extensive intercourse, throw serious obstructions in the way of the principal staples of the United States. In such a position of things, the United States cannot exchange with Europe on equal terms; and the want of reciprocity would render them the victim of a system which would induce them to confine their views to agriculture, and refrain from Manufactures ... It is for the United States to consider by what means they can render themselves least dependent on the combinations, right or wrong, of foreign policy.[134]

The theory of free trade between nations was, at that time, only a theory, quite new and untried. Pitt in England, Napoleon in France, and Hamilton in America faced international conditions during the 1790's that made free trade an ideal economic state, wonderful in theory, but quite unrealizable in fact. The economic policy of the great European powers was aggressively to promote their own trade and to restrict or curtail that of other nations in order to obtain the most favorable balance of trade for themselves.

Facing a world of belligerent nations, each fighting for economic domination or survival, Hamilton proposed a policy of rapid industrialization as a means of making the United States free from economic dependence on foreign powers:

> Not only the wealth, but the independence and security of a Country appear to be materially connected with the prosperity of manufactures. ... The possession

of these is necessary to the perfection of the body politic; to the safety as well as to the welfare of society.... The extreme embarrassments of the United States during the late wars from an incapacity to supply themselves, are still a matter of keen recollection. A future war might be expected again to exemplify the mischiefs and dangers of a situation to which that incapacity is still in too great a degree applicable, unless changed, by timely and vigorous exertion. To effect this change, as fast as shall be prudent, merits all the attention and all the zeal of our Public Council; 'tis the next great work to be accomplished.[135]

Hamilton then went on to explain in detail his program to promote industrial growth by a flexible system of commodity taxes or duties on imported commodities to encourage the growth of industries considered essential to the *general welfare*. It was Hamilton who first appropriated for the national government the *plenary* power to raise money under the *general welfare* clause of the Constitution, a doctrine that John Marshall, a follower of Hamilton, later elaborated and confirmed by decisions of the Supreme Court.

The greater part of Hamilton's report was devoted to replying to arguments against the protective tariff as a policy of economic growth through commodity taxation directed by the central government. The arguments in favor of the plan were less elaborate and were based on modifying and improving tariff regulations and procedures and increasing, by rather small amounts, duties on certain selected items. The very moderation of Hamilton's tax proposals may have been designed to allay fears of states rights adherents to a policy that promoted the growth of Federal power. In a government less than 3 years old, still used to thinking in terms of sovereign states united only for common defense, Hamilton's national economic plan directed by the Federal government, with vast tax powers, seemed to many a return to a form of despotism against which the country had just rebelled.

The Hamiltonian concept of protection was that the sovereign state had the right, indeed, the duty, to intervene in the economy for the promotion of the general welfare. In Hamilton's plan, intervention took the form of subsidies to manufactures under the guise of import taxes on the commodities that competed against domestic manufactured commodities. This protection was to serve the national interest and to encourage the industrial growth of the nation, which Hamilton regarded at that time to be the most urgent national priority, overriding all others. Hamilton was a nationalist, a believer in American greatness and American industrial power. As a political philosopher, he believed America could achieve its destiny only by a strong central government that overrode private in favor of public interests. This philosophy was, of course, directly opposed to the Jeffersonian concept of limited government and nonintervention in the private economy. Jefferson was very close to Rousseau in his social ideas and in many ways a disciple of Locke, who taught that private property was a natural right of man and that governments existed primarily for the defense of individual property rights. Hamilton followed Hobbes' political doctrine, in which the rights of the individual were always subordinate to those of the sovereign state. When Hamilton, a 19-year-old captain of artillery, joined Washington's army, he carried with him a few books, one of which was by Hobbes and another by

178

Rousseau. It is not difficult to guess which political philosopher made the more lasting impression on Hamilton.

The history of the protective tariff in later years took on aspects that not only were unforeseen by Hamilton, but very likely would not have been approved by him. Perhaps the greatest aberration was the gradual subversion of the tariff by private interests so that it came to serve the interests of a special class or group of producers rather than the public interest or the general welfare. The producers, both industrial and agricultural, formed power blocs that exerted tremendous political pressure on Congress and obtained tax rates on imported commodities that guaranteed them huge profits. Critics of Hamilton charge that this was a natural development of Hamilton's doctrine of protection and that Hamilton was a known admirer of wealth and aristocracy and an enemy of democracy. Jefferson, who was a wealthy aristocrat, could make this charge, but Hamilton, who was born and died a poor man, was not a believer in plutocracy. His reports on *The Public Debt, The National Bank,* and on *Manufactures* are masterful treatises on economics, not briefs for special interests. No American political leader of his day or later matched Hamilton's genius for public finance. In all his works the underlying principle was the furtherance of national power and greatness and the promotion of the general welfare. In none of his papers is there an advocacy of narrow sectional, class, or private interests as being paramount or preeminent over the public interest. The principle of protection may have been subverted later by selfish interests for personal gain, but certainly Hamilton would not have tolerated this subversion. Neither did the political heirs of Hamilton — Clay, Lincoln, and McKinley — advocate protectionism in a narrow partisan or selfish sense. To them, as to Hamilton, the protective tariff was the best way to build up America and make her independent, united, and powerful.

In a cynical age it is customary to regard patriots as chauvinists and nationalists as jingoists. But men of Hamilton's caliber are not motivated by thoughts of personal greed or of selfish gain. It is unfair to charge them with a betrayal of their own ideals by accusing them of motives alien to their character and purpose. Hamilton, for example, would never have condoned the use of the protective tariff for the personal or class interests of manufacturers. Once the tariff had accomplished its work, Hamilton would not have kept it to protect industries grown fat and arrogant on subsidies no longer needed. There is ample evidence of this view in his writings.

Hamilton was killed in a political duel while still in his forties. His great opponent, Jefferson, took the reins of government from the Federalists and passed them on to his disciple Madison. For 16 years the tariff issue lay dormant. The doctrine of laissez-faire became the official policy. The views of the Jefferson-Madison administrations on the tariff issue were probably best summarized by Albert Gallatin, Jefferson's Secretary of the Treasury:

> Every individual, in every community, without exception, will purchase whatever he may want on the cheapest terms within his reach. The most enthusiastic restrictionist, the manufacturer, most clamorous for special

179

protection, will, each individually, pursue the same course, and prefer any foreign commodity or material, to that of domestic origin, if the first is cheaper, and the law does not be forbidding him. All men ever have acted, and continue, under any system, to act on the same principle. . . . The advocates of the tariff system affirm, that what is true of all men, individually, is untrue when applied to them collectively. We cannot consider the adherence of enlightened nations to regulations of that description, but as the last relic of that system of general restrictions and monopolies, which had its origin in barbarous times. . .

Jefferson's own views on the tariff were expressed in a letter to his friend Pierre du Pont de Nemours:

We are all the more reconciled to the tax on importations, because it falls exclusively on the rich, and with the equal partition of intestate's estates constitutes the best agrarian law. . . . Our revenues once liberated by the discharge of the public debt and its surplus applied to canals, roads, schools, etc., and the farmer will see his government supported, his children educated, and the face of his country made a paradise by the contributions of the rich alone, without his being called upon to spare a cent from his earnings.[136]

The idea of using the tariff to tax luxuries only is certainly a commendable one, but Jefferson did not have the economic knowledge or executive ability to translate this dream into a practical system of taxation. The farmer and the planter as it turned out, were the ones who suffered most from the tariff, according to their own spokesmen.

Despite the personal views of Jefferson and Madison and the official laissez-faire policy of their administrations, it was during their years in office that the United States first put into effect severe import restrictions that spurred the rapid growth of American manufactures. These import restrictions were imposed, not by high tariffs, but by the Embargo of 1807 and the War of 1812. But the economic effect was to stop all imports and, thus, in an unexpected way, Jefferson and Madison demonstrated the successful application of Hamilton's basic idea of a protective tariff.

Professor F. W. Taussig who, in general, takes the position that protective duties were not needed for encouraging American industrial development, states that the rapid growth of the cotton industry, the most important manufacture of the times, was caused by the application of protection:

Before 1808 the difficulties in the way of the introduction of this branch of industry were such that it made little progress. These difficulties were largely artificial . . . arising from ignorance of the new processes and from the absence of experienced workmen . . . combined with the stimulus which the condition of foreign trade gave to agriculture and to the carrying trade, to prevent any appreciable development . . . if the period before 1808 had come to an end without a jar, the eager competitions of well-established English manufactures, the lack of familiarity with the processes, and the long-continued habit, especially in New England, of almost exclusive attention to agriculture, commerce, and the carrying trade, might have rendered slow and difficult the change, however inevitable it may have been, to greater attention to manufactures. Under such circumstances there might have been room for the legitimate application of protection to the cotton manufacturing as a young industry. But this period, in fact, came to an end with a violent shock, which threw industry out of its accustomed grooves, and caused the striking growth of the cotton manufacture from 1808 to 1815. The transition caused much suffering, but it took place sharply and quickly. The intensification of trade was equivalent to a rude but vigorous application of protection, which did its work thoroughly.[137]

In 1808, 15 cotton mills were built, running 8000 spindles. In 1809 the number of mills built shot up to 62, with 31,000 spindles. Taussig reports that in 1811 the total numbered 80,000 spindles and that by 1815 it had jumped to 500,000. In 1800 the cotton textile industry had consumed only 500 bales of cotton and in 1805 only 1000 bales. In 1815 it was consuming 90,000 bales annually. The import restrictions imposed by the embargo and war had provided a powerful stimulus to the growth of the domestic cotton industry. There were other causative factors, of course, but the rapid growth of this industry during a period of almost complete protection was a vindication of Hamilton's theory. The rising class of manufacturers and their political allies who formed a new middle class were not slow in learning the lesson. They took up Hamilton's theory of protection and made it a potent political weapon, unfortunately not always used for the general welfare as Hamilton understood it.

4. The Great Tariff Debate

According to Horace Greeley, the period following the war of 1812 was a difficult one for the new industries that had grown up in wartime, protected from foreign competition:

> At the close of the second war with England, peace found this country dotted with furnaces and factories which had sprung up under the precarious shelter of embargo and war. These not yet firmly established found themselves suddenly exposed to a relentless and determined foreign competition. Great Britain poured her fabrics, far below cost, upon our markets in a perfect deluge. Our manufacturers went down like grass before the mower, and our agriculture and the wages of labor speedily followed. Financial prostration was general and the presence of debt was universal. In New England, fully one-fourth of the property went through the sheriff's mill, and the prostration was scarcely less general elsewhere. In Kentucky the presence of debt was simply intolerable. In New York, the leading merchants, in 1817, united in a memorial to Congress to save our commerce as well as our manufactures from utter ruin, by increasing the tariff duties.[138]

When Hamilton submitted his *Report on Manufactures*, the doctrine of government protection of industry by commodity taxation was discussed on theoretical grounds, and Congress could afford to ignore the *Report* with impunity. There were no pressure groups pushing it. Hamilton's economic arguments were admired, but were probably beyond the comprehension of the average Congressmen drawn from farms, plantations, and the law. The Federalist party was smashed by internal dissension and by the Jefferson

181

agrarian majority and so could not fight for the economic policies of Hamilton.

The situation in 1816 was quite different. Protection was no longer a matter of theory. The manufacturers who had sprung up in the 1808-1815 period represented a powerful and vocal power bloc with vested interests. They petitioned Congress for help from foreign competition, and they found a powerful ally in the press, which took up their case and carried it to the people. Public opinion swung over sharply in favor of protection. The majority of the people were convinced that protection was to their best interest. The full impact of an aroused public opinion was felt in Congress in favor of the protective tariff for the first time. Besides the pressure of public opinion, Congress felt the financial pressure of a large public debt accumulated during the war. Although the customs duties were doubled in 1812 as a wartime measure, the tax receipts fell from $13 million in 1813 to $6 million in 1814. The war and the British navy virtually put an end to the import trade and to import duties. The Treasury was forced to depend on loans and Treasury notes. Congress imposed a few direct taxes on houses, lands, and slaves and some excises, but popular pressure forced Congress to repeal them after the war. The tariff was then left as the sole source of revenue, and Congress had the added incentive for raising duties, to replenish the treasury as well as to protect American industry.

The dual function of the tariff as a revenue measure for financing government operations and as an instrument of national economic policy for promoting industrial growth was brought to a head in 1816. The Tariff Act of 1816 did not resolve the problem presented by the dual functions of the tariff. Some historians, however, believe that for the first time in American history "protection was adopted as the primary principle of the fiscal system and revenue was treated as secondary to industrial needs."[139]

Congress never did divorce the revenue function from the political control function of the tariff. The result was that, in times of war or depression, the tariff rates were raised for revenue purposes, and after the crisis the higher rates tended to become the base rates for more protection later. Industries formed powerful blocs with a vested interest in the higher protective rates. Protection was addictive; once used to protection, it was difficult for industries to do without, or so they claimed:

> The connection between tariff legislation and the state of the revenue has been almost constant in our history. In 1842 an empty treasury was followed by the passage of a high protective tariff. In 1857 an overflowing revenue caused a reduction of the duties. In 1861 the Morrill tariff was passed partly in order to make good a deficit. During the war the need of money led to the Act of 1864. The ten per cent reduction of 1872 was called out largely by the redundant revenue; its abolition in 1875 was excused by the falling off in the government income.

Although, as Professor Taussig states, there was a constant connection between revenue and protection in United States tariff history, the connection was never spelled out by Congress. Hamilton had spelled out with great clarity and logic the political and economic costs and benefits of the protective tariff as it applied to the economic conditions of the 1790's. As the economic conditions of the nation changed, the tariff neccessarily changed with them, and the politicians altered the political objectives of the tariff to meet the needs of the times: protection of labor, of agriculture, and of the home market. But no one with the genius of Hamilton arose to reappraise the tariff and clearly to define and separate the economic and the political benefits.

As a result, Congressional debate over the tariff became heated with political animus; the clash of economic interests dominated the debates; and class and regional rivalries influenced tariff legislation. After 1816 the industrial North generally favored high protective duties, with revenue secondary, and the agrarian South stood for a revenue tariff with no protection. This political alignment developed slowly, with groups changing sides from time to time, in both the South and the North.

When the Tariff Act of 1816 increasing duties on imports was passed, John C. Calhoun, the spokesman of the South, voted for it. This consensus did not last long. After 1816 the South took a strong antitariff position, and Calhoun became the recognized leader of the antitariff or free-trade movement. The South soon recognized that it was dependent on foreign markets for its cotton and tobacco exports and that duties on commodities imported were not simply a subsidy to Northern manufactures but a tax on Southern exports. After 1816, the tariff became a political issue, with clearly recognized class and regional interests aligned on both sides.

Despite the bitter opposition of the South, the rest of the country remained strongly in favor of protection. Farmers and workers aligned themselves with manufacturers. The farmers, in the depression of 1818-1820, saw farm prices drop to a disastrously low level. Flour fell from $14 a barrel in 1817 to less than $4 in 1819. Farmers saw their export market for farm products dry up and were convinced by tariff advocates that protection to manufactures would build up the home market for farm products. The depression of 1818-1820 also produced the phenomenon, for the first time in America, of industrial unemployment. The number of unemployed Philadelphians in 1819 was estimated at from 7288 to 20,000 of a total population of 110,000. In Pittsburgh employment fell one third between 1815 and 1819. The workers were convinced that competition by cheap foreign labor was causing their unemployment, and they supported the factory owners in petitioning Congress for protection and higher duties.

The rising tide of protectionist sentiment reached a peak in 1828 when the Tariff Act of that year raised duties on imports higher than at any other time before the Civil War. It was called a Tariff of Abominations by the South. South Carolina called a state convention, which declared the Tariff Act of 1828 unconstitutional and threatened to secede from the union unless it was repealed. President Jackson rejected the state's right of nullification and threatened to use Federal troops against South Carolina. The crisis passed with the adoption of the Compromise Tariff of 1833, which provided for a gradual lowering of duties over a ten-year period back to the general level of the 1816 Tariff.

The period between the Tariff Act of 1816 and the Compromise Tariff of

1833 was probably the most crucial in American tariff history. The tariff was the hottest political issue of the times. No other subject aroused so much interest, or was discussed more passionately pro and con in the decade following the War of 1812. The great political leaders of the day — Clay, Calhoun, Webster, John Quincy Adams, Jackson, and Van Buren — were forced to take positions on this issue, and their speeches, especially those of Clay, Calhoun, and Webster, are still read for their oratorical brilliance, as well as for their economic arguments. The newspapers became mouthpieces of "protectionists" on one side and of "free traders" on the other, with each side trying to out-shout the opposition. The general public was drawn into the controversy because each and every citizen felt that his personal interest was at stake; the farmer, the planter, the worker, the merchant, the manufacturer, each had a vital stake in the tariff, for the rates set for specific commodities could bring disaster or prosperity to his own calling or business. Probably in no other period of American history was the general public so deeply involved in national economic legislation.

Today under the income tax system the numerous national economic plans are conceived by experts — economists, sociologists, social engineers, urbanologists, criminologists, agronomists, ecologists and production, marketing, advertising and finance specialists — all working in the planning or budget office of the executive branch. Government plans, when perfected, are presented to the Congress for funding. The role of the citizen is reduced to that of a pawn moved around by the planners. The role of the legislative assembly is reduced to that of a funding agency, rubber-stamping appropriations already budgeted.

Under the tariff, national economic plans were debated and hammered out in Congress, and the average citizen followed the debate because he was involved in the issues, they were vital to his own interests, and he was called upon to decide them by his own vote.

The great spokesman for those favoring the protective tariff in the period between the War of 1812 and the Civil War was Henry Clay. Like Hamilton, Clay never attained his ambition of becoming President and saw that office fall to lesser men. His influence, nevertheless, was profound, not only on the general public, but on such future leaders as Lincoln. In the style of the times, he was a flamboyant speaker. He lacked Hamilton's genius for economics, but he had great political ability and knew how to present complex issues in simple imaginative word pictures that moved and convinced his constituents, many of whom, like Lincoln, had no formal schooling.

Clay carried on the Hamiltonian tradition of linking protectionism with the rising nationalism. Clay was more successful than Hamilton in winning popular support for his ideas, possibly because they were unencumbered with the technical details of abstract economics. Where Hamilton was an organizer, Clay was a popularizer. Clay's ideas of protectionism were simple and patriotic:

> The greatest want of civilized society is a market for the sale and exchange of the surplus of the produce of the labor of its members. This market may exist at home or abroad, or both, but it must exist somewhere, if society prospers, and wherever

184

it does exist, it should be competent to the absorption of the entire surplus production. It is most desirable that there should be both a home and a foreign market. But, with respect to their relative superiority, I cannot entertain a doubt. The home market is first in order and paramount in importance. The object of the bill under consideration is to create this home market, and to lay the foundation of a genuine American policy . . . We have seen that an exclusive dependence upon the foreign market must lead to still severer distress, to impoverishment, to ruin. We must then change somewhat our course. We must give a new direction to some portion of our industry. We must speedily adopt a genuine American policy. Still cherishing a foreign market, let us create also a home market, to give further scope to the consumption of the produce of American industry.

Clay was a true Hamiltonian who was not bothered by Jeffersonian or Jacksonian inhibitions on the impropriety of state intervention in the private economy:

. . . it is the solemn duty of Government to apply a remedy to the evils which afflict our country, if it can apply one. Is there no remedy within the reach of the Government? Are we doomed to behold our industry languish and decay yet more and more? But there is a remedy, and that remedy consists in modifying our foreign policy, and in adopting a genuine American system. We must naturalize the arts in our country, and we must naturalize them by the only means which the wisdom of nations has yet discovered to be effectual — by adequate protection against the otherwise overwhelming influence of foreigners. This is only to be accomplished by the establishment of a tariff . . . The bill may be postponed, thwarted, defeated. But the cause is the cause of the country, and it must and will prevail.

This speech by Clay in support of the Tariff Bill of 1824 was answered by Daniel Webster, who was the spokesman for the New England maritime interests and who was not, at that time, entirely in favor of the tariff. Webster had no difficulty disposing of Clay's logic or lack of it:

Gentlemen tell us that they are in favor of domestic industry; so am I. They would give it protection; so would I. But then all domestic industry is not confined to manufactures. The employment of agriculture, commerce, and navigation, are all branches of the same domestic industry; they all furnish employment for American capital and American labor.

Clay's American system was misguided chauvinism, according to Webster:

One man makes a yard of cloth at home; another raises agricultural products, and buys a yard of imported cloth. Both of these are equally the earnings of domestic industry, and the only questions that arise in the case are two: The first is, which is the best mode under all the circumstances, of obtaining the article; the second is, how far this question is proper to be left to individual discretion. There is no foundation for the distinction which attributes to certain employments the peculiar appellation of American industry; and it is, in my judgment, extremely unwise to attempt such discriminations.

The Southern viewpoint on the tariff was eloquently expressed in Congress by the representative from South Carolina, George McDuffie, who joined the debate with a speech on April 16, 1824. McDuffie, in sarcastic tones, observed

185

testily that the inevitable result of a protective tariff was the destruction of commerce:

> If we make everything we consume at home we will, of course, import nothing; and if we import nothing it is a self-evident proposition that we can export nothing...But this wonder-working bill, it seems, is to furnish a substitute for those branches of our foreign commerce that it will destroy...But, can it be seriously contended that manufactures, which cannot hold a competition with the foreign in our own market, with the heavy duties which have existed for the last eight years, but require the additional protection provided in this bill, can maintain a successful competition in foreign markets?

McDuffie then went on to deflate the farmers' hopes of getting benefits from protection which, he said, were an illusion. "The great majority of farmers can produce no more than they consume in their families. It will be the wealthy farmers, therefore, who will realize the advantages...This is a combination, not only of the few against the many, but of the wealthy against the poor; we take from those who have not, and give to those who have.".

The bitterness of McDuffie's speech and his emotional appeal to class interests were a portent of the drastic nullification act and threat of secession by South Carolina in 1832. This extreme Southern position was justified by McDuffie in a speech in Congress on April 29, 1830. McDuffie went into a detailed analysis of the effects of tariff on the exports of cotton and concluded the analysis with these words:

> From this estimate, it will be seen that the prohibition of foreign imports has resulted in curtailing the entire demand for cotton in the markets of the whole world, including our own, two hundred and fifty thousand bales. In addition, then, to the annual burden he bears in paying the duties upon imports he is still permitted to bring into the country, the planter sustains an annual loss of seven million five hundred thousand dollars, being the candid value of the cotton for which he has lost a market, in consequence of the unjust restrictions imposed upon his lawful commerce by the suicidal policy of his own government...

McDuffie's remarks show how bitter the Southern states had become over the tariff question and how explosive the tariff issue was becoming. The specter of secession and civil war emerged as a very real possibility. Calhoun talked of the doctrine of States Rights, which implied the right to secede when, in the opinion of the state, the Federal government had exceeded its constitutional authority. The threat of secession was averted by Jackson, who refused to be intimidated by the Tariff Nullification Act of South Carolina, and by Clay, who swallowed his protectionist principles and engineered the Compromise Tariff of 1833. This tariff, with its promise of gradually declining duties, defused the explosive situation and pacified the South. Gradually the tariff question receded in importance as the question of slavery took over the attention of Congress and of the American people.

However, up to the eve of the Civil War the tariff remained, next to slavery itself, the most explosive issue in the South and one that aroused the most intense feelings of sectional rivalry. When the new Republican Party elected Lincoln on a platform that stood for a protective tariff and against the spread of slavery, it is likely that the South took umbrage from both planks and felt that both were aimed directly at the two most vital elements of the Southern economy — its export markets and its manpower — neither of which it could afford to give up without a fight.

The great tariff debates that had taken place in Congress between 1816 and 1833 brought to the fore most of the arguments that were later used for and against the tariff; because of the caliber of the speakers, these arguments were never again so eloquently stated. In many respects the economic policy debates in Congress during that period and the speeches on the tariff question by Clay, Calhoun, Webster, McDuffie, James Hamilton, and others represent a high-water mark in the politicoeconomic history of the United States. Never again was economic policy debated in Congress with such intense emotion or by speakers of such stature and eloquence. Neither were economic policy debates in Congress ever followed before or since with such rapt attention by the electorate and the press. How much of this feeling of interest and participation by the electorate can be attributed to the eloquence of the Congressional leaders and how much to the economics of the situation, specifically to the relationship of the taxpayer to the commodity tax system, remains an unanswerable question. Undoubtedly, both elements played a key part in sparking public interest in the legislative battle over the tariff.

The battle was not confined to the floor of Congress. Public debates and meetings were held throughout the country on the tariff. Although most of the meetings in the North were in favor of protectionism, there were some who spoke against it. In a Free Trade Convention held in Philadelphia in 1831 Albert Gallatin, Jefferson's former Secretary of the Treasury, spoke in favor of the Southern position and against protectionism and pleaded with the protectionists not to "persevere in a course which disturbs the peace of the country and alienates the affections of a numerous portion of their fellow-citizens."[140]

But the North was predominantly protectionist, and the protectionists were regarded by the South as a threat to their economy almost as dangerous as the abolitionists.

5. British Tariff Policy

Before closing this chapter on the early history of the American tariff, it may be instructive to note briefly the British experience. In many ways it provided a striking contrast to the American experience. In England during the first half of the 19th century agriculture, not manufacture, was protected by the tariff. The manufacturing class, represented and championed by two leaders dedicated to the theory of free trade, Richard Cobden and John Bright, fought a long and bitter struggle against the protective tariff.

During the Napoleonic Wars, English agriculture was protected by import taxes and export subsidies and by the effects of the war on foreign competition. At the close of the war period, in 1815 English landlords demanded and obtained continuance of the protection that the Corn Laws gave them. "Corn" in this instance was a generic term for all grains. The importation of wheat was almost prohibited by high import taxes. Keeping the price of grains high helped the landlord, but it raised the level of food prices to the consumer. As a result, in times of poor harvests hundreds of thousands of English workers and their families were brought to the verge of starvation by the high price of bread. For the industrialist, this spelled equal disaster. Since wages must keep pace with food prices, the Corn Laws meant higher labor costs and smaller profits. With all his available income spent on food, the average worker had little left with which to purchase industrial goods. Cobden stated that agricultural laborers had less than $7.50 a year — the value of about three bushels of wheat — to spend on manufactured articles. However, in the House of Commons the landlords had a four-to-one majority over their opponents, and they resisted all efforts to change the Corn Laws.

David Ricardo laid the theoretical foundation for the successful campaign against the Corn Laws and the landlords. Ricardo was a successful business man who made a fortune and retired before the age of 42. He was, for a time, a member of Parliament, but it was as an economist that he achieved worldwide fame. His *Principles of Political Economy and Taxation*, published in 1817, was influential in mobilizing English public opinion against the Corn Laws and against a policy favoring agriculture. Ricardo was an open and bitter enemy of the landlords. As early as 1815 he wrote: "The interest of the landlords is always opposed to the interests of every other class in the community." It must be remembered that, up to that time, the English country gentlemen was considered the paragon of nature. All the great English leaders, from Richard The Lion-Hearted to Wellington, the conqueror of Napoleon, had been nurtured in the stately country homes of England. To besmirch this heroic legend and brand the landlord as a villain was a form of radicalism almost as daring as Marx's attack on the private industrialists a few decades later.

Of course, Ricardo required something more substantial than moral indignation to convince the English people that landlords were villains. He did possess something very solid — an elaborate, logical, complete theory of economics, so beautifully constructed that even Marx admired and envied it and stole his idea of surplus value from it.

Ricardo was able to convince the English people that rents, paid the landlord for the use of the land, were unearned and were a drain on society. They added nothing to production. It was a tax, levied on the producer by the owner for the use of his land, that was passed on to the consumer in the form of higher prices. Ergo, the landlord was a burden, not an asset to the economy.

Proceeding from the labor theory of value and "unearned" rents, Ricardo then attacked the agrarian economy as having a poor growth potential. Agriculture, he said, was subject to the law of diminishing returns. Good land is limited and cannot be replaced or enlarged. Adding more workers and fertilizers increases production, but at some future date the point at which the land cannot and will not produce more will be reached. A society that is based on agriculture is doomed to be a "stationary" society; it cannot progress beyond a certain point. On the other hand, industry is not subject to the limitations of agriculture. Energy can be applied to industrial production in ever-increasing increments, and the result is a higher rate of production. Therefore, the same investment applied to industry will, in the long run, return a better profit or yield than when applied to agriculture. An industrial nation enjoys an advantage over an agricultural nation because it creates wealth faster. It is able to acquire the food it needs by exchanging industrial products at a better than even exchange or "parity" price. Such an industrial nation has a greater growth potential.

Ricardo's attack on the English agricultural interests was successful. How much influence he exerted on the final outcome is debatable, but it was significant. His most severe critic, Keynes, who had a talent for hyperbole, probably exaggerated its importance when he stated, "Ricardo conquered England as completely as the Holy Inquisition conquered Spain."

As a result of the work of Cobden, Bright, and other free traders, the English Parliament finally removed the tariff shelter for agricultural products in 1846. Repeal of the Corn Laws was a pivotal event in English history. It may not by itself have changed England from an agricultural to an industrial nation, but it hastened the change by several decades. It made coal, not grain, the country's staple product.

The British experience did not contradict Hamilton's theory of protection, which applied specifically to young or unborn industries. England was the world leader in the industrial revolution at this time. British manufacturers were much more advanced than others; they had no competition from foreign manufactures and feared none. Their main concern was to find markets for their rapidly expanding production. It was to their interest, therefore, to buy agricultural products from America so that they, in turn, could sell manufactured products in the American and world markets.

British industrial hegemony, however, was relatively short-lived. During the latter half of the 19th century two new industrial giants challenged British supremacy: the United States and Germany. In both countries Hamilton's theory of protection of the home market had considerable popular and political support. In Germany this theory was introduced by Friedrich List, who had lived in the United States and was a disciple of Hamilton. It was later amplified by German economists into a more complete theory of economic nationalism.

At the turn of the century American and German competition had reached a point where it posed a serious threat to British industry. The theory of free trade began to lose its appeal to British manufacturers, and a strong protectionist movement headed by Joseph Chamberlain began to develop at the turn of the century. Chamberlain was a successful businessman who made a fortune in Birmingham and retired at 38. He entered politics and exhibited the same prodigious energy and ability to get things done that had marked his business career. He attacked the national policy of free trade, not with theories, but with facts. In 1903 Chamberlain argued that since 1870 Germany and the United States, with protective tariffs, had outstripped England in trade. He proposed a 10 per cent duty on imported manufactured goods. He spoke of the need for retaliation against foreign tariffs, not only by protecting the English market, but by limiting the free trade area to the British Empire. England had a world empire, and Chamberlain wanted protection for her colonial markets. But the British government had the income tax, in addition to the tariff, to rely on for revenue. England had a large income from overseas investments, insurance, and banking and shipping interests. For these and other reasons protection was not, for England at the beginning of the 20th century, as crucial a problem as it was for Germany. Nevertheless, foreign competition was a factor of increasing importance that forced Britain to abandon its traditional policy of free trade and to adopt a protective policy after World War I.

British experience demonstrated that the tariff could be used for the protection of interests other than manufactures. Prior to 1846 it had been used for the protection of agriculture. It was repealed by the industrialists to serve their purpose, which was theoretically free trade, but in reality against subsidies to agriculture. When free trade no longer served their purpose, English industrialists quickly adopted a protective tariff policy.

6.   The Pro-Labor Tariff

After the Civil War the problems of reconstruction absorbed the energy of the Republicans, the victorious war party, which stood solidly behind the protective tariff. It was not until 1884 that the Democrats, led by Cleveland, were successful in defeating the Republicans, largely on the issue of corruption. In 1887 President Cleveland challenged the Republicans on the tariff issue by sending to Congress his annual message devoted entirely to a single subject, the tariff. Never before had a chief executive devoted his entire annual message to a single topic. Cleveland stated that the Treasury had a surplus and that there was no need for protection. The tariff, he said, should be reduced in the interests of the general public. The Democratic tariff bill introduced on April 2, 1888 was the work of Roger Q. Mills of Texas, an ardent free-trader. It called for a general reduction of rates and free entry of raw materials, including wool.

Rep. William McKinley of Ohio spoke against the bill and immediately became a national figure by challenging the President on this central issue. "We are uncompromisingly in favor of the American system of protection," said McKinley, speaking in the style of Clay, whom he greatly admired. "We protest against its destruction as proposed by the President and his party. They serve the interest of Europe; we will support the interest of America. Its abandonment has always been followed by general disaster to all interests, except those of the usurer and the sheriff. We denounce the Mills bill as destructive to the general business, the labor, the farming interests of the country..."[141]

In 1888 the Republicans defeated Cleveland, largely on the tariff issue; the

190

election was taken as an endorsement of the protective tariff. The Democrats did not seriously challenge the Republican position on this issue again until 1913.

McKinley was successful in tying the protective tariff to the interests of labor. Son of an Ohio ironworker whose business had been hurt by imports, McKinley was deeply convinced that American labor needed protection from cheap foreign labor. "It was a deep conviction, almost a religion with him," according to Robert La Follette, the leader of the Republican progressive wing. In his first major address on the tariff, McKinley stated categorically: "Reduce the tariff and labor is the first to suffer."[142] Again in another speech, "He who would break down the manufactures of this country strikes a fatal blow at labor. It is labor I would protect."[143]

McKinley, like Clay, was passionately committed to the protective tariff and could speak on it with evangelical zeal. Said his biographer: "His campaign tours brought him in contact with thousands of workers, and he never failed to explain patiently why he stood for protection. More than one grimy head nodded in agreement as he toured factories and mines. It was said that he could make a tariff schedule read like poetry . . . He never forgot the lesson of his childhood — cheap foreign iron ruined domestic production, then raised prices. He insisted that the tariff was not paid by the consumer but by the foreign producer. Revenue must be raised and so the selective tariff was most effective, and it both produced funds and protected home industry."[144]

To the academic arguments of economists in favor of free trade McKinley replied that protection might not be "favored in the colleges [but] it is taught in the school of experience, in the workshop, where honest men perform an honest day's labor . . ."

By identifying the interests of labor with the protective tariff, McKinley laid the basis for a broad coalition of labor and industry that was able to resist the Populist revolt of the farmers, who followed William Jennings Bryan into the Democratic party. The tariff was a burning issue in the 1890's until the outbreak of the Spanish-American war in 1898. Thereafter, it was pushed into the background by war and the spread of American involvement in Cuba, Puerto Rico, the Philippines, Panama and, after 1914, in Europe.

After McKinley's death President Theodore Roosevelt captured the attention of the nation with his "trust-busting" campaign, and the Congress was embroiled in the fight to make the income tax constitutional. It was not until 1930 that the protective tariff became the center of a major political battle.

In 1929, just prior to the market crash, the United States seemed to be enjoying a period of prosperity and in no need of higher tariff rates either for revenue or protection. However, agriculture was not sharing in the general prosperity, and it was to bring relief to this sector of the economy that the Smoot-Hawley Tariff Act was enacted.

In a minority report attached to H. R. 2667 dated May 11, 1929, Cordell Hull stated the traditional Democratic stand against the tariff bill and raised the specter of overproduction:

The major effect of tariffs is to transfer wealth from one class to another without affecting the Nation's total. It is safe to say that our productive capacity today is 25 per cent in excess of our ability to consume. . . . If American plants today were unloosed at full production capacity, they would flood all domestic markets within ninety days, and many artificial parts of our economic structure would topple and fall. It is my individual view that these glaring facts and conditions soon will compel America to recognize that these ever-increasing surpluses are her key economic problems, and that our neglect to develop foreign markets for surpluses is the one outstanding cause of unemployment. . . . The conclusion is inescapable that this nation, faced with large and growing surpluses, can advance its economic welfare to a far greater extent by developing these wonderful foreign-trade opportunities than by rejecting them for the sake of an air-tight tariff structure. . . .[145]

A protest against the tariff bill was signed by 1028 economists including many leaders of the professions such as Professor (later Senator) Paul H. Douglas, Professor Irving Fisher, Professor F. W. Taussig, and many others from the leading universities. The protest began with these words:

The undersigned American economists and teachers of economics strongly urge that any measure which provides for a general upward revision of tariff rates by Congress be denied passage, or if passed, be vetoed by the President. We are convinced that increased restrictive duties would be a mistake. They would operate, in general, to increase the prices which domestic consumers would have to pay. By raising prices they would encourage concerns with higher costs to undertake production, thus compelling the consumer to subsidize waste and inefficiency in industry. At the same time they would force him to pay higher rates of profit ro established firms which enjoyed lower production costs. A higher level of duties, such as contemplated by the Smoot-Hawley bill, would therefore raise the cost of living and injure the great majority of our citizens.[146]

The Republican position was stated by the Secretary of the Treasury, Andrew W. Mellon:

Our tariff policy has been mainly responsible for the development of manufacturing in America. Our tariff policy has brought to labor the highest real wages in history. The development of manufacturing has been accompanied by improved methods and quantity production, and we have been able to make and distribute at a relatively low price, considering the high cost of labor. In many lines we more than meet foreign competition with its low labor costs. In turn high wages have created a great consuming population, which has been the principal factor in our reaching quantity production and thus low costs. A study of the industries in this country shows a very small margin of profit per unit and large profits in the aggregate possible only through large turn-over. . . . The trend of trade during the past few years convincingly confirms the contention that the overall volume of imports is controlled by the purchasing power of the nation rather than the rate of import duties assessed. . . . No economic survey of world conditions can reach correct conclusions unless this major factor — the high purchasing power of the United States — is taken into account and its effect intelligently understood.[147]

Secretary Mellon spoke of the danger of tempting manufacturers to move to areas of low labor costs:

If the tariff is taken off, a larger share of manufacturing will be done abroad, where the costs are less. The United States is the largest customer in the world today.... It is inconceivable to me that American labor will ever consent to the abolition of protection, which would bring the American standard of living down to the level of that in Europe; or that the American farmer could survive if the enormous consuming power of the people in this country was curtailed and his market at home destroyed.

The Republican majority assured the passage of the Smoot-Hawley Tariff Act in 1930, but the protectionists' moment of triumph was short-lived. When the depression struck, the Smoot-Hawley Tariff was blamed as one of the principal causes. However, a study of the total drop in imports from the high of 1929 to the low of 1932 indicates that about two-thirds of the decline came before the Smoot-Hawley Tariff Act became effective. The history of the United States imports seems to bear out the contention that there is no significant correlation between tariff rates and imports. Nevertheless, the depression shattered the Republican myth of being the party of prosperity; the tariff was part of the myth. Before the depression the average American believed the tariff to be a major safeguard for the maintenance of employment and of domestic industrial prosperity. After 1930 he no longer thought so.

Most statesmen such as Hamilton would be willing to concede that, in a world of peace and perfect competition, trade should flow without restrictions so that all nations would benefit from the advantages of the international division of labor and the natural advantages of climate and soil.

The world being imperfect and international competition being, in the nature of things, less than perfect, politicians are forced to initiate policies and programs to protect the national interest of their respective countries. The tariff was an effective and flexible instrument of national economic policy, as proved by its long and continuing history. In the 19th century statesmen used it to further the particular national goals chosen by the nation or its leaders.

In the preindustrial or postfeudal age, the tariff was used by Walpole and Pitt the elder in England, by Colbert in France, and by other European statesmen to build up the national power of the central government, to accumulate capital by a favorable balance of trade, and to invest this capital in colonial or national expansion.

In the late 18th century European and American statesmen began to realize that national power was a function of industrial power, that without industry a nation was defenseless, as well as economically backward. This seems a truism today, but in the 18th century the Rousseau-Jefferson reaction against urban society and the Quesnay-Smith doctrines of agrarian GNP as the measure of wealth were the leading ideologies of the time. James Watt, Arkwright, Eli Whitney, Hargreaves, and other inventors were creating a revolution, but their names were not known. Hamilton was the first statesman to see the full implication of the industrial revolution before it had yet become a reality in America, and he was the first statesman to develop an economic plan to bridge the transition from an agricultural to an industrial economy. His adaptation of the tariff for the purpose of stimulating industrial growth was a sound and practical plan, although, of course, Hamilton had other recommendations to go with the tariff: on banking, public debt, credit, excises, and subsidies.

The protective tariff became so dominant in American life and history that it is difficult for Americans to realize that the tariff is merely a system of commodity taxation and that, whether it is protective or neutral or whether it protects manufactures or some other such facet of the economy as commerce, labor, consumers, or farming, it is determined entirely by those who frame the tariff law. This versatility of the tariff was amply demonstrated by the American and British experience. The Hamiltonian concept of protection for young industries was a brilliant and farsighted exercise of statesmanship at the earliest stage of industrial development. Protection for industry became less relevant as American industry established itself. By the 1840's the chief argument in favor of protection was that it was needed to protect high-paid American labor against low-paid foreign labor. During the Populist revolt of the 1880's and 1890's the tariff was attacked by the farmer groups, but later these same farmers clamored the loudest for protection. The Smoot-Hawley Tariff of 1930 was chiefly the work of Senator Smoot, who sought protection for the beet sugar and other agricultural interests. After the Civil War agriculture was rapidly mechanized and became as much an industry as any other. Whether it needed protection is a debatable point, but the agricultural industry saw no reason why other industries should receive all the tax benefits from the tariff while it was left out in the cold.

Oswald Garrison Villard, a well-known editor and ardent free trader commented acidly:

> That beet sugar company which produced 48 per cent of the American crop in 1892 increased its earnings in that year no less than 171 per cent, earning $11.22 a share on its stock, which has a par value of $25, while passing itself off as an infant industry in the process of being ruined by Cuban competition, and therefore in need of a still higher tax. It is the height of economic injustice to favor these people when there are other useful industries that struggle along without government aid. It is political and social, as well as economic injustice, that the bulk of the American people should be taxed to support a privileged few, and insure them vast profits.[148]

The Hamiltonian concept of a tariff policy devoted to the national welfare had been forgotten in the rush of each producer to grab as much of a tax subsidy as he could.

To summarize this chapter on the tariff, it is obvious that the tariff is not a simple tax standing by itself, but that it is a part of a large complex system of commodity or consumption taxation. It is a system that may be adapted to a great variety of economic interests and social conditions. The use to which the tariff was put in the United States was as wide and varied as the imagination and ingenuity of lawmakers, and this indicates the flexibility inherent in a system of commodity taxation.

This brief and necessarily sketchy outline of tariff history serves to illustrate a few simple facts: that commodity taxation existed in the United States for a long period of time; that it financed the operations of the Federal government over a century of progress in peace and war; and that it was a system adaptable to changing conditions and had many excellent features not found in a system of personal taxation.

194

Considering its long and successful role as the chief American revenue tax, why did the Roosevelt administration turn its back on it in 1932 and place its faith and hope on direct taxes?

There are many reasons. The tariff, especially the Smoot-Hawley tariff of 1930, was associated with the unpopular Republican administration of Hoover. The Republican Party "Proclaimed year after year that theirs was the party of prosperity, and that the high tariff was the grand instrument of prosperity."[149] This economic strategy had been very successful for the Republicans until 1930, when the Smoot-Hawley tariff act and the great depression left the Republicans with their economic strategy completely shattered. The Democratic Party had, since Cleveland's time, been associated with a low-tariff policy. It was natural, therefore, for Roosevelt to incline toward a tariff policy that had been traditional with the Democratic Party, a policy he had inherited from his great predecessor and teacher, Woodrow Wilson. Nevertheless, undoubtedly a much greater inducement was the fact that the income tax offered greater possibilities for revenue. Revenues derived from the tariff were limited by the volume of imports, which amounted in 1932 to $1.3 billion, or 2.3 per cent of the GNP. This was too small and narrow a base on which to build a tax system large enought to fund the ambitious New Deal welfare programs. The New Deal politicians and economists felt that the income tax could reach vast new sources of wealth untouched by the tariff and thus greatly expand total government revenues.

It was becoming apparent in the 1930s that the conditions of the international market were making tariffs obsolete. The tariff works best where international trade flows along established trade channels without smuggling, corruption, or political interference. Starting about 1930, the nations of the world began to initiate policies of direct manipulation of the economy in the form of currency and exchange controls, import and export subsidies, wage and price controls, investment credit, and the entire panoply of monetary and fiscal policies that are now used by all governments under a "managed" economy. These political controls subvert the function of tariffs and render them almost useless except as a revenue tax measure. Currency controls and internal economic controls are more important today in controlling and directing foreign trade than the tariff policy.

For these and other reasons, Roosevelt decided to shift the tax base from consumption to income. The income tax rates were substantially increased and the income base broadened. The relative ease with which this was accomplished can be explained by the economic crisis, which made the people accept income tax rates they would normally have resisted. The tariff was relegated to a minor role in the tax structure. For the first time in American history the tariff was relieved of what had originally been its primary function — revenue. Tax revenues were obtainable from the income tax on a gradually expanding scale. The government tax collectors now had the entire internal wealth of the country to draw on, not just the relatively small segment represented by imports. At that time the potential of the income tax seemed inexhaustible. Never before had so much untapped wealth been turned over legally to the agents of the United States Treasury. Of course, this wealth had been laid bare in 1913, when the income tax act was passed, but Congress had not had the temerity to expropriate the private wealth of the nation on the scale that Roosevelt did and probably would not have been permitted to do so by public opinion before the depression.

With the revenue problem taken care of by the income tax, Roosevelt was free to adjust tariff rates to suit his foreign policy. The mood of the Democratic Party was in favor of reducing barriers to world trade, that is, to adopt as close to a free-trade policy as political conditions permitted. Instead of lowering rates by passing a new tariff bill, however, Roosevelt asked and received executive powers to adjust tariff rates. The Reciprocal Trade Agreement Act was passed in 1934 as an amendment (Section 350) to the Tariff Act of 1930. It is ironic that the two measures that killed the tariff — the Income tax act and the Reciprocal Trade Agreement Act — were both passed as *amendments* to a tariff act.

When the Reciprocal Trade Agreement Act was passed, the tariff issue ceased to be a domestic issue of any consequence. The tariff problem passed out of the hands of Congress and became part of the executive power, specifically an economic weapon used by the President in the conduct of foreign affairs.

The decline of the tariff as an effective tool of economic policy is the result of the emergence of the income tax as the primary revenue law and the increasing use of nontariff measures to control foreign trade. The nontariff measures include, but are not limited to, state trading, embargoes, quotas, licensing, artificial exchange rates, blocked currency, direct subsidies to exporters, government-to-government loans, barter deals, bilateral trade agreements, exchange retention systems, tax relief measures, lower interest rates, insurance, guarantees to exporters, and other measures

Historically, the tariff policy of the United States developed on a unilateral basis. It was assumed that, in determining tariff policy, Congress did not need to be concerned with the effect such a policy might have on foreign interests, which were regarded as relatively unimportant compared to domestic interests. Under the Reciprocal Trade Agreement Act, tariff-making becomes a bargaining process in which other nations participate. Executive tariff-making is based on the premise of reciprocity and is the result of international negotiation rather than domestic legislation.

To avoid the need for Congressional approval, the tariff agreements worked out by the President with foreign powers are called executive agreements. The Republicans at first fought this method as unconstitutional but, after coming to power in 1954, they found that they could not unravel the executive agreements already made and were likewise unable to restore to Congress the tariff-making power.

The complexity of the economic controls used by all governments to control their import-export trade has forced the Congress to continue the policy of letting the executive deal with the problem by negotiation, since tariff barriers, per se, appear to be easily bypassed, and only the executive is in a position to carry on negotiations with representatives of other governments on nontariff obstructions.

In his trade message to Congress on April 10, 1973 President Nixon enumerated the various barriers to trade and noted that,

> Nontariff barriers have greatly proliferated as tariffs have declined. These barriers to trade, in other countries and in ours, presently cost the United States several billion dollars a year in the form of higher consumer prices and the inefficient use of our resources.... I am confident that our free and vigorous American economy can more than hold its own in open world competition. But we must always insist that such competition take place under equitable rules. The key to success in our coming trade negotiations will be the negotiating authority the United States brings to the bargaining table.

The President pleaded for a new Trade Reform Act of 1973 to give him greater powers to negotiate tariff and nontariff concessions with foreign powers. The tariff, as a system of commodity taxation, under Congressional control, for influencing the domestic economy has ceased to exist.

Despite the eclipse of the tariff, it does not follow that consumption taxation is obsolete or has been permanently abandoned. The undue and total dependence of the United States government on income taxation for tax revenues has reached a dead end. It is not likely that the income tax will be entirely abandoned, but it does seem likely that consumer taxes will be brought back and applied in some new form to the problems of public finance.

Commodity taxes collected from the consumer have many excellent qualities that make them superior to personal income taxes.

1. They are neutral and impersonal in application.
2. They are automatic in collection.
3. They are voluntary in payment.
4. They are readily applicable to a variety of economic conditions.
5. They can be made progressive and selective in their rate schedules.
6. They can be applied to internal and/or external trade.
7. They can be incorporated into the market price system and, for that reason, do not require a substitute redistributive agency or bureaucratic apparatus.
8. They can be controlled by Congress through the legislative process of debate and consensus and, for that reason, do not require the undue expansion of executive power and rule by administrative orders.

It would be misleading, however, to claim that commodity taxes are in themselves the perfect and complete answer to all tax problems or that Congress is incapable of making mistakes in carrying out a commodity tax program. The long history of the tariff proves that Congressional tax powers under the tariff were sometimes exercised in the national interest by high-minded statesmen and at other times in an atmosphere of corruption and deceit by politicians who were influenced by special interests. F. W. Taussig, the leading authority on the American tariff, wrote: "Everyone knows that the traditional ways of framing tariff legislation have been in the highest degree haphazard... Our tariffs have been settled in ignorant and irresponsible fashions. Of this we have become painfully aware and it is natural that we should look for some sort of remedy."[150] Professor Taussig wrote this criticism in 1920; the remedy he had in mind was the appointment of a permanent tariff commission to aid Congress in its deliberations on tax policy. The remedy that was applied to the tariff a few years later was much more drastic — its almost complete liquidation by Roosevelt and its replacement by income taxation. It was not as successful a remedy as had been anticipated.

7.   The American Tradition

The principle that a government is responsible for the welfare of its people is accepted by all nations and is inscribed in the United States Constitution. However, the Constitution does not lay down an economic plan to achieve this objective. In the United States the birth of the government coincided with the birth of laissez-faire capitalism — *The Wealth of Nations* and the Declaration of Independence both appeared in 1776. The birth of the United States also coincided with the death of mercantilism, the economic system by which in the 17th and 18th centuries national governments managed and controlled the economy in very minute detail; the American revolution started as a reaction to taxes imposed for the benefit of the British East India Company, a government-controlled monopoly. At the very outset, therefore, the United States government was influenced by economic and political theories and events that were against any form of direct government intervention in economic affairs and in favor of leaving the market free to allocate resources and set priorities.

In Europe, on the other hand, 18th century mercantilism remained as a very strong political tradition and was associated, not with colonial submission, as in the United States, but with imperial power: the reign of Louis XIV in France and the rise of Parliament in England. Theories of state control were, therefore, more easily accepted in Europe than in America. State control and management of the economy in Europe was never regarded as a totally foreign and repugnant theory. It was, in fact, more natural and less alien than the American theory of absolute individual economic freedom and independence. The European peasant and the American pioneer were worlds apart. Europe had long since outlived its pioneer or frontier days. It had long ago accepted the fact of state supremacy and of individual dependence on the state. The French revolution was not followed by Jeffersonian democracy, but by the dictatorship of Napoleon and the restoration of the monarchy. Of course, there were varying shades of economic and political dependency. In England political and economic freedoms were well established and protected by law, although an aristocratic tradition exercised a strong influence over the economy and the government. In other countries, a rule by a strong paternalistic government was never seriously challenged. In Russia the revolution of 1917 merely changed one form of absolutism for another; the Russian people are still totally dependent on the government. There is no independent legislative assembly; the executive power is supreme, as it was under the Tsars. Western European governments are strongly paternalistic; the concept of national welfare tends toward the Socialist ideal, that is, the concept of government ownership and/or control of the economy, with the individual totally dependent on the state from the cradle to the grave.

This concept was, until very recently, altogether alien to the American tradition of individualism and of independence from the state. This tradition was shattered by the great depression. The New Deal adopted Keynesian and Socialist policies imported from Europe. Since then the European influence has continued. World War II brought a great number of European intellectuals to America. Their intellectual eminence exercised a strong hold on American political thought. Einstein in the physical sciences, Keynes in the social sciences, and Freud in the behavorial sciences are examples of the quality of the European intellectuals who came to dominate American intellectual life after the 1930's.

The European influence was probably inevitable, given the advance in communications and transportation and the active participation of the United States in world affairs. Undoubtedly it has contributed to the quality of American thought and has given it a world outlook that it certainly did not possess before World War I. The scholarship of the middle-European scientists was especially outstanding and exercised a profound influence.

In the social sciences the European intellectual was steeped in the tradition of state absolutism, which had a long European history, not only in practice, but in theory, from Plato to Hegel and Marx. A few Europeans such as Ludwig von Mises and Leo Strauss were enemies of the collectivist society; others such as Keynes were Fabian Socialists rather than Marxists; but many, perhaps a majority, were like Herbert Marcuse, so thoroughly steeped in the Hegelian philosophy of state absolutism that they would be incapable of understanding American political history and philosophy, even if they read it.

In fact, it is doubtful that they did. European intellectuals have always regarded European science and philosophy as incomparably superior to the American. The United States, they claim, has produced no great philosopher or scientist. They point out that the best exposition of American democracy was written by de Tocqueville and that the leading American philosopher was Santayana, who was born in Spain. America has produced no Newton, no Darwin, no Einstein, no Spinoza, no Hegel. The European intellectual, even when he emigrates to America, retains this innate belief in European intellectual superiority and is likely to ignore or belittle American political and economic history and theory.

The American intellectual, especially in the social sciences, is likely to stand in awe of such intellectual giants as Spencer, Comte, Marx, Freud, Ricardo, Walras, Pareto, Weber, Durkheim, and Keynes. Only in rare cases has America produced a world-recognized genius of comparable stature; William James and John Dewey are two such rare cases.

The result has been, since World War I, the gradual Europeanization of American intellectual life, the deliberate deemphasis of American political thought. How many American college students are familiar with the Constitutional theory of the division of powers, the *Federalist* papers, Calhoun's theory of consensus, the basic principles of Jeffersonian and Jacksonian democracy, the economic theories of Hamilton, or the political philosophy of Madison and Adams?

The emphasis in modern American colleges is on Hegelian-Marxist socio-political philosophy and the numerous deviations or sects it has spawned. The American political heritage is all but forgotten. This is not a healthy condition, for a nation, like an individual, cannot cut its own roots and not feel the loss. A European-born economist has observed:

> The welfare of the individual depends on the extent to which he can identify himself with others, and that the most satisfactory individual identity is that which identifies not only with a community in space but also with a community extending over time from the past into the future ... and there is a great deal of historical evidence to suggest that a society which loses its identity with posterity and which loses its positive image of the future loses also its capacity to deal with present problems, and soon falls apart.

It is true, of course, that America, South as well as North, has always looked upon Europe as its cultural mother and teacher. The dependence was even stronger during the early days. The Founding Fathers drew heavily on European culture and thought, both ancient and recent. The influence of Locke, Montesquieu, Harrington, Rousseau, Smith, Hume, and Hobbes is obvious. There were then no native cultural resources to draw on. But, by one of those historical accidents that occur without known causes, the American revolutionary period, like similar periods in Elizabethan England, Renaissance Italy, and Periclean Greece, produced an extraordinary crop of talented men. They combined the imported ideas with their own native genius and produced a new and original creation — the American Republic — which was distinctly and uniquely American and not a copy of a European model. As the nation grew into a new unexplored frontier, it acquired further cultural characteristics and traditions that further differentiated it from European models. Early American leaders such as Lincoln, for example, were able to formulate their political philosophies and achieve a remarkable purity and profundity of thought without going to political sources other than the works of the Founding Fathers.

In the 19th century the European intellectual influence was still very strong. But the American culture — raw, by European standards — was already set. It was individualistic, pragmatic, and utilitarian. The philosophies of Bentham and Spencer were favored because they fitted the American pattern. Marxism was rejected by the Populists and the Progressives, by Bryan, La Follette, and Theodore Roosevelt, as well as the party regulars, Cleveland and McKinley. These leaders found their inspiration in Jefferson, Hamilton, Madison, Adams, Clay, Webster, and Lincoln, not in European statesmen and theorists. At the start of the 20th century America already felt it had a manifest destiny of its own and was beginning to suspect that European culture was old and decadent, living in the past.

To most Americans, as well as to the poorer classes of Europe, America was the land of the future. Except in medicine, Americans felt they had nothing to learn from Europe. Faith in American political and economic institutions was supreme. American intellectuals who were not in tune with this nationalistic culture followed Henry James to Europe. In 1917 President Wilson sent the American army to Europe to "make the world safe for democracy," that is, to teach Europe American-style democracy.

Two world wars and a great depression exploded the American conceit. Although victorious, the Americans were thrown into intimate contact with the older European cultures and realized that they still had much to learn from them. Americans asked von Braun to take them to the moon; Fermi and Teller to help them conquer the atom; Keynes to teach them macroeconomics; Toscanini and Stokowski to lead their orchestras; Picasso to teach them art; Einstein to instruct them in physics; and Stravinsky to broaden their concept of music.

In the field of social sciences the Europeans humbled the American spirit. The natural sciences are neutral — they have no effect on the spirit, except perhaps to teach it humility. But in the social sciences the spiritual effect is paramount. New ideas can shatter traditional beliefs and shake the faith in established institutions. The Marxist-Leninist-Maoist theories of Socialism wrapped in Hegelian dialectics and brilliantly expounded by such men as G. B. Shaw, H. G. Wells, Benedetto Croce, Bertrand Russell, J. M. Keynes, and Herbert Marcuse had an overwhelming impact on American thought directly through their original books and indirectly through the teaching of their European disciples who came to America before and after World War II and took leading posts in American universities. The effect on the postwar generations is evidenced by a marked decline of student interest in American political and economic theory; a loss of faith in American institutions; and a decided preference for European political philosophy of the Socialist variety. The American university student of today is more likely to be "turned on" by Mao's Little Red Book than by the *Federalist* papers.

The present passion for European sociopolitical theory is not unhealthy, but the denigration of American political thought certainly is. In the political and social history of Europe there is nothing to equal the American experience. This experience is unique. It has given rise to certain political institutions that also are unique. They have been copied by Europeans, but not duplicated. American political life has a dynamic that is missing from European politics. American political theory may be inferior to European in abstract or metaphysical content, but it is superior in its pragmatic and humanistic approach. This finds its roots in the fact that political theory in the United States has been the work, not of theorists, but of statesmen. Jefferson, Adams, Hamilton, Webster, Madison, Lincoln, Calhoun, Wilson, and the two Roosevelts were not philosophers in the academic sense, but their state papers and speeches on politics helped to form political policies and institutions that are quintessentially American and in many ways superior to the European variety.

Solutions to problems of American life are more likely to be found in the American experience and thought than in the theories and experiences evolved in European societies. This is not to deny that some ideas may have universal application. Hamilton's ideas were greatly admired and copied in Hegelian Germany. Nevertheless, in the life of a community, as in the life of an individual, there are unique experiences that shape its destiny and character. It is these unique experiences that set one nation apart from another and make policies that work in one country unworkable in another.

In the field of taxation the long American acquaintance with the protective tariff is an invaluable experience from which much may be learned. The principles of selective taxes based on national interest; the incorporation of a differential tax into the price system; the use of the legislative process to define and execute broad economic policy; the rejection of inquisitorial personal or direct taxes; the avoidance of a nonmarket redistributive system in the government sector — these and other principles make the Hamiltonian approach to taxes one that could serve as a model for a modern system of commodity taxation.

Chapter
VI

NEW TAXES ON CONSUMPTION

1. Shifting from Income to Consumption.

The selectivity, flexibility and versatility of commodity taxes have not been lost on modern legislators, and increasingly they are turning to such taxes for additional revenues. These modern commodity taxes have assumed new forms and new names and are better known in some countries as "purchase taxes," "turn-over taxes," "value-added taxes," and "sales taxes."

In England during World War II the traditional excises on liquor and tobacco were supplemented by the purchase tax (sales tax) on many products at rates as high as 100 per cent. The turn-over tax is the tax presently favored by the Soviet government. It is an excise tax levied on a commodity at each stage of its production or distribution.

A variation of the turn-over tax is the value-added tax invented by the Frenchman Maurice Laure in 1954. To avoid the pyramiding effect of the turn-over tax, Laure introduced the idea of taxing only the value that each producer adds to the product. A table that passes through three stages of production and distribution — lumber mill, furniture factory, retail store — is taxed three times, but each time only on the value that each has added to the product. The value-added tax has become the world's fastest growing revenue producer. In 1971 it produced 52 per cent of France's $30 billion of taxes and 25 per cent of Germany's $51 billion of taxes. It raised one-third of the tax revenues in Belgium in 1971 in its first year and 26 per cent in Holland. Italy and Britain adopted it in 1973.

The element of social value is incorporated in the value-added tax, but not with the completeness of the tariff schedule. The sales tax in California, like those of many other states, incorporates social value in a limited way. It exempts food and drugs from the tax. In France the standard rate adds 23 per cent to the retail prices of most goods and up to 33 per cent to "luxury" goods. The Brussels Commission has suggested a standard rate for the Common Market of about 15 per cent. In 1972 British tax experts recommended that the national sales tax be abolished and replaced by a value-added tax of zero rate on food and housing and 10 per cent on other items.

In February 1972 the President's Advisory Commission on Intergovernmental Relations was asked to study and report on the draft of a White House plan to impose a 3 per cent national value-added sales tax. It is estimated that this tax would raise $16 billion dollars a year and could be used to finance education and take some of the load off the property tax. The value-added tax has been strongly opposed by liberal politicians and labor leaders. Most economists — Paul A. Samuelson, for example — feel that the value-added tax is just a sugarcoated sales tax. In their opinion, it is less visible than a sales tax, but just as unfair to the poor. It is, in the economists' jargon, "regressive" or unfair as compared to the graduated income tax, which is "progressive" or fair.

It appears that the value-added tax is comparable to the older excise taxes, which emphasized the social value of luxuries and necessities on a sliding scale, with luxuries and potentially harmful products — liquor or tobacco — getting the highest tax rate. However, this social value aspect of the value-added tax appears, at this stage, to be a minor consideration, with the major emphasis being laid on its high yield, enforceability, and neutral effect on competition. To obtain the full effect of social value in taxation, the politicians would have to turn to the tariff or to a similar complete system of commodity taxation made applicable to domestic commodities. Under such a system the income tax would decline in relative importance, and the tax base would be shifted from income to consumption.

Substituting consumption for income as a tax base would not necessarily alter the broad political objectives of the tax system according to economist Richard Goode.

The most important difference between income and consumption as tax bases resides in the difference in allocation *of the base* among individuals and over time for any one person. In the aggregate, the difference cannot be great because most disposable personal income is consumed. From 1950 to 1963 personal consumption expenditures in the United States were never less than 92 per cent nor more than 94 per cent of disposable personal income in any year. For particular families and individuals, of course, the difference is greater than for the aggregate, since the total includes units with consumption and income ratios above and below the average. But for a large fraction almost the same arithmetic result would be obtained by applying an income tax and an expenditure tax schedule that would yield the same total revenue.... Consumption is a genuine rival to personal income as an index of ability to pay taxes and as a basis for the assessment of progressive taxes. Citing Hobbes, Kaldor has contended that it may be just and expedient to tax people with reference to what they take out of the common pool [the national product] rather than what they contribute and has suggested that consumption may be a better tax base than income.[152]

Prior to 1913 consumption, not income, was the base of the United States Federal tax system. The battles over national economic priorities and tax policy were fought in Congress over the tariff, which was a complete system of commodity taxation.

After studying the experiences of European nations with various types of commodity taxes, it has been suggested that the United States also should restore commodity taxation in some form that would incorporate the ideals of fairness, equity, and ability to pay. The basis of taxation would be shifted from income to expenditure or consumption. Kaldor makes a strong case for a spending tax:

> The point is that no definition of income, which is a plausible one for purposes of tax assessment, can measure taxable capacity. Accruals from the various sources cannot be reduced to a common unit of spending power on any objective criteria. But each individual performs this operation for himself when, in the light of all his present circumstances and future prospects, he decides on the scale of his personal living expenses. Thus a tax based on actual spending rates each individual's spending capacity according to the yardstick which he applies to himself. Once actual spending is taken as the criterion all the problems created by the non-comparability of work-incomes and property-incomes, of temporary and permanent sources of wealth, of genuine and fictitious capital gains resolve themselves; they are all brought into equivalence in the measure in which they support the actual standard of living.[153]

Kaldor disposes of the argument that a spending or consumption tax is regressive or less progressive than an income tax by stating that "it would be perfectly possible to vary the rate of progression" in one as in the other. As to the moral or ethical superiority of the income tax, Kaldor follows Hobbes and takes a contrary position:

> An inhabitant from Mars, admiring the highly intricate arrangements whereby men in society satisfy their needs in common through mutual cooperation, would surely be puzzled to discover that each individual's contribution to the finance of socially provided benefits depends not on the sum of benefits he receives from the community but on his personal contribution to the wealth of the others. It is only by spending, not by earning or saving, that an individual imposes a burden on the rest of the community in attaining his own ends. In all his other activities his own interests and the interests of the community run not counter to one another but parallel. Why should 'he which laboureth much and sparing of the fruits of his labour, consumeth little, be more charged than he that liveth idlely, getteth little, and spendeth all he gets'? It is by the 'luxurious waste of private men', and not by the praiseworthy activities of Working, or Saving or Risk Taking, that 'the Commonwealth is defrauded.' The implication of this argument is that in considering what constitutes the fairest tax system we cannot stop short of reflection on the social consequences of individual behaviour, and the effect of the behaviour on the tax system itself. Though questions of incentives are usually regarded as quite distinct from questions of equity, in the last analysis it is impossible to arrive at any ultimate criteria of 'fairness' without taking the economic and social repercussions of individual behaviour into account.

However, Kaldor's recommended expenditure tax was based on *total* expenditures to be used as the basis of assessment. This presented practical difficulties that politicians judged to be insurmountable.

Another alternative system of commodity taxation is a modified tariff system that would apply to domestic commodities the same principle of taxation that the tariff has always applied to foreign commodities — the principle of social value. In tariff policy debates this principle is usually called "the public interest" or "the national interest" principle. In setting tariff rates legislators have sometimes been motivated by narrow sectional, personal, or class interests but, since the tariff rates are set by the Congress and not by any one legislator, the national interest cannot be ignored. It is expected that in a system of commodity taxation similar to the tariff but applied to domestic commodities — an internal tariff system — the principle of social value and national interest would prevail over class or sectional interests. Is such an internal tariff system practical and, if so, how would it be constructed and by whom would it be administered?

In the first place, the internal tariff would not require any basic structural changes in the government or require a Constitutional amendment, as was required by the income tax law. The power to tax would still be lodged in Congress, but the internal tariff would make that power more real. The economic power of the executive would be reduced, but not abrogated. The Federal budget would continue to be a very powerful instrument for guiding the economy. Budget appropriations for defense, education, health, public roads, space, and other government programs would still be required, and their impact on the national economy would continue to be significant. The preparation of the budget would still remain in the hands of the executive, but under the internal tariff the Congress would take over many of the economic functions now handled by him. The allocation of resources would be accomplished mainly through the internal tariff, and the setting of national economic priorities in *both* the private and public sectors would be controlled *directly* by Congress. Under the present system resources are squeezed out of the private sector by the income tax and diverted to the public sector, where the executive in many cases must redistribute them to the private sector in the form of grants, subsidies, and loans.

The internal tariff would make this circular distribution redundant. The internal tariff would not tax income and then return income for need. The needed commodities would be provided directly by a social value added tax that would (1) make commodities available as needed, (2) eliminate the bureaucracy that is required to levy the income tax, and administer the welfare aid programs, the farm support programs, the various subsidy programs, and the food-stamp programs that the government now uses to redistribute income and regulate the lives and consumer habits of its poorer citizens. The internal tariff tax would be an automatic regulator of needed commodities providing a basic level of commodity consumption to satisfy primary needs.

This is not to say that basic commodities such as milk, bread, housing, and clothing would be free to all. All commodities would cost something, with or without a tax. However, the regulation of the amount added or detracted as social value by Congress would automatically regulate the distribution *in the aggregate* of the taxed commodity. The distribution of socially needed commodities — basic food, clothing, and shelter — would be guaranteed on a need or use basis, although market competition would not be restricted but encouraged in the production of the commodities. All commodities would be marketed under open competition and sold according to consumer preference and disposable income.

Khrushchev once boasted that at a future date the Russian consumer would be given *free* 50 per cent of all goods and services that the consumer in the West had to buy at exorbitant prices. This is good political propaganda, but economic nonsense. It makes no difference economically if people are taxed directly or indirectly for goods the government provides free or whether the consumer buys those goods in a free market with his own untaxed income. In England, for example, the consumer is taxed about 13.5 per cent of his income for *free* National Health Service. Economists in Russia, as well as those in the West, know that there are no *free* goods. In a world of scarce and limited resources, all goods produced by man carry a price in energy consumed, human and inanimate. Free distribution is possible where consumers are not free to choose, as in a prison or in the army, or in a mobilized economy, or under a government aid program. In a market economy the consumer is free to make a choice. This freedom would be preserved under the internal tariff system. Although basic essential commodities would be priced low, they would carry a price and be subject to consumer choice and market competition.

Many goods and services now provided by the government through budget allocation could be handled through the traditional channels of market competition under the internal tariff system. The extent to which the internal tariff is used to restore consumer choice and to relieve the government of direct management responsibility for providing goods and services would be determined by the people through their elected representatives. Public goods and services that are provided by the government need not be made by the government. The United States government uses submarines, but does not make them. Whether the government should be in the pollution-control business, transportation business, health care business, housing and construction business, electric power business, or child-care business is not determined by the nature of the product or service, but by the government's economic policy.

Some social needs cannot be supplied entirely by the market — national defense, public roads, and public sanitation, for example — although the market can be used to supply services and goods to government departments. In some cases the nature of the product makes market competition impracticable: the consumer does not need more than one telephone or electric company or one water system. In these cases government regulations or government ownership may be indicated.

Where the element of free choice is possible, the market provides the best mechanism for balancing demand and supply. The internal tariff would preserve the market price mechanism wherever it can be used. At the same time it would break down the barriers between the private and public sectors of the economy and bring both within a unified economy using the same priorities.

The conflict that exists between the two sectors promotes national disunity and makes it difficult to pursue common national goals.

In 1970 Congress cut back funds for high-technology research, space research, and the supersonic transport on the ground of economy, although the American people were undoubtedly in favor of these projects. It was a question of priorities, however, and Congress felt that the tax funds were needed for more urgent tasks such as fighting environmental pollution, urban renewal, health and welfare, education, and other social welfare needs. The nation could not afford the Apollo program, according to Congress; so the moon exploration program was abandoned and the $25 billion written off as a dead-end publicity stunt to prove that Americans could beat the Russians to the moon. Yet, based on 1969 averages, the United States could afford to spend five times as much for highway construction as it did on the Apollo program; twice as much for cigarettes and tobacco; twice as much for soap and toilet goods; ten times as much for gasoline; twice as much for household appliances; as much for toys and sporting goods; as much or more for tires; as much or more for paying farmers not to grow crops; as much for jewelry, silverware, notions and greeting cards; twice as much for foreign travel; five times as much for public assistance; twice as much for veterans' programs; 50 times more for social welfare; as much or more for soft drinks and beverages; 26 times more for cars and automotive products; five times as much for liquor; eight times as much for advertising; twice as much for laundry and dry cleaning; as much or more for beauty shops and barber shops; and over twice as much for auto repairs.

Obviously, for the United States it was not a question of being able to afford lunar exploration; it was a question of intersectoral priorities. The priorities set within the public sector were not applicable to the private sector. There can be, in a two-sector economy, no trade-offs between goods and services in all sectors of the economy. The private sector has its own priorities based on market values, and these cannot be reconciled with the priorities in the public sector based on political or nonmarket values. A high national priority could be given to advanced technology and scientific research, not only in the field of space and aviation, but in many other fields in which the United States is falling behind other nations. The priorities of the mass consumer market in the private sector will not permit it, however. National priorities are applicable only for the public sector and are set only through the Federal budget.

2. The Internal Tariff

The internal tariff would be a method of incorporating the principle of social value in the price system through the medium of commodity taxation. This principle has been used from colonial times in the protective tariff; in a few selected excises on luxury goods in wartime; in the current price-support programs for farm products; in excises on tobacco and alcoholic beverages under current United States laws; in sales taxes that exempt food and drugs; and in the new types of excise taxes that have become popular in many European countries. Of all known taxes, the protective tariff as conceived by Hamilton is the one that best demonstrates the principle of social value.

No modern nation allows all foreign products to enter its domestic market freely and indiscriminately. Even where the tariff is used mainly for raising revenue, there are multiple rates of duty that reflect the social value the nation places on certain imported products. It selects those that come in free and those that pay low or high taxes according to a schedule based on its own criteria of social values. The scale of values incorporated in the tariff may be misguided, shortsighted, and economically unsound, but all nations base their tariff rates on their scale of social value, that is, on their own concept of what is beneficial or injurious to their own national interests. This is a value judgment, and the tax on imports is a method of incorporating social value in the imported commodity.

Market prices alone are not usually considered sufficient criteria of value for setting a tax rate on imported commodities. The ideal of "free trade," that is, competition between nations on a straight market price basis, has been popular at times in countries enjoying superior economic advantages. England was the dominant industrial power in the 19th century and after 1846 favored free trade. However, competition from the United States, Germany, and Japan forced England to adopt, early in the 20th century, a tariff incorporating "safeguarding" taxes on imported goods she considered injurious to the national interest.

The theory of "comparative advantage" in world trade has been modified in England and most other countries by a national tariff system in which the national interest is protected by a graduated selective import tax that corresponds to the social value of the imported commodity and may or may not correspond to its cost or market price.

In the United States, as in most other industrial nations, competition between domestic and imported products has seldom been permitted on a strictly market price basis. There is a "free list," allowed in duty-free, consisting of such goods as coffee or tea that are not produced in the United States. All other goods are assessed a duty or tax based on their value to the United States economy. This value is usually referred to in tariff debates as the "national interest" or "public interest" and corresponds to the social value placed on the imported commodity — that is, on its value to society as a whole rather than its price value to the consumer.

Under the tariff system the free list represents a political value judgment. The fact that some commodities are allowed entry duty-free is not because the United States believes in free trade, but rather because "free" commodities are considered valuable to the economy and do not compete with domestic commodities. Those that are taxed with the highest duties are those that the Congress regards as having the lowest social value or those that would cause the greatest potential injury to the domestic economy.

Social values are the basic criteria of the external tariff. Duties are assessed according to the need to protect the public interest or national interest. However, the "public interest" is a general concept allowing of many interpretations. In the 19th century United States import duties were high on manufactured products. The government considered it in the public interest to protect American manufacturers. After World War II, the United States emerged as the only great industrial power, and a considerable body of public opinion favored "free trade" or a drastic reduction in tariffs. There was after 1946 no serious competition from foreign manufacturers and it was to the public interest to allow foreign competition on a strictly market price basis. American industry had nothing to fear from foreign competition, over which it had a tremendous productive and technological superiority. Tariffs were reduced and a foreign aid program, the Marshall Plan, was put into effect to restore the productive capacity of wartorn foreign industries.

After 1960 competition from Japan and European countries caused Congress to be less favorably disposed in principle to free trade. There was increasing evidence that imports in such fields as textiles, shoes, electronics, automobiles, and steel were beginning to hurt American producers, and they asked Congress for protection. Finally on August 15, 1971 President Nixon, in the face of disastrous deficits in the balance of payments, announced new monetary and import policies designed to protect American industry. Peter S. Peterson, Secretary of Commerce, called for an end to postwar "generosity" and declared that the "new realities" demanded a "clearer, more assertive version of new national interest...I believe we must dispel any 'Marshall Plan psychology' or relatively unconstrained generosity that may remain. This is not just a matter of choice but of necessity..." The new economic policy reflected a change in economic conditions rather than a change in altruism. The United States could afford to be "generous" in 1946 because imports could not compete with American-made products. In 1972 imports could compete with American products on a market-price basis in many cases. It was necessary to revaluate the "new realities" and inaugurate a new policy to protect the public or national interest. This, of course, was and is the traditional function of the tariff. Unfortunately, the protective tariff on imported commodities has lost its effectiveness to regulate world trade and has been bypassed by state control over exchange rates and the internal market.

An internal tariff would require Congress to set up a tax schedule on *all* commodities by specific commodity or by commodity groups, with a tax rate that varies according to the relative social value such commodity or group bears to the public interest, as defined by public opinion and economic priorities set by Congress. The tax would be collected on the manufacturer's, vendor's, or importer's invoice price to the wholesaler-retailer. It would differ from a sales tax in that the rate is variable and is not collected on the retail sales price. It would differ from the value-added tax or turn-over tax in that it is not a flat tax added to a product at each step of its processing and distribution. It would be more closely related to a selective manufacturer's excise tax, with the added feature that it has variable tax rates that correspond, in inverse ratio, to the social value of the commodity — the higher the social value, the lower the tax rate.

Under the internal tariff the tax levied on each commodity and service would represent the social value of the commodity or service in its relation to all other commodities and services. The criteria of social value and of public interest would remain the same as in the external tariff. The basic difference would arise from the economic interests of the parties involved. In the external tariff the economic interests of domestic producers and consumers must be considered in relation to the interests of foreign producers and foreign consumers. A tax on an imported commodity is a tax on the domestic consumer and a subsidy to the American producers. It reduces production in the exporting country and reduces the ability of that country to buy American goods. The conflict of interests is rather complex, and a tariff schedule never can please all parties. The determination of national interest calls for the highest order of legislative wisdom and statesmanship. It is not a formula that can be applied indiscriminately to all commodities in all cases.

An internal tariff would involve the economic interests of every citizen as a consumer, on the one hand, and as a worker, on the other. These interests would, of course, conflict with each other, not only along class and occupational lines, but along regional lines. How these conflicting personal, class, and regional interests would be resolved by Congress in the "national interest" is a difficult but not an unsolvable problem.

Neither computers nor economists nor a crystal ball could help Congress solve the problem of the relative social values of commodities. In an authoritarian state the task might be given to a state planning bureau such as the Soviet Gosplan working under the orders of an all-powerful dictator or an élite Central Committee. In a democratic legislative assembly, however, the task would necessarily be done by trial-and-error and open debate and compromise. This system may provoke tedium and aggravation, filibusters, and some injustices, but it is a system that can also produce the eloquence of some new Webster or a new Clay. This is the special glory of the democratic process, which will never be matched by a computerized planning bureau or a Communist central committee.

In general, Congress would determine the social value of a commodity or service according to the criteria of:

1. Relative social utility. How useful is the commodity or service to society in relation to *all* other commodities and services?

2. Relative social cost. How much *total* energy does the commodity or service consume, including human labor?

The objective of the internal tariff schedule would be to conserve energy and penalize waste by discouraging production of goods that are inherently wasteful, superfluous, and socially and environmentally harmful and by charging for energy costs in relation to their value to society.

Setting up a comprehensive rate schedule for all commodities and services could not be done overnight. It would take considerable time and effort and force Congress to take a hard look at many current practices that encourage extravagant misuse of energy and natural resources. Hitherto Congress has either ignored these practices — many lie outside the public sector — or has not thought out clearly the side effects of some of its laws or has enacted

211

legislations in piecemeal fashion without considering the overall effect on the future needs of the economy.

According to Professor Lynton K. Caldwell:

> The present energy system is the product of disjunctive, incremental decision making — if not wholly inadvertent — is nevertheless based on narrow, economy-oriented considerations. It has powerfully influenced the shaping of America's physical environment, chiefly through the automobile and the distribution of electricity. American society has been profoundly influenced by its almost inadvertent preference for fossil fuels rather than an energy system developed to serve considered and articulated goals of society. A new energy system cannot be designed without specifying certain assumptions about the society of the future. If it is true that the present social system has been heavily influenced by an energy system which cannot be sustained indefinitely, then reliance upon the present uses and distribution of energy as a basis for future policy is highly questionable. Until a policy for America's future environment is developed, at least in broad outline, no one can say what kind of energy system should be sought.[154]

A comprehensive system of commodity taxation would force Congress to have a comprehensive policy for all energy uses. The setting of priorities by taxation for all commodities and services would require a general economic policy or goal by which such priorities would be compared. Without such a comprehensive policy, no commodity rate schedule could be worked out. General policies of this type are usually a part of a party's platform and are voted on by the people at general elections. They are then regarded as a mandate for Congressional action and are implemented and articulated in specific tax bills. The setting of priorities by taxation for all commodities and services would control the rate of growth and the growth pattern of all industries in a coordinated manner, but without a formal plan. This is a formidable task. The question may also be asked: if Congress cannot do it, who can? Leaving the task entirely up to the free market has been found to be, since 1929, unworkable because the market is no longer free. Leaving the task to be decided by confrontation between capital and labor leaves the public interest a poor third. Letting a technocratic government bureau set up price controls and economic plans under the executive presents a serious challenge to individual liberty and has not proved infallible. The power to tax commodities by progressive rates set by Congress is no greater or more dangerous than the power Congress now has to tax income by progressive rates. The end-result is the same. Income is diverted, in the one, when it is earned; in the other, when it is spent. The basic difference is that one requires a huge executive bureaucracy to administer social services for which the taxpayer is paying through the income tax, whereas the other effects the same distribution through the market price system without bureaucratic intervention.

That the task of setting up a master schedule of rates for all commodities and services — an internal tariff — can be accomplished by the Congress is not at all an unreasonable expectation. The Congress has had the experience with the external tariff to serve as a guide. The members of Congress need not all become experts on all commodities; neither, for that matter, could any executive officer. There are several hundred members of Congress, and the Congress has the power to appoint committees of experts to help its deliberations.

The internal tariff would not conflict with the external tariff; neither does it imply an autarchic self-sufficiency. The benefits of the international division of labor are too well-known to need proof at this late date. Where a foreign country has a natural advantage in the production of a commodity and can make it cheaper and better, it would be a shortsighted policy to prohibit its import and devote greater material and human resources to duplicate it. This applies to motorcycles and radios as well as to tea and coffee. But the social value of an industry cannot be ignored, either. The answer to this problem is not a simple one. Congress has many options: it can raise external and internal tariff rates; it can impose import quotas; it can subsidize the domestic industry to a point where it can be competitive; or it can encourage domestic production of the foreign product by a license. Once established, the criteria of social value will suggest the correct solution.

Appropriate Senate and House committees could be formed to deal with groups of commodities. Subcommittees with technical staffs could make studies and recommendations. Advisory committees of producers, consumers, and workers could be formed and consulted. The usual public hearings could be held to give all interested parties an opportunity to be heard.

As in the past, when the external tariff was the chief business of Congress, there will be Congressmen who will specialize in the commodities or products that are native to their districts. The Congressmen from Florida would, no doubt, want to be represented on the committee dealing with oranges; those from Texas would become members on the committees dealing with oil and cattle; those from Michigan with automobiles; those from Oregon with timber; those from Idaho and Maine with potatoes; those from California with movies; and those from Ohio with tires and machine tools.

There would be a certain amount of logrolling or compromise between conflicting local interests. But this is the democratic way of settling differences, and in many ways it is preferable to decisions made *in camera* by so-called experts who, with all their graphs, statistics, computers, and parabolic curves, are not immune from making mistakes.

The setting of economic priorities through the internal tariff would involve considerable experimentation, tumultuous debates, bitter sectional rivalries, maddening delays, and tremendous pressures on Congressmen from local and special interest groups; in comparison with the silent unanimity of the GOSPLAN, the Congressional method of economic planning would seem disorderly and "unscientific." However, bringing economic priorities into the Congressional arena, where they may be debated in the glare of full publicity, will have some compensations. Economic power, the "power of the purse," belongs in Congress. The concentration of this power in the executive branch has been a move away from the democratic process and away from the principle of taxation by representation. The executive branch is governed by the authoritarian principle. An executive gives orders or obeys them. If an order is debated or questioned, it ceases to be an order. A legislative body, in

213

which laws are made only after long and serious deliberation and only after all points of view have been expressed, is the proper place for crucial economic decisions that affect the public interest. As the highest legislative body in the land, the Congress is the proper and logical forum where the highest economic policy questions may be debated and decided.

A congressman acts in the capacity of a people's tribune. Congress is not an executive or authoritarian body. As a legislative assembly, it is responsible and very sensitive to the desires of consumers who are also voters. The process of setting priorities for goods and services by commodity taxation would involve the people as consumers and workers, as well as Congress. They would be vitally affected by Congressional action. Their jobs as well as their consumer preferences would be at stake. The people would be drawn into the arena of economic decision-making in a very real and even painful sense. But this is also part of the democratic process. The decision on these matters should be made by the people — not by a board of economic planners — responsible to one supreme executive authority. The people in America do not want to become like the Russian people, who are not consulted about economic priorities. The GOSPLAN is revealed to the Russian public only *after* it is put into effect and then only in the form of target quotas. Nor do they wish to be like the Swedish or French people who, under their current systems of *dirigisme,* are presented with a plan for economic priorities as a *fait accompli.* It is one thing to have the power to veto or approve a massive national budget or economic plan; it is quite another to be involved in the decisions that go into the making of the plan. This involvement in the decision-making process is the essence of democracy.

It is very difficult for the citizen to become involved with or to participate in executive administrative bodies, whether they belong to the Department of Defense, or State, or Labor, or Commerce, or Transportation. In its relations with the citizen, the executive branch of the government appears as a bureaucratic, coercive, or regulatory body. It taxes, drafts, regulates, commands, punishes, orders, and compels. The citizen has no recourse against the executive power except through the courts, which is a costly and difficult defense. Only when he is on welfare or working for the executive branch does the citizen feel he is benefiting from the relationship; for that reason, the growth of bureaucracy and welfare strengthens the executive branch. The average citizen appears before the executive official as a petitioner or defendant. The executive official is not dependent on the citizen petitioner for his job. He is, therefore, unconcerned or even arrogant in his relations to those citizens coming under his authority.

The relationship of the citizen to the legislative branch is on an entirely different plane. As a voter, the citizen is always welcomed by his representative, since he needs his vote. The successful legislator makes every effort to keep in close touch with his electorate. Although he may not realize it or may not take advantage of it, the average voter has the ear of the legislator; if he represents a group interest or a popular cause, and not merely a personal grievance, he will find the legislator very receptive to his suggestions. If the representative loses touch with his voters, he will soon be out of office. It is this dependent relationship between voter and legislator that makes it democratic.

Undoubtedly, if Congress were again to become the arena of battle for setting economic priorities, the individual citizen as a voter would feel directly involved and follow the Congressional debate with deep personal interest, which he would communicate to his congressman. It is not difficult to imagine the pressures from the electorate "back home" that would fall on the Congressman from Michigan when taxes on automobiles were being debated, for example.

The feeling of participating in the economic decisions made by his representatives in Congress would give every citizen a new spirit of confidence in himself and in democracy. The feeling of alienation, of being a helpless pawn in a game manipulated by invisible economic forces beyond his control, would be replaced by a feeling of mastery and control. The decisions made would not always be the right decisions, but in any case they would be his decisions, not made for him by a bureaucratic executive board.

The internal tariff is not suggested as a panacea for all the economic and social ills of modern society. It will not solve the problems arising out of labor-management relations, education, productivity, innovation, foreign investments, fiscal policy, international balance of payments, inflation, defense budgets, monopoly, and other crucial economic problems. However, it is likely that it could have a beneficial effect on some of these problems or reduce their intensity. The list of benefits it can reasonably be expected to generate as a tax measure, however, is sufficiently large to make it worthy of consideration. The following represent some of the most potential significant benefits of the internal tariff over the present income tax.

1. It will generate adequate tax revenues for the general welfare.

2. It will be completely neutral in its effect on market competition.

3. It will be collected without involving the IRS in the internal private affairs of the buyer or seller and with a minimum of expense and red tape.

4. It will be a highly effective tool for economic planning in a democratic society. The priorities for consumer goods will be set by the consumers themselves and by their elected representatives.

5. It will introduce the element of social value into the price system in a responsible democratic manner.

6. It will eliminate negative work incentives and tax penalties for exceptional effort.

7. It will reduce the need for direct bureaucratic controls over the private economy.

8. It will provide for better allocation of material and manpower resources.

9. It will distribute the tax burden in a more equitable manner.

The internal tariff is, in a sense, a social-value-added tax, or a selective excise, or a domestic version of the protective tariff; in short, it is a commodity tax system and, as such, has an ancient and respectable tradition. It has been given its best theoretical exposition by Alexander Hamilton. Whatever merits the internal tariff may have, originality is not one of them, for the structure of the tax is derived from the Hamiltonian concept.

The case for a return to nondirect taxes rests, not only on the ground that direct taxes have proved a failure but, more positively, on the ground that only through nondirect taxes can desirable social welfare goals be achieved in a democratic, noninquisitorial manner. Nondirect taxes on commodities have always been imposed by governments and their use, according to J. S. Mill, is justified on moral and political grounds:

> But it must be remembered that taxation for fiscal purposes is absolutely inevitable; that in most countries it is necessary that a considerable part of that taxation should be indirect; that the State, therefore, cannot help imposing penalties, which to some persons may be prohibitory, on the use of some articles of consumption. It is hence the duty of the State to consider, in the imposition of taxes, what commodities the customers can best spare; and *a fortiori*, to select in preference those of which it deems the use, beyond a very moderate quantity, to be positively injurious.

Although Mill was applying a narrow, moral criterion to commodities — the usual criterion for excises — the protective tariff has demonstrated that the wider criteria of public interest or social value can be applied in a system of nondirect taxes and that such a system is perfectly compatible with the democratic legislative process and the market economy.

3. Minimum Consumption Standards

All taxes must ultimately be paid by production. Without production, there is no wealth and no income. Transferring taxes from income to consumption merely transfers the locus of payment. Income taxes are collected at the source by the government before the income is spent. Consumption taxes are collected by the government at the time income is spent on goods and services.

Disregarding for the moment questions of equity, justice, and ability to pay, it is obvious that tax rates on commodities can be set according to whatever schedule is necessary to raise the desired level of revenues. However, the question will naturally arise: what is the essential difference between levying taxes on consumption and levying taxes on income? Are they not equally painful to the taxpayer? The answer is: No. A raise in income tax rates is nonselective. The individual income tax is a class or "volumetric" tax. Despite individual class rates, despite numerous exemptions and allowable deductions, the income tax remains a volumetric tax applying without discrimination to a broad class of taxpayers. The individual income tax can neither be tailored to the individual nor be made applicable to an individual transaction. The income tax is like a blunderbuss or a shotgun in its effect. Being a commodity tax, the internal tariff is, on the contrary, very selective. It is like a sharp knife in the hands of the taxpayer, enabling him to select the commodity he needs from those he does not need or cannot afford.

In *The Federalist* (No. 21) Hamilton made this comment on consumption taxes: "Imports, excises and in general all duties upon articles of consumption may be compared to a fluid which will in time find its level with the means of paying them. *The amount to be contributed by each citizen will in a degree be at his own option.*" Under a tax on articles of consumption, the taxpayer has the option to avoid or reduce his tax by foregoing the purchase of items carrying a heavy tax or choosing others that carry a smaller tax. Under the income tax law he has no such option. The internal tariff *leaves the consumer with more discretionary buying power than the income tax.* An example will make this clear. Under the present tax system John Smith earns $100 per week and, after paying $20 income tax, receives $80 in tax-free income. (Other payroll deductions are disregarded in this example.) It is assumed that Smith pays from his weekly wages $40 for rent, $20 for food, $10 for car upkeep, and $5 for miscellaneous expenses, leaving him $5 as "discretionary" income, that is, income available for purchases other than those required for absolute necessities on his standard of living. When Smith goes shopping, he finds items he can buy for one week's discretionary income, $5 or even less. Other items will take several weeks to pay off.

Under the internal tariff Smith is paid the same wages, $100 per week, but there is no income tax deduction, so his tax-free pay is $100. It is assumed, for the sake of simplicity, that his living expenses are the same. This means that Smith will now have a disposable income of $25, $20 of which represents the income tax not deducted from his paycheck. When he goes shopping, he now finds that prices on some items have increased substantially, while others have not. Since he has more discretionary income, he finds that he has more purchasing power than before, but he also finds that many luxury items cost more and that he must work longer for them. These high-priced items cost more because the Congress has set a higher tax on them to discourage their consumption. Higher prices on some luxury goods will tend to offset his increased buying power, but overall the economic condition of people such as Smith at the bottom of the income tax pyramid could be substantially improved under the internal tariff.

It is very difficult to provide for the poor and hungry under the income tax system. The income tax law divides the people into income classes or income brackets. The theory of the income tax is that the richer must pay more taxes to support or subsidize the poor. But those in the higher income bracket resent having a large portion of their income taxed to support those who, they feel, did not work as hard as they did to earn it. Those in the lower income brackets resent being shut out from employment and career opportunities for a variety of reasons that they regard as unfair and discriminatory.

Attempts by the government to reconcile these conflicting interests between the low-income and the high-income classes have so far proved futile. Under the income tax system any attempt by the government to subsidize the poor — by welfare payments or guaranteed income by a negative income tax — tends to institutionalize the condition it seeks to correct. The tax subsidy gives a vested interest in the poverty program to those who benefit from tax benefits, both the bureaucrats and the recipients. This is why the welfare rolls are always highest in the richest states and continue to climb even in times of prosperity. This is why the program to aid families with dependent children seems miraculously to propagate and multiply dependent children. That is why aid to the unemployed never solves the unemployment problem. Under the income tax system the program to abolish poverty merely institutionalizes poverty and creates a bureaucracy with a vested interest in the poverty program and a subclass of welfare dependents who demand free income as a right. The level of free income for this subclass becomes both an economic and a political right.

Under the internal tariff the problem of poverty would be attacked from a different angle. The tariff would include a tax-free list of necessities that would be so low in price as to be available to all, regardless of income. Like the external tariff, the internal tariff would contain a full range of selective rates from a basic free list, that is, a list of goods on which no tax applies, to a high-tax list of goods on which prohibitive rates apply. The free list would include all basic necessities of life — some, but not all, items of food, clothing, and shelter to which, it is now generally agreed, all citizens have a right, a right that was not denied to a medieval serf. The high-tax list would consist of goods that, because of their low social value or extreme luxury, are taxed at a rate to discourage their consumption.

The question of supplying the basic necessities of life would be separated from income. They would be available to all on an equal basis, regardless of income class. The rich would not be taxed directly to support the poor. The poor would not receive income derived from taxes on the rich. The free list would emancipate the special subclass of welfare dependents supported by the tax contributions of those in a higher income class. The free list would carry no stigma of social inferiority such as is now attached to welfare or relief payments or to food stamps, or be identified with any class. The free list would be for all, rich or poor, employed or unemployed. The poor would be amply supplied with the basic necessities but, to acquire the luxury goods and the status symbols of wealth, they would be required to work for them. Poverty and hunger on the subsistence level would be abolished. However, under the internal tariff, the incentive to work for the amenities of life would not be removed; if anything, they would be accentuated. It is a well-known fact that luxury goods are not valued in themselves, but serve mainly as status symbols. The possession of an object is valued because it carries a high price tag. In many cases the owner may not appreciate it or even know its true value. Under the internal tariff luxury goods would carry a very high tax that, in turn, would make them much more desirable as status symbols. The paradox of a man or woman on welfare driving up to collect government checks in a luxury car would no longer be possible. The luxury car would be completely out of the range of the low-income family, but such a family would no longer feel deprived of the basic minimum necessities of life to which they are entitled as a right.

One of the significant benefits of the internal tariff would be that it would establish a system of economic priorities for consumer goods *set by the consumers themselves.* Officially, the Congress would set the tax rates but,

218

because Congress is made up of elected representatives, it is very responsive to public opinion. A congressman normally would not vote for tax rates that are opposed by his constituents. The consumers, therefore, would have a powerful voice in deciding the taxes on all commodities and services. The tax would represent the opinion of the citizen in his dual capacity as a voter *and* consumer.

As a consumer, in his daily purchase of goods and services, he would be voting with his dollars. His "dollar vote" would influence the market allocation of resources among the most efficient producers. As a voter, the citizen would influence the vote of his congressman on any tax measure in which his vital interests were concerned. The internal tariff would not diffuse the economic interests of the consumer, but would pinpoint them, item by item. The tax rate on a specific item would be of vital concern to the citizen who stood to gain or lose by the tax rate, as a producer or consumer of the item. The potato growers would certainly be concerned when a tax on potatoes was considered, as would producers and consumers of other products.

The dual control over economic resources by the citizen as a consumer-voter under the internal tariff would be quite different from the nominal control or veto power exercised by the citizen over the economic plans of state planning agencies. Under present forms of *dirigisme* the citizen can approve or disapprove the plans only *after* the economic decisions have been made in the planning stages. The distinction is vital for, as Gardiner C. Means so aptly put it, "A consumer veto over wasteful use of resources is by no means the same as the consumer control over their use."[155]

The internal tariff does not interfere with consumer choice, and the principle of marginal utility will be fully operative within the market. The range of prices will change when social value is added to the cost price as a tax but, since this tax is uniform, it does not distort production cost price or relative market value. The producer who has the cheapest cost price will still have the cheapest market price. By the same token, the consumer will be given the same relative choice of market values between the lowest-cost and the highest-cost producer. The internal tariff may change the absolute prices of commodities and services by adding a social value tax, but since this tax is added on to the cost price in uniform increments or uniform rates within a commodity group or service group, it tends to preserve the economic effect of disparate production costs with little or no distortion in market values. The preservation of price competition within the market is enhanced rather than endangered by the internal tariff. The factory market price under the internal tariff system would be closer to the true cost-of-production price than under the income tax system. The internal tariff tax would not distort or cancel the cost-of-production price advantage of one firm over another. Under the present tax system, market prices are distorted by noneconomic pressures that may nullify comparative cost-of-production advantages. Efficient producers are penalized in many cases by higher taxes. In other cases subsidies tend to favor one producer over another. For many reasons prices in the market do not reflect true cost-of-production values since they are no longer determined by pure market competition. Under the internal tariff, these nonmarket influences would be eliminated or sharply reduced, and true market competition would be restored.

An internal tariff presupposes that production is in private hands or corporate bodies distinct from the government. Under Communism, production is state-owned and managed. Under *dirigisme* the state intervenes in the production process by direct and indirect controls. Under the internal tariff system there would be no government ownership or control of production. There would be no attempt by the government to influence or subsidize one producer in favor of another. The producer would stand on his own feet and compete for the available market with other producers or vendors. There would be no appeal from the verdict of the market or of the profit-and-loss statement. If the firm could not produce efficiently and at a competitive price and operate at a profit, it would not survive. The internal tariff would not in any way interfere with production planning, corporate management, or the internal operations of a company. Political control of a company, in any form, does not as a rule increase efficiency and, once insulated from the discipline of market competition and the profit-and-loss statement, companies tend to become bureaucratic and indifferent to costs.

Under the internal tariff system, the tax problem in business would not exist and market prices would not be distorted by discriminatory rates of income taxation. The abolition of the income tax would eliminate the unhealthy preoccupation of corporate managers with taxes and leave them free to concentrate on production problems. Inefficient and wasteful practices adopted for "tax reasons" would not exist. Efficient producers would not be penalized by higher tax rates. The product would be priced to sell at the best competitive price. The tax would be added to the manufacturer's price, and the manufacturer's price would not be distorted by it in any way. The effect of the tax on the marketability of his product would be the same for him as it would be for all his competitors. It would not be possible for him, as a producer, to evade it, alter it, or discount its effect. The manufacturer's product or vendor's service would be placed on the market free of discriminatory tax influences, and the price would more accurately reflect the true costs of production. This would apply equally to all manufacturers and vendors on a nationwide basis. Corporate managers could plan production without having to consider tax advantages and disadvantages or the use of "tax dollars."

The corporation income tax distorts market price competition, not only between small firms that are exempt from the tax and large firms, but also between firms of the same size that, because of peculiar tax situations or capable tax managers, are able to shift all or part of the tax. Representative Charles A. Vanik of Ohio sponsored a study on "corporate Federal tax payments and Federal subsidies to corporations for 1972." Mr. Vanik discovered an astounding variation in corporate tax levies. Thus, General Motors paid an effective Federal tax rate of 44.6 per cent on its earnings, close to the statutory 48 per cent corporate tax rate, while International Telephone and Telegraph paid either 1 per cent, according to Mr. Vanik, or 9.5 per cent, according to ITT. Eleven giant corporations paid no Federal tax, although they all had "substantial profits." Said Mr. Vanik, "These corporations have done nothing illegal in lowering their tax rate. They have simply taken advantage — quite effectively — of the multitude of tax subsidies which have been enacted into the tax laws over the years."[156]

In setting up a schedule of commodity taxes the Congress would, in effect, be taking some of the tax priorities out of the hands of large corporations, subjecting taxation to the criteria of social value.

The tax under the internal tariff will be in some cases a major component of the price to the consumer. Even where there is no tax, the effect would still be decisive, for the absence of tax, under this system, acts as a subsidy or tax credit. The tax added to the cost price of the commodity would represent the *social value* as determined by Congress and indirectly by public opinion. The factory price or the production cost price would be determined by competition between producers.

Before setting the internal tariff tax, the Congress would have to determine the social value of the commodity. The criteria would be quite different from either production cost (which is reflected in the factory price) or market value (which is the retail price *without* the tax). By setting a tax on the commodity, Congress is altering the sales price in a decisive manner, or in effect putting a new price on the commodity. To determine the tax, Congress must first determine the social value of each commodity. Whatever tax it sets on one commodity would be related to the tax it sets on other commodities; the relative tax rates would be a composite index of the relative social value of all commodities.

The social value of commodities and services is not assessable by fixed measurement standards; it is a relative value determined by human judgment and arrived at after the commodities and services have been studied in relation to each other and in relation to the economic goals and priorities of the current administration, public opinion, and the Congress.

In the past, when excise and sumptuary taxes were levied, the rate was based on social need. Luxury items or nonessential items were taxed; food and other necessary items were exempt. It is not now possible to divide commodities into two separate classes: (1) necessities and (2) luxuries. This might have been possible in times past when only the rich could afford luxury goods and there was a marked distinction between the possessions of the wealthy and the poor. The poor could seldom afford such luxury goods as silk dresses, silk stockings, satin and velvet goods, wel-turned furniture, houses with carpets and elaborate bathrooms, sailing boats, tailor-made suits, bone chinaware, sterling silver, walking sticks, gloves, wigs, jewelry and expensive watches, riding horses, golf clubs and golf club memberships, and other luxury goods and privileges reserved only for the wealthy. Today in the United States, except for a very few specialty items such as private aircraft and yachts, almost every luxury is within the reach of the large middle class. What has happened is that all commodity groups now exhibit a complete range of values from low-priced economy models to expensive luxury types. This is true, for example, in clothing, food, appliances, watches, boats, TV's, sports equipment, autos, furniture, housing, radios, pianos, and air conditioners. In

221

all these various commodity groups the division between luxury and economy-type goods must be made *within* the commodity group rather than *between* commodity groups. This condition will have the effect of bringing almost all commodities within the taxable schedule of the internal tariff. There would be a free list of basic necessities at the bottom and a list of pure luxury products at the top. In between would be the great mass of commodities and services comprising both luxury and economy types and taxed according to relative social value.

It is obvious that a highly selective tax system with variable rates for each commodity or service would offer Congress the power to make either minor or major adjustments in the economy. It would give Congress the power to wipe out entire industries by prohibitive tariff rates, if it chose to do so. On the other hand, Congress could also make very minor adjustments in any industry by raising or lowering tariff rates by fractional amounts. The effects would be comparable to those observable in the domestic market by the raising or lowering of external tariffs or by the intervention of government in the price-support programs. Nevertheless, there are some important differences between the internal tariff system and a system of government price controls such as is used in Socialist economics. It is true that Soviet Union prices are set to include social value as determined by the political authority. Production costs are considered in the Soviet price formula, but social value is a much more important consideration. Prices in Communist countries, therefore, strike Western economists as "artificial", "uneconomic," and "unreal." Products and services that are very costly in capitalist countries — rent, medical care, transportation, and education — are free or have a very low price in the Soviet Union and China. On the other hand, products such as automobiles, homes, and motorboats are extremely expensive or unobtainable. Prices in the Soviet Union and China are not ordinarily set by the market or by production costs. They are fixed by the government according to a formula in which price, market demand, and production are all derived from a central plan.

In Russia, according to Professor Franklyn D. Holzman: "The state independently sets the price of each commodity with a view to receiving both equilibrium in separate commodity markets and aggregate fiscal stability. The turn-over tax is then used to draw into the budget the bulk of the difference between price and cost." The tax is not applied capriciously. Says Professor Holzman: "The state first establishes the turn-over tax for individual commodities or groups in such a way as to adjust price roughly to correspond with market demand. This is accomplished on a *centralized* basis for the nation as a whole."[157]

The setting of prices by Soviet decree or by Congressional act seems a difference in degree, and the question naturally arises: are they fundamentally the same and do they vary only in political form rather than in economic content? The answer is that they are quite different in both respects. In an authoritarian state, rule by decree is accepted as the norm. There may be times in the United States when the executive seems to override the legislative and judiciary, but to date there has never been a complete abdication of lawmaking power by Congress, and the executive still must obtain Congressional approval for executive programs and money to fund them. Assuming that the Soviet and American governments both set prices by law, the differences in political form between the two governments alone would guarantee a radically different price system.

The two price systems differ radically in economic content. In the internal tariff system social value is *added* to the cost of production and does not distort market values *within the commodity group.* In the Soviet Union prices do not reflect economic costs of production with any degree of fidelity, and official prices reflect instead the priorities of the current five-year plan. Absolute control over the economy gives the Soviet government the power to regulate prices without having to consider the market values or consumer preferences. In a completely politicized economy such as Russia's, the price system is not a decisive mechanism for allocating resources. The major decisions are political judgments that allocate credits according to the master plan, which determines production of consumer goods, the only goods placed on the market. Consumer buying power operates within the restricted sphere of available goods; when they are sold out, the consumer has no power to generate new production.

An internal tariff system would have significant economic differences from the Soviet model of price control and price-fixing. These include (1) the use of capital and currency standards of value set by competition, (2) the use of competitive production costs to determine the market price, and (3) the use of market competition to set marginal utility value. None of these are applicable to the Soviet Communist price system. Capital in Communist economies is controlled by the state, and its value is determined by fiat or decree. The American dollar has a value set by the government, but the dollar is not insulated from market pressures.

The internal tariff tax would be reported and paid by manufacturers, importers, and prime vendors, making tax collection automatic and impersonal. The reporting firm would pay the tax on a monthly basis, or other reporting period, and the process would be quite uncomplicated, involving a simple calculation based on gross sales. There would be a minimum of red tape and expense and no need for inquisitorial methods to audit, verify, or probe into personal or corporate records. There would be no need for a centralized bureaucracy for policing the economy and for investigating the income records of taxpayers. If a modified income tax is retained (perhaps an excess profits tax or a surtax on high incomes) the internal tariff system tax would be entirely compatible with the income tax. This tax does not preclude the use of other taxes if found useful and desirable; at the beginning, it would be much more practicable to phase in the new tax and phase out the old taxes gradually as experience and intelligence indicate.

The rates shown in the internal tariff schedule that follows are, of course, hypothetical and serve only to illustrate the wide range of tax rates that may be applied by the Congress to any specific commodity. The Congress, as is customary in such cases, could authorize the executive to change rates by executive order where necessary to prevent injury to a domestic industry. This power would be used only under specified conditions. Normally, the rate schedule set by the Congress would govern until changed by Congressional action. The opportunity, under this system, of making quick emergency rate changes, by specific commodity and for each industry, gives the internal tariff system a flexibility not possessed by the more rigid income tax system.

Another aspect of this flexibility involves the setting of rates on specific commodities on a gradual basis. It is unlikely that, at the beginning, the Congress would have either the time or the knowledge to establish a tax schedule for all commodities and services with any degree of finality. A totalitarian planning agency such as the Russian GOSPLAN can set rates arbitrarily on one or all commodities, but a democratic body such as Congress would undoubtedly take a tentative pragmatic approach to the problem. The internal tariff system is already operating effectively in two large industries — those producing tobacco and alcoholic beverages. The Congress would probably add only one or two other large industries at the start to initiate the internal tariff schedule. The initial rates would be set low to give the affected industry a chance to adjust, and further increases in rates would be made after experience indicated that there are no undesirable side effects and that such increases are in line with the approved goals of the government and are backed by public opinion.

After it is proved by experience, the internal tariff system could be expanded to cover all commodities and services. Whether this expansion is rapid or slow would depend entirely upon the success of the program and its acceptance by the electorate.

Unquestionably, the advantages of the new tax would soon become apparent to the taxpayers and consumers. The price of a commodity or service under the income tax system is determined by a formula that ignores or disregards social costs. Adding social costs to production costs would make certain luxury consumer goods higher in price, but this would be offset by the increased abundance of other goods to provide a uniform level of consumption that would benefit *all* consumers. Under the income tax system a rich country such as the United States finds it impossible to eradicate poverty or to provide medical care and educational opportunity and adequate housing and food for all. There are poorer countries that seem to be able to afford these benefits. In collectivist economies the state abolishes the market and imposes a uniform level of consumption by force. The eradication of poverty in China (by Chinese standards) and the general availability at very low prices, or free, of education, health care, housing, and basic foods is considered a remarkable achievement in such a poor country. But it has been achieved at a high cost — the complete suppression of freedom of choice. Under the internal tariff system the uniform level of consumption to guarantee a minimum comfortable standard of living by American standards would be established without sacrificing consumer choice or market efficiency.

4. The Internal Tariff Schedule

Table I, which follows, is a hypothetical schedule of rates for internal tax. This schedule uses the official external tariff schedule of the United States as a guide for commodity numbers and descriptions and also shows the official tariff rates as shown in *Tariff Schedules of the United States Annotated (1972)*, Washington, U.S. Government Printing Office.

There are, of course, many omissions from the official tariff schedule, which contains over 585 pages of tax rates applicable to imported commodities. The reason for using the official United States Tariff as a guide is to utilize a format already established and to compare, within limited space, the differences between the internal and external tariff.

The selection of commodities for the internal tariff schedule is arbitrary and incomplete. The schedule is not meant to be, in any way, representative or even suggestive of the rates that might be passed by Congress. No one can anticipate, of course, the tax schedule that eventually would be passed by the Congress as an internal tariff bill. The future rate schedule will be determined only after considerable debate. The process would involve the give-and-take of democratic action, with all affected groups having an opportunity to be heard for each commodity or commodity group or industry. Setting a tax on a commodity or service will, of course, have a direct and perhaps decisive effect on its marketability and this, in turn, will determine the growth or decline of the industry affected.

The amount of tax revenues needed to fund government budget appropriations will determine the overall average rates of taxation. The exact revenue load that the internal tax system is expected to carry will determine the tax rates applicable to all commodities and services. After a few years' experience, it will be a simple matter to calculate the revenue that may be realized from a given tax rate levied on a specific commodity.

It has been estimated that a broad-based Federal retail sales tax of 2.2 per cent would raise $12 billion in revenues. By that rule, a 22 per cent sales tax would be needed to raise $120 billion.

In 1971, personal consumption expenditures, according to the United States Department of Commerce, were $662 billion. In 1971 the government raised $86.5 billion from the individual income tax and $30.1 billion from the corporation income tax, a total of $116.6 billion. The income tax represents, therefore 17.6 per cent of personal consumption. However, there are many other income and consumption factors involved that make this ratio inexact. For the purposes of this discussion it is not important to develop an exact ratio. It is sufficient to assume that an average consumption tax of 25 per cent would be necessary to replace the revenues lost from the income tax. In looking at the internal tariff schedule the reader therefore should realize that a tax of 25 per cent does not represent an increase over present taxes, but rather an average tax rate roughly comparable to the one he is now paying on his income. A rate of 35 per cent represents a 10 per cent increase, a 50 per cent rate is a 25 per cent tax increase, and so on. On the other hand, a 10 per cent rate is equivalent to a reduction of 15 per cent, and a free rate is equal to a 25 per cent tax reduction from present tax rates.

The element of social justice requires that taxes be levied according to ability to pay. In the internal tariff this end is achieved by graduated progressive rates on commodities. This corresponds to the graduated progressive rates on incomes. However, it is not possible under the internal tariff to shift the burden of taxes. The wealthy would not be able to escape their tax liability. Every commodity and service would carry the extra tax that is applicable to the type of luxury goods used to support a high standard of living.

The following pages illustrate what some of these tax rates might be under the internal tariff. The rates used for this tariff are, of course, hypothetical and serve no purpose other than to illustrate how rates may be applied and how they may vary from item to item. The concept of social value is used to determine comparative rates. Social value as a working hypothesis for taxation may be broken down into the following criteria:

1. Ability to pay or sharing the burden of taxation, placing higher taxes on luxury goods, lower taxes on essential goods, and putting basic necessities on the free list.

2. The waste of energy in any form is discouraged and its conservation encouraged by appropriate tax rates. The need for this is obvious.

3. Pollution of the environment is taxed to compensate society for the loss of or damage to natural resources.

4. Social disutility is taxed. Social utility is determined by Congress according to current national priorities. In wartime, guns would have higher priority than butter and consumer goods. In a peacetime economy, consumer goods would have a high priority, but some consumer goods (drugs, foods, and clothing) would merit a higher priority than others (cosmetics, foreign travel, and motorboats).

5. Products that have a harmful effect on public safety, public health, and public morals are discouraged by taxation — tobacco, alcohol, pornography, and guns. The reader, if he has skipped over the first chapters of this book, may object that morals are no concern of taxation or that it is not the function of taxation to regulate morals. Taxation, to repeat the obvious, affects public morals, whether or not designed to have this effect. Taxing income will prevent consumers from buying certain items just as effectively as taxing commodities. Whether the selection is done by Congress through income tax rates or through internal tariff rates is not, from an ethical viewpoint, a significant difference. From an economic viewpoint, it is quite different.

6. Obsolescense is taxed. The idea of planned obsolescence is discouraged by taxing items that have a short life cycle. A rapid turnover helps sales and profits in a particular industry, but in the long run it is wasteful and creates disposal problems for society. Commodities planned for quick replacement are usually inferior in quality. A tax on obsolescense is a tax in favor of quality and long life.

7. Market competition would impose its own tax on each product, and this may be called a tax on inefficiency. The least efficient producer would be taxed

the heaviest. That is, he would have the highest prices; other things being equal, the higher price would reduce his market acceptance. The consumers would buy the lower-priced goods of his competitors. The producer would be forced to be competitive or go out of business. This automatic tax on inefficiency is the classic function of market competition and forces producers continually to strive for efficiency, product improvement, and productivity. This function of the market would be retained under the internal tariff undistorted by tax considerations or tax penalties on efficiency.

5. The Free List

In addition to the items already classified as free in the regular tariff schedule, the free list could include the following which would not be taxed:

1. Charges for repair and maintenance services made to prolong the useful life of the article, including, but not limited to, auto repairs, shoe repair, laundry and dry cleaning, appliance and electrical repairs, and painting, for example.

2. Charges and fees for medical, dental, and health services; fees for legal services; tuition fees for any course of instruction taken for self-improvement; and fees for accounting, insurance, engineering, architectural, and other professional services.

3. Retail and wholesale trade. Since the internal tariff tax is levied on the manufacturer, importer, or prime vendor, the retail and wholesale dealer merely pass the tax on to the end-user or consumer. It would be too complicated to levy the tax on the retailer. Unlike the sales tax, the internal tariff would be too complex to levy on the retailer because of its individual rates and commodity classifications.

4. Raw materials, components, primary metals. Any material sold for fabrication or incorporation into another before it is sold would normally be free of tax, since it would be taxed when it is eventually sold to the consumer. Items that are classified as both raw materials and consumer goods would be taxed, with the primary supplier charging no tax on items sold to a manufacturer.

5. Industrial machinery would not be taxed, on the theory that its cost is included in the taxable product it produces. Machines that are used outside of business — typewriters and sewing machines, for example — would be taxed.

SCHEDULE 1
INTERNAL TARIFF

Item	Articles	U. S. TARIFF Internal	U. S. TARIFF External
661.20	Airconditioning Machines, comprising a Motor-driven fan and elements for changing the temperature and humidity of air..................		5.5% ad val.
	Window or wall-type air conditioners under 10,000 BTU	25% ad val.	5.5% ad val.
	Other machines over 10,000 BTU	35% ad val.	5.5% ad val.
661.35	Refrigerators and refrigerating Equipment, whether or not electric		5% ad val.
	Under 9.5 cubic feet valued under $300 ea.	20% ad val.	5% ad val.
	Under 9.5 cubic feet valued over $300 ea.	35% ad val.	5% ad val.
	Under 13.5 cubic feet valued under $350 ea.	30% ad val.	5% ad val.
	valued over $350 ea.	45% ad val.	5% ad val.
692.10	Automobiles, Passenger		3% ad val.
	New, under $2,800 in value each	35% ad val.	3% ad val.
	New, under $4,000 in value each	45% ad val.	3% ad val.
	New, over $4,000 in value each	90% ad val.	3% ad val.
	Used, under $1,000 in value each	10% ad val.	3% ad val.
	Used, under $2,000 in value each	15% ad val.	3% ad val.
	Used, over $2,000 in value each	25% ad val.	3% ad val.
692.50	Motorcycles		5% ad val.
	Having engines with total piston displacement:		
	Under 50 cubic centimeters	25% ad val.	5% ad val.
	Under 90 cubic centimeters	45% ad val.	5% ad val.
	Under 190 cubic centimeters	65% ad val.	5% ad val.
	Over 190 cubic centimeters	85% ad val.	5% ad val.
732.8	Bicycles, valued under $10 each	10% ad val.	15% ad val.
	valued under $50 each	10% ad val.	15% ad val.
	valued over $50 each	20% ad val.	15% ad val.
607.10	Iron or Steel waste and scrap Tin plate waste or scrap	FREE	FREE
	Articles made entirely of waste & scrap..............	FREE	
	Articles containing 25% of waste & scrap...........	20% tax credit	
	Articles containing 50% of waste & scrap...........	30% tax credit	
	Articles containing over 50% of waste & scrap...	50% tax credit	
	Photographic Cameras, motion picture		
722.02	Valued under $50 each	25% ad val.	12% ad val.
722.04	Valued $50 or more each	50% ad val.	6¢ ad val.
	Still cameras other than fixed focus		
722.14	Valued not over $10 each	25% ad val.	17% ad val.
722.16	Valued over $10 each	50% ad val.	7.5% ad val.
	Beef and veal, prepared or preserved cured or pickled		
107.40	Valued not over 30¢ per pound.......................	FREE	3¢ per lb.

Item	Articles	Internal	External
107.45	Valued over 30¢ per pound	20% ad val.	10% ad val.
	Fish, salted or pickled, whether or not whole, but not otherwise prepared or preserved, and not in airtight containers:		
111.22	Cod, cusk, haddock, hake, and pollock; whole; or processed by removal of heads, fins, viscera, scales, vertebral columns, or any combination thereof, but not otherwise processed.	FREE	FREE
	Fish, prepared or preserved in any manner, in airtight containers:		
112.01	Anchovies	25% ad val.	12.5% ad val.
112.05	Bonito and yellow tail	FREE	6% ad val.
112.08	Herring	FREE	4% ad val.
112.18	Salmon	30% ad val.	7.5% ad val.
112.30	Tuna	35% ad val.	6% ad val.
112.73	Sardines, in oil, not over 30¢ per lb.	35% ad val.	15% ad val.
112.74	Sardines, in oil, not over 30¢ per lb. skinned or boned	40% ad val.	30% ad val.
112.79	Sardines, in oil, valued 45¢ or more per lb.	45% ad val.	6% ad val.
112.86	Sardines, in oil, valued 45¢ or more skinned or boned	50% ad val.	24% ad val.
	Meat, including meat offal, not fit for human consumption:		
184.60	Raw, whether or not chilled or frozen, horsemeat	25% ad val.	FREE
184.65	prepared or preserved	30% ad val.	4% ad val.
184.70	Byproducts obtained from the milling of grains, mixed feeds.		
	Pet food packaged for retail sale	30% ad val.	FREE
166.10	Non-alcoholic beverages Consisting chiefly of water & artificial flavorings and syrups	35% ad val.	1.5¢ per gal.
166.30	Vegetable and fruit juices	10% ad val.	1¢ per gal.
167.05	Ale, porter, stout, and beer	35% ad val.	6¢ per gal.
167.10	Champagne and other sparkling wines		
	Valued not over $6 per gal.	40% ad val.	$1.17 per gal.
	Valued over $6 per gal.	80% ad val.	$1.17 per gal.
167.30	Stillwines produced from grapes containing not over 14% of alcohol by volume		
	Valued not over $4 per gal.	40% ad val.	37.5¢ per gal.
	Valued over $4 per gal.	80% ad val.	37.5¢ per gal.
167.37	Stillwines produced from grapes containing over 14% of alcohol by volume		$1 per gal.
	Valued not over $5 per gal.	40% ad val. + $5 per proof gal. on alcohol content.	
	Valued over $5 per gal.	80% ad val. + $5 per proof gal. of alcohol content.	
168.19	Brandy & other spirituous beverages	$2 per gal. +	
	Valued at not over $9 per pf gal.	50% ad val.	62¢ per gal.

Item	Articles	Internal	External
168.20	Brandy & other spirituous beverages	$2 per gal. +	
	Valued over $9 per pf gal.	80% ad val.	$1.25 per gal.
182.25	Bread made with the use of yeast as the leavening substance	FREE	FREE
182.20	Biscuits, cake, cakes, wafers & similar baked products	20% ad val.	3% ad val.
149.50	Other fruits, fresh	FREE	5.5% ad val.
149.60	Prepared or preserved	20% ad val.	17.5% ad val.
182.30	Cereal breakfast foods and similar cereal preparations, by whatever name known.		
	Processed further than milling		2.5% ad val.
	Less than 15% protein by weight	40% ad val.	2.5% ad val.
	More than 12% protein by weight	20% ad val.	2.5% ad val.
	Organic unprocessed other than milling	FREE	
	Wood, veneers, not reinforced or backed		
240.00	Birch, maple	40%	4% ad val.
240.93	Other, hardwood	40%	5% ad val.
	Other, softwood	25%	5% ad val.
	Paper-making materials: Wood pulp; rap pulp; and other pulps derived from cellulose fibrous materials		
250.02	Sulphate, unbleached, hardwood	35%	FREE
	Sulphate, unbleached, softwood	25%	FREE
	Sulphate, bleached, hardwood	45%	FREE
	Sulphate, bleached, softwood	35%	FREE
250.04	Waste paper and paperboard, and scrap paper and paperboard products fit only for remanufacture	FREE	FREE
270.25	Books, not specially provided for	FREE	FREE
	Comic books, periodicals containing wholly or chiefly articles and pictures without educational value	50% ad val. +- 50% adv. rev.	
270.55	Newspapers	50% adv. rev.	FREE
270.63	Periodicals	50% adv. rev.	FREE
	Articles, chiefly used for preparing, serving, or storing food or beverages:		
533.11	Of coarse-grained earthenware	FREE	2.5% ad val.
	Of fine-grained earthenware:		
533.14	valued not over $1.50 per doz. articles	10% ad val.	6% ad val.
533.16	valued over $1.50 per doz. articles	25% ad val.	6% ad val.
533.23	valued not over $3.30 per doz. articles	35% ad val.	5¢ per dz. + 14% ad val.
533.25	valued over $3.30 per doz. articles	45% ad val.	10¢ per dz. 21% ad val.
533.26	valued not over $12 per doz. articles	55% ad val.	10¢ per dz. 21% ad val.
533.28	valued over $12 per doz. articles	65% ad val.	5¢ per dz. + 10.5% ad val.
546.11	Glassware containing by weight over 24% lead monoxide valued not over $1 each	20% ad val.	20% ad val.
546.13	Valued over $1 but not over $3 each	40% ad val.	14% ad val.
546.17	Valued over $3 each	60% ad val.	10.5% ad val.
	Other glassware: Smokers' articles		
546.42	Valued not over $3 each	60% ad val.	22.5% ad val.

Item	Articles	Internal	External
546.43	Valued over $3 each	80% ad val.	22.5% ad val.
546.48	Perfume bottles valued not over $3 each	60% ad val.	17.5% ad val.
546.49	Perfume bottles valued over $3 each	80% ad val.	17.5% ad val.
653.60	Sterling silver tableware	80% ad val.	12.5% ad val.
653.75	Coated or plated with gold	60% ad val.	20% ad val.
653.80	Coated or plated with silver	40% ad val.	8.5% ad val.
653.85	Not coated or plated with precious metal	FREE	4% ad val.
678.45	Industrial cigarette-making machines	100% ad val.	6% ad val.
	Cotton, not carded, not combed, and not similarly processed:		
300.10	Having a staple length under 1-1/8″	FREE	FREE
300.15	Having a staple length 1-1/8″ or more but under 1-11/16″	10% ad val.	3.5¢ per lb.
300.20	Having a staple length 1-11/16″ or more	20% ad val.	1.75¢ per lb.
400.40	Waste of cotton, hard waste (yarn and thread waste)	FREE	FREE
	Yarn of man-made fibers (multifilament)		
310.01	Valued not over $1 per lb.	20% ad val.	12.5¢ per lb.
310.02	Valued over $1 per lb.	40% ad val.	16% ad val.
	Woven fabrics, of wool		
336.55	Valued not over $2 per lb.	20% ad val.	$1.135 per lb.
336.60	Valued over $2 per lb.	40% ad val.	37.5¢ per lb.
	Floor coverings of wool,		
361.46	Valued not over 40¢ per sq. ft.	30% ad val.	7.5% ad val.
361.48	Valued over 40¢ per sq. ft.	60% ad val.	15% ad val.
	Tapestries, of wool		
364.20	Valued not over $2 per lb.	40% ad val.	37.5¢ lb + 9% ad val.
364.22	Valued over $2 per lb.	80% ad val.	37.5¢ lb. + 7% ad val.
	Underwear, of cotton, men's, boys' women's, girls', infants', knit		
378.10	Valued not over $4 per lb.	10% ad val.	25% ad val.
378.15	Valued over $4 per lb.	40% ad val.	15% ad val.
	Men's wearing apparel, of wool, knit		
380.57	Valued not over $5 per lb.	10% ad val.	37.5¢ per lb. + 30% ad val.
380.59	Valued over $5 per lb.	40% ad val.	37.5¢ per lb. + 15.5% ad val.
	Sweaters valued over $18 per lb., Wholly of cashmere	80% ad val.	37.5¢ per lb. + 15.5% ad val.
	Women's, girls' or infants' wearing apparel of cotton, not knit:		
382.09	Coats and raincoats not over $4 ea.	10% ad val.	16.5% ad val.
382.12	Coats and raincoats Over $4 each	40% ad val.	8% ad val.
791.15	Fur coats	80% ad val.	10% ad val.
435/440	Drugs and related products	FREE	Various
460.05	Aromatic or odiferous substances obtained from natural substances, containing no alcohol	50% ad val.	FREE
460.90	Ditto, containing over 10% alcohol by weight	50% ad val.	8¢ per lb. + 7.5% ad val.

Item	Articles	Internal	External
461.05/45	Perfumery, cosmetics, and toilet preparations:		
	Women's	40% ad val.	Various
	Men's	80% ad val.	Various
	Industrial diamonds, natural or synthetic not suitable for use in the manufacture of jewelry:		
520.19	Miners' diamonds	FREE	FREE
	Precious and semi-precious stones, cut but not set, and suitable for use in the manufacture of jewelry:		
	Diamonds weighing not over 0.5 carat	100% ad val.	4% ad val.
	Diamonds weighing over 0.5 carat	200% ad val.	5% ad val.
	Rubies and sapphires	100% ad val.	4% ad val.
	Emeralds	100% ad val.	FREE
	Yachts or pleasure boats:		
696.05	Valued not over $15,000 each..........................	60% ad val.	2% ad val.
696.10	Valued over $15,000 each	100% ad val.	5% ad val.
	Valued under $5,000 each	40% ad val.	
	Valued under $1,000 each	25% ad val.	
730.10	Muskets, shotguns, rifles, pistols, and revolvers designed to fire shot, pellets, or bullets	100% ad val.	FREE
756.02/15	Cigar and cigarette lighters	100% ad val.	12/25% ad val.
660.25	Steam engines and parts thereof	25% ad val.	4% ad val.
660.44	Internal Combustion engines, piston-type		
	Rated not over 100HP	50% ad val.	4% ad val.
	Rated not over 200HP	60% ad val.	4% ad val.
	Rated not over 300HP	80% ad val.	4% ad val.
	Rated over 300HP	100% ad val.	4% ad val.

SCHEDULE II
INTERNAL TARIFF

		U. S. TARIFF	
Item	Articles	Internal	External
1.	Dwellings; single family:		
	Not over $30,000 value	FREE	
	Between $30,000/$50 000 value	25% ad val.	
	Between $50,000/$100,000 value	50% ad val.	
	Between $100,000/$250,000 value	75% ad val.	
	Over $250,000 value	100% ad val.	

Item	Articles	Internal	External
2.	Mobile homes, trailers, and campers:		
	Not over $1,000 value	20% ad val.	
	Between $1,000/$5,000 value	30% ad val.	
	Over $5,000 in value	40% ad val.	
3.	Dwellings, multiple-unit:		
	Not over $20,000 per unit value	20% ad val.	
	Between $20,000/$40,000 per unit value	40% ad val.	
	Between $40,000/$60,000 per unit value	80% ad val.	
	Over $60,000 per unit value	100% ad val.	
4.	Swimming Pools,		
	Above ground, not over $500 in value	25% ad val.	
	Above ground, between $500/$1000 in value	30% ad val.	
	Above ground, between $1000/$2000 in value	40% ad val.	
	Above ground, over $2,000 in value	60% ad val.	
	In ground Not over $5,000 in value	60% ad val.	
	In ground between $5,000/$10,000 value	80% ad val.	
	In ground Over $10,000 in value	100% ad val.	
5.	Admissions to theaters for public performances live or filmed:		
	Rated G	20% ad val.	
	Rated GP	40% ad val.	
	Rated X	100% ad val.	
6.	Admission to spectator sports events	30% ad val.	
7.	Passenger fares on government licensed transportation, air, water and land:		
	Domestic	35% ad val.	
	Foreign	50% ad val.	
8.	Charges, fees or dues, rents for occupancy in publicly licensed hotel, motel, lodge, club, whether charged on hourly, daily, weekly, monthly or any other basis whether open to public or private members; regardless of type of services or accommodations offered; but excluding educational institutions	35% ad val.	
9.	Electric power:		
	Private residences	50% ad val.	
	Industrial users	25% ad val.	
	Commercial users	40% ad val.	
10.	Telephone service	20% ad val.	

A brief explanation of the Internal Tariff Schedule rates in Tables I and II follows:

Item 661.20 Air Conditioners. Since it is assumed that Congress will regard the room air conditioner as a necessity in many areas of the country, a 25 per cent average rate tax is shown. A 10 per cent higher rate is placed on large deluxe units. The external tariff duty is a flat 5.5 per cent; in this, as in almost all other items, the external rate does not favor the lowest cost price. In many cases the external rate favors the higher-priced item.

Item 661.35 Refrigerators. A small refrigerator is a basic necessity in the

United States and a tax rate of 20 per cent, which represents a tax subsidy of 5 per cent is shown. Higher rates are shown for larger or deluxe models.

Item 683.40 Cooking Stoves and Ranges. A tax preferential rate is given to microwave ovens because they are greasefree, smokefree, and odorless and therefore cleaner and less polluting than regular cooking ranges. In general, home appliances may be rated on their consumption of energy, as well as on initial cost price. If energy consumption becomes critical in relation to available production, it may be more desirable to discourage consumption by taxing certain nonessential current-using appliances, such as heaters and toasters, than to increase the cost of electric power. Many household items that use electric power are extremely inefficient and wasteful. The light bulb is a good example. Industry can make light bulbs that virtually never burn out. Still, in the face of a world shortage of tungsten and an energy crisis, the industry makes light bulbs that burn out quickly. A tax based on the efficiency and life of a light bulb would automatically correct this wasteful practice.

Item 692.10 Automobiles. The low rates of 10 and 15 per cent for used cars are designed to encourage owners to maintain and preserve their cars and to cut down the enormous waste of resources in new car manufacture. New and deluxe models are charged higher rates to divert the resources from this sector to other more essential needs. To allow the affected industry to adjust, a rate of 90 per cent would not, of course, be set except after a considerable time. A 90 per cent rate may seem too high for large luxury automobiles, but Congress could state with some justification that anyone who drags 5000 pounds of steel around should pay for the privilege, especially if it is a gasguzzling, airpolluting, mankilling, fireeating monster.

Each year 200 million tons of pollutants are discharged into the atmosphere of the United States; most of this comes from about 105 million motor vehicles. The total cost of transportation in the United States is estimated at $110 billion, of which $90 billion is accounted for by the personal automobile. The love affair of the American public with the automobile has cooled somewhat as consumers are awakening to the threat it poses to life, property, and the environment. The social costs of the automobile have never been reckoned. The United States is the world's first fully motorized society, and the automobile is the most costly and important artifact of American life. Nevertheless, no sociologist or economist, as far as the author knows, has ever made an in-depth study of the total interrelated effects of the automobile on American life or estimated the overall costs to society in terms of total resources, man-hours, and dollar value in its production, distribution, upkeep, financing, and after-sale service; the social cost of constructing and maintaining highways; police surveillance and traffic control; government bureaucracies to register and control motor vehicles; medical and hospital costs consequent on auto accidents; or the cost of maintaining the petroleum industry, the auto parts industry, the steel and glass and rubber industries, and the myriad of other industries that "feed on" or are supported by the automobile. It has been estimated that $15 billion is paid for automobile insurance premiums; over $5 billion is paid by victims of automobile accidents; over $1 billion is received by lawyers in connection with automobile accident cases; over $1 billion is paid for car repairs; and over $35 billion is carried by auto buyers in installment debt and interest cost of over $2 billion. The total costs of the automobile to the American economy are truly astronomical.

The United States government is beginning to tackle the social problem of the automobile. Special taxes have been levied on tires and gasoline to build up a highway trust fund to improve and build highways. This is a form of social value taxation, but it does not go far enough, and its effect was offset by the removal of the excise tax on automobiles in 1971. The funds used by the Department of Transportation to combat auto pollution emission and develop auto safety standards are derived from general tax revenues. Under the present tax system, no effort is being made or can be made to evaluate the full costs, as well as benefits, to society of the automobile or to add these costs to the price of the automobile. The automobile is a monster that has been allowed annually to consume billions of gallons of gasoline, which cannot be recycled; kill over 56,000 people a year and maim over 3 million; change completely the pattern of American social life in its most fundamental aspects; and yet its cost price to the consumer reflects none of these social costs. It has been tacitly assumed that the benefits it brought society far outweighed its costs. This assumption is no longer unquestioned.

On May 9, 1972 Eugene J. McCarthy, former Senator from Minnesota, said: "We should be concerned about the automobile industry and our 'automobile culture.' Cars are too big, too expensive, and major sources of pollution. We should control the size of cars through selective excise taxes, or even direct regulation."[158] There is already considerable regulation, according to Richard C. Gerstenberg, Chairman of the Board, General Motors Corporation:

> The government today has a prominent part in many of our operations — and in all our planning. Government standards — for safety, emission control, repairability, and even noise reduction — dictate much of the designs of our products and our plants. The government tells us not only how to design and build our products, but how to advertise them, how we must warrant them to the customer, and most recently, how much, in effect, we can pay our work force, and even what price we can ask.[159]

It would appear that more government regulations are not the answer. However, the alternate suggestion of Senator McCarthy that selective excise taxes be used to control public use of the automobile is, of course, the precise remedy offered by the internal tariff.

Item 692.50 Motorcycles. A motorcycle is not in most cases an essential item, but a small model could be used as cheap transporation, so a progressive graduated scale of rates is shown, with a high rate of 85 per cent on very large models used for sport and racing.

Item 732.08 Bicycles. The bicycle receives a favorable low rate because it does not use gas, is not dangerous or wasteful of resources, and is cheap healthful transportation.

Item 607.10 Scrap and Waste. The need for recycling recources is recognized by all and a tax subsidy or free rate is applied to encourage the reuse of scrap and waste.

Item 116.10 / 168.20 Beverages. The rates suggested are to encourage the drinking of nonalcoholic or low-alcoholic beverages in line with current and past public policy. Beer cans and pop bottles represent a serious litter and solid-waste problem. Despite ecological concern and local attempts to ban them, nonreturnable soft drink bottles have increased from 5 per cent in 1965 to 26 per cent in 1971, and nonreturnable beer bottles from 17 per cent in 1965 to 22 per cent in 1972. Beer cans amount to 54 per cent of beer packaging. To combat the litter problem, the social costs involved in handling the disposal of nonreturnable containers should be added to the cost of beverages so packaged

Item 182.25 / 184.70 Foods. Basic foods such as bread, fruits, meat, fish should be free of tax, which corresponds to a subsidy of 25 per cent on today's market. Where foods are processed, refined, and packaged, and such processes involve additional use of scarce resources or reduce the nutritional value of the food, a graduated tax should be imposed to offset the loss of food value and to encourage consumption of healthful, nutrional foods. Sugar is a food that has its place in the diet but, because of its cheap price, it is consumed in excessive amounts that make it a major cause of tooth decay, obesity, diabetes, and other serious hazards to health. Its low price relative to more nutritional food leads to unhealthful overconsumption, which can be reduced by either numberless regulations restricting its use or by a tax that raises its price and discourages consumption. Gourmet foods of all types would carry a tax higher than foods required for a healthy basic diet.

Items 722.02 / 722.16 Cameras. A low tax is set on inexpensive cameras and a higher tax on de luxe models. The external tariff rate is just the opposite. It was set, no doubt, to protect the low-cost camera producers in the United States. Producers of expensive American cameras do not need protection, since they do not exist.

Item 240.00 Wood Veneers. Wood is a basic natural resource, and taxes would be set by Congress to encourage the use of this resource in the manner best suited to protect the nation's timber reserves. Some hardwoods are becoming scarce, and this scarcity should be recognized and offset by a higher tax on the endangered lumber species. The case of redwoods is a prime example.

Items 250.00 / 250.04 Paper. Wood pulp is used in paper-making in huge quantities. If some of this paper could be reused, a natural resource could be protected. Every ton of recycled newsprint saves an estimated 17 trees. Chicago alone supplies 50 million pounds of waste pulp to one company for reuse, thereby saving 147 square miles of woodland each year. This development should be encouraged by putting recycled print on the free list. Other types of paper should be tax-rated according to their use of natural resources and their contribution to waste and pollution.

Since 1971 Federal and local governments have specified recycled waste paper content in certain paper and paperboard they purchased. This was done to encourage use of waste paper, to conserve fiber, and to relieve the serious solid-waste disposal problem. Some companies are now actively promoting the sale of printing papers made entirely from recycled paper waste, but the prices are higher than comparable paper made from virgin fiber. Under the internal tariff the social costs of lumber depletion and solid-waste disposal would be reflected in a preferential tax for recycled paper, thereby making it more economical to produce.

The problem of waste disposal is a serious one in the paper industry. The packaging industry alone produces about 50 million tons of solid waste annually. Recycling levels can be increased by tax incentives; it may be necessary to tax certain paper items produced for easy disposal to reflect social costs of disposal and waste, as well as consumer convenience.

According to the Department of Commerce:

> It has been difficult to determine whether a particular sanitary paper product is an item of necessity or luxury. The industry uses sophisticated advertising and aggressive marketing techniques to offer products of such varying grades and prices that they range from basic necessities to obvious luxuries. For example, toilet papers, facial tissues and towels are marketed in a wide price and grade range including single-ply and multi-ply grades of varying thickness, weight, strength, absorbency, scent, color, and texture (creped or embossed, soft or coarse). It is difficult to separate essential from luxury items among the many combinations of these characteristics.[160]

Nevertheless, the attempt must be made to set a social value or to account for all social costs in paper products to abate the damage to forest resources and to reduce solid-waste disposal problems caused by the "free" disposal of such items. As the government statement indicates, it is not an easy problem. How, for example, is the social value to be set on disposable diapers? This is a new product, but in 1971 $200 million worth was sold. In 1980 sales are expected to reach $1 billion. This presents a serious disposal problem against which the convenience to mothers must be balanced. Even Solomon might have been reluctant to pass judgment on this item.

Items 270.25 / 270.63 Advertising. Advertising is the Pied Piper that charms the millions of consumers to buy what is available on the market. It is an educational medium, that is, it teaches the consumer to want a product he may not have even heard of or known about. The advertising message creates the desire to buy. It is a creative merchandising tool used to develop and expand the market for new and established products. By expanding the market, it increases production and reduces unit costs. Advertising is not, contrary to popular opinion, a cause of higher prices. It reduces units costs; unless it does so, it is not economical to use. Advertising is an expense, and no firm willingly assumes an expense that is not necessary for profitable operation. In short, advertising is creative, necessary, and profitable.

Having said this, it must also be admitted that advertising is overdone, misleading, irritating, and socially irresponsible. Advertising expenditures in all media were about $22.8 billion in 1972 and are estimated to reach $26 billion in 1975 and $36 billion in 1980. These are huge amounts of money spent solely to inform the consumer where to buy what he needs. These huge sums of money have an effect on the media far beyond the content of the message. The media are dependent on advertising revenues for their existence. It is this dependence that causes advertising to have a social cost or significance apart from its function as a means of consumer education.

In considering a tax on advertising, this social cost must be evaluated. How much does advertising contribute to the tremendous consumption of newsprint, about 7 million tons in 1970? Is this use of scarce timber resources necessary, or is it largely wasted? How much does advertising contribute to media news content, from which it is theoretically divorced? How much does advertising contribute to the consumption of shoddy, unhealthy, meretricious merchandise by false claims, invidious comparisons, and prurient allusions? How much does advertising contribute to the low cultural level of the programs shown on TV and heard on the radio?

Advertising as a merchandising tool is legitimate and serves an economically useful function, but it goes beyond that function and becomes the arbiter of social values and cultural standards and the chief sponsor of the news media. Advertising has assumed a very crucial role in society, the role of social and cultural arbiter. It is a role for which advertising is not fitted, which it does not want, which is forced upon it by consumerism, and for which it is castigated unmercifully. The values of a consumer society are the values expressed in advertising, which tells the consumer what to eat, what to drink, what to wear, what to read, what to see on TV, what to hear on radio, what to take when he feels indisposed, where to go when he travels, how to lose weight, gain weight, win friends, be sexually attractive, and how to judge people by the clothes they wear, the cars they drive, the places they frequent, and the food they eat.

The standards set by advertising are largely the product of consumerism, of which the advertising man is himself an unconscious agent. He is just doing his job; most advertising men are at a loss to explain why their work arouses such intense moral and social concern. To him the social effects of advertising are secondary — the economic results are what count. The social and moral effects are beyond his control. He may feel somewhat guilty about them if he is a moralist or if his advertising message is socially harmful or unethical, but in most cases he does his job and ignores the social effects.

Placing ethical or social values on advertising cannot be done by advertisers while they operate under the market pressures of consumerism. The social value of a product must be placed on it by nonmarket forces. The internal tariff does it by taxation. In some cases this might not be enough. Cigarettes, for example, have been heavily taxed to discourage consumption. Taxation alone did not work; its effect was offset by massive consumer advertising that portrayed smoking as chic. Finally, cigarette advertising itself was regulated and reduced by law.

By taxing advertising revenues, the undue influence of consumer advertising on the cultural and news media would be reduced. Hopefully, artistic and cultural standards may then be substituted for mass-consumption standards. This may be done by the allocation of specific channels for mature adult listeners, others for news, others for pop shows, others for children. The criterion of popular appeal would still apply, but would be applicable to a specific audience. The plays of Shaw and O'Neill and Chekhov would not be ignored because there is a larger audience for cowboy and private eye stories, nor would Stravinsky, De Falla, or Debussy be banned because they are not as popular as the Beatles or the Rolling Stones. Popular art is vital and popularity is a valuable criterion, but it should not be the only standard. The tendency of consumerism to reduce all culture to the lowest common denominator is not healthy. Divorcing the artistic and cultural media from dependence on advertising would go a long way toward breaking up this homogenized culture.

The influence of advertising on the selection of consumer products would be considerably reduced by the internal tariff. Advertising would still play its part, but the addition of a tax based on social value to the price of an item would influence its marketability as much as or more than advertising appeal.

Advertising gives Americans "free" TV and radio and cheap newspapers and magazines. If it were actually free, it still would not be a bargain. At a cost of $22.8 billion, it is a tragic waste of resources.

Items 678.45 / 756.15 Cigarette Machines, Paper. In addition to taxes on tobacco products, not listed here, it may be desirable to levy taxes on machines and paper and other raw materials used in cigarette manufacture. Smokers' articles should also be taxed in line with public policy to discourage consumption of tobacco.

Current taxes on tobacco products are an example of taxation according to the principle of social value. To discourage consumption and to add the social cost of medical and hospital care for lung diseases, a pack of cigarettes is taxed heavily — 8¢ Federal tax, up to 21¢ state tax, and up to 7¢ local tax. Total taxes derived from cigarettes alone in 1971 were $4.7 billion. This is certainly a high revenue from a single commodity. It suggests that taxation by social value when applied to a commodity and backed by public opinion can produce tremendous tax revenues.

Items 533.11 / 653.85 Household Articles. The tax rate on these articles follows the pattern of placing basic necessities on the free list and using a graduated progressive tax schedule to tax nonessential or de luxe items.

Items 300.10 / 364.22 Fabrics, Cotton, etc. These rates are based on United States Tariff commodity descriptions and costs, which may be somewhat obsolete, but they are meant to be indicative of the rate flexibility and range rather than an attempt to fix *a priori* rates to these items.

Items 378.10 / 791.15 Apparel. A low rate is set on simple inexpensive clothing and progressively higher rates on more expensive high-style goods, in line with the "progressive" or "ability to pay" theory of taxation.

Items 435 / 440 / 461.45 Chemicals. No tax should be laid on drugs and related health products. Chemicals and raw materials in general should not be taxed, since they will be taxed eventually in the finished article. There may be exceptions such as that on raw materials for perfumes. Perfumes and cosmetics may be classified as nonessential or essential, depending on whether a man or a woman is passing judgment. However, the growth in male cosmetics, euphemistically called "grooming aids", from $340 million to $1 billion in a decade is a rather obvious example of superfluous consumption, except for such basic items as shaving cream. Trade sources estimate that the men's fashion industry has tripled in the last 15 years, is now at a peak of $20 billion a year, and is growing at a rapid rate. Male concern for fashion and beauty may be a healthy psychological development bespeaking a more assertive and self-confident male ego, but from an economic viewpoint it must definitely rate a lower value than supersonic transport, lunar exploration, free medical care, free school lunches, and other goals to which $20 billion dollars could be allocated.

Item 502.19 Precious Stones. Industrial diamonds could be classified in the free list, along with other types of industrial tools and raw materials. However, precious stones for jewelry naturally are in the highest class of luxury goods and taxed accordingly.

Items 696.05/10 Yachts. Another example of progressive taxation applied to a class of products that ranges from low to very high.

Item 730.10 Firearms. Deaths and crimes caused by these weapons make them eligible for the highest tax rates. The negative social value of guns is acknowledged by all, yet they are sold at cut-rate market prices. A social value tax such as the internal tariff would take them out of the bargain category and make them less easy to buy.

Items 660.25 / 660.44 Engines. In the schedule a high tax is placed on the gasoline piston-type engine. However, if the engine is "cleaned up" so that it does not pollute the air, the tax may be reduced to a level comparable with that on other "clean" engines. However, the higher rates for increased horsepower are directly related to the potential of the larger engines to injure and kill and to the waste of fossil fuel resources.

Internal Tariff Schedule II contains a short list of important items that are not covered by the external tariff, which, of course, does not include construction, buildings, and services. Many of these are quite important, but only a few are described and listed here.

Item 1/3 Construction. Congressional policy on housing will determine tax rates on homes. If the Congress wishes to encourage single-family dwellings, it can do so under the internal tariff by putting small homes on the free list and increasing the rates on a progessive scale on luxury homes. The rates set on single-family residences relative to rates set on mobile homes and apartment houses will determine to a large degree the future growth of the housing industry. By passing the FHA law and other subsidies, Congress made possible the growth of suburbia and indirectly contributed to the decline of the urban areas, but these results were largely unexpected and unplanned. One of the advantages of the internal tariff is that it creates a process of rational decision-making that is both open and responsible to the people. Hidden tax subsidies are eliminated. The internal tariff forces on Congress the necessity of open choice on every commodity or service. The choices must be made clear and understandable, their advantages and disadvantages fully stated, and alternatives brought into the open.

What are the advantages of single-family residences? What is the ultimate cost of urban sprawl in terms of highways and automobile costs, lost farm land, increased pressures on family life caused by isolation, and economic and social discrimination? Is the family no longer a cohesive unit? If so, are single-family homes socially useful? Are apartment homes more adaptable to modern life? What social value should be placed on design and environmental adaptation? In the Southwest, the Pueblo Indians built homes of thick adobe walls with small windows that were better adapted to the environment than modern thin-wall homes with large glass areas that require enormous amounts of energy for environmental protection. Should social value be expressed in taxes on homes according to built-in environmental protection or should such value be expressed in taxes on building components such as insulation materials and air-conditioning units? Should social value, in the form of preferential rates, be placed on quality and long life? Lending institutions now influence house design by approving or disapproving loans on homes that are different or unusual or inferior to accepted standards. Quality could be subsidized or given tax preference by grading housing units into classes according to life expectancy. A home built to last over 50 years could be given a tax preference over one that is built to last 15 years, either in the form of a tax on purchase price or depreciation allowance. Under the present tax system depreciation allowances favor rather than penalize buildings with short life expectancy.

Taxes in the form of preferential rates to express social value are more democratic than public housing, for they leave the choice of occupancy with the buyer. Public housing that forces people into occupancy by income criteria are patently undemocratic. Public housing should be left to special classes under government jurisdiction: prisoners, military personnel, students, and other groups where regimentation is temporary and unavoidable.

Tax preference or tax subsidies should be given to the construction of schools, hospitals, scientific projects, and other structures with a high social value. This is in line with past government tax policy, which has subsidized land grant colleges and railroad rights of way. The criteria of social value will naturally change with the social needs of the times.

Present government policy of tax relief and special low-interest loans to certain classes of buyers is not incompatible with the concept of tax rates set according to social value.

In commercial and industrial construction, also, the internal tariff rates should set standards of social value, but leave freedom of choice to the buyer. The criteria of social utility should emphasize environmental adaptation, minimum energy consumption, and effects on population. Present tax policies do not follow these criteria. Manufacturers in so-called ghetto areas are penalized with high tax rates and high insurance rates and are induced to move into new areas by special tax subsidies and lower insurance rates. The new areas may be undeveloped and lack manpower and energy resources, public schools, public roads, and other public services but, since these social costs are not borne by the builder or occupant, they are disregarded. Social value taxation would not inhibit freedom of movement, but it would try to prevent callous disregard of social costs in such movements. A wise assessment of social value in new industrial construction would go a long way to prevent the uneconomic utilization of manpower and energy resources. Population movements are affected by many social factors, but economic factors of employment, welfare benefits, and housing are decisive, and these are to a great extent now determined by government policy.

Present policy appears to encourage the building of second homes. In the 1940's, second homes were built at a rate of 20,000 per year. It is estimated that in the 1970's second homes will be built at an average rate of 130,000 per year. This is the type of consumer affluence that is largely untouched by current tax policy. The social value of a second home is certainly not as great as that of the first home, but where social value is not a criterion, the two homes are treated equally for tax purposes.

Heavy taxes on standard-construction dwellings cause people to seek nonstandard dwellings that are not so heavily taxed. Whether intended as deliberate or not, such a policy is subsidizing instant slums, or homes that have a rapid built-in obsolescence. Two such types are motor homes and mobile homes. Both consume billions of dollars of scarce resources. Both are doomed to rapid decay and deterioration. The question here is not whether such structures are "good" or "bad", desirable or undesirable. The fact remains that the tax policy of the government is forcing the development of these structures on the home-buying public without giving serious thought to the ultimate consequences and without considering alternate tax policies that could divert the construction to more aesthetically pleasing and more architecturally efficient dwellings. Under the internal tariff system, legislators would be forced to make explicit choices from many alternate construction programs, and each would be debated in light of long-term public interest, civic services, permanence, appearance, architectural beauty, and function. Today the tax system ignores social costs; consequently, the construction industry builds for a quick sale and a high return on investment. The result is a nation with the highest per capita income in the world living in urban ghettos, mobile home parks, and clapboard and stucco cottages that are potential slums.

In Europe construction is more premanent and less subject to pure market pressures. The Europeans know that unrestrained construction is out of the question. The master plan for the Paris region, for example, calls for 13 regional shopping centers and no more. This is in sharp contrast to such American areas as Long Island and Southern California, where shopping centers have multiplied without regional planning. In contrast to city development based on highest returns per square foot of available space, there is in Europe a criterion of social value based on permanence, beauty, and livableness. This is not true everywhere, of course, but high standards of city planning are found in many countries, especially in Germany. The view obtained from an apartment tower in Asenwald, four miles from Stuttgart, could not be duplicated in a large American city. On one side is a public forest, on the other farmlands unchanged since the Middle Ages. In downtown Stuttgart there is a 60-acre strip of lawns, ponds, and playgrounds. It would be difficult to find such vistas in downtown American cities because uncontrolled urban sprawl has destroyed farms and orchards near metropolitan areas.

The internal tariff would not automatically create beautiful cities, but it would discourage the construction of temporary, mobile, tract-type, nondescript dwellings built for quick profits, rapid depreciation, and low taxes. The tax advantage under the internal tariff would encourage long life and architectural quality. Beyond that, city development would be in the hands of the city government.

Item 4. Swimming Pools. Taxes on swimming pools follow the philosophy of the Internal Tariff in putting a higher tax on luxury goods that the rich can afford.

Items. 5/6. Admissions. Public spectacles are proper subjects for taxation. Through taxation, certain types of offensive or degrading shows may be discouraged.

Item 7. Travel. Travel is a form of sumptuous consumption and, therefore, subject to tax according to the progressive theory of taxation. The taxes suggested are relatively low for domestic travel and somewhat higher for foreign travel.

Item 8. Occupancy. Occupancy or membership in hotels and clubs is another form of conspicuous consumption and is a logical target for taxation based on the principle of ability to pay.

Item 9. Electric Power. The high rates suggested are merely indicative of the concern expressed over the energy crisis and the still unresolved problem of waste disposal from both fossil fuel and nuclear plants. If energy becomes the predominant problem in the near future, drastic measures will be required to curtail its consumption. The lower rates for industrial users are designed only to postpone the tax until the finished industrial product is made and sold, when it will be rated again for tax purposes.

Item 10. Telephone Service. The social cost of the telephone is represented in ugly poles and transmission lines that deface the environment. The tax of 20 per cent is not punitive since it falls below the 25 per cent level set as the average tax load now carried by consumers.

The items described have been rated for demonstration purposes only according to the six criteria of (1) ability to pay; (2) conservation of energy; (3) pollution control; (4) social utility; (5) health and safety risks; and (6) obsolescence.

The seventh criterion of *efficiency* would be a function of market competition and would not be included in determining tax rates. Of the six criteria, four are noncontroversial, that is, everyone is willing to concede that considerations of ability to pay, conservation of energy, pollution control, and health risks are not to be ignored in the making of tax and price policy.

Social utility is, of course, highly controversial. It is easy to agree *in principle* on the goal of maximum social utility, but the problem of achieving it presents insurmountable difficulties. The free market under laissez-faire was not able to achieve the Benthamite ideal of the greatest good of the greatest number; the Marxist ideal of distribution according to need has foundered on the rocks of production legistics and *Realpolitik*. The ideal of maximum consumer satisfaction or maximum social utility or happiness is one that is difficult to achieve, since no consumer can ever be completely satisfied or happy for long. The pursuit of happiness is a never-ending quest, not a definite economic goal. Leaving it to Congress to set priorities for the guidance of the consumer market will not solve what is an unsolvable problem, but it puts the problem within the reach and the control of the people. It is the people who will be called upon to vote on the economic programs that will be presented to them by the major parties and Congressional candidates seeking office. It is their vote that will decide the basic direction of price and tax policy. The taxes that will be imposed by Congress on all goods must be judged by their effect on the general goals set by political consensus and party platform. If these goals are not reached, the people have the power to vote for a new party and a new legislator.

The other controversial criterion is that of obsolescence. Here again, it is easy to agree *in principle* on the desirability of product quality and long life. However, the American economy has been built on the foundation of maximum sales and rapid turnover. What would happen to the automobile industry if cars lasted 500,000 miles instead of 100,000? What would happen to the lamp industry if lamps lasted 10,000 hours instead of 1000? What would happen to the housing industry if houses were built to last 100 years instead of 50? What would happen to industries such as clothing, furniture, and recreation, which are built on the transient trends of fashion? Obviously almost all industries would suffer a severe drop in sales as a result of a tax on obsolescence. The people affected adversely will *not* agree on the desirability of quality and long life, but will champion the opposite ideal of model and style changes as beneficial to progress.

The question of taxes on obsolescence is one that cannot be decided *a priori* or arbitrarily. This would require debate on each specific item, followed by agreement on what degree of obsolescence is desired. Too high a tax would retard obsolescence, but would freeze design and retard innovation. No tax or too light a tax on obsolescence would continue wasteful production of inferior, throw-away, impermanent, shoddy goods destined for a short life and the junk heap.

Kenneth Boulding has touched on the need for correcting the price system to put a premium on obsolescence:

> What is clear is that no serious attempt has been made to assess the impact over the whole of economic life of changes in durability, that is, in the ratio of capital in the widest sense to income. I suspect we have under-estimated, even in our spendthrift society, the gains from increased durability, and that this might very well be one of the places where the price system needs correction through government-sponsored research and development.[161]

It would appear that the government tax system would provide the best correction for the price imbalance that is now so heavily weighted in favor of obsolescence, although government-sponsored research in development of longer-lasting products would also be helpful. The current market price system makes obsolescence profitable. The profit system need not be abolished or replaced by a government bureaucracy that specifies how products are to be made more durable. A tax on obsolescence would create an incentive to make goods more long-lasting and of a higher quality and make it unprofitable to design goods built for a short life and a quick profit. In a market economy, to reduce built-in obsolescence it is necessary to make obsolescence unprofitable.

The fear that making products with more quality and a longer life will create unemployment is unfounded; rather, it is founded on the false theory that employment is a function of consumption.

A significant feature of the internal tariff is its comprehensiveness. Without this feature, the setting of national economic priorities would be impossible. The tax included in the price of one commodity can be significant only in relation to the prices of all other commodities within a general system of priorities. Myrdal has cautioned: "The effect of a tax must never be examined in isolation, but must be seen in its setting amongst other measures in the complex system of price formation."[162]

Under the internal tariff system legislators would be forced to examine each specific commodity and service and rate it in relation to all others in a complex, comprehensive system of price formation.

6. Economic Planning by Legislative Process

Obviously, the brief list in the preceding pages can give only a very incomplete idea of the scope and range of the internal tariff. The items listed represent only a few of many thousands of related items in the same commodity group. The official United States Tariff takes about 585 pages of fine print to describe all imported commodities. The internal tariff would be larger because there are more items made and sold than are imported, and it must list services as well. When it is realized that services provide a greater portion of the national income than manufacturing, the size of this addition to the schedule becomes apparent.

Does this mean that the task of preparing such a schedule is too great? Not at all. With modern computers it is a simple matter to solve the technical aspects of compiling data for Congress and keeping the members up-to-date on economic factors affecting commodity prices. The very breadth and scope of the schedule would ensure that the system would be complete and that, when all rates have been approved and passed by Congress, the whole will represent a complete and balanced economic system.

Unlike the external tariff, which can be changed only after considerable negotiation with foreign powers, the internal tariff may be changed by a simple act of Congress whenever evidence is presented that a tax rate is causing unforeseen harm or is no longer serving a useful purpose.

In a previous chapter the income tax was compared to the volume control on an amplifier that could do no more than make the volume of revenues go up or down by broad classes. It could never be used as a tool for "fine-tuning" the economy. The internal tariff, on the contrary, is like a conductor who can orchestrate the entire economy and increase or decrease revenue from each of many thousands of different commodities or services in large or fractional amounts. It affords Congress the opportunity to channel economic and manpower resources in a manner consistent with its goals for social welfare and to set national economic priorities on all important economic activities without interfering with market competition.

The internal tariff would encounter difficult but not insurmountable problems. There would be strong opposition from industries that felt penalized by the tax. This problem would best be met by a policy of gradualism. As the internal tariff is levied on a specific industry, the rate could be set on a graduated scale, with the final rate taking effect in five, seven, or even ten years. The initial rate could be offset by the cancellation of the corporate income tax. As one industry after another came under the internal tariff and management and labor saw that it was not causing any injurious effects, the acceptance of the new tax by all industry would follow in due course.

The reader who has followed this exposition this far may now begin to wonder if the internal tariff could be *too* successful and, if so, what might be the consequences. The internal tariff being an indirect and impersonal tax, the Congress would eventually find that the rates could be raised on many commodities to a point where the total revenue produced would be much higher than was possible under a direct, personal tax such as the income tax. The reader may have already mentally calculated that, if a cigarette tax can produce $4 billion and there are thousands of taxable commodities, the internal tariff might be a veritable cornucopia with unlimited revenue potential.

Another reader may wonder if the success of the internal tariff might not bring a disastrous depression. The object of the internal tariff is to conserve manpower, energy, and material resources and to reduce pollution and waste. In many industries, such as the automotive, the tax would probably cut employment by reducing model changes and size of cars. Gasoline consumption would also be reduced, and some loss would take place in the auto service industry.

It is true that production and employment would be reduced in some industries, for the tax is designed to discourage production of some items. However, it is also designed to encourage the production of others. The flexibility of the rate schedule makes it possible to balance production in any desired "mix."

It must be kept in mind that the object of the internal tariff is not only to raise revenue, but also to give Congress the opportunity to plan economic growth in a democratic manner. The raising and lowering of tariff rates permits Congress to do so without direct controls. It also allows Congress to set priorities on nonconsumer projects. The projects available to it are endless in the realms of national defense, advanced energy technology, aerospace technology, public transportation, modernization of cities, cleaning of rivers and lakes, education, and medical care, for example. The problem is not one of finding projects on which to work and use manpower; it is one of setting priorities among many competing projects. The Council on Environmental Quality reported on Sept. 17, 1973 that about $274.2 billion would be needed to combat all kinds of pollution in the period 1972 through 1981. Cleaning up the nation's water to make it safe to drink and to bathe in will cost about $121.3 billion. Much of the money will be allocated for sewage treatment plants. This is only one of several urgent projects that can absorb all the available energy, manpower, and capital available from the United States economy.

In the internal tariff the Congress would have a democratic method for setting priorities over the private economy and a flexible tax base that would support any public program backed by public opinion. The power in the hands of Congress would be tremendous; there is no guarantee that it would be used wisely and that the priorities it set would be in the highest national interest. In a democratic society the people must place their faith in the wisdom of their elected representative. The Congress as the highest representative assembly is the organ that has, or should have, the responsibility of deciding national priorities according to the public interest.

Up to now the priorities of the private economy have been left to the market, to advertising, and to labor-capital power struggles over prices and wages. The government has intervened by tax policy and fiscal policy, but its intervention has served merely to divert revenues by income taxation from the private to the public sector. Within the private sector it has not established priorities. The production and consumption of commodities have been left alone, as if the principle of laissez-faire market competition were still operative or as if consumer priorities in the private sector had no relation to priorities in the public sector. As a result of this tax policy, there is the extraordinary phenomenon of consumer affluence coexisting with poverty and lack of money for vitally needed high-priority tasks. The economy can spend over $100 billion on automobiles, but has no money for space exploration. It can spend over $100 billion on luxury homes, second homes, and suburban developments, but has no funds available for cleaning up urban ghettos; it can spend over $25 billion on men's fashions and cosmetics, but it is not able to fund adequate health care. The contrast between private affluence and public poverty has been noted by J. K. Galbraith and others much better qualified to describe it and need not be pushed any further. The point to be made is that the priorities of the private sector need to be evaluated and considered in the national interest as much as the priorities of the public sector. There is only one economy. The public sector is not hermetically sealed from the private sector. They are two parts of the same body, directed by the same political organs, using the same system of communication, and the same currency is in circulation in both.

The internal tariff would allow Congress the opportunity to make long-range national economic plans. Up to now this has been impossible because consumer demand is unpredictable and outside the control of Congress. Under the internal tariff the Congress would not control demand in a literal sense, but it would set the priorities for each segment of the consumer market, and economists would be able to advise Congress with reasonable accuracy the exact production-consumption levels for each commodity group for planning purposes. Even under present unplanned market conditions, the variation in total output in any industry or commodity group, whether measured in dollar value or in physical output, is relatively stable and predictable. Under these new game rules, Congress would be free to plan ahead and establish bold new programs that would give overall guidance to the economy. The Apollo program is an example of the type of long-range planning that Congress would be able to make. This type of long-range planning has been the unique advantage of Socialist governments. Under the internal tariff the Congress would have the same capability without the bureaucratic regimentation of Soviet-type planning.

At present, private industry plans for the future, insofar as it is able to do so, without knowledge of future government plans or priorities. The United States government is limited to the resources of the tax-financed public sector; since the planning by fiscal and monetary policy is done through the executive branch, such plans are made on an annual basis and limited to a four-year period in long-range terms. At the end of the period, the executive faces the possibility of losing office and having his plans revised or cancelled. No effective long-range planning is possible under these conditions.

To be effective, government economic planning must be complete, that is, it must bring the private sector into the plan as an active participant, and it must be long-range. Only through the Congress would it be possible to establish a basic economic policy with both continuity and long-range goals. The policy of Congress in the internal tariff would be analogous in terms of long-range policy with the tariff policy of the 19th century, although, naturally, much more comprehensive.

The internal tariff could not give the Congress a blank check to finance whatever programs it chose. The responsibility of careful choice and wise preparation is inherent in any good planning procedure. The Congress would still have ceilings on its revenues, and there would be a definite fiscal limit to what it could spend on any and all programs. The difference is that, for the first time, the Congress would have a much wider range of options with regard to funding long-range programs. At the present time the Federal budget acts as a straitjacket that restricts the Congress and the President to very few options. The Federal budget for fiscal year 1974 is *already overcommitted for the next four or five years.* That is, without any new programs, the money collected by current tax laws is already committed to fund existing programs that will continue for that length of time. Under the circumstances, the options open to Congress for funding new programs are almost nil. At most, it has two: (1) divert funds from one program to another and (2) raise new revenues by new taxes. The first has been attempted by Congressmen who have succeeded in diverting some funds budgeted for supersonic transport, the space program, and national defense for use elsewhere. The second option is being toyed with by the Congress, but there is a reluctance to increase current taxes that, at their present levels, are already very painful.

The options available to the Congress under the internal tariff would be considerably greater. There would be the opportunity for trade-off between priorities in *all* sectors of the economy, both private and public. The money for a new space program need not come from national defense needs — it could come from increased tariff rates on motel rooms, advertising novelties,

248

amusement park admissions, men's toiletries, pet foods, beverage dispensers, electric bulbs, jewelry, detergents, and fur coats. The industries taxed would present their views through their Congressional representatives from their districts and through their trade organizations and chambers of commerce, and their opinions and objections would be taken into consideration. Business leaders do not like taxes, but it is easy to overestimate their resistance to new taxes of this type. In the first place, the tariff rate would apply to *all* commodities. Second, the rate increase would be, in most cases, applied in small increments. Third, the increase would apply to *all* producers within a commodity group so that the *relative* competitive position of all producers would remain unaffected by the rate increase.

That is not to say that the internal tariff tax would not be painful and resented by the affected parties. There is no way to remove the sting from taxation altogether. What the internal tariff does is *widen* the choice of options available to Congress and at the same time give it the opportunity to spread the tax load over a *wider* range of commodities, thereby lessening the hardship on the individual industry or trade.

How much greater the overall tax load that would be placed on the economy under the internal tariff than under present taxes is not determinable in advance. However, since the internal tariff is an indirect tax, the chances are that it would carry a greater load than direct taxes such as the income tax. But Congress would not be able to set tax rates arbitrarily on any commodity. The consumers and producers would both apply pressure to prevent it. The effective maximum rate would necessarily be a trade-off between the expected benefits from the program for which taxes are levied and consumer inconvenience from higher prices. The Congress would have to use its oratorical skill to convince the voters that they are giving up something (a higher price on a consumer item) for something else of greater value (a new hospital program). Unless the country were sold on the new program, the taxes could not be levied. Public opinion and participation are essential under the internal tariff.

Under present government economic policies the public is excluded from policymaking by the nature of the process, which is undemocratic and beyond the control and the understanding of the general public. Although the Medicare program is designed to help the poor, it indirectly subsidizes hospitals and medical personnel; although food stamps help feed the hungry, they subsidize farmers and food processors; student loans and free tuition subsidize school teachers and administrators; school milk programs subsidize the dairy industry; housing programs subsidize builders, bankers, and real estate developers; welfare programs subsidize a huge bureaucracy. The government sets priorities and guides economic growth, but the process is undemocratic and inadvertent and achieves results that often are not what had been originally intended or desired.

Under the internal tariff the indirect subsidies to producers who are sometimes the chief beneficiaries of welfare programs for the needy would be impossible. The internal tariff tax will make it necessary for the legislators to face explicitly *all* the social benefits, direct and indirect, that the tax will produce. Questions of social benefits and national priorities will necessarily be faced and debated on specific commodities, not generalized in grandiose welfare plans that mask indirect subsidies.

The question of leadership in economic affairs is a crucial one under the internal tariff, as under any other tax system. In the United States and in most parliamentary democracies, the Congress or legislative assembly holds the power of the purse, the economic power. In Europe the executive branch or cabinet is an arm of the legislative assembly so that there is, theoretically, no conflict between the executive and the legislative in the exercise of economic power. This has not prevented the development of bureaucratic planning that, under various forms of *dirigisme,* is essentially authoritarian and undemocratic.

In the United States the President has taken the initiative in economic leadership; under the present income tax law it is difficult to see how Congress could regain the economic power and initiative it had in the past and that the Constitution specifically confers on it.

The internal tariff would help to restore the mantle of economic leadership to Congress. It would involve Congress in continuous economic decision-making and planning on both a short-term and long-term basis. With the added power would come added responsibility and work. How Congress would discharge this responsibility of leadership is not predictable. It is, of course, possible that a strong President, as a party leader, may mobilize public opinion behind a bold economic program and leave Congress with the duties of carrying out its details.

However, unless Congress abdicates its power through weakness, indecision, or submission, it retains, under the internal tariff, the instrument for wielding economic control over the economy, and it is not likely that it would fail to exercise it. The internal tariff is essentially a legislative form of economic planning. The economic goals may be enunciated by the President, but it is in Congress and in the legislative process that the plan would take shape. The responsibility for "selling" the economic plan to the public would lie with Congress; and it is this responsibility that the Congress, above all other government bodies, is uniquely fitted to carry out as the peoples' representative.

Today the legislature in a two-sector economy acts as a rubber stamp for the automatic approval of executive economic plans or budgets. It is not directly involved in the planning process. It cannot be, for the planning process is under the executive and is not a legislative or democratic procedure. The legislature is not directly involved in setting economic priorities. This is true even where the planning is done under the direction of a minister who is also a member of the legislature. The legislature does not debate the priorities. It merely approves or rejects them. For economic planning to be truly democratic, it must be a legislative process. Every aspect of the plan must be debated in Congress and priorities set by compromise between the various interests represented in Congress: labor, capital, states, classes, districts, and industries, for example. The executive cannot represent these interests. Powerful executive department heads or bureau chiefs are not elected representatives, and the only influence to which they are subject to is that of powerful special interest lobbies. The experience of the Congress with the protective tariff indicates that economic planning by Congress is quite different from executive planning. It is not necessarily more efficient, wiser, or more successful than executive planning, but it *is* more democratic.

Under the internal tariff the two sectors would merge into a unified national economy, with the legislature performing the political functions of economic guidance and making tax policy and the private market producing goods under rules of effective price competition. Under this system the vast bureaucratic apparatus for managing tax-funded social programs would no longer be required, and bureaucratic executive power would decline. This would be in itself a considerable achievement.

According to Karl Mannheim: "The problem of the democratic constitution of a planned society mainly consists in avoiding bureaucratic absolutism. It all depends on whether we can find ways of transferring democratic, parliamentary control to a planned society. If this control is destroyed in the effort to establish a planned society, planning will be a disaster not a cure."[163]

The debate over the internal tariff would force Congress to make explicit choices on specific commodities. Questions of conservation of resources, quality of life, poverty, health, food, and housing would be focused on each item in the tariff, not generalized in vast social welfare programs that the Secretary of HEW confessed in October 1973 did not always achieve the desired results: "We have added enormous amounts of money to the so-called Great Society programs since they began in the mid-1960s, but the problems we had then for the most part have gotten worse."[164]

Under the internal tariff law Congress would have to estimate for tax purposes the social value of a pair of shoes or of a quart of milk. This is much more difficult than passing laws to create the Great Society.

Chapter
VII

BEYOND THE TWO-SECTOR ECONOMY

1. Income Support

According to textbooks, the economic problem facing any nation is the fair and efficient allocation of *all* material and human resources between competing objectives. There is the difficult task of allocating resources between the consumer market (the private sector) and the government (the public sector.) Within the private sector there is the controversial question of the division between labor and capital. Within the public sector there is the dilemma of choosing between defense requirements and the welfare needs of the country. Within each sector there are further subdivisions until the ultimate consumer is finally reached and is satisfied or deprived. Human appetites being insatiable, there is no possibility that any society will ever devise a completely satisfactory system for allocating all resources, that is, a system that will satisfy everybody. For that reason, special provisions must be made, usually by the government, for those who are left out of the general distribution or who are denied a fair share of the gross national product.

In the United States, until the great depression, it was thought that only beggars or bums would accept government relief, and acceptance carried the stigma of social inferiority. The principle that people on welfare should work for what they get from society is an Anglo-American tradition that goes back to the beginning of the welfare system. Queen Elizabeth enacted the first English Poor Law "and made a condition of setting the poor to work" for benefits received. President Roosevelt in his message to Congress in 1935 stated that his Social Security program was designed to take the government out of "this business of relief" and make workers pay for their own welfare through payroll contributions. The Family Assistance Plan of 1969 was a guaranteed income plan, but it had work incentives built into it and was advocated by President Nixon for that very reason. The principle of income by right rather than by work has not been accepted as yet in America as a principle of welfare. However, the stigma attached to welfare has almost disappeared, and welfare recipients in the United States are becoming better organized, more conscious of their "rights," more militant in their attitude, and less ashamed of their position than formerly.

In England in times past those who accepted relief because of circumstances beyond their control were called "the deserving poor." It was assumed that they were unwilling victims of an economic crisis and that, when work was again available, they would take jobs. This was to distinguish them from the chronic drunkards, beggars, or idlers who did not want to work and would not accept a job when it was available. In America the poor have, in the past, gone to extreme lengths to stay off the relief rolls. To be "on relief" was a social disgrace to be avoided at all costs. Even the lowest-paid worker felt that acceptance of relief meant a loss of pride and self-respect, in addition to being a social stigma. This attitude is not so prevalent today.

The values of the welfare state are the values of a consumer society in which every consumer has a right to a share of the gross national product. According to Keynesian economics, full employment is based on full consumption; to maintain full employment, the consumer should be subsidized whether he works or not. Redistribution of income through progressive income tax rates further erodes the doctrine of work as the only basis of money claims on consumption. The advent of the welfare system has brought into existence powerful groups that have a vested interest in its perpetuation. The Federal bureaucracy, now being organized as a labor union, is vitally interested in keeping and expanding its power and jobs. The welfare recipients themselves are finding leaders eager to organize them into a political pressure group or a political party that could, as in ancient Rome, determine national elections. Marxist politicians and intellectuals are eager to complete the proletarianization of the unemployed. The welfare class would be much easier to radicalize than organized labor, which now is highly paid and conservative. Under these circumstances, the old values associated with work, self-reliance, and pride and the values associated with welfare — loss of self-respect and social esteem — are no longer widely held. Instead, there is a growing belief in the doctrine of income as a right and in the right of the government to distribute income according to "need". The American citizen now feels, as the Roman citizen once did, that he has a right to a share in the spoils of the state, or of the gross national product, as the national wealth is now called. To deprive him of this right may prove as difficult to modern statesmen as it was impossible for Caesar or Augustus. It is also widely believed, not only by the welfare recipient, but by others, that to deprive him of his right to free income would be an act of injustice. Prior to 1930 such an attitude toward work and welfare would have been almost inconceivable; the American dream of rags to riches by hard work and capital savings was still believed almost religiously.

Before 1920 government aid was extended only to war veterans — a program started in the Revolutionary war — and in the military retirement program started in the Civil War. In 1920 a Federal civil service retirement program was started. In 1935 the Social Security program was passed under Roosevelt's New Deal. Although it was sold to the public as an insurance program to care for the aged, the destitute, and the disabled, it is now generally recognized that it is only partly a contributory insurance program and much more a social welfare income support program. Originally, workers paid a 1 per cent payroll tax on the first $3000 of annual wages and the employer matched the tax. There have been numerous raises in tax rates since then. The combined rate in 1973 for both worker and employer was 11.7 per cent on the first $10,800 of earnings. The program provides retirement benefits and survivor benefits for covered workers. There have been substantial increases in both the number of workers covered and in benefits paid. In 1956 disability benefits were added to the Social Security programs. By 1972 disability benefit payments alone exceeded $3 billion. In 1966 the government added medical and hospital benefits (Medicare) for the elderly. It is expected that the Social Security program of income support will be broadened to a point where, in the near future, it will cover every citizen from the cradle to the grave with complete social and health benefits, a type of coverage already in effect in Sweden, West Germany, Norway, Denmark, England, Holland, Austria, France, and some other European countries.

The Social Security law of 1935 also provided unemployment benefits funded by a 1 per cent payroll tax on the first $3000 of earnings, paid only by the employer. The rate in 1972 was 3.2 per cent on the first $4200 of earnings. In 1972 about 8 million workers collected unemployment benefits totaling $5.8 billion. Average weekly benefit was about $53, but there are wide variations between states because the program is state-administered.

Another income-support program for the poor is the food stamp program established in 1964. A family of four, according to the 1971 law, with an annual income under $3600 is eligible for food stamps worth $108 a month. As income rises, a charge is made for food stamps, reaching 25 per cent of income at $2000 annual income and 27 per cent at $4000 annual income. A poor family uses the food stamps as scrip money to buy food. In 1971 about 10.5 million persons were buying food with food stamps. Other government food subsidy programs include food subsidies to the aged ($221 million), the disabled ($97 million), families with dependent children and unemployed persons ($3 billion), and children not classified as needy ($602 million). Total food subsidies in 1971 amounted to $3.9 billion.

Public housing is available to the poor, who are charged no more than 25 per cent of a tenant's income, although eligibility rules vary from community to community. In 1973 the Federal government spent $1.8 billion dollars for low-cost housing for the poor. About 500,000 units were built. It is estimated that 6 million such units will be constructed by 1978 at an eventual cost of about $7.5 billion a year. Other income-support programs include subsidies to farmers and to students.

Income support by the government represents the reverse or the "negative" side of income taxation. The obvious and perhaps the most logical type of income support under an income tax system is a negative income tax, as originally proposed by economist Milton Friedman. Under such a program every individual with an income that falls below a specified "minimum" level would receive a tax subsidy or government check to bring his income up to the legal national minimum income level. If a taxpayer earned $3000 annual income and the legal minimum income was $4,000, he would receive a tax subsidy of $1000 under the negative income tax law.

The advantages of a negative income tax program are that it is simple, eliminates the need of a welfare bureaucracy, and does away with the stigma attached to welfare aid. The disadvantages are that it establishes the doctrine of income by right, opens the door to continuous pressure in Congress to raise the minimum income level — like the minimum wage level — and weakens further the incentive to work, already eroded by the income tax.

William Cavala and Aaron Wildavsky wrote a penetrating study on "The Feasability of Income by Right" and reached the conclusion that a guaranteed income such as a negative income tax would not pass Congress for three basic reasons: (1) policies that provide unearned income run counter to widely held and deeply felt American values such as achievement, work, and equality of opportunity; (2) to fund such programs new taxes must be imposed or present taxes raised, and the tax system is already overburdened; and (3) labor unions fear that a guaranteed income would render them superfluous. Militant black leaders take the same position for a similar reason. The same fear is felt by militant welfare leaders and the entrenched welfare bureaucracy, both of which see in the negative income tax a threat to their survival.

The pressure for some type of income support for the poor is not new. As far back as 1949 Senator Robert A. Taft of Ohio proposed that the Federal government maintain a "minimum standard floor under subsistence" so as to guarantee all Americans a "minimum standard of decent living...all children a fair opportunity to get a start in life."

The present system of income-support programs represents a mixed bag of reform or meliorative social programs started under the New Deal and financed largely by the income tax and payroll taxes. Some of the programs, such as the Social Security system, were copied from German and English programs that had been tested and proved by experience for decades. Others were experiments at social engineering carried out under the theory that social ills are completely curable by legislation. It appears, however, that some social conditions such as idleness, poverty, educability, population growth, family unity, crime and antisocial behavior cannot be completely controlled by legislation because of complex underlying causes that are not yet fully understood.

In the field of welfare dependency there is really very little that is known absolutely, according to one man who probably knows more about the subject than any one else in American political life, Daniel P. Moynihan:

The actual process of welfare dependency — how it comes about, what it is,

255

how it is sustained, what diminishes it — remains virtually unexamined. Some few persons have ventured into the field, often at cost to themselves, and rarely with any great reward in terms of findings. In large terms there is nothing unusual about this absence of knowledge. What forms of human behavior are understood? Even so, in most areas of social policy there are quite extensive research efforts which recurrently produce results of proximate value; but not in the area of welfare dependency. [165]

Lack of understanding of the causes of poverty and welfare dependency coupled with a blind faith in government bureaucracy has been followed since the 1960's by growing public disillusionment with the results achieved. Unemployment insurance has not ended unemployment; urban renewal programs have not improved housing in the cities; Social Security has not ended welfare dependency; billions spent to fight poverty have not improved the lot of the poor; billions spent on public schools have not improved the quality of education; and billions spent on aid to families with dependent children have not restored broken families. But the solution offered by bureaucrats, when faced with failure, is not to cut out government aid, but to increase it and overlay one layer of bureaucracy with another.

The number of government agencies dealing with welfare is so large and the welfare function enters into so many government activities that it is impossible to give an accurate account. The 1973 Federal budget shows that welfare takes about 39 per cent of total expenditures — over $100 billion. In terms of people it is sad to note that in 1971 the Department of Health, Education, and Welfare reported that more than 10 per cent of the residents of the nation's 20 largest cities were on welfare. In Boston one in five persons was on welfare. The total number of people on welfare grew from 6,052,000 in 1950 to 15,069,000 in 1972, yet 1972 was considered a year of prosperity. The figures are for Federal welfare aid. Add city, state, and county benefits paid to the poor, and the total would be much larger. Henry Hazlitt estimates that between 1935 and 1971 there was a 29-fold increase in expenditures for welfare at the Federal level and a 23-fold increase at the local level.[166]

The vast Federal bureaucracy devoted to welfare is engaged in such programs as food stamps, job training, public housing, rent supplements, model cities, community action projects, legal services for the poor, neighborhood health centers, "alphabet" agencies such as OEO (Office of Economic Opportunity), Medicaid, OAA (Old Age Assistance), AB (Aid to the Blind), APTD (Aid to the Permanently and Totally Disabled), AFDC (Aid to Families with Dependent Children), GA (General Assistance), CAP (Community Action Programs), and VISTA. Some of these agencies may be defunct by the time this is read, but their functions and personnel probably will have been absorbed in or transferred to other agencies.

In 1969 Mrs. Edith Green, a Congresswoman from Oregon, asked the Library of Congress to compile the total welfare benefits a family of five (mother and four children) could receive under existing government programs. Total benefits available were reported as follows:

The family could collect $2800 from public assistance; $618 from medical assistance because of AFDC; $336 in cash value for food stamps; about $200 from OEO for legal services and health care; $406 to $636 in public housing or rent supplements; $1050 for one preschool child enrolled in Head Start; $1440 in services from Upward Bound to a child in high school; $500 to $1000 for education grants available to the son in college; $475 for a work-study program; and, if mother wanted to participate in the job opportunity program, this would be worth $3,000. The Library of Congress came up with possible total benefits of $11,513 for a hypothetical family of mother and four children. This, of course, is a possible rather than an actual figure, but it illustrates the spread of welfarism and the difficulty of confining the policy within manageable limits once the principle of welfare according to need is established. There are no known limits to needs.

In 1970 Robert Finch, Secretary of HEW, stated before the Senate Finance Committee:

> A low income woman and her family can receive food stamps, State supplementation, Medicaid benefits, public housing, day care, legal services, and a variety of other service benefits. For example, a non-working mother with three children in New York city who receives State supplementation, Medicaid, food stamps (using the current schedule), and public housing, has a total income — of both money and in-kind payments — of $7,405, exclusive of day care benefits.

Although the vast majority of people on welfare are genuinely in need of aid and are often pathetic cases, it is also true that there are welfare "chiselers" and many who are on welfare through cheating, lying, and misrepresentation. Just how serious is this problem? Routine spot checks by official agencies and independent surveys always uncover a large percentage of fraudulent welfare cases. James S. Dwight, Jr., administrator of the Social and Rehabilitation Service of the Department of Health, Education, and Welfare, reported in August 1973 that payments to ineligible welfare cases and overpayments cost the American taxpayers nearly $1 billion in one year. This is a large sum, even when contrasted with total outlays of $19 billion, which Mr. Dwight estimated as the total cost, state and Federal, required to care for the 10 million persons dependent on welfare. To solve the problem of welfare chiseling, HEW proposed to add 400 more Federal financial managers, which it was confident would solve the problem. But the basic problem is not cheating, as Moynihan has pointed out: "The fact is, the more one knows about welfare the more horrible it becomes, but not because of cheating, rather because the system destroys those who receive it, and corrupts those who dispense it."[167]

Added to the welfare problem of fraud is the inherent inefficiency of most government institutions. For example, according to the governor of Illinois, it costs the state $25,000 a year to keep a delinquent in a state correctional institute. For a fifth of that amount he could be attending Harvard or Princeton.[168]

Disillusionment with government welfare, or relief, has been expressed officially and unofficially by all American political leaders since the system was started in the 1930's. In 1935 President Roosevelt declared: "The Federal Government must and shall quit this business of relief...continued dependence upon relief induces a spiritual and moral disintegration, fundamentally destructive to the national fiber." Thirty-two years later in

1967 President Johnson said: "The welfare system in America is outmoded and in need of a major change." When he launched his War on Poverty, he stated that he hoped to make "tax payers" out of "tax eaters."

The War on Poverty did not end poverty, but it did create jobs for a large number of government social workers at salaries well above the poverty line:

> There were 100,000 workers in Community Action Agencies, established under the office of Economic Opportunity after 1964. One of the major tasks of this legion was to tell poor people about welfare, accompany them to welfare agencies, argue for them, organize them in sit-ins, distribute simplified accounts of the rules governing welfare and the benefits available. In short, there were 100,000 recruiters for welfare that were not there before. In addition, there were at least 1,800 lawyers paid by OEO projects in 1968; one of their functions was to challenge the restrictions around the granting of welfare. [169]

According to Governor Daniel Walker of Illinois in November 1973:

> The War on Poverty is a prime example of a program that was supposed to solve the housing problems of the underprivileged by massive public outlays for public housing. We spent billions of dollars, but poverty remains and insubstantial housing pockmarks our cities. Giant public housing projects remain breeding grounds for crime, delinquency, and despondency. The ghetto monuments to urban renewal all too frequently consist of blocks of empty land, abandoned buildings and broken glass. I hope we have learned that massive amounts of money and Washington bureaucracies are not a viable response to the nation's domestic problems.

President Nixon in a major television address to the American people in his first term expressed the general feeling of disappointment over welfare:

> A third of a century of centralizing power and responsibility in Washington has produced a bureaucratic monstrosity, cumbersome, unresponsive, ineffective. A third of a century of social experiment has left us a legacy of entrenched programs that have outlived their time or outgrown their purposes. . . . Nowhere has the failure of government been more tragically apparent than in its efforts to help the poor and especially in its system of public welfares. Whether measured by the anguish of the poor themselves, or by the drastically mounting burden on the tax payer, the present welfare system has to be judged a colossal failure.

President Nixon listed among the failures:

> The welfare system stagnates enterprise and perpetuates dependency.
> It is bringing states and cities to the brink of financial disaster.
> It is failing to meet the elementary human, social and financial needs of the poor.
> It breaks up homes. It often penalizes work. It robs recipients of dignity. And it grows.
> The present system creates an incentive for desertion. . . . A father is unable to find a job at all or one that will support his children. So, to make the children eligible for welfare, he leaves home . . .
> The present system often makes it possible to receive more money on welfare than on a low-paying job. This creates an incentive not to work; and it is also unfair to the working poor. It is morally wrong for a family that is trying to make ends meet to receive less than the family across the street on welfare. This has been

bitterly resented by the man who works, and rightly so — the rewards are just the opposite of what they should be. Its effect is to draw people off payrolls and onto welfare rolls — just the opposite of what government should be doing. To put it bluntly and simply — any system which makes it more profitable for a man not to work than to work, or which encourages a man to desert his family rather than to stay with his family, is wrong and indefensible.

In 1969 President Nixon introduced a new welfare plan called the Family Assistance Plan (FAP), the brainchild of Daniel P. Moynihan. The plan was a combination of the negative income tax and a work incentive plan. The FAP provided for direct Federal payments to *all* families with children with incomes below stipulated levels. It included both families with unemployed fathers and working fathers, as well as fatherless families. In this respect, it was similar to a negative income tax with a minimum income level of $1600 for a family of four. The plan, however, had built-in work incentives. Families could earn additional income and still receive welfare payments. Up to a specified maximum income level, the welfare family would be able to work and keep over 50 per cent of the earned income above $1600. A basic element of FAP was the requirement that all applicants register with the Employment Service and be available for work or job training. There was also provision for child-care services for working mothers. The Family Assistance Plan passed the House, but was defeated in the Senate.

Moynihan wrote a book, *The Politics of a Guaranteed Income*, in which he described the fate of the FAP in its first Congressional ordeal. The most savage opposition to the Family Assistance Plan came from the entrenched Federal bureaucracy, which saw its jobs threatened, and from the National Welfare Rights Organization, which saw it as a threat to its efforts to organize welfare mothers into a powerful political bloc. The NWRO believes in income by right and regards as a form of "slavery" any attempt to force people on welfare to work. This view has been upheld by some court decisions and finds considerable support among social workers and liberal politicians. "In the end the bill was defeated in the Senate Finance Committee by liberal votes," wrote Moynihan, describing the fate of the Family Assistance Plan. "Welfare militants were jubilant. Congressmen . . . saw in the 91st Congress that anyone trying to replace the welfare system with a guaranteed income would be attacked by welfare militants with a violent and abusive rhetoric that would do damage to a liberal or moderate reputation. In particular, any suggestion that income maintenance be associated with work incentives would be excoriated as repression."

What was the motivation behind the liberal attack on the Family Assistance Plan? Said Moynihan:

It is only required that the question be raised: *Who* gets *what?* Whatever is precisely the case, the general point is that the growth on welfare dependency and the initiating of federally financed welfare and antipoverty activities under successive Democratic Presidents had by the end of the 1960s created a large and strategically placed interest group. This interest group had to be affected by the Family Assistance Proposal, and this in turn would be affected by the group's response. How *would* the heirs of the Webbs, 'their allies in the

259

higher ranks of the civil service, in the Left Wing of the labor movement and among the Liberal intellectuals in the constituencies' respond? In a word, they did all in their power to insure that a guaranteed income was not enacted.

A welfare plan based on work incentives presents insuperable difficulties under an income tax system. The concept of income as a right undermines the justification of tying welfare benefits to work. The logical solution to welfare in an income tax system would appear to be a negative income tax, with income guaranteed to a minimum base figure consistent with need. The same justification that takes income from those who earned it can be used to give it to those who did not earn it. Just as the positive income tax takes more from the salaried worker as his earnings increase, so the negative income tax would give less to the working poor as his earnings increased. The negative income tax is no more irrational than the positive income tax. Both are based on the same rationale.

The case for a guaranteed minimum income has been stated by Galbraith: "An affluent society that is also both compassionate and rational would, no doubt, secure to all who needed it the minimum income essential for decency and comfort. The corrupting effect on the human spirit of a small amount of unearned revenue has unquestionably been exaggerated as, indeed, have the character-building values of hunger and privation."[170]

Galbraith assumes that in the "affluent society" poverty is eliminated or can be. But is this assumption realistic? Henry Hazlitt does not think so:

> Can the State undertake to provide adequate relief to everybody who really needs and deserves it without finding itself supporting the idle, the improvident, and the swindlers? . . . Can the State, again, provide really 'adequate' relief for any extended period even to the originally 'deserving' without undermining or destroying their incentives to industry, frugality, and self-support? If people can get an 'adequate' living without working, why work? Can the State, finally, provide 'adequate' relief to all the unemployed, or, even more, guaranteed incomes for all, without undermining by excessive taxation the incentives of the working population that is forced to provide this support? Can the State, in sum, provide 'adequate' relief to all without discouraging and gravely reducing the production out of which all relief must come — without letting loose a runaway inflation/ — without going bankrupt?[171]

Hazlitt points out that there is no record in history of a relief system or welfare system solving the problem of poverty. The experiences of the Roman and English doles, both forms of guaranteed or free income, were disastrous and do not auger well for future experiments of this type.

2.   Economic Dependency

Surprising as it may seem, it is nevertheless true that the major social legislation on which the welfare state is based was the work, not of liberal politicians or progressive economists, but of conservative statesmen. The

Tory Prime Minister, Pitt the younger, was the originator of the modern income tax, which has funded most of the social programs of the welfare state. Prince Bismarck, the Iron Chancellor, was the first to establish a comprehensive social security system, based on compulsory insurance, to protect the worker against accident, sickness, and old age. In 1909 Winston Churchill, then Tory President of the Board of Trade, drafted legislation establishing compulsory unemployment insurance, "The boldest item of social legislation in the history of industrial democracy," according to Daniel P Moynihan. Pitt's act was opposed by the classic economists, Bismarck's act was fought by the Marxists, and Churchill's acts antagonized the Webbs and the Fabian Socialists. The most "radical" piece of social legislation proposed in the United States since a Republican President abolished slavery was The Family Assistance Plan, advanced in 1969 by a Republican President, Richard M. Nixon. It was defeated in the Senate by "liberal" votes. The problem of work and welfare in a complex one, full of paradoxes such as this.

Aid to the poor in ancient times was left to the family and to kin groups of the needy and to "good Samaritans." Organized state relief appears in early Rome under the rule of the Gracchi. The influx of captives from conquered lands and their employment on slave-operated *latifundia* drove farmers into Rome, where they formed a large class without means of support and totally dependent on government relief. They naturally supported those politicians who promised them land or bread. Tiberius Gracchus was the first Roman politician to make a serious effort to help the unemployed by agrarian reform. He passed a law that no person should own more than 500 *jugera* of land — about 300 acres — plus 250 *jugera* more for each son. Tiberius was assassinated in 133 B.C. and was succeeded by his younger brother Gaius, who continued his brother's social welfare program. He ordered public granaries to be built and wheat sold to the poor at a fixed price — about half of market price. Gaius was assassinated in 122 B.C., but the custom of feeding the Roman poor at state expense, once started, was never stopped and survived the Republic. The Romas senate, which had engineered the death of the Gracchi brothers, did not dare take away the dole. It was temporarily suspended by the dictator Sulla, but reinstated. Thereafter the dole became a "right" enjoyed by all the Roman poor:

> The hundreds of thousands of Roman citizens who lived in Rome cared little for political rights. They readily acquiesced in the gradual reduction of the popular assembly under Augustus to a pure formality, they offered no protest when Tiberius suppressed even this formality, but they insisted on their right, acquired during the Civil war, to be fed and amused by the government. None of the emperors, not even Caesar or Augustus, dared to encroach on this sacred right of the Roman proletariat. [172]

Henry Hazlitt draws two conclusions from the Roman experience with welfare programs:

> The first, which we meet again and again in history, is that once the dole or similar relief programs are introduced, they seem almost inevitably — unless surrounded by the most rigid restrictions — to get out of hand. The second lesson

is that once this happens the poor become more numerous and worse off than they were before, not only because they have lost self-reliance, but because the sources of wealth and production on which they depended for either doles or jobs are diminished or destroyed.[173]

The Roman welfare system has been called a contributing if not a major factor in the decline of Roman power. The Roman citizen, it is said, became a ward of the state, lost his self-reliance, and lived on "bread and circuses." Taxation to support the army and the idle on welfare reached confiscatory levels and eventually exhausted all revenue sources. The imperial government resorted to currency debasement and wage and price controls. Inflation became uncontrollable. By the time of Diocletian the price of a bushel of wheat *(artaba)* had jumped from 7 or 8 drachmas to 120,000 drachmas!

England was the first modern nation to establish a national system of welfare, called poor relief. The English poor law goes back to the reign of Queen Elizabeth, who in 1572 imposed a national system of handling poor relief. By the end of the 17th century, according to the English historian Trevelyan, about one in five were drawing some type of poor relief. There were complaints then, as now, that the relief benefits were too high and that the poor on welfare were better off than common laborers.

The English were also the first to experiment with a guaranteed minimum income. This has been called the Speenhamland system because it originated in the town of that name in 1795. The law specified that income below a specified minimum should be supplemented by welfare benefits according to size of family.

In 1832 a royal commission was appointed to investigate the state welfare program, which had become a source of public discontent. The report ran to 362 pages and raised the same questions and the same answers that similar welfare commissions have reported for the last 150 years. It makes familiar reading today, and some of its paragraphs could have been lifted from contemporary Presidential or Congressional reports on welfare:

> The laborer under the existing system need not bestir himself to seek work; he need not study to please his master; he need not put any restraint upon his temper; he need not ask relief as a favor. He has all a slave's security for subsistence without his liability to punishment. As a single man, indeed, his income does not exceed a bare subsistence but he has only to marry, and it increases.... Small as the usual allowance of 2s. a head may be, yet when there are more than three children, it generally exceeds the average wages in a pauperized district. A man with a wife and six children, entitled, according to the scale, to have his wages made up to 16s. a week, in a parish where the wages paid by individuals do not exceed 10s. or 12s., is almost an irresponsible being. All the other classes of society are exposed to the vicissitudes of hope and fear; he alone has nothing to lose or to gain...[174]

The welfare militants on relief were able to intimidate the welfare agents and local proprietors by threats of violence:

> The assistant overseers [welfare agents] are reluctant to make complaints for neglect of work, lest they should become marked men and their lives rendered uncomfortable or even unsafe. Farmers permit their laborers to receive relief,

262

founded on a calculation of a rate of wages lower than that actually paid; they are unwilling to put themselves in collision with the laborers, and will not give an account of earnings, or if they do, beg that their names not be mentioned.... Farmers are afraid to express their opinions against a pauper who applies for relief, for fear their premises would be set fire to ... the apprehension of this dreadful and easily perpetrated mischief has very generally affected the minds of the rural parish officers of this country, making the power of the paupers over the funds provided for their relief almost absolute...[175]

The effect of welfare on districts with heavy relief rolls was to reduce property value because taxes in such districts were high, and tenants were reluctant to rent property in such depressed areas.

The American experience with Aid to Families with Dependent Children (AFDC) was foreshadowed by the 1832 report, which stated that the relief system encouraged vice:

To the women, a single illegitimate child is seldom any expense, and two or three are a source of positive profit... The money she receives is far more than sufficient to repay her for the loss her misconduct has occasioned her, and it really becomes a source of emolument.... The sum allowed to the mother of a bastard is generally greater than that given to the mother of a legitimate child; indeed the whole treatment of the former is a direct encouragement to vice...[176]

The commission found that guaranteed relief tends to discourage the working poor and to encourage the growth of the dependent poor:

Throughout the evidence it is shown, that in proportion as the condition of any pauper class is elevated above the condition of independent laborers, the condition of the independent class is depressed, their industry is impaired, their employment becomes unsteady, and its remuneration in wages is diminished. Such persons, therefore, are under the strongest inducement to quit the less eligible class of laborers and enter the more eligible class of paupers.[177]

The English poor law reform of 1834 threw out guaranteed relief or income support for the poor and instituted stringent new provisions that called for a system of workhouses, where the poor were made to work for their money. These workhouses were continued in England until 1908, when the Old Age Pension Act was passed, and 1911, when the National Insurance Act was passed, 24 years before the American Social Security Act came into being.

The workhouse system of relief for the poor was considered cruel and inhumane by many observers. Dickens probably did more than anyone to arouse public opinion against the system. The English had tried guaranteed income with disappointing results; they had tried relief tied to work, and again the results were disappointing.

There appears to be no happy medium. If the state provides ample benefits or a guaranteed income, there is the cry that the state will be impoverished and that the people's character and industry will be ruined. If the benefits are niggardly, the tender-hearted will cry out that the poor are being exploited and deprived of their rights to a decent minimum standard of living.

When economic dependency is institutionalized and supported by tax revenues, it is difficult to avoid social friction and class conflicts. Dependency can be ended only when all workers are integrated into what are considered normal social and economic activities. The dependent subculture will then be assimilated into the cultural mainstream. Poverty may still exist, and other class conflicts may continue, based on racial, social, religious, or political anatagonisms, but the subculture of dependency with its custodial bureaucracy would no longer exist.

The problem of a guaranteed income or free income without work obligation is not a moral problem, although it is often presented as such. It is basically both an economic and a political problem. Can the political and economic goals of society be reached where work is not required as a condition of receiving income? If the answer is yes, then free income is socially acceptable and "right." If it is not, then it is socially unacceptable and "wrong."

Assuming that solar energy has been harnessed and cybernetics perfected to a degree of complete automation, then work would be unnecessary and man would have a "right" to free income, as he has a right to free air. It might even be written into the Constitution as an inalienable right for all Americans. The only problem left would be to find something for men and women to occupy their leisure time.

This should present no social problem, according to Bertrand Russell, who once said that "leisure is essential to civilization" and "the morality of work is the morality of slaves, and the modern world has no need for slaves." Machines, according to Russell, have replaced slaves and men today need not work more than a few hours a day. This view is based on the assumption that energy is inexhaustible and that other nations would also reduce their work day and join with the United States in its pursuit of culture through leisure rather than continue working hard for economic and military power.

On the other hand, if the United States is faced with tough international competition and declining natural resources, it may be forced to maintain a high rate of productivity to safeguard its standard of living and national security. Nations do not stand still; they either move forward or backward in relation to other nations. Assuming that work in necessary for economic growth and military power and assuming that work is downgraded or made nonobligatory in the United States, then it may be necessary to change some national goals. Military supremacy or consumer affluence may be sacrificed or the war on poverty abandoned, for example.

When Nixon was elected President in 1968, the American public was surfeited with President Johnson's War on Poverty, which had not ended poverty and had been accompanied by ugly urban riots in Los Angeles, Detroit, Newark, and other cities. The riots may not have been caused by the antipoverty program, but the public was inclined to believe they were. The Black Panther party was started in an OEO office in Oakland by two social welfare workers, Bobby Seale and Huey P. Newton. The radicalization of the poor by government social workers, some drawing princely salaries, made the public angry. The Nixon administration was eager to find another solution to the problem of dependency, and the negative income tax seemed the best

264

option available: "With little public debate and almost no public notice the economist planners in government opted for negative income tax as the basic instrument of an income strategy. By the time Nixon took office planning for a negative income tax was well advanced, and there were no plans for any alternate approach."[178]

Moynihan changed the direction of government welfare policy by converting Nixon to the Family Assistance Plan, which "envisioned a level of payment sufficient to maintain a reasonable, if low, standard of living. A negative income tax would provide just such a guaranteed income. In this sense they were identical proposals. In another sense, however, they were profoundly different."[179]

The difference was more apparent than real. President Nixon defined it thus: "A guaranteed income would undermine the incentive to work; the Family Assistance Plan that I propose increases the incentive to work. A guaranteed income establishes a right without any responsibilities; family assistance recognizes a need and establishes a responsibility."

But this was mere political rhetoric. As Moynihan explains:

> While it was readily enough agreed in the White House that if FAP was to have any chance in Congress it would have to be geared to 'work', behind this tactical analysis was a strategic one that saw employment with income supplementation as the most likely long-run solution to the problem of dependency. Most of the President's advisers gradually came to see the true nature of their proposal, but they only dimly, almost subliminally. It might have seemed obvious enough: under FAP thirteen million people were to begin receiving income payments who had not previously received any. This surely was the largest feature of the proposal: a guaranteed income.[180]

Commenting on the fact that this proposal was made by a Republican president and defeated by a liberal Democratic Congress, Moynihan writes:

> "And yet this same president proposed, and one body of that Congress passed, and the other might well have passed, one of the half-dozen or dozen most important pieces of social legislation in American history. It adduced much favorable comment in the United States, although the more complex analyses tended to come from abroad. A Yugoslav Marxist, for one, was reported as commenting within his circles that were it to pass it might well be the most important social legislation in history in that it would finally free the individual and his family from the myriad and inescapable forms of coercion which society exerts through the employment nexus.[181]

These passages illustrate the tortured logic liberals sometimes use to justify income as a right. While President Nixon was justifying the Family Assistance Plan as an incentive to work, the authors of the plan knew that it was a form of guaranteed income and that its justification was that it would "finally free the individual and his family from the myriad and inescapable forms of coercion which society exerts through the employment nexus." In other words, the individual would finally be free from the obligation to work to earn income. This is the heart of the argument, sometimes obscured by passing off guaranteed income as a form of work incentive. The debate in

Congress over FAP did not come to grips with the central issue of guaranteed income — that it breaks the "coercion which society exerts through the employment nexus." Society in America and in other democratic countries has already partially broken the nexus through various forms of free income. If Congress cuts it completely by establishing free income as a right, the coercion society exerts on the individual through the obligation to work to earn income will need to be replaced by some other type of discipline. It would be appropriate to have some discussion on what options are available before abandoning the obligation to work for income. Once abandoned, it may be difficult to reinstate. The options available in Marxist economies seem to be: work based on coercion backed by police power, piecework with income tied directly to work performed, the use of conscript labor in agriculture, and psychological coercion through control of all media of communication. Coercion involved in Marxist economies to enforce work requirements is much more severe than the simple obligation to work for income. Freeing men from the obligation to work for income "might well be the most important social legislation in history." It might also be the most disastrous.

Welfare dependency is peculiarly an Anglo-American problem. Other countries have no comparable dependency problem, although they have much less gross national income. In most other advanced countries, however, distribution of basic commodities and social services is more universal, not restricted by income. According to Moynihan:

> The French had no welfare problem: they had no welfare program. Which is not to say that there are no poor in France, no dependent persons. There is a sufficiency of both. But there is no program which caters to the special needs of the dependent poor, and which maintains a vast bureaucratic machinery that depends on this class of persons for its own existence. Harsh, essential facts. The French have family allowances, social insurance, medical care; if anything an overfull panoply of social services, but with it all the assumption remains that people have to look after themselves. The custodial quality of American welfare is not to be encountered elsewhere. [182]

Welfare recipients whose total benefits may be equal to an annual earned income of $5000 or $6000 would not be classified as poor in countries such as Chile, Egypt, or China. The problem of dependency is not the same at that of poverty. The problem of dependency is that of being dependent on government for income or lacking an independent means of support. The obvious cure for dependency is jobs, but there are difficulties. For example, how can mothers without husbands work and still raise a family? Moynihan gives an example of how the French do it:

> "Female-headed families were not unknown in France, where the illegitimacy ratio had settled at about 6 per cent, down from 9 per cent in the early twentieth century, but about that of the early nineteenth. But there was no dependent class, simply — it must be assumed — because there was no provision made for dependency. There were family allowances, maternity allowances, housing allowances, the working class Family Help Association, and Family Holiday Hostels, with *aide sociale* funds available for emergencies. But these were universal provisions which made no distinction whatever in favor of the female-

266

headed household, in consequence of which, in the view in any event of French officialdom, there was no problem of dependent female-headed household."[183]

In China the per capita income is extremely low, but there is no class of welfare dependents because everyone is required to work, and basic necessities are distributed on a universal basis. In France family benefits are paid only on proof that the family head is gainfully employed, unless he is incapacitated, "with a view to excluding the willfully unemployed who could be tempted to live on their children's allowances." Such a condition, however, can be imposed only where employment is guaranteed by law.

The problem of welfare dependency boils down to involuntary unemployment, the only cure for which is guaranteed jobs. The right to income without work is also an answer if the state wishes to subsidize unemployment, but thise leads to other problems of an even more serious nature. The right to a job would seem to offer the less dangerous and more productive solution to welfare dependency.

In countries where there are no welfare aid programs, the state has generally followed one of two basic rules, or both:

1. Everyone who can work is guaranteed a job.

2. Basic necessities of life are provided free or at a cost within the reach of all.

These two rules apply, not only to such two-sector economies as France and Sweden, but to one-sector economies such as China and Russia. It is unlikely that welfare dependency can be cured unless these two preconditions are met. The wealth of the country is not the decisive factor. It has been noted, since de Tocqueville first pointed it out, that welfare is often accompanied by high national income. Observing the rise in welfare dependency during the years 1966-1970, Moynihan commented: "If poverty had seemed a straightforward affair, clearly welfare dependency was not. *Across the nation it had become a general rule that as poverty declined, welfare dependency increased.*"[184]

Almost everyone is willing to agree that a guaranteed job, rather than guaranteed income without a job, is the best answer to dependency. Even the United States Chamber of Commerce subscribes to the objective of full employment. It has been the official policy of the American government since 1946. The difficulty is that, under the present tax and market price system, it is an unattainable ideal. Employment under the present system is a function of consumption. Artificial stimulation of consumption through unemployment relief and welfare grants helps to raise the level of consumption and employment, but the side effect is economic dependency. The private sector cannot hire personnel it does not need or cannot afford to pay. The public sector can absorb workers, but in a two-sector economy it is limited by tax revenues and fear of inflation. A guaranteed job, while it is economically and morally superior to a guaranteed income, is difficult of achievement in a two-sector economy.

Under a system of commodity taxation on the tariff principle, the nexus between employment and consumption would be broken. Consumption would be controlled within general limits by the tariff schedule. There would be no direct control on the consumer, but the differential commodity tax rates would inhibit wasteful consumption of superfluous commodities and encourage a more general distribution of basic commodities and services. Poverty would remain, for poverty is a relative term. Some people will still be poorer than others, but no class would be denied rights to basic consumption needs to sustain a decent minimum way of life by American standards. With employment no longer tied to consumption and consumer basic needs adequately provided for, manpower could be allocated according to priorities that are selected by public consensus according to national needs.

Employment need not be a function of consumption. It is not, in mobilized war economies or in Communist economies. Tying employment to consumption leads to artificial stimulation of consumption by such absurd and uneconomic methods as paying people not to work or, to follow the classic Keneysian prescription for unemployment, digging holes and then filling them up again.[185] It makes the economy dependent on consumer "confidence," which is unpredictable and based on fashion trends, advertising slogans, and other noneconomic factors. Consumer sovereignty whipsaws the economy from peaks of overconfidence and inflationary buying sprees to depressions of overanxiety and deflationary hoarding. Breaking the nexus between employment and consumption does not mean that consumer sovereignty is nullified; it is only dethroned. Consumer demand would still control distribution of consumer goods, but consumer demand would no longer control employment, total volume of business, and the major priorities of the economy. The tax fixed by Congress on each commodity and service could be the dominant factor in setting national economic priorities and employment levels.

3. Servants and Services

According to sociologist Daniel Bell:

> The United States is the first post-industrial society in that the service sector accounts for more than half the gross national product. It is the first nation in which the major portion of the population is engaged neither in agrarian nor in industrial pursuits. Shortly after the turn of this century, only 3 in every 10 workers were in service industries. By 1950, the weight had shifted to just over 5 in every 10. By 1968, the proportion was almost 6 in every 10. And by 1980, according to the projections of the U.S. Department of Labor, of a 100 million person labor force in U.S., almost 7 out of every 10 workers (about 68 million) will be in service industries. This is a major shift from a goods-producing society to a service economy.[186]

This shift has been noted by other observers; the conclusion usually drawn from it is that this is a symptom of a mature "postindustrial" society that, they say, has solved its production problems and has left-over or excess capacity and manpower that must, therefore, go into service industries. This trend is bound to continue as manufacturing becomes more automated and requires less manpower. This theory makes some assumptions that are questionable.

The myth of consumer affluence popular in the 1960s is hardly credible in the 1970s in the face of shortages and poverty evident everywhere, even in the United States. The people living in the depressed rural areas of Appalachia, the deep South, and in urban ghettos are badly in need of production goods of all kinds such as housing, furniture, appliances, apparel, and cars.

So are the underdeveloped nations of the world that control the critical raw materials needed for modern technology: copper, petroleum, bauxite, cobalt, nickel, manganese, tin, chromium, and rubber, for example. It is hardly realistic to believe that these nations will continue to supply the "affluent" nations with raw materials to support a postindustrial economy of services while they are still trying to establish an industrial base.

Even in such a basic necessity as food the problem of production remains unsolved. The United Nations Food and Agriculture Organization estimates that more than two-thirds of the 800 million children now growing up in developing countries will suffer some physical and mental impairment brought on or aggravated by malnutrition.

Many economists believe that poverty is unnecessary and that the production problem is already solved. Faulty market distribution alone prevents the poor from enjoying the boundless productivity of American farms and factories. The market is blamed for the unequal distribution, and the recommended remedy is to shift a larger share of the gross national product to the public sector so that the government may distribute the needed goods and services where they are most needed. In other words, the production of much that is now going into *private goods* for the market should be diverted to *public goods* for the government. Is this view realistic?

In the first place, the production problem has not been solved and probably never can be. There will always be more demand for farm and industrial products than can be produced, given the insatiable appetite of consumers and the known limits of energy and natural resources. If the consumption standards of an affluent American with an annual income of $20,000 or more were to be shared by the world's poor, or even America's poor, the strain on the world's raw material and energy resources would lead to a production crisis beyond the control of any government. It must therefore be concluded that there exists at present a serious shortage of industrial goods and that this shortage will continue to exist when measured against the ideal standard of living of the affluent consumer. Equal distribution on the Marxist plan would solve the distribution problem, but not the production problem. In Communist societies the consumers are just as dissatisfied and demanding as in capitalist countries. The shortages of industrial consumer goods are as serious in socialist economies as in capitalist economies and probably will continue to be.

In the face of existing shortages in production, the relative decline of industrial output and the relative increase in service industries raise questions of priorities, which have not been sufficiently investigated. Why are resources being diverted from productive industries to service industries at a time when there are large segments of the United States with large unfilled needs and when many of the world's poor still face, not only deprivation, but severe malnutrition or starvation?

It is true, of course, that many service industries, such as health services and educational services, are as necessary as manufactured products. It is also true that many manufactured products, such as luxury cars and yachts, are not basic necessities and that increased production in such luxury goods can be of no benefit to the poor. Nevertheless, it cannot be denied that most service industries are in the luxury class or provide services that are normally available only to those above the poverty level.

In a mass consumer society, services available to the wealthy are also available to the middle-class and the poor, but the degree of use is sharply reduced as income declines. In consumer products the division between luxuries and necessities is no longer defined by class, as already noted in another chapter. Instead, there are economy and luxury models within each class of goods. The same distinction applies to consumer services. They are available to all, but within each service industry there are clearly marked divisions that separate those services normally available to the wealthy consumer and those available to the poor. This is in strong contrast to past ages, when services were performed by personal servants — maids, cooks, gardeners, chauffeurs, and valets — who were employed directly by the rich for their exclusive service. Today personal servants are rare even among the wealthy, but the range of services available to the wealthy has increased rather than diminished. They are available on a purchase, hire, rental, lease, or contract basis. The growth of one glamorous service industry — the travel industry — may be cited as an example.

Tourism and the whole gamut of travel services is a huge industry. According to the Department of Commerce, Americans spent $47.5 billion in domestic tours in 1970 and $4.3 billion in foreign travel in 1971. The department estimates that total foreign and domestic tourism by Americans in 1980 will cost $126.9 billion. To support the travel industry there is a tremendous investment in hotels, motels, automobiles, trains, gas stations, restaurants, pool service, airports, airplanes, and vessels. In 1973 the United States alone had about 52,000 motels with 2,551,007 rooms. A very large class of employees, from the airplane pilot to the bus boy, are trained to deliver special services to the tourist. The poor travel occasionally and, in the United States, they may avail themselves of the services provided by motels, airports, gas stations, and restaurants. But this utilization bears no relation to that of the "jet set" tourist who travels first class in the air, on land, and over water and who is almost constantly moving from one hotel to another, from one city to another, from one country to another. The travel industry is a service industry that caters to the wealthy consumer and provides him with luxury accommodations sometimes enjoyed by the middle class, but seldom available to the poverty class. The travel industry utilizes scarce resources and skilled manpower on a very large scale. Whether these luxury services should be encouraged or discouraged by taxation is an appropriate subject of Congressional debate. Under a commodity tax system, on the tariff principle the travel services would be subject to the same scrutiny as other services, and commodities and the trade-offs would have to be made between travel service and health services, educational services, and housing and other services. Under the income tax system these trade-offs cannot be made.

As a result, an increase in health services may have to be made at a cost of reduced public services for the poor. Travel services for the wealthy consumer are in the private sector and therefore not subject to public sector priorities.

Under the present system in the United States there is very uneven medical coverage. Some segments of the population — the wealthy and those covered by their employers or unions — enjoy excellent medical coverage. The very poor and the elderly are now provided free medical care under various state and Federal laws. The middle class and the working poor who are not covered by adequate medical insurance face financial disaster when serious illness strikes the family. The gross and obvious injustices of the present system are recognized by both political parties; it is only a question of time before Congress will enact one of several national health plans now under consideration.

Of course, "free" medical services are not really free; they are paid for by taxes, either voluntarily or involuntarily. In a two-sector economy the transfer of health services to the public sector will put a tremendous tax burden on the private sector. Under the present income tax system there is no way to compensate for the health services by a reduction in some other services in the private sector. The public health services must be paid by the general tax funds; if they are insufficient to cover all government services, the health services must compete with other vital public services for available funds. The enactment of a national health plan could bring about a decrease in the quality of health services or a reduction in budgets for public education, law enforcement, armed services, space exploration, and other public services.

Under a comprehensive commodity tax system there would be trade-offs between health services and other private as well as public services. Congress might decide, for example, to reverse present priorities and set a higher priority on first-class hospitals than on first-class hotels.

Automotive services consume a considerable portion of the average citizen's disposable income in the United States. It has been estimated that the average motorist pays about $150 a month for the privilege of driving his private car. If this figure is reduced to $100 a month and multiplied by the 100 million cars in the United States the figure is still impressive, $10 billion a month or $120 billion a year, about equal to the entire revenue collected by the individual income tax.

The automobile provides a service to the consumer; it transports him wherever he wants to go. However, to provide him with this service, many industries must contribute their products and services. Besides the basic automobile manufacturing industry to provide the automobile, there is the petroleum industry to provide the gasoline and the service stations, the automobile dealers to provide car distribution and service, the banks and finance companies to provide the credit for car purchases, the insurance companies to provide the liability insurance, the auto replacement parts industry, the construction companies to provide the roads and bridges, the food service industry to provide the restaurants along the highways, the rubber industry to provide the tires, the steel industry to provide the sheet metal, the glass industry to provide the windows and windshields, the car rental industry to provide car users with short-term leases, the auto maintenance industry to provide garages and mechanics to make necessary repairs (this item alone runs to $1.25 billion a year), and the paint industry to paint new and used cars. The list is almost endless. Every American is connected with the automobile industry in some way either as a consumer or as a worker.

Taxes are assessed against automobile and truck users to help pay for roads and bridges. These taxes take the form of license fees, highway tolls, gasoline taxes, and special road use taxes for trucks. This does not pay all expenses incurred by society to maintain the highway system, but motorists do pay special taxes for the privilege of using the highways and, since practically all Americans own cars, the contribution made by the general tax fund must also come mainly from the pockets of motorists. The Federal freeway system has been financed by gasoline taxes; until 1973 the funds of the Highway Trust Fund could not be used for any purpose other than building roads. In 1973 Congress authorized diversion of some of these funds to finance development of mass transit systems.

Despite the special taxes laid on the motorist for road-building, it is undoubtedly true that they represent only a small portion of the social costs of the automobile. Some of these costs have already been enumerated — the loss of life (up to 2 million American dead by the automobile, as of 1973), the maiming and crippling of millions more every year; the huge financial burden the automobile industry imposes on society; the cost to the government in providing law enforcement on the highways; the tremendous pollution problem caused by the automobile that is only now being recognized; the drain caused by the automobile on natural resources, some of which, like oil, are irreplaceable; the severe adverse effect in the American balance of payments by the importation of foreign oil; and many other costs.

Against these serious charges must be weighed the obvious desire, not to say passion, of the consumer for the automobile. In a consumer society, where the consumer is king, nothing is allowed to stand in the way of the "love affair" of the American consumer with the automobile. But the love affair seems to be cooling off. The automobile is no longer a romantic plaything or an invitation to adventure. It has become an economic necessity, a cruel tyrant that eats up the owner's income, a costly status symbol, a torture chamber that transports its owner to and from his job through streets choked with traffic, a deadly missile that exposes the occupant to a higher fatality and casualty risk than conventional warfare.

The amount of the United States gross national product devoted to the automobile and related service industries is very large. Whether it is excessive is a matter of judgment. Under present economic policies, it is almost impossible to evaluate the priority that the automobile should have in the American economy. No serious effort has been made to assess the social costs of the automobile and its effect on American social and economic life. The automobile has transformed the American city and the American countryside, but this transformation has been unplanned and largely unforeseen. The automobile appeared like some powerful genie uncorked by Henry Ford and immune from government control. It demanded that roads be built; cities strangled; it commanded the American exodus to suburbia; it ordered the killing of over 2 million Americans and the crippling of millions more; it caused thousands of oil wells to be drilled, supertankers to be built, and turned the sands of Arabia into gold.

Government desire to control the automobile has been frustrated by the dependence of the American economy on the automobile industry. General Motors is the largest manufacturing corporation in America, and the automobile industry is probably the most influential industry in American economic life. A slow-down in automobile production has a depressing effect on all industries. America is a motorized society; when automobile production slows down, all American industry slows down with it.

The dependence of the American economy on the automobile is contrived and even unnatural. The consumer dependence on the automobile for transportation is derived from consumer sovereignty and from the market's inability under the present price system to charge the automobile with all its social costs, which must be paid by society. Under a comprehensive commodity tax system the Congress would be given an opportunity to assess the automobile in its proper relation to other forms of transportation. The true social costs of the automobile as a mankilling machine, as a polluter, as a destroyer of natural resources, as a major source of drain on foreign exchange, as a cause of urban decay, as an agent of social unrest and population dispersion — all these and other costs would be explicitly faced and fully investigated when taxes are assessed. When all social costs are placed on the automobile, the industry will be faced with the problem of competitive prices, not from other automobiles, domestic and imported, but from other transportation services that are inherently superior, safer, and less wasteful. There is a place for the private personal automobile in modern life, but it should be fixed in relation to other available means of transportation and in relation to the social costs that make up its true price to society. This evaluation would be forced upon Congress when it comes to set internal tariff tax rates on the automobile and the service industry it supports. It must then decide whether to continue to subsidize the automobile or whether it is time to assess the true social costs of the private car and price it accordingly.

When the affluent consumer is not traveling, he avails himself of services that are not normally available to the poor. The food service industry devotes considerable capital and manpower to gourmet restaurants; the entertainment industry has plush clubs where the tab is too high for low-income groups; the sports industry has many exclusive clubs where only sportsmen who pay high membership fees can play; the fashion industry employs large numbers of designers, hairdressers, decorators, and other workers who cater to the beautification of the well-dressed, well-fed, well-heeled consumer. When in their homes, the wealthy command the services of

273

gardeners, plumbers, electricians, chauffeurs, maids, cleaners, carpenters, and other servicemen to maintain their estates in prime condition. Legal services, investment services, and banking services are also available to the wealthy and are rarely used or available to those in the lower income brackets.

The rich lament that servants are no longer available and that they must wait on themselves. The servant class has changed, but it is still there — today it is called the service industry.

A private apartment complex in the beach city of Marina Del Rey, California advertises for occupants by offering these services:

> A staff of one hundred fifty makes each resident feel as if he were the only resident. We will answer your phone, send up a dinner, care for your children, do your laundry, drive you to the airport, cater your party and reserve an apartment for your out-of-town guests. And naturally our security staff quietly protects your domain twenty-four hours a day. One of the city's finest gourmet dining rooms and an intimate lounge featuring live entertainment crown our three-story club house, with three dining rooms, each unique, three new lounges and banquet facilities for private parties. For our yachtsmen we supply slips, power, storage, instruction, rentals, charters, brokerage services...

With this type and variety of service available, who needs personal servants?

Instead of a chauffeur, the affluent consumer rents a car or airplane; when he drives, he commands the service of hordes of gas-station attendants and auto mechanics. He may not have servants to maintain his house, but he commands the services of caterers, restaurant employees, laundries, carpet and drapery cleaners, upholsterers, gardeners, pool cleaners, and others. When he travels, he enjoys such services as those of motel and hotel personnel, travel agents, taxis, and entertainers. The extent of his command over the services available on the market or on a contract basis are limited only by his income or credit. These services are normally not available to those without high income.

In general, the growth of the service industries represents an increase in consumer affluence, but the benefits are tipped in favor of the richer consumers. Services performed by well-paid employees, usually organized into unions and often fiercely independent — the airline pilots' union, the plumbers' union, the carpenters' union, and the teamsters' union, for example — may seem to be quite different from those performed by the menial servants of the rich, but the distinction is social rather than economic. The captain of a ship on a vacation cruise may enjoy a different social status than the pilot of a private yacht, but both are performing services for the benefit of well-to-do consumers. The same could be said of the personal valet of a nobleman and a steward on an ocean liner or on a Boeing 747. When valet services are performed by independent unionized employees, there is a tendency to forget the economic basis of the work performed. The *illusion* is created that such work is socially necessary and quite different from the menial work performed by servants of the rich in the agrarian economy.

Under a system of national priorities set by Congress through a comprehensive commodity tax system, the priorities to be placed on services of

274

all kinds would be evaluated in the same light as commodities. If the services provided are luxurious and tend to be wasteful of energy resources, there is no reason why they should be exempted from the heavier tax load that normally would be placed on commodities of the same category. The guiding principle would be, not to encourage or discourage the growth of any specific service industry, but to bring them all within a rational system of national economic priorities and tax each according to its relative social value.

4.   A House Divided

After World War II the United States led the world in developing new technologies. These gave rise to giant new industries: jet aircraft, computers, television, and Xerography, to name the four leaders. The technological leadership was not seriously challenged until October 4, 1957, when Russia launched Sputnik, the first man-made satellite, starting a traumatic shock wave felt across America. For the first time in decades the United States saw a hated and despised rival take over technological leadership in a new vital area — space. The country made a desperate all-out effort to recapture leadership in this area with the Apollo program and put the first man on the moon. But Sputnik I was only a signal of a general revival in technology, not only in Russia, but in Japan and Western Europe, all of which now seriously challenge our technological leadership in many fields.

The United States is falling behind Japan and Western Europe in superspeed trains and behind England, France, and Russia in supersonic air transport. Russia has produced the supersonic TU-111. France and England have together produced the supersonic Concorde. The United States Congress killed development of our supersonic transport as an economy measure. In 1970 the European Economic Community passed the United States as the world's largest trading entity, with total trade amounting to $45 billion compared to our total of $43 billion; more automobiles were produced in Europe than the United States, and West Germany replaced America as the world's largest exporter of manufactured goods. In 1971 the Soviet Union passed the United States in steel production. Russia also completed the world's first large prototype breeder reactor; the world's first successful MHD power generator (MHD is an advanced system for generating electricity directly from a high-temperature, high-velocity stream of ionized gases, derived from coal, oil or natural gas); announced the success of experiments involving a new thermionic method that converts nuclear energy directly to electric power; and reported the completion of 11 geothermal projects, as against only one in the United States. According to Dr. Edward Teller, eminent physicist and "father" of the hydrogen bomb: ". . . the Russians are getting ahead of us in the development of the applications of science in technology. We should keep in mind that today the world's largest high quality science center is Akademgorodak, near Novosibirsk. And it is open. It is the largest *visible* portion of the Russian technological iceberg. In contrast the interest in defense, and even in science is rapidly declining in American colleges and universities."[187]

For the 80 years preceding 1950, the United States productivity growth rate exceeded that of Europe by 60 per cent and that of Japan by 70 per cent. Since 1965 the United States has *trailed* Europe by 35 per cent and Japan by 60 per cent. The United States now ranks *last* among the 20 leading industrial nations in *rate of productivity growth*. Productivity is the key to gross national product growth. It has been estimated by John M. Stewart, executive director of the National Commission on Productivity, that even a tenth of 1 per cent increase in productivity in the American economy would generate $1 billion in growth of the gross national product.

American imports of complex technological products have been growing more than twice as fast as our exports of those products. Between 1965 and 1972 United States trade with Japan in sophisticated technological products ran a deficit of $1 billion. In short, the United States appears to be falling behind in advanced technology and industrial efficiency, the field in which only recently she had undisputed leadership. The trend has been sufficiently alarming to cause President Nixon to increase Federal spending for civilian research in 1971 by $700 million, 15 per cent more than in 1970 and 65 per cent more than in 1969, and to give technological research and development one of the top priorities in government plans. Will these efforts restore undisputed technological leadership to the United States? It is doubtful. Our lag in technology will probably continue to widen vis-à-vis Russia, Japan, and Western Europe in many important areas unless a much higher priority is placed on technological research. The trend today in the United States seems to be toward a deliberate deemphasis of technology. In 1964 the Federal govenment funded 57 per cent of the research and development performed by industry; in 1971 that figure had dropped to 41 per cent. A higher priority on technological research — especially in "pure" nonmarket areas — must compete for limited tax funds with other high-priority projects. It is not allowed to compete against wasteful and nonessential projects in the private sector.

A nation's security is the first and the highest obligation of government. Since technology affects national security, it is natural that it should have a very high priority, but sometimes it does not. In a democracy a soldier is a hero in wartime and a bum in peacetime. It is very difficult for the military leadership to maintain high morale in the armed forces during peacetime or to convince the Congress that a huge peacetime budget is justified. In a market economy, the citizen is too busy making a living to worry about future wars, and he resents being taxed heavily for military preparedness in peacetime. The consumer is likely to believe the politician who promises him more social welfare services paid for by cuts from the Pentagon budget. Since the consumer has more votes that the soldier, the pressure is uneven and in favor of consumer affluence.

Even the most urgent priorities — those involving national defense — are the subject of heated controversy. Such is human nature that, if a spaceship could be sent to Heaven, there would be Congressmen who would vote against the appropriation! It is futile, therefore, to speak of economic planning or of setting national priorities as if this were a technical subject that could be solved by computers or technical experts. The setting of priorities is a matter of judgment and decision, involving the consideration of intangible values and the weighing of imponderables and, to be frank, of educated guesses about the future course of events. This is particularly true in matters relating to foeign policy and national security. The defense budget of the United States has a high priority when the nation feels itself threatened; when no visible enemy threatens its security, the United States government tends to embrace policies of "peaceful coexistence", "détente", isolationism, and pacifism and to downgrade defense priorities.

Most Congressmen would probably agree that the major threat to the national security of the United States today is posed by Soviet militarism. The Soviet Union appears to be determined to become the world's greatest military power. At one time Russian military policy was dictated by a fear of capitalist encirclement. Now it appears to be a policy dictated by many complex factors — Russian nationalism, fear of China as well as fear of the United States, fear of consumer sovereignty, Communist imperialism, and other factors outside the scope of this discussion. Russian militarism is no idle threat. Russia already has the world's greatest army, and at the present rate of growth it may soon surpass the United States in both air and naval power, if it has not already done so.

How can the Soviet Union with an economy inferior to that of the United States achieve a position of military superiority? The answer is that the Soviet Union is able to divert a larger share of the Russian gross national product to national defense than the United States. According to official figures, the Soviet Union spends about 10 per cent of the gross national product on defense. The United States defense budget for 1973 represents 6.4 per cent of the gross national product and 30 per cent of the Federal budget.

If the American economy is more than twice as large as the Russian, it appears that the United States is spending more on defense needs than the U.S.S.R. The figures are $75.8 billion for the United States in 1972 and an estimated 26.7 billion rubles for the Soviets in 1972. However, there is no general agreement among experts on the ruble-dollar exchange value in military hardware. In the 1972 Defense Report, Secretary of Defense Melvin R. Laird estimated that Soviet military spending was about equal to that of the United States. Unofficial estimates vary widely. Some place Soviet military expenditures as high as 50 per cent of the Russian gross national product or about 80 billion rubles ($108.2 billion dollars at current exchange rates). Andrei Sakarov, inventor of the Soviet H-bomb has said: "In no country does the share of military expenditures in relation to national income reach such proportions as in the Soviet Union — over 40 per cent."

The Russian military-industrial complex is an indivisible part of the Soviet economy. There is no clear demarcation between the civilian and military establishments. The Soviet budget is planned, approved, and administered by the executive branch (there being no independent legislative or judicial branches) and covers the entire economy. Since there is no market mechanism for setting prices, prices, taxes, and wages are set by executive decree. Under the Soviet system, consumer demand can be kept under severe restraints and investments diverted to the military-industrial complex in any amount considered desirable by political and military leaders.

In the United States, placing severe restraints on consumer demand would be politically and economically unthinkable and contrary to public policy except in wartime. The official Keynesian policy of consumer prosperity and full employment requires subsidizing consumer demand. Restraining consumer demand would result in a reduced volume of sales, a drop in gross national product, loss of income, unemployment, and a generally depressed economy. This effect is unavoidable in a two-sector economy. The public sector derives its support from the gross *income* of the private sector; therefore, the affluence of the consumer market in the private sector largely determines the tax revenues of the public sector available for national security. The continued growth and prosperity of the private sector is of utmost importance to the United States government for the protection of its tax revenues, by which the public sector is supported.

However, restraining consumer demand need not always be followed by a reduction in gross national product. In a fully mobilized economy, where the private sector of the economy is taken over by the government, as in the United States during wartime or in the U.S.S.R. in peacetime, production and employment do not decrease with a reduction in consumer spending. On the contrary, during World War II the economy of the United States achieved full employment and the highest industrial output up to that time. In the U.S.S.R., unemployment is not a problem; and despite consumer demand, Russia continues to pur huge resources into military technology. Experts claim Russian funds for research in this area are 50 per cent greater than those spent by the United States. In March 1973 Dr. John W. Foster, outgoing United States director of defense research and engineering, told Congress: "Our national security will be in jeopardy unless we find some way to sustain and significantly increase and improve the resources dedicated to R & D for our military forces.... No projection shows that we are holding our own against the Soviet's determined effort to wrest military technology superiority from us."

Obviously, in a fully mobilized economy consumer demand may be disregarded with impunity. The state, having complete control of the means of production, can produce what it wishes to produce and distribute it as it sees fit. In China, Cuba, and Russia, the state has been able to keep the consumer poor but reasonably satisfied. The problem of consumer resistance is minimized because:

1. The state is able to convince the people that consumer affluence must be sacrificed for national goals of a higher order — building a future perfect society, protecting the homeland from foreign aggression, helping allies destroy imperialist or colonial powers, and providing cheap or free public education, public health, public transportation, and other public goods.

2. The state controls the media of information and education and can

278

indoctrinate the people with its policies and suppress opposition.

3. The state can keep the people isolated by preventing contact with foreign cultures that provide examples of superior standards of consumer affluence.

At this time, the Soviet state seems quite able to maintain a high level of industrial production with a low level of consumer affluence. China is building an industrial base that may, in time, be as great as or greater than Russia's; from all indications, China is determined to sacrifice consumer goods for public goods and armaments. Despite a primitive consumer level, it already has atomic bombs. The Communist challenge to the United States is both military and economic. On both fronts the threat springs, not from greater productivity or a greater gross national product, but from the ability of the Communist states to suppress consumer demand in favor of public goods and services that the state can use for military build-up and economic penetration of uncommitted "third-world" nations. While "rich" countries such as Japan, West Germany, and England cannot "afford" to maintain a minimal military defense establishment, Russia and China, with "poor" economics, are able to maintain and expand large military establishments and are penetrating Africa, Asia, and the Middle East with increasing force, both military and economic. The suppression of consumer demand in the Communist economies appears as a positive source of strength and leads to increased national power rather than to depression and unemployment, as in the two-sector economies of the West.

In a democracy, the military is used to implement foreign policy, but in an authoritarian state the military serves to implement, not only the foreign policy of the state, but its domestic policy as well, for it too is based on authority backed by force, rather than on popular consent. In Russia and China, in peacetime as well as in wartime, the military structure and attitudes fit much better with the political structure, which is also authoritarian and hierarchic.

For these and other reasons the military in Russia and China is a favored class and enjoys considerable honor and prestige. It commands, and will continue to command, a much higher share of the gross national product than in democracies. Their lower standard of consumer affluence will enable them to put more men into combat units than democracies, whose soldiers are used to electric blankets, air conditioners, and other consumer luxuries.

In 1973 Senator John Stennis inquired: "Why, for example, do we put only 13 Army divisions in the field with an active Army strength which will total 814,000? ... Can the armed services afford to assign more than a million men to support duties?" The Soviet military, by contrast, can field 160 army divisions — 96 motorized, 56 tank, and 8 airborne — on an active army strength of two million. The Russians are able to squeeze much more from their defense ruble than the United States gets from its defense dollar. Most of the U.S. military budget goes for salaries, services, and nonmilitary goods. Only 35 cents goes for weapons. Two-thirds of the Russian ruble goes for weapons.

The United States has pioneered in military technology in many areas: airplanes, atomic bombs, and nuclear submarines. It appears that the next major war may be decided in space and probably by nuclear-powered space ships. Will these spaceships be American? Or Russian? The Russians are pushing ahead with increasing energy and investments to develop a military space capability, while the budget for the military space program is being reduced in the United States.

Although it is twice as wealthy as the Soviet Union, the United States claims that it does not have the money to keep up with the Russians in military and space technology. More accurately, it has the money, but prefers to use it on sibsidizing consumption.

In 1959, for example, the United States spent $11 billion in advertising, $7 billion on tobacco products, and $15 billion in automobile purchases as opposed to total public and private spending of $10.2 billion for research and development. G. Myrdal has observed: "There is no other road to economic development than a compulsory rise in the share of the national revenue which is withheld from consumption and devoted to investment."[188]

The economies of Communist states may not be as efficient or productive as those of the Western democracies, but they do enjoy a marked military advantage in being able successfully to suppress consumer demand and in being able to invest a larger share of national income in nonconsumer fields.

Military leaders in the United States have expressed grave concern over the decline of American military power vis-à-vis the U.S.S.R. There is increased demand for cutting down the national defense budget from such powerful Congressional leaders as Senators Fulbright, Proxmire, McGovern, and others. The news media are highly critical of the industrial-military complex which, it claims, is taking too large a share of the national budget. Consumer affluence not only robs the budget of funds it could use on defense needs, but saps the military morale of the people. Historically, rich nations have been "soft" nations, unwilling to give up their luxuries for the Spartan simplicity of a war economy or the hardships of combat. Some military leaders in the United States are afraid that their country is emulating the disastrous historical course that Athens and Rome followed in the past. This view seems unduly pessimistic.

The problem of financing national defense is primarily a tax problem. As long as the income tax supports a two-sector economy, there will be a bitter struggle over funds for the public sector. Since the national defense budget takes the largest share of the Federal budget — about 30 per cent, or $88 billion, in 1974 — the Pentagon will continue to be the major target of those who wish to reduce the tax burden. Senator Proxmire charged President Nixon with overspending on the military budget and said: "The President chose the space shuttle, aircraft carriers, and Pentagon procurement over money for schools, health, housing, mass trasnit, the environment, and other needed programs. With the freeze on food-stamp money, he also cut a vital program already starved for funds. He reordered priorities, but he reordered them in the wrong way."[189]

The priorities of the antimilitary political leaders are not necessarily misplaced. Health and welfare are as deserving of tax funds as the Pentagon. The problem is that, in a two-sector economy, priorities are not set for the private sector. In a two-sector economy prices are not charged a differential tax for national defense; the tax load is distributed uniformly over the price system. As a result, necessities such as food, housing, and clothing are charged the same for national defense as luxuries such as foreign travel, luxury cars, yachts, and furs. When defense needs rise under a two-sector economy, the private sector is squeezed harder to supply the extra tax revenues, but the squeeze, being uniform, is felt hardest in the low-income groups because, when prices rise, the pinch is felt hardest by those who must pay more for the necessities of life. The rich can afford to pay more for their luxuries or can dispense with them.

Charging for national defense according to ability to pay has always presented politicians with their most difficult tax problem. During a war the taxes for the support of the war effort can be a crushing burden. The tax system of a country at war is put to a severe test to distribute the tax load on a fair and equitable basis. If the tax load falls heavily on the poor, while the rich are exempt, there is an obvious injustice that rankles and produces discontent, resistance, or rebellion. The sight of a privileged class or group enjoying luxuries during wartime is especially galling to those who are suffering privation and hardship. It is for these reasons that politicians are able at such a time to impose taxes on the rich that under ordinary circumstances would be considered unnecessary or oppressive. During all wars differential or excise taxes are imposed on luxury goods. Taxing the rich on their consumption spares the poor some of the sacrifice of paying for the national defense, and some of the burden is shifted to the rich.

Taxes on luxury items are usually dropped after the war on the ground that such taxes interfere with consumer sovereignty. In the United States it has been considered preferable to tax the rich on their income rather than on their consumption. In practice, the income tax has been found to be successful for diverting tax revenues from the private to the public sector, but has not been successful in equalizing the tax burden within the private sector. A system of commodity taxation according to the tariff principle would give the government the option to charge defense costs against the more superfluous consumer goods, the reduction of which would cause the consumer little or no hardship.

Today the United States is divided into two sectors — the private and the public. The two have divergent aims and conflicting priorities, making the economy a house divided against itself. In times of peace and plenty this division can be sustained without undue strain. In times of national emergency and war this division creates severe economic strain and hardship, and the entire economy is mobilized under the public sector. After the war the economy is demobilized to restore market freedom and consumer sovereignty to the private sector.

The division of the nation into two sectors in peacetime is not healthy if the two sectors do not cooperate on national goals. National security should have as high a priority in the private as in the public sector. War and peace affect civilians as well as soldiers. The artificial division of the economy into two sectors by the income tax creates difficulties in working toward a unified policy of national security. Under a system of commodity taxation on the tariff principle, both would work toward common goals, and the priorities of national defense would apply to both.

Under a unified economy the needs of national defense would not be weighed only in relation to the needs of public health, education, and welfare. They would be weighed also in relation to the needs for men's cosmetics, car washes, vacation homes, winter cruises, juke boxes, sports cars, and other consumer goods and services. National defense needs would be freed from the restrictions imposed by consumer sovereignty, and foreign policy would be governed by strategic considerations of national, not consumer, interest. It would not, of course, guarantee that such foreign policy would be the best or the wisest. However, under a unified economy, with the legislative branch setting national economic priorities, the United States would be in a much stronger strategic position to ward off the military and economic threat from the mobilized economies of the Communist states.

5.   The Balanced Economy

Expansion of the public sector has been a striking phenomenon of the late 19th and especially of the 20th century. The trend may have been encouraged by Marx and the theory of Communism, but even in non-Marxist countries such as imperial and democratic Germany and the American republic the trend toward greater government control of the economy has been apparently inevitable and beyond the control of conservative politicians. In the view of market purists and rabid anti-Marxists, this development has been a colossal error. Their faith in the classic market system of laissez-faire remains unshaken. If the market had not been subverted by liberal and Socialist politicians, there is no reason, they claim, why the market economy could not perform the functions it once did. They favor the lifting of all political controls and say that the market law of supply and demand alone should set prices, wages, and interest rates and that the medium of exchange should be a nonpolitical commodity such as gold or silver. The champions of a free market society want the market to regulate all economic life; the fact that the market is blind to social and moral values does not deter them. Said F. von Hayek:

> A society in which the position [reward] was made to correspond to human ideas of moral merit would therefore be the exact opposite of a free society. It would be a society in which people were rewarded for duty performed instead of for success.... But if nobody's knowledge is sufficient to guide all human action, there is also no human being who is competent to reward all efforts according to merit.

Hayek revives the myth, now generally exploded, that the free market is above and apart from human beings and, because it is based on "natural" laws, is beyond human judgment and political control.[190] That the classic laissez-faire market can be revived is highly improbable. This nostalgic desire is no more realistic than the romantic yearnings of Ortega y Gassett and de Tocqueville for the aristocratic culture of the 18th century. The expansion of the political sector was forced upon such recalcitrant and die-hard conservatives as Churchill and Eisenhower by the logic of events. In all nations where the public sector has expanded, the conservative market-oriented politicians have been unable to roll it back. Once in power, they have not only been powerless to reverse the trend toward greater government control of the market; they have themselves been forced to impose more controls. In the United States the public sector has grown during all Republican administrations since the New Deal: in England it has grown under the Conservatives.

Stating this fact of expansion is not to say, as Adolf Wagner did, that there is an economic "law" that decrees this expansion or that such an expansion is historically inevitable according to some abstract theory, as Marx claimed. Men are not gods; despite all claims to the contrary, they cannot see into the future. Men can only make educated guesses about the future and make future projections based on past historical experience and trends. The trend away from individualism is an historic cycle dictated by the need for large-scale industrial organizations. According to Bertrand Russell:

> It seems not improbable that the movement toward individual liberty which characterized the whole period from the renaissance to nineteenth century liberalism may be brought to a stop by the increased organizations due to industrialism. The pressure of society upon the individual may, in a new form, becomes as great as in barbarous communities, and nations may come increasingly to pride themselves upon collective rather than individual achievements. This is already the case in the United States.... The same attitude pervades the philosophy of the Soviet Government.[191]

The trend toward collectivism and greater government planning and controls over the economy is still in process, but it is very doubtful that this trend will continue indefinitely. In economic affairs the use of force is too costly, too cumbersome, and ultimately exhausting. Economic incentives based on the worker's self-interest and desire to improve himself are usually more productive in the long run.

The political system is not an efficient mechanism of production because it is noncompetitive and protected from failure. A bureaucracy generally operates on a seniority system; it has a guaranteed source of income; it does not compete in the market; it cannot go bankrupt; and since it cannot fail, it is under no compulsion to improve.

When market controls are inoperative, no restraint is placed on costs. A bureaucracy, therefore, sees no reason why it cannot give itself wage raises or fringe benefits or additional personnel. In a private enterprise, when market competition is operative, there are fundamental reasons for keeping costs within bounds; otherwise, the company fails. These cost restraints do not apply to government enterprises.

The economic tasks the public sector does best are redistribution of resources through taxation, regulation (not operation) of industries, and policy planning for long-term growth. It is generally acknowledged that only the national government has the resources and the political power to plan massive long-term projects such as the Manhattan project for nuclear research, the Apollo program, the nuclear submarine project, the national mass transit project, the national highway project, and similar programs. Projects of this type require long-term planning and resources available only to the national government. Regulation of industries is a proper function of government. Private industry cannot police itself, for there are always unethical or unscrupulous competitors who will evade standards of health, safety, and morals to achieve market success. Only the government can impose and enforce standards to protect the public interest. The tax function is a primary function of government and one that well befits its capabilities and powers. No private organization can assume this function.

The production and distribution of goods is one task that does not fit government capabilities and is done better under free-market conditions of price competition. However, through its regulatory, planning, and taxing powers the government must spell out the ground rules for market competitions, applicable to all and set priorities on what economic activities are desirable for the long-term national interest. The tax power inherent in a commodity tax system of the tariff type would be appropriate for this function. It would preserve the market economy, but superimpose a social value on the market free system without direct intervention or direct controls.

The alternative is to mobilize or nationalize the economy, to absorb the private sector into the public sector. The management function is taken over by the government bureaucracy. The English Labor party is committed to this program. When economic power is concentrated in government hands, a loss of private power centered in labor unions and in private corporations follows. Of course, political controls over the market are always imposed in the name of social security, better wages, better employment benefits, and other desirable objectives. This is an old political conception, according to Henry C. Simons, who first analyzed it in 1938:

> In the name of justice (fair wages, fair prices, parity prices, and other derivatives of the medieval conception), we are preventing and destroying the free enterprise, free market, and competitive free trade which are essential to representative government and to orderly political life on a large scale. We are deliberately displacing competition within economic groups, which is essentially peaceful, orderly, productive, and mutually advantageous, by organized economic and political action which is inherently exploitative, destructive, and violent. Thus we move toward the politician's millenium where politics has crowded competition entirely out of the picture — toward the economy of organized negotiation which, once achieved, would immediately necessitate the introduction of a supreme negotiator who, in turn, would either liquidate the organizations or utilize them to consolidate his own dictatorial powers. [192]

In totalitarian regimes political laws enforced by the police power of the state control the allocation of all material and manpower resources. Regimes of this type were common in ancient times. In Europe medieval feudalism was followed by a commercial age in which free markets substituted money and credit for force and coercion as determinants in economic behavior. Credit became the decisive factor, but credit is nothing but belief in somebody's word or promise and therefore largely a matter of faith.

"Wealth, in a commercial age, is made up largely of promises," said Roscoe Pound:

> I suggested, as a jural postulate of civilized society, that in such a society men must be able to assume that those with whom they deal in the general intercourse of the society will act in good faith, and as a corollary must be able to assume that those with whom they so deal will carry out their undertakings according to the expectations which the moral sentiment of the community attaches thereto. Hence in a commercial and industrial society, a claim or want or demand of society that promises be kept and that undertakings be carried out in good faith, a social interest in the stability of promises as a social and economic institution, becomes of the first importance.[193]

In a commercial society credit is based on voluntary savings, character, and promise to pay. In a politically dominated economy public credit is based on compulsory savings extracted by taxes. In the extension of credit the ephemeral element of faith is replaced by heavy-handed regulations covering disbursements of public funds.

The individual in a competitive market economy is free to work, buy, sell, invest, save, and otherwise influence the allocation of resources. He is permitted to build up economic power that he can manipulate without police interference. He is subject to financial and monetary pressures rather than direct commands of the political authority. He is paid to do things rather than ordered to do them.

In a politically dominated economy incentives — better wages, higher profits, and fear of capital losses — are replaced by political laws or plans backed by the military-police power of the state; the self-regulation of the market is replaced by government regulations. Credit ceases to be a contractual obligation based on mutual trust and confidence and becomes instead a government grant or dispensation based on political status and expediency. The relationship of creditor and debtor becomes that of patron and client. When the economy is dominated by the political power of the state, it becomes politicized or mobilized, depending on the extent and duration of the domination. A democratic state may adopt a policy of mercantilism or *dirigisme* or economic mobilization in wartime, but these periods are usually followed by a return to an economy of greater voluntary action and free choice. Of course, the individual may sometimes be willing to trade political liberty for economic security, as the Roman proletarian did. In Russia, China, and other countries without democratic traditions this trade-off may be accepted willingly, but in countries with long-established democratic institutions, the loss of private economic power, individual or corporate, will not be accepted meekly, except as a result of war or grave national crisis.

Such a grave national crisis may come as a result of the displacement of competition by "organized economic and political action," that is, by the political acts of organized groups, labor, consumers, and producers acting outside the government. These groups are in effect taking the law in their own hands and using power or the threat of power to coerce the government to grant their demands. The coal miners' strike in Britain in February 1974, which forced the resignation of the Conservative government, is an example of economic groups using political power to achieve their ends as a result of the politicalization of the economy, against which Simons warned.

In the meantime the power of the individual to govern himself through democratic political institutions decreases. An elitist ideology is propagated to the effect that the individual is unable to cope with, understand, or decide the complex socioeconomic issues of the times and that the decisions must be left to the "experts" with their superior scientific training and their problem-solving computers. Unfortunately, neither the sciences nor computers have all the answers to political problems. Catastrophes such as the Vietnam war and the Bay of Pigs are the results of bad political judgments based on technical data derived from computerized analytical tools operated by highly intelligent experts. Very few experts have much faith in the ability of the people to make decisions; by definition, the expert is one who knows better. The élitist ideology erodes faith in the ability of democratic institutions to serve the people, and provides an ideological cover for militant and terrorist groups that seek political solutions outside the ballot box.

Nevertheless, the Jefferson-Lincoln tradition of popular government is hard to suppress and eventually will reassert itself. This assumption is based on two premises. The first is that the political struggle between liberty and authority is incapable of permanent solution according to any absolute or transcendental or scientific formula. Events are beyond the absolute control of human beings; since events determine politics, it is only common sense to assume that future political-economic evolution will continue to be a political struggle between the forces of individual liberty and collective authority and that each generation must work out the precise accommodation between these two irreconcilable ends. If one generation could achieve a permenent utopian solution of this problem, there would be nothing left for future generations to do! It is much more likely that the political-economic struggle will go on and that history will continue to record cyclical swings between the extremes of anarchy and despotism, with the more fortunate nations momentarily achieving a happy mean or a stable equilibrium between the two extremes.

The second premise is that the problem of economics — the production and distribution of goods and services — is not one that can be resolved solely by political means if one defines political power as the power to make laws enforced by the police power of the state. The political power controls the economic sphere and defines the rules of the game under which it operates. Within the economic sphere, however the incentives to growth and progress are provided by economic rewards: money or financial power. These incentives and rewards are better distributed by a market mechanism than by a political bureaucracy. The potential of the market mechanism as a distributive agency is probably unlimited. The growth of the regulatory bureaucratic redistributive system in the public sector does not mean that the market mechanism has become obsolete and can no longer be economically useful. The failure is a failure to adapt the market mechanism to new conditions. It may mean that market capabilities have not been sufficiently understood or utilized; that outdated market rules and regulations are inhibiting the market from performing its exchange functions; or that people are incapable of acting as independent agents in a free market or prefer to be protected and directed by political authority.

When the market mechanism breaks down, the political power must provide a viable alternative, but it is a mistake to assume that the politicalization of the economy is a permanent solution. The economic function of the market can never be completely suppressed and will reassert itself in black markets or eventually in a new political framework. The political power overreaches itself when it tries to operate the economy. It is more economical to pay a man to work than to force him to labor. The politicians should not try to run the economy for the same reasons that they should not try to fight wars or operate the police establishment. The political power can set the goals and the priorities, but the actual management of the economy is best left to those who have developed the specialized capability to do so.

Plato defined social justice as the maintenance of the precarious balance between the dominant classes of society — workers, soldiers, and lawmakers. In the ideal society each class performs its function and does not interfere unduly with the other, for "meddling of one with another is the ruin of the State ... This then is injustice; and on the other hand when the trader, the auxiliary, and the guardian each do their own business, that is justice ..." The economic power overreached itself during the 19th and early 20th century and tried to dominate the political power. In the United States it was widely believed before World War I that most senators were in the pay of the big trusts and that most large cities were governed by political machines controlled by money, not votes. Today the political power is overextending itself into the econimic sphere, and the effects are equally unfortunate. The Platonic concept of a balanced social order is a dynamic concept underscoring the inherent instability of social institutions. It is less reassuring than the Marxist belief in a perfect future society, but probably more true to life. It is hard to avoid the suspicion that life in utopia must be rather boring and in an economic utopia even more so.

The concept of a balanced economy recognizes that there is friction and antagonism between separate and unequal interests — labor, management, capital, consumers, and taxpayers. It leaves it up to the government to provide the unity of purpose, the legal machinery, and the national goals that will keep these interests pulling together as a team, working cooperatively rather than against each other.

In the 19th century the concept of Congressional hegemony in economic affairs was accepted by the American people as natural and according to the

Constitution. During the years of the protective tariff the great economic issues were debated in Congress, and that debate was concerned with taxes on individual commodities and prices. The rise of giant corporate trusts after the Civil War transferred much of this economic power to private corporate owners — the Vanderbilts, Rockefellers, du Ponts, Fords, Harrimans, Carnegies, and Mellons, for example. This corporate power has been considerably abridged and is no longer dominant. The economic power of private corporations is generated by profits that are included in prices, but the profit share of prices is no longer the major share, being about 5 per cent of manufacturers' prices.

The rise of labor power after the New Deal gave organized labor a powerful voice in economic policy, directly through its control of labor and indirectly through its influence on politicians. Labor now has a major voice in setting prices. Labor's share of prices is not determined by corporate owners or the market, but largely by labor itself, and represents about 66 per cent of manufacturers' prices.

The government, of course, still has great economic power, and it is increasing. Nevertheless, since the 16th Amendment and since the collapse of the tariff system in the 1930's, the economic power of the government has been concentrated in the executive department. Because the executive department is an authoritarian bureaucracy, the economic hegemony it exercises is intrusive, regulatory, inquisitorial, and oppressive.

Restoration of the tariff principle of commodity taxation to both external and internal trade would restore economic hegemony to Congress and bring economic planning within the democratic legislative process. The economic powers of the consumer, the worker, and the owner would not be suppressed, as in Socialist states; neither would any single class or interest be sovereign. The sovereign economic power would reside where the Constitution placed it — in Congress.

NOTES

1 Henry C. Simons, *Personal Income Taxation*. Chicago: University of Chicago Press, 1965. P. 2.
2 Louis I. Bredvold & Ralph G. Ross (Eds.), *The Philosophy of Edmund Burke*. Ann Arbor: University of Michigan Press, 1967. P. 88.
3 Walter W. Heller, "Taxation." *Encyclopaedia Britannica*, 1966. Vol. 21, p. 839.
4 James Coffield, *A Popular History of Taxation*. London: Longmans, Green, 1970. P. 78.
5 *Ibid.*, p. 95.
6 *Ibid.*, p. 108.
7 *Ibid.*, p. 105.
8 *Ibid.*, p. 27.
9 Sidney Ratner, *Taxation and Democracy in America*. New York: John Wiley, 1967 p. 272.
10 Roy G. Blakey & G. C. Blakey, *The Federal Income Tax*. New York: Longmans, Green, 1940. P. 38.
11 C. Northcote Parkinson, *The Law and the Profits*. Boston: Houghton, Mifflin, 1960. P. 55.
12 J. S. Mill, *Principles of Political Economy*. W. J. Ashley (Ed.). London: Longmans, Green, 1929. P. 814.
13 J. H. Perry, *Taxes, Tariffs and Subsidies*. Toronto: University of Toronto Press, 1955. Vol. 1, p. 316.
14 Richard Goode, *The Individual Income Tax*. Washington: The Brookings Institution, 1964. P. 308.
15 Richard A. Musgrave, *Fiscal Systems*. New Haven: Yale University Press, 1969. Pp. 137-141.
16 Coffield, *op. cit.*, pp. 3, 8.
17 *Ibid.*, p. 5.
18 Goode, *op. cit.*, pp. 13, 14.
19 Nicholas Kaldor, *An Expenditure Tax*. London: Allen & Unwin, 1955. Pp. 14, 45.
20 Simons, *op. cit.*, p. 105.
21 Adam Smith, An *Inquiry Into the Nature and Causes of the Wealth of Nations*. New York: Modern Library, 1937. P. 800.
22 David E. Apter, *The Politics of Modernization*. Chicago: University of Chicago Press, 1965. P. 454.
23 *Los Angeles Times*, Oct. 31, 1971.
24 Samuel D. Warren & Louis D. Brandeis, "The Right to Privacy." *Harvard Law Review*, Dec. 15, 1890.
25 *Los Angeles Times*, May 24, 1973.
26 Stanley S. Surrey, "Definitive Problems in Capital Gains Taxation." In *Tax Revision Conpendium*. Washington: House Ways & Means Committee, 1959. Vol. 2, p. 1203.
27 Art Buchwald, "A Taxpayer Reflects on his Return — Amen." *Los Angeles Times*, Apr. 17, 1972. Reprinted by permission of the author.
28 Johnnie M. Walters, "Your Chances of a Tax Audit." *U. S. News & World Report*, May 15, 1972.
29 Coffield, *op. cit.*, p. 201.
30 Ralph W. Emerson, *Complete Essays and Other Writings*. New York: The Modern Library, 1950. Pp. 556, 562, 606.
31 *Los Angeles Times* Oct. 5, 1969.
32 Goode, *op. cit.*, pp. 283, 284.
33 Steve Harvey, "Why Loopholes Were Created." *Los Angeles Times*, Apr. 1, 1973.
34 Coffield, *op. cit.*, p. 201.
35 *Los Angeles Times*, Oct. 31, 1971.
36 Walters, *op. cit.*
37 Simons, *op. cit.*, p. 40.
38 *Ibid.*, pp. 134, 135.
39 *Forbes Magazine*, Mar. 1, 1973.
40 Musgrave, *op. cit.*, p. 129.
41 Aristotle, *The Politics of Aristotle*. Ernest Baker (Ed.). Oxford: Oxford University Press, 1958. P. 21
42 Murray N. Rothbard, *Man, Economy and State*. Los Angeles: Nash, 1970. P. 847.
43 Smith, *op. cit.*, pp. 388, 389.
44 Mill, *op. cit.*, pp. 199, 200.
45 Karl Marx, *Capital*. Frederick Engels, (Ed.). New York: The Modern Library, Pp. 423, 425.
46 V. I. Lenin, "The Three Sources and Three Constituent Parts of Marxism," in *Capital, The Communist Manifesto and other Writing of Karl Marx*. Max Eastman (Ed.). New York: The Modern Library, 1959. P. XXIV.
47 Marx, *op. cit.*, pp. 45, 46.
48 William S. Jevons, *The Theory of Political Economy*. New York: Kelley & Millman, 1957. Pp. 1, 2.
49 Smith, *op. cit.*, p. 28.
50 Committee on Interior and Insular Affairs, *Selected Readings on the Fuels and Energy Crisis*. Washington: Government Printing Office, 1972. P. 3.
51 Gerard Piel, *The Acceleration of History*. New York: Alfred A. Knopf, 1972. P. 126.
52 Philip H. Abelson, *Science*. May 1971. P. 815.
53 Thorstein Veblen, *The Theory of the Leisure Class*. New York: The Modern Library, Pp. 31, 32.
54 *Ibid.*, pp. 96, 97, 103.
55 Jose Ortega y Gasset, *The Revolt of the Masses*. New York: W. W. Norton, 1957. Pp. 58, 60.
56 J. A. Hobson, *Work and Wealth*. New York: Macmillan, 1914. P. 138.
57 Thorstein Veblen, "The Independent Farmer," in *The Portable Veblen*. Max Lerner (Ed.). New York: Viking Press, 1965. P. 404.
58 *The Politics of Aristotle, op. cit.*, p. 67.

289

59 S. L. Jones, *Commerce Today*. Washington: U. S. Dept. of Commerce. Sept. 3, 1973.
60 *Wall St. Journal*, Mar. 28, 1972.
61 David Granick, "The Red Executive," in D. T. Bazelon, *The Paper Economy*. New York: Vintage Books, 1963. P. 434.
62 Robert Bleiberg, in speech in Town Hall, Los Angeles, Nov. 13, 1973.
63 *Los Angeles Times*, Nov. 22, 1973.
64 James Daniel, "He Manages the Nation's Money Supply." *Reader's Digest*, January 1972.
65 Advertisement in *Fortune*, Nov. 1973.
66 C. C. Zimmerman, *Family and Civilization*. New York: Harper, 1947. Pp. 631, 632.
67 Hobson, *op. cit.*, p. 166.
68 Kenneth E. Boulding, *Beyond Economics*. Ann Arbor: University of Michigan Press, 1968. P. 286.
69 William Proxmire, *Uncle Sam: The Last of the Big Time Spenders*. New York: Simon & Schuster, 1972. Pp. 31, 32.
70 Robert L. Heilbronner, *The Future as History*. New York: Harper, 1960. Pp. 155, 156.
71 H. B. Acton, *The Morals of the Market*. London: Longmans Group, 1971.
72 Gunnar Myrdal, "The Relentless Drive Toward Egalitarianism", in *Business and Society Review/Innovation No. 7*, 1973, p. 18.
73 Simons, *op. cit.*, p. 22.
74 Boulding, *op. cit.*, p. 218.
75 Gunnar Myrdal, *The Political Element in the Development of Economic Theory*. Paul Streeten (Trans.). New York: Simon & Schuster, 1954. P. 135.
76 R. W. Davies, *The Development of the Soviet Budgetary System*. Cambridge: Harvard University Press, 1958. P. 193.
77 Arthur M. Okun, in speech in Town Hall, Los Angeles, Mar. 16, 1972.
78 Simons, *op. cit.*, p. 72.
79 *Los Angeles Times*, June 8, 1973.
80 Joseph A. Pechman, *Federal Tax Policy*. Washington: Brookings Institution, 1971. Pp. 45, 44.
81 Proxmire, *op. cit.*, pp. 28, 29.
82 Gerhard Colm, *Essays in Public Finance and Fiscal Policy*. New York: Oxford University Press 1955. P. 258.
83 E. B. Staats in speech in Town Hall, Los Angeles, Mar. 7, 1972.
84 Neil Jacoby, "The Fiscal Policy of the Kennedy-Johnson Administration," *The Journal of Finance, Papers and Proceedings*, May 1964. Pp. 353, 369.
85 Proxmire, *op. cit.*, pp. 36, 37.
86 *Los Angeles Times*, Feb. 3, 1973.
87 N. Glazer, "The Limits of Social Policy." *Commentary*, Sept. 1971.
88 C. Jackson Grayson, Jr., "Let's Get Back to the Competitive Market System," *Harvard Business Review*, Nov.-Dec. 1973.
89 Robert L. Heilbronner, *The Future as History*. New York: Harper, 1960. P. 43.
90 W. G. Sumner, *Earth Hunger and Other Essays*. Freeport, N.Y.: Books for Libraries Press, 1970.
91 Sidney Fine, *Laissez Faire and the General Welfare State*. Ann Arbor: University of Michigan Press, 1969. P. 211.
92 *Ibid.*, p. 263.
93 *Ibid.*, p. 264.
94 *Ibid.*, p. 267.
95 Daniel Bell & Irving Kristol (Eds.). *Capitalism Today*. New York: Basic Books, 1971. Pp. 91, 92.
96 Benjamin N. Cardozo, *The Nature of the Judicial Process*. New Haven: Yale University Press, 1973. P. 54.
97 *Ibid.*, p. 56.
98 *The Philosophy of Edmund Burke, op. cit.*, p. 212.
99 B. B. Seligman, *Main Currents in Modern Economics*. New York: Free Press of Glencoe, 1963. P. vi.
100 Myrdal, *Political Element, op. cit.*, p. 206.
101 G. Santayana, *Dominations and Powers*, New York: Scribner, 1951. P. 184.
102 Boulding, *op. cit.*, p. 30.
103 J. K. Galbraith, *The New Industrial State*. Boston, Houghton, Mifflin, 1967. P. 408.
104 *Business Week*, Jan. 1, 1972.
105 Simon Kuznets, *Economic Growth and Structure*. New York: W. W. Norton, 1965. Pp. 63, 64.
106 Simons, *op. cit.*, p. 45.
107 *Newsweek*, Apr. 12, 1973.
108 Fred Cottrell, *Energy and Society*. New York: McGraw-Hill, 1955. P. viii.
109 Arnold Toynbee, *A Study of History*. D. C. Somervell (Ed.). New York: Oxford University Press 1947. Pp. 195, 196.
110 Roy A. Rappaport, "The Flow of Energy in an Agricultural Society." In *Energy and Power*. San Francisco: W. H. Freeman, 1971. P. 80.
111 *Los Angeles Times*, Nov. 22, 1973.
112 *Business Week*, Nov. 19, 1973.
113 *Ibid.*
114 *Newsweek*, Nov. 19, 1973.

115 Robert Riggs, *The Transformation of the American Economy 1865-1914*. New York: John Wiley, 1971. P. 56.
116 *Ibid.*, p. 55.
117 Cardozo, *op. cit.*, pp. 79, 80.
118 Boulding, *op. cit.*, pp. 33, 34.
119 Thomas Jefferson, *The Writings of Thomas Jefferson*. Paul L. Ford (Ed.). New York: Putman. Vol. 8:127.
120 Carl S. Shoup, *Ricardo on Taxation*. New York: Columbia University Press, 1960. P. 220.
121 Smith, *op. cit.*, pp. 636-637.
122 *Ibid.*, pp. 421, 423, 424.
123 *Ibid.*, p. 434.
124 *Ibid.*, pp. 612, 613.
125 *Ibid.*, p. 612.
126 *Ibid.*, p. 900.
127 Thomas Jefferson, *The Life and Selected Writings of Thomas Jefferson*. A Koch & W. Peden (Eds.). New York: The Modern Library, 1944. Pp. 279, 280.
128 *Ibid.*, p. 127.
129 Alexander Hamilton, *The Reports of Alexander Hamilton*. Jacob E. Cooke (Ed.). New York: Harper & Row, 1964. P. 4.
130 Smith, *op. cit.*, p. 630.
131 Hamilton, *op., cit.*, pp. 118, 119.
132 *Ibid.*, p. 136.
133 Smith, *op. cit.*, pp. 437, 384.
134 Hamilton, *op. cit.*, pp. 137, 138.
135 *Ibid.*, pp. 161, 162.
136 Dumas Malone (Ed.). *Correspondence Between Thomas Jefferson and Pierre Samuel du Pont de Nemours 1798-1817*. Boston: Houghton, Mifflin, 1930. Pp. 133-134.
137 F. W. Taussig, *The Tariff History of the United States*. New York: Putnam, 1931. Pp. 33, 34.
138 D. G. Harriman, *American Tariffs from Plymouth Rock to McKinley*. The American Protective League, 1892. P. 25.
139 Ratner, *op. cit.*, p. 35.
140 F. W. Taussig (Ed.). *State Papers and Speeches on the Tariff*. Cambridge: Harvard University Press, 1893. P. 119.
141 H. Wayne Morgan, *William McKinley and His America*. Syracuse: Syracuse University Press, 1963. Pp. 113, 114.
142 *Ibid.*, p. 60.
143 *Ibid.*, p. 61.
144 *Ibid.*, p. 64.
145 Julia E. Johnsen (Ed.). *Free Trade*. New York: Wilson, 1930. Pp. 119ff.
146 *Ibid.*, p. 124.
147 *Ibid.*, pp. 149, 156.
148 *Ibid.*, p. 111.
149 Taussig, *Tariff History, op. cit.*, p. 521.
150 F. W. Taussig, *Free Trade, The Tariff and Reciprocity*. New York: Macmillan, 1920. P. 215.
151 Boulding, *op. cit.*, pp. 283, 284.
152 Goode, *op. cit.*, p. 22.
153 Kaldor, *op. cit.*, p. 53.
154 L. K. Caldwell, "Energy and Environment: The Bases for Public Policies." *Annals of the American Academy of Political and Social Sciences*, Nov. 1973. P. 136.
155 Gardiner C. Means, *The Corporate Revolution in America*. New York: Collier Books, 1954. P. 69.
156 *Christian Science Monitor*, Aug. 4, 1973.
157 Franklin D. Holzman, *Soviet Taxation*. Cambridge: Harvard University Press, 1955. P. 90.
158 Speech in Town Hall, Los Angeles, May 9, 1972.
159 R. C. Gerstenberg, "The Automobile Industry." *Saturday Evening Post*, Fall Issue, 1972.
160 *U. S. Industrial Outlook*. Washington: U. S. Department of Commerce, 1972. Pp. 29-35.
161 Boulding, *op. cit.*, p. 285.
162 Myrdal, *Political Element, op. cit.*, p. 188.
163 Karl Mannheim, *Man and Society In An Age of Reconstruction*, New York: Harcourt, Brace & World. P. 380.
164 *Nation's Business*, Oct. 1973.
165 Daniel P. Moynihan, *The Politics of a Guaranteed Income*. New York: Random House, 1973. P. 19.
166 Henry Hazlitt, *The Conquest of Poverty*. New Rochelle, N. Y.: Arlington House, 1973. Pp. 95, 96.
167 Moynihan, *op. cit.*, pp. 81, 82.
168 Gov. Daniel Walker of Illinois, speech in Town Hall, Los Angeles, Nov. 15, 1973.
169 Nathan Glazer, *New York* magazine Oct. 11, 1971.
170 John K. Galbraith, *The Affluent Society*. New York: New American Library, P. 255.
171 Hazlitt, *op. cit.*, pp. 83, 84.
172 M. Rostovzeff, *The Social and Economic History of the Roman Empire*. Oxford: Clarendon Press, 1957. P. 81.
173 Hazlitt, *op. cit.*, p. 71.

174 *Ibid.*, pp. 75, 76.
175 *Ibid.*, pp. 76, 77.
176 *Ibid.*, p. 78.
177 *Ibid.*, p. 79.
178 Moynihan, *op. cit.*, p. 126.
179 *Ibid.*, p. 224.
180 *Ibid.*, p. 355.
181 *Ibid.*, p. 4.
182 *Ibid.*, p. 93.
183 *Ibid.*, p. 95.
184 *Ibid.*, p. 35 (italics in original).
185 *National Review*, July 1972.
186 Daniel Bell, "The Post-Industrial Society — Expectations for the 1970s and 1980s." In *The Future of the Corporation.* Herman Kahn (Ed.). New York: Mason & Lipscomb, 1974. P. 20.
187 *National Review*, July 1972.
188 Gunnar Myrdal, *Economic Theory and Under-Developed Regions.* London: Duckworth, P. 84.
189 Proxmire, *op. cit.*, p. 16.
190 *Capitalism Today, op. cit.*, p. 7.
191 Bertrand Russell, *In Praise of Idleness and Other Essays.* New York: Simon & Schuster, 1972. P. 168.
192 Simons, *op. cit.*, pp. vii, viii.
193 Roscoe Pound, *An Introduction to the Philosophy of Law.* New Haven: Yale University Press, 1969. P. 133.

INDEX

295

296

Renaissance, 59
Report on Manufactures (A. Hamilton), 169-70, 174, 175, 179, 181
Report on the National Bank (A. Hamilton), 174, 179
Report on the Public Credit (A. Hamilton), 174, 179
Ricardo, David, 57, 62, 67, 151, 154, 199; ignores income tax, 166; Keynes's view of, 189; opposes Corn Laws, 188-89; *Principles of Political Economy and Taxation,* 188
Ricardo-Marx labor theory of value, 14, 69
Ricardo on Taxation (Shoup), 166
Riggs, Robert, 161
"robber barons," 19
Robinson, J., 116
Roman Empire: tax system of, 18, 27
Roosevelt, Franklin D., 39, 53, 151, 153-54; design of, for Social Security, 252-53; initiates *dirigisme,* 122; shifts tax base, 195-96
Roosevelt, Theodore, 191, 200
Ross, Edward A., 148
Rostovtzeff (Michael), 18
Rothbard, Murray D., 60
Rousseau (Jean Jacques), 100, 156, 178
Rowell-Sirois Commission, 25
Russell, Bertrand, 12, 68, 201, 264, 283

Saint-Simon, Henri de, 69, 144-45, 148
Sakarov, Andrei, 277
sales tax, 51, 203, 204, 225
Samuelson, Paul E., 155, 204
Santayana, George, 152, 199
Say, J. B., 72, 73, 78, 88
Say's Law, 78, 87
Schumpeter, Joseph A., 44, 151-52, 154
Scipio Africanus, 58
Seale, Bobby, 264
Seligman, E. R. A., 146
service industries, 268-75
Setting National Priorities — The 1972 Budget (Brookings Institution), 109
Shakespeare, 77
Shape of Things to Come, The (Wells), 145
Shaw, G. B., 201
Sherman, John, 23
Shoup, Carl S.: *Ricardo on Taxation,* 166
Simon, William E., 160-61
Simons, Henry C., 11, 51-52, 117, 155, 284; defines *income,* 29; *Individual Income Taxation,* 54
Sismondi (Jean), 78
16th Amendment, 171, 288; and erosion of property rights, 162
Skinner, B. F., 150
slavery, 186-87
Smith, Adam, 21, 43, 57, 67, 77, 154; admired by Hamilton, 165; on protective tariff, 167-69; tax principle of, 35; teachings of, opposed to Keynes's, 88; *The Wealth of Nations,* 61-62, 167
Smoot (senator), 194
Smoot-Hawley Tariff Act, 191, 192, 193, 194-95
Social Security, 56, 93, 254, 263; F. Roosevelt's design for, 252-53
Social Security tax, 105

Socialism, 78, 87, 145, 222; influence of Marxian, on America, 201; scientific, 148-49
Solon, 100, 158
Soviet Budgetary System, The (Davies), 124
Speenhamland system, 262
Spencer (Herbert), 199, 200
Spinoza, 199
stamp tax, 11
States Rights: doctrine of, 186
Stewart, John M., 276
Stokowski (Leopold), 201
Stone, Richard, 153
Story, Joseph, 162
Strauss, Leo, 199
Stravinsky (Igor), 201
Sumner, William Graham, 145, 146
supply and demand: law of, 124, 125
Supreme Court, U.S., 35
Surrey, Stanley S., 34

Taft, Robert A., 255
tariff, 47-48. *See also* external tariff; internal tariff; protective tariff
Tariff Act of 1928, 11
Tariff Schedules of the United States Annotated (1972), 225
Taussig, F. W., 180, 192, 197-98
Tax Foundation, 105
Tax Institute of America, 35
tax loopholes, 46, 51
Tax Nullification Act of South Carolina, 186
Tax Reform Act of 1969, 34, 132, 133
tax shelters, 37, 51
taxation: in the Bible, 17; and consumption, 105-11, 117; in history, 17-23; legislative process regarding, 131-35; "progressive" principle of, 26; punitive, 76
technological lag, 275-82
Teller, Edward, 201, 275
Theory of the Leisure Class, The (Veblen), 83
tithe, 27
Tocqueville, Alexis de, 199, 283
Toscanini (Arturo), 201
Toynbee (Arnold), 158
Train, Russell E., 160
Treasury, U.S. Department of, 33, 39, 137
turn-over tax, 203, 210
two-sector economy, 88, 111-12, 250, 271, 280-81; beyond the, 252-88; priorities in, 128-31; and unemployment, 91

U.S. Steel Corporation, 122, 127
utilitarianism, 63-64

value-added tax, 203-4
Vanik, Charles A., 220-21
Veblen, Thorstein, 68-69, 82-83, 85, 106, 115, 116, 146; *The Engineers and the Price System,* 148; *The Theory of the Leisure Class,* 83; urges technocracy, 148
vested interests, 55
Vietnam war, 286
Villard, Oswald Garrison, 194
voluntary tax, 27

297